GROWING UP

ISSUES AFFECTING AMERICA'S YOUTH

ISSN 1939-084X

GROWING UP

ISSUES AFFECTING AMERICA'S YOUTH

Melissa J. Doak

INFORMATION PLUS® REFERENCE SERIES
Formerly Published by Information Plus, Wylie, Texas

Detroit • New York • San Francisco • New Haven, Conn. • Waterville, Maine • London

THOMSON

™

GALE

Growing Up: Issues Affecting America's Youth
Melissa J. Doak
Paula Kepos, Series Editor

Project Editors
Kathleen J. Edgar, John McCoy

Permissions
Edna Hedblad, Jhanay Williams

Composition and Electronic Prepress
Evi Seoud

Manufacturing
Cynde Bishop

ISBN-13: 978-0-7876-5103-9 (set)
ISBN-10: 0-7876-5103-6 (set)
ISBN-13: 978-1-4144-0759-3
ISBN-10: 1-4144-0759-9
ISSN 1939-084X

This title is also available as an e-book.
ISBN-13: 978-1-4144-2948-9 (set), ISBN-10: 1-4144-2948-7 (set)
Contact your Gale Group sales representative for ordering information.

Printed in the United States of America
10 9 8 7 6 5 4 3 2 1

TABLE OF CONTENTS

PREFACE

Growing Up: Issues Affecting America's Youth is part of the *Information Plus Reference Series*. The purpose of each volume of the series is to present the latest facts on a topic of pressing concern in modern American life. These topics include today's most controversial and most studied social issues: abortion, capital punishment, care of senior citizens, crime, the environment, health care, immigration, minorities, national security, social welfare, women, youth, and many more. Although written especially for the high school and undergraduate student, this series is an excellent resource for anyone in need of factual information on current affairs.

By presenting the facts, it is the Gale Group's intention to provide its readers with everything they need to reach an informed opinion on current issues. To that end, there is a particular emphasis in this series on the presentation of scientific studies, surveys, and statistics. These data are generally presented in the form of tables, charts, and other graphics placed within the text of each book. Every graphic is directly referred to and carefully explained in the text. The source of each graphic is presented within the graphic itself. The data used in these graphics are drawn from the most reputable and reliable sources, in particular from the various branches of the U.S. government and from major independent polling organizations. Every effort was made to secure the most recent information available. The reader should bear in mind that many major studies take years to conduct, and that additional years often pass before the data from these studies are made available to the public. Therefore, in many cases the most recent information available in 2007 dated from 2004 or 2005. Older statistics are sometimes presented as well, if they are of particular interest and no more-recent information exists.

Although statistics are a major focus of the *Information Plus Reference Series*, they are by no means its only content. Each book also presents the widely held positions and important ideas that shape how the book's subject is discussed in the United States. These positions are explained in detail and, where possible, in the words of their proponents. Some of the other material to be found in these books includes: historical background; descriptions of major events related to the subject; relevant laws and court cases; and examples of how these issues play out in American life. Some books also feature primary documents, or have pro and con debate sections giving the words and opinions of prominent Americans on both sides of a controversial topic. All material is presented in an even-handed and unbiased manner; the reader will never be encouraged to accept one view of an issue over another.

HOW TO USE THIS BOOK

Childhood and adolescence are perhaps the most critical period in any person's life. The education one receives during this time, the environment one is raised in, and the way one is treated by family, friends, and society, go a long way toward determining how the rest of an individual's life will turn out. This volume addresses various factors that affect youth, including family income, who cares for children, health and safety issues, educational matters, and teen sexuality and pregnancy. Also, crime, violence, and victimization are addressed, including gang violence, school violence, and crime prevention and punishment.

Growing Up: Issues Affecting America's Youth consists of ten chapters and three appendixes. Each of the chapters is devoted to a particular aspect of youth in America. For a summary of the information covered in each chapter, please see the synopses provided in the Table of Contents at the front of the book. Chapters generally begin with an overview of the basic facts and background information on the chapter's topic, then proceed to examine subtopics of particular interest. For example, Chapter 7, Juvenile Crime and Victimization, begins by discussing several major surveys of crime and victimization in the United States. It then delves into crime trends and the juveniles who commit offenses, and continues on to review the risk factors of youth violence. The chapter presents an overview of juvenile victims of crime and concludes with sections on child abuse and neglect, missing children, abducted youth, runaways, and thrownaways. Readers can find their way through a chapter by looking for the section and subsection headings, which are clearly set off from the text. Or, they can refer to the book's extensive Index, if they already know what they are looking for.

Statistical Information

The tables and figures featured throughout *Growing Up: Issues Affecting America's Youth* will be of particular use to the reader in learning about this topic. These tables and figures represent an extensive collection of the most recent and valuable statistics on growing up in America, as well as related issues—for example, graphics in the book cover the number of children without health insurance, the percentage of students who consume alcohol, the rate of teens having abortions, the number of youth in gangs, and the presence of violence at school. The Gale Group believes that making this information available to the reader is the most important way in which we fulfill the goal of this book: to help readers understand the issues and controversies surrounding youth in America and reach their own conclusions.

Each table or figure has a unique identifier appearing above it, for ease of identification and reference. Titles for the tables and figures explain their purpose. At the end of each table or figure, the original source of the data is provided.

In order to help readers understand these often complicated statistics, all tables and figures are explained in the text. References in the text direct the reader to the relevant statistics. Furthermore, the contents of all tables and figures are fully indexed. Please see the opening section of the Index at the back of this volume for a description of how to find tables and figures within it.

Appendixes

In addition to the main body text and images, *Growing Up: Issues Affecting America's Youth* has three appendixes. The first is the Important Names and Addresses directory. Here the reader will find contact information for a number of organizations that study children, adolescents, and families. The second appendix is the Resources section, which can also assist the reader in conducting his or her own research. In this section, the author and editors of *Growing Up: Issues Affecting America's Youth* describe some of the sources that were most useful during the compilation of this book. The final appendix is the Index.

ADVISORY BOARD CONTRIBUTIONS

The staff of Information Plus would like to extend its heartfelt appreciation to the Information Plus Advisory Board. This dedicated group of media professionals provides feedback on the series on an ongoing basis. Their comments allow the editorial staff who work on the project to make the series better and more user-friendly. Our top priorities are to produce the highest-quality and most useful books possible, and the Advisory Board's contributions to this process are invaluable.

The members of the Information Plus Advisory Board are:

- Kathleen R. Bonn, Librarian, Newbury Park High School, Newbury Park, California

- Madelyn Garner, Librarian, San Jacinto College–North Campus, Houston, Texas

- Anne Oxenrider, Media Specialist, Dundee High School, Dundee, Michigan

- Charles R. Rodgers, Director of Libraries, Pasco-Hernando Community College, Dade City, Florida

- James N. Zitzelsberger, Library Media Department Chairman, Oshkosh West High School, Oshkosh, Wisconsin

COMMENTS AND SUGGESTIONS

The editors of the *Information Plus Reference Series* welcome your feedback on *Growing Up: Issues Affecting America's Youth*. Please direct all correspondence to:

Editors
Information Plus Reference Series
27500 Drake Rd.
Farmington Hills, MI 48331-3535

CHAPTER 1
CHILDREN AND FAMILIES IN THE UNITED STATES

DEFINING CHILDHOOD AND ADULTHOOD

Exactly when childhood ends and adulthood begins differs among cultures and over periods of time within cultures. People in some societies believe that adulthood begins with the onset of puberty, arguing that people who are old enough to have children are also old enough to assume adult responsibilities. This stage of life is often solemnized with special celebrations. In the Jewish tradition, for example, the bar mitzvah ceremony for thirteen-year-old boys and the bat mitzvah ceremony for thirteen-year-old girls commemorates the attainment of adult responsibility for observing Jewish law.

Modern American society identifies an interim period of life between childhood and adulthood known as adolescence, during which teens reach a series of milestones as they accept increasing amounts of adult responsibility. At age sixteen most Americans can be licensed to drive. At eighteen most young people leave the public education system and are eligible to vote. At that time they can be tried as adults in the court system and join the military without parental permission. There are contradictions in the rights and privileges conferred, however. In many states teens under the age of eighteen can marry but cannot view or purchase pornographic material.

In general, American society recognizes twenty-one as the age of full adulthood. At twenty-one young men and women are considered legally independent of their parents and are completely responsible for their own decisions. They are allowed to buy alcoholic beverages and become eligible to apply for some jobs in the federal government.

According to the Federal Interagency Forum on Child and Family Statistics, in *America's Children in Brief: Key National Indicators of Well-Being, 2006* (http://childstats.gov/americaschildren/pop.asp), in 2004 seventy-three million children younger than the age of eighteen lived in the United States, almost a million more than in 2000. This number is expected to increase to eighty million by 2020.

However, because the country's entire population will increase, the percentage of children in the population is projected to remain fairly steady, decreasing slightly from 25% in 2004 to 24% by 2020.

BIRTH AND FERTILITY RATES

Fertility is measured in a number of ways. One such measure, called the crude birthrate, is the number of live births per 1,000 women in the population, regardless of their age, in any given year. In 2004 the crude birthrate was 14 live births per 1,000 women. The crude birthrate for Hispanic women (of any race) was considerably higher (22.9) than for Asian and Pacific Islander women (16.8), non-Hispanic African-American women (15.8), Native American or Alaskan Native women (14), and non-Hispanic white women (11.6). (See Table 1.1.)

Another way to measure the number of births is the fertility rate, the number of live births per 1,000 women in the population between the ages of fifteen and forty-four years in any given year. These are the years generally considered to be a woman's reproductive age range. During the first ten years of the baby boom that immediately followed World War II (1939–45), fertility rates were well over 100 births per 1,000 women per year. (See Table 1.1.) In contrast, the fertility rate for American women in 2004 was 66.3 births per 1,000 women, just over half the 1960 fertility rate of 118 births per 1,000 women. However, some groups in American society have much higher fertility rates than average. In 2004 the fertility rate for Hispanic women was 97.8 births per 1,000 women; for Asian and Pacific Islander women, 67.1; for non-Hispanic African-American women, 67; and for non-Hispanic white women, 58.4.

Birth Trends

In "Projected Total Fertility Rates by Race and Hispanic Origin, 1999 to 2100" (January 13, 2000, http://www.census.gov/population/projections/nation/summary/

TABLE 1.1

Crude birth rates, fertility rates, and birth rates by age of mother, according to race and Hispanic origin, selected years 1950–2004

[Data are based on birth certificates]

Race, Hispanic origin, and year	Crude birth rate[a]	Fertility rate[b]	10–14 years	15–19 years Total	15–17 years	18–19 years	20–24 years	25–29 years	30–34 years	35–39 years	40–44 years	45–54 years[c]
All races						Live births per 1,000 women						
1950	24.1	106.2	1.0	81.6	40.7	132.7	196.6	166.1	103.7	52.9	15.1	1.2
1960	23.7	118.0	0.8	89.1	43.9	166.7	258.1	197.4	112.7	56.2	15.5	0.9
1970	18.4	87.9	1.2	68.3	38.8	114.7	167.8	145.1	73.3	31.7	8.1	0.5
1980	15.9	68.4	1.1	53.0	32.5	82.1	115.1	112.9	61.9	19.8	3.9	0.2
1985	15.8	66.3	1.2	51.0	31.0	79.6	108.3	111.0	69.1	24.0	4.0	0.2
1990	16.7	70.9	1.4	59.9	37.5	88.6	116.5	120.2	80.8	31.7	5.5	0.2
1995	14.6	64.6	1.3	56.0	35.5	87.7	107.5	108.8	81.1	34.0	6.6	0.3
2000	14.4	65.9	0.9	47.7	26.9	78.1	109.7	113.5	91.2	39.7	8.0	0.5
2002	13.9	64.8	0.7	43.0	23.2	72.8	103.6	113.6	91.5	41.4	8.3	0.5
2003	14.1	66.1	0.6	41.6	22.4	70.7	102.6	115.6	95.1	43.8	8.7	0.5
2004	14.0	66.3	0.7	41.1	22.1	70.0	101.7	115.5	95.3	45.4	8.9	0.5
Race of child:[d] white												
1950	23.0	102.3	0.4	70.0	31.3	120.5	190.4	165.1	102.6	51.4	14.5	1.0
1960	22.7	113.2	0.4	79.4	35.5	154.6	252.8	194.9	109.6	54.0	14.7	0.8
1970	17.4	84.1	0.5	57.4	29.2	101.5	163.4	145.9	71.9	30.0	7.5	0.4
1980	14.9	64.7	0.6	44.7	25.2	72.1	109.5	112.4	60.4	18.5	3.4	0.2
Race of mother:[e] white												
1980	15.1	65.6	0.6	45.4	25.5	73.2	111.1	113.8	61.2	18.8	3.5	0.2
1985	15.0	64.1	0.6	43.3	24.4	70.4	104.1	112.3	69.9	23.3	3.7	0.2
1990	15.8	68.3	0.7	50.8	29.5	78.0	109.8	120.7	81.7	31.5	5.2	0.2
1995	14.1	63.6	0.8	49.5	29.6	80.2	104.7	111.7	83.3	34.2	6.4	0.3
2000	13.9	65.3	0.6	43.2	23.3	72.3	106.6	116.7	94.6	40.2	7.9	0.4
2002	13.5	64.8	0.5	39.4	20.5	68.0	101.6	117.4	95.5	42.4	8.2	0.5
2003	13.6	66.1	0.5	38.3	19.8	66.2	100.6	119.5	99.3	44.8	8.7	0.5
2004	13.5	66.1	0.5	37.7	19.5	65.0	99.2	118.6	99.1	46.4	8.9	0.5
Race of child:[d] black or African American												
1960	31.9	153.5	4.3	156.1	—	—	295.4	218.6	137.1	73.9	21.9	1.1
1970	25.3	115.4	5.2	140.7	101.4	204.9	202.7	136.3	79.6	41.9	12.5	1.0
1980	22.1	88.1	4.3	100.0	73.6	138.8	146.3	109.1	62.9	24.5	5.8	0.3
Race of mother:[e] black or African American												
1980	21.3	84.9	4.3	97.8	72.5	135.1	140.0	103.9	59.9	23.5	5.6	0.3
1985	20.4	78.8	4.5	95.4	69.3	132.4	135.0	100.2	57.9	23.9	4.6	0.3
1990	22.4	86.8	4.9	112.8	82.3	152.9	160.2	115.5	68.7	28.1	5.5	0.3
1995	17.8	71.0	4.1	94.4	68.5	135.0	133.7	95.6	63.0	28.4	6.0	0.3
2000	17.0	70.0	2.3	77.4	49.0	118.8	141.3	100.3	65.4	31.5	7.2	0.4
2002	15.7	65.8	1.8	66.6	40.0	107.6	127.1	99.0	64.4	31.5	7.4	0.4
2003	15.7	66.3	1.6	63.8	38.2	103.7	126.1	100.4	66.5	33.2	7.7	0.5
2004	16.0	67.6	1.6	63.3	37.2	104.4	127.7	103.6	67.9	34.0	7.9	0.5
American Indian or Alaska Native mothers[e]												
1980	20.7	82.7	1.9	82.2	51.5	129.5	143.7	106.6	61.8	28.1	8.2	*
1985	19.8	78.6	1.7	79.2	47.7	124.1	139.1	109.6	62.6	27.4	6.0	*
1990	18.9	76.2	1.6	81.1	48.5	129.3	148.7	110.3	61.5	27.5	5.9	*
1995	15.3	63.0	1.6	72.9	44.6	122.2	123.1	91.6	56.5	24.3	5.5	*
2000	14.0	58.7	1.1	58.3	34.1	97.1	117.2	91.8	55.5	24.6	5.7	0.3
2002	13.8	58.0	0.9	53.8	30.7	89.2	112.6	91.8	56.4	25.4	5.8	0.3
2003	13.8	58.4	1.0	53.1	30.6	87.3	110.0	93.5	57.4	25.4	5.5	0.4
2004	14.0	58.9	0.9	52.5	30.0	87.0	109.7	92.8	58.0	26.8	6.0	0.2

np-t7-a.pdf), the U.S. Census Bureau indicates that total fertility rates among racial and ethnic groups are expected to differ markedly in the twenty-first century. Total fertility rate refers to the average number of children a woman will give birth to in her lifetime. The total fertility rate of white women is expected to rise slightly through the century but not to reach the population replacement rate (the fertility rate needed to keep the population stable). The total fertility rate for African-American, non-Hispanic women will remain steady at about the population replacement rate. Native American and Asian total fertility rates are expected to decrease slightly but remain well above the population replacement rate through the twenty-first century. The Hispanic total fertility rate is also expected to decrease from a high of 2,920.5 births per 1,000 women over their lifetimes in

TABLE 1.1

Crude birth rates, fertility rates, and birth rates by age of mother, according to race and Hispanic origin, selected years 1950–2004

[CONTINUED]

[Data are based on birth certificates]

Race, Hispanic origin, and year	Crude birth rate[a]	Fertility rate[b]	10–14 years	15–19 years Total	15–17 years	18–19 years	20–24 years	25–29 years	30–34 years	35–39 years	40–44 years	45–54 years[c]
Asian or Pacific Islander mothers[d]						Live births per 1,000 women					
1980	19.9	73.2	0.3	26.2	12.0	46.2	93.3	127.4	96.0	38.3	8.5	0.7
1985	18.7	68.4	0.4	23.8	12.5	40.8	83.6	123.0	93.6	42.7	8.7	1.2
1990	19.0	69.6	0.7	26.4	16.0	40.2	79.2	126.3	106.5	49.6	10.7	1.1
1995	16.7	62.6	0.7	25.5	15.6	40.1	64.2	103.7	102.3	50.1	11.8	0.8
2000	17.1	65.8	0.3	20.5	11.6	32.6	60.3	108.4	116.5	59.0	12.6	0.8
2002	16.5	64.1	0.3	18.3	9.0	31.5	60.4	105.4	109.6	56.5	12.5	0.9
2003	16.8	66.3	0.2	17.4	8.8	29.8	59.6	108.5	114.6	59.9	13.5	0.9
2004	16.8	67.1	0.2	17.3	8.9	29.6	59.8	108.6	116.9	62.1	13.6	1.0
Hispanic or Latino mothers[e, f]												
1980	23.5	95.4	1.7	82.2	52.1	126.9	156.4	132.1	83.2	39.9	10.6	0.7
1990	26.7	107.7	2.4	100.3	65.9	147.7	181.0	153.0	98.3	45.3	10.9	0.7
1995	24.1	98.8	2.6	99.3	68.3	145.4	171.9	140.4	90.5	43.7	10.7	0.6
2000	23.1	95.9	1.7	87.3	55.5	132.6	161.3	139.9	97.1	46.6	11.5	0.6
2002	22.6	94.4	1.4	83.4	50.7	133.0	164.3	139.4	95.1	47.8	11.5	0.7
2003	22.9	96.9	1.3	82.3	49.7	132.0	163.4	144.4	102.0	50.8	12.2	0.7
2004	22.9	97.8	1.3	82.6	49.7	133.5	165.3	145.6	104.1	52.9	12.4	0.7
White, not Hispanic or Latino mothers[e, f]												
1980	14.2	62.4	0.4	41.2	22.4	67.7	105.5	110.6	59.9	17.7	3.0	0.1
1990	14.4	62.8	0.5	42.5	23.2	66.6	97.5	115.3	79.4	30.0	4.7	0.2
1995	12.5	57.5	0.4	39.3	22.0	66.2	90.2	105.1	81.5	32.8	5.9	0.3
2000	12.2	58.5	0.3	32.6	15.8	57.5	91.2	109.4	93.2	38.8	7.3	0.4
2002	11.7	57.4	0.2	28.5	13.1	51.9	84.3	109.3	94.4	40.9	7.6	0.5
2003	11.8	58.5	0.2	27.4	12.4	50.0	83.5	110.8	97.6	43.2	8.1	0.5
2004	11.6	58.4	0.2	26.7	12.0	48.7	81.9	110.0	97.1	44.8	8.2	0.5
Black or African American, not Hispanic or Latino mothers[e, f]												
1980	22.9	90.7	4.6	105.1	77.2	146.5	152.2	111.7	65.2	25.8	5.8	0.3
1990	23.0	89.0	5.0	116.2	84.9	157.5	165.1	118.4	70.2	28.7	5.6	0.3
1995	18.2	72.8	4.2	97.2	70.4	139.2	137.8	98.5	64.4	28.8	6.1	0.3
2000	17.3	71.4	2.4	79.2	50.1	121.9	145.4	102.8	66.5	31.8	7.2	0.4
2002	16.1	67.4	1.9	68.3	41.0	110.3	131.0	102.1	66.1	32.1	7.5	0.4
2003	15.9	67.1	1.6	64.7	38.7	105.3	128.1	102.1	67.4	33.4	7.7	0.5
2004	15.8	67.0	1.6	63.1	37.1	103.9	126.9	103.0	67.4	33.7	7.8	0.5

— Data not available.

*Rates based on fewer than 20 births are considered unreliable and are not shown.

[a]Live births per 1,000 population.

[b]Total number of live births regardless of age of mother per 1,000 women 15–44 years of age.

[c]Prior to 1997, data are for live births to mothers 45–49 years of age per 1,000 women 45–49 years of age. Starting with 1997 data, rates are for live births to mothers 45–54 years of age per 1,000 women 45–49 years of age.

[d]Live births are tabulated by race of child.

[e]Live births are tabulated by race and/or Hispanic origin of mother.

[f]Prior to 1993, data from states lacking an Hispanic-origin item on the birth certificate were excluded. Rates in 1985 were not calculated because estimates for the Hispanic and non-Hispanic populations were not available.

Notes: Data are based on births adjusted for underregistration for 1950 and on registered births for all other years. Starting with 1970 data, births to persons who were not residents of the 50 states and the District of Columbia are excluded. Starting with *Health, United States, 2003*, rates for 1991–1999 were revised using intercensal population estimates based on the 2000 census. Rates for 2000 were computed using the 2000 census counts and starting in 2001 rates were computed using 2000-based postcensal estimates. The race groups, white, black, American Indian or Alaska Native, and Asian or Pacific Islander, include persons of Hispanic and non-Hispanic origin. Persons of Hispanic origin may be of any race. Starting with 2003 data, some states reported multiple-race data. The multiple-race data for these states were bridged to the single race categories of the 1977 Office of Management and Budget standards for comparability with other states. Interpretation of trend data should take into consideration expansion of reporting areas and immigration.

SOURCE: "Table 4. Crude Birth Rates, Fertility Rates, and Birth Rates by Age, Race and Hispanic Origin of Mother: United States, Selected Years 1950–2004," in *Health, United States, 2006, with Chartbook on Trends in the Health of Americans*, Centers for Disease Control and Prevention, National Center for Health Statistics, 2006, http://0-www.cdc.gov.mill1.sjlibrary.org/nchs/data/hus/hus06.pdf (accessed February 6, 2007)

1999 to 2,333.8 births per 1,000 women in 2100—a rate still well above the population replacement rate and well above the rates of other ethnic and racial groups. As a result, the proportion of American children who are non-Hispanic white is expected to decrease from 59% in 2004 to 53% in 2020, and the proportion of children who are Hispanic is expected to increase from 19% in 2004 to 24% in 2020, whereas other race and ethnic groups will proportionally stay about the same. (See Figure 1.1.)

FIGURE 1.1

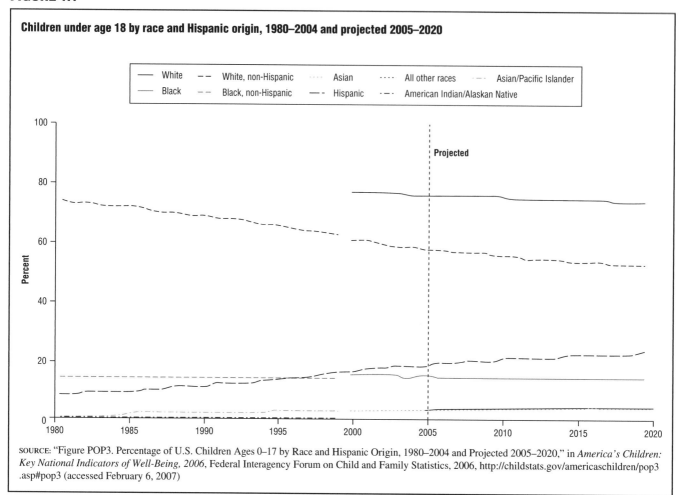

Children under age 18 by race and Hispanic origin, 1980–2004 and projected 2005–2020

SOURCE: "Figure POP3. Percentage of U.S. Children Ages 0–17 by Race and Hispanic Origin, 1980–2004 and Projected 2005–2020," in *America's Children: Key National Indicators of Well-Being, 2006*, Federal Interagency Forum on Child and Family Statistics, 2006, http://childstats.gov/americaschildren/pop3 .asp#pop3 (accessed February 6, 2007)

After 2020 Hispanic births are expected to add more people each year to the U.S. population than all other non-white racial/ethnic groups combined. By 2010 the Hispanic-origin population will likely become the nation's second-largest group. The white, non-Hispanic population will drop from 69.4% of the total population in 2000 to 50.1% in 2050, whereas the Hispanic population will rise from 12.6% of the total population in 2000 to 24.4% in 2050. (See Table 1.2.)

As a result, the youth segment of the U.S. population is becoming more racially diverse. Between 1980 and 2004 the non-Hispanic white share of the under-eighteen population dropped from 74% to 59%. (See Figure 1.1.) During the same period the non-Hispanic African-American share of this population remained stable, increasing only slightly from 15% to 16%. In contrast, the Asian and Pacific Islander share of the under-eighteen population increased from 2% in 1980 to 4% in 2004. The Hispanic share of the under-eighteen population showed the highest increase, from 9% in 1980 to 19% in 2004. In 2004 almost one out of every five children in the United States (19%) was of Hispanic origin.

Evidence also suggests that racial and ethnic lines became less rigid in the United States in the last two decades of the twentieth century, as people from different ethnic and racial backgrounds parented children together. People who reported in the 2000 census that they came from more than one ethnic or racial background had a significantly younger median age than all single-race groups, at 22.7 years. (See Figure 1.2.) Almost one out of two people (41.9%) with a mixed ethnic or racial background were under the age of eighteen. This finding may indicate that distinctions between racial and ethnic groups in the United States will continue to blur in the twenty-first century.

CHANGING FAMILY
Family and Household Size

The composition of households in American society changed markedly in the twentieth century. According to Frank Hobbs and Nicole Stoops, in *Demographic Trends in the 20th Century* (November 2002, http://www.census .gov/ prod/2002pubs/censr-4.pdf), in 1950 families accounted for 89.4% of all households; by 2000 that number had decreased to 68.1%. The proportion of married-couple households that included at least one child under the age of eighteen had also decreased. In 1980 nearly 80% of all family groups with children were married-couple households; that

TABLE 1.2

Projected population of the United States by race and Hispanic origin, selected years 2000–50

[In thousands except as indicated. As of July 1. Resident population.]

Population or percent and race or Hispanic origin	2000	2010	2020	2030	2040	2050
Population total	282,125	308,936	335,806	363,584	391,946	419,854
White alone	228,548	244,995	260,629	275,731	289,690	302,626
Black alone	35,818	40,454	45,365	50,442	55,876	61,361
Asian alone*	10,684	14,241	17,988	22,580	27,992	33,430
All other races	7,075	9,246	11,822	14,831	18,388	22,437
Hispanic (of any race)	35,622	47,756	59,756	73,055	87,585	102,560
White alone, not Hispanic	195,729	201,112	205,936	209,176	210,331	210,283
	100.0	100.0	100.0	100.0	100.0	100.0
White alone	81.0	79.3	77.6	75.8	73.9	72.1
Black alone	12.7	13.1	13.5	13.9	14.3	14.6
Asian alone	3.8	4.6	5.4	6.2	7.1	8.0
All other races*	2.5	3.0	3.5	4.1	4.7	5.3
Hispanic (of any race)	12.6	15.5	17.8	20.1	22.3	24.4
White alone, not Hispanic	69.4	65.1	61.3	57.5	53.7	50.1

*Includes American Indian and Alaska Native alone, Native Hawaiian and other Pacific Islander alone, and two or more races

SOURCE: "Table 1a. Projected Population of the United States, by Race and Hispanic Origin: 2000 to 2050," in *U.S. Interim Projections by Age, Sex, Race, and Hispanic Origin*, U.S. Census Bureau, March 18, 2004, http://www.census.gov/ipc/www/usinterimproj/natprojtab01a.pdf (accessed February 6, 2007)

percentage had dropped to only 72% by 2003. (See Figure 1.3.)

The American family shrank in size during the twentieth century. In 1900 most households consisted of five or more people. By 1950 two-person families became the most common family type and remained so to the end of the century. (See Figure 1.4.) The proportion of one- and two-person households increased from 1970 to 2003, whereas the proportion of households with three or more people steadily decreased. In addition, Jason Fields notes in *America's Families and Living Arrangements: 2003* (November 2004, http://www.census.gov/prod/2004pubs/p20-553.pdf) that the average household size declined from 3.14 people in 1970 to 2.57 in 2003. This was true partly because the population was getting older, which meant that a smaller proportion of households consisted of parents and their children.

Fewer Traditional Families

One of the more significant social changes to occur in the last decades of the twentieth century was a shift away from the traditional family structure—a married couple with their own child or children living in the home. The Census Bureau divides households into two major categories: family households (defined as groups of two or more people living together related by birth, marriage, or adoption) and nonfamily households (consisting of a person living alone or an individual living with others to whom he or she is not related). As a percentage of all households, family households declined between 1970 and 2003. According to Fields, in 1970 family households accounted for 81% of all households.

By 2003 that figure had dropped to 68%. The rise in nonfamily households is the result of many factors, some of the most prominent being:

• People are postponing marriage until later in life and are thus living alone or with nonrelatives for a longer period.

• A rising divorce rate translates into more people living alone or with nonrelatives.

• A rise in the number of people who cohabit before or instead of marriage results in higher numbers of nonfamily households.

• The oldest members of our population are living longer and often live in nonfamily households as widows/widowers or in institutional settings.

Although family households were a smaller proportion of all households in 2000 than in 1950, they were still the majority of households. The Census Bureau breaks family households into three categories: married couples with their own children, married couples without children, and other family households. This last category includes single-parent households and households made up of relatives (such as siblings) who live together or grandparents who live with grandchildren without members of the middle generation being present.

Of the three categories, the "other family household" grew the most between 1970 and 2003, growing from 10.6% of all households in 1970 to 16.4% in 2003. (See Figure 1.5.) The traditional family household experienced the greatest decline during this same period. Married couples with their own children made up 40.3% of households in 1970 but only 23.3% in 2003.

FIGURE 1.2

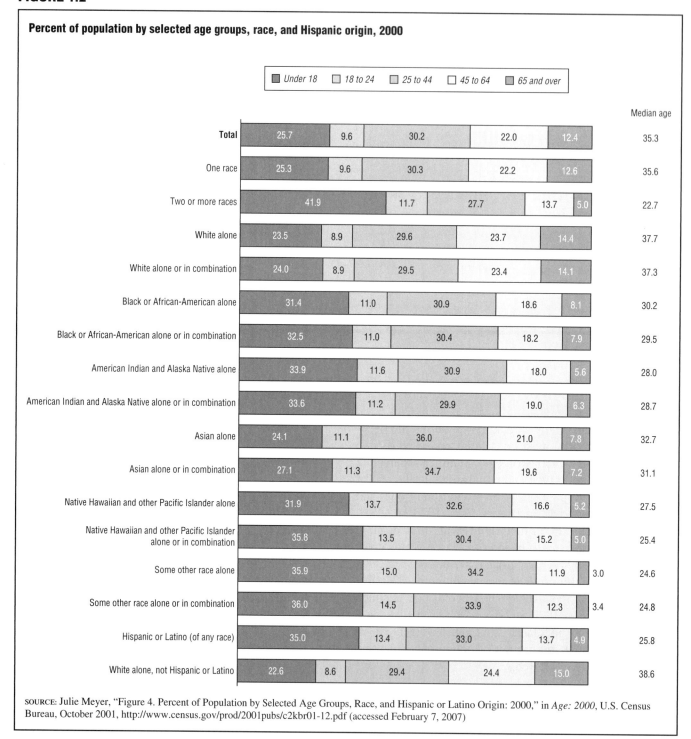

Percent of population by selected age groups, race, and Hispanic origin, 2000

	Under 18	18 to 24	25 to 44	45 to 64	65 and over	Median age
Total	25.7	9.6	30.2	22.0	12.4	35.3
One race	25.3	9.6	30.3	22.2	12.6	35.6
Two or more races	41.9	11.7	27.7	13.7	5.0	22.7
White alone	23.5	8.9	29.6	23.7	14.4	37.7
White alone or in combination	24.0	8.9	29.5	23.4	14.1	37.3
Black or African-American alone	31.4	11.0	30.9	18.6	8.1	30.2
Black or African-American alone or in combination	32.5	11.0	30.4	18.2	7.9	29.5
American Indian and Alaska Native alone	33.9	11.6	30.9	18.0	5.6	28.0
American Indian and Alaska Native alone or in combination	33.6	11.2	29.9	19.0	6.3	28.7
Asian alone	24.1	11.1	36.0	21.0	7.8	32.7
Asian alone or in combination	27.1	11.3	34.7	19.6	7.2	31.1
Native Hawaiian and other Pacific Islander alone	31.9	13.7	32.6	16.6	5.2	27.5
Native Hawaiian and other Pacific Islander alone or in combination	35.8	13.5	30.4	15.2	5.0	25.4
Some other race alone	35.9	15.0	34.2	11.9	3.0	24.6
Some other race alone or in combination	36.0	14.5	33.9	12.3	3.4	24.8
Hispanic or Latino (of any race)	35.0	13.4	33.0	13.7	4.9	25.8
White alone, not Hispanic or Latino	22.6	8.6	29.4	24.4	15.0	38.6

SOURCE: Julie Meyer, "Figure 4. Percent of Population by Selected Age Groups, Race, and Hispanic or Latino Origin: 2000," in *Age: 2000*, U.S. Census Bureau, October 2001, http://www.census.gov/prod/2001pubs/c2kbr01-12.pdf (accessed February 7, 2007)

One- and Two-Parent Families

Among all families with children, two-parent families accounted for 87.2% of families in 1970 and 67.4% in 2005. (See Table 1.3.) Overall, most households with children are still headed by married couples. However, the decline in the percentage of children being raised in two-parent households has been the subject of much study and attention.

In 2005, 12,835 (or 32.6%) of all families with children were maintained by just one parent, compared with just 3,803 (or 12.8%) in 1970. (See Table 1.3.) In 2005 mothers were single parents 4.2 times as often as fathers. In 1970 that figure was 8.7 times as often; in 1970 there were few single-father families. During that thirty-two-year period, the number of single-father families increased more than fivefold, whereas single-mother households increased threefold.

The proportion of families headed by a single parent increased between 1980 and 2005 in all racial and ethnic

FIGURE 1.3

Family groups with children, by type of family group, 1970–2003

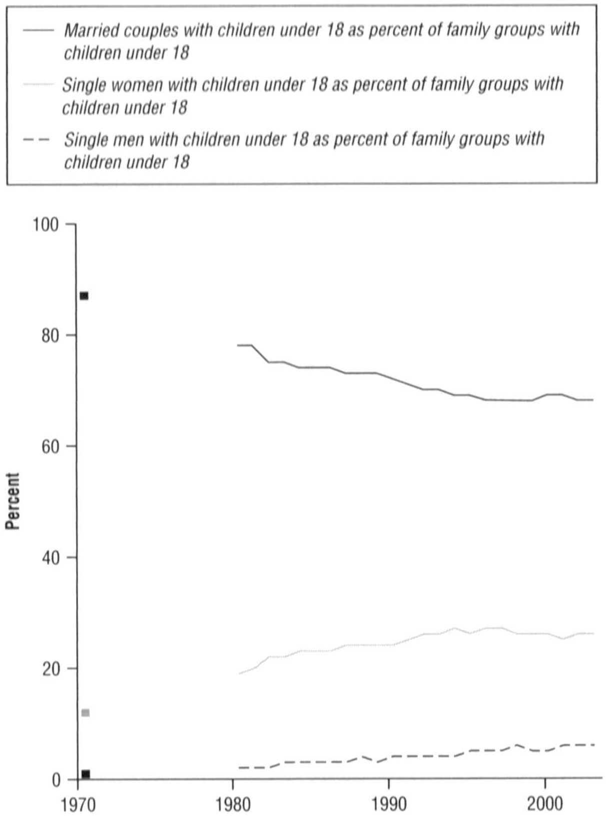

—— Married couples with children under 18 as percent of family groups with children under 18

—— Single women with children under 18 as percent of family groups with children under 18

— — Single men with children under 18 as percent of family groups with children under 18

Note: Family groups are family households plus all related and unrelated subfamilies. These subfamilies may consist of either married couples or parent-child units, and the reference person of that family group may be either related or unrelated to the householder.

SOURCE: Jason Fields, "Figure 1. Family Groups with Children by Type of Family Group: 1970 to 2003," in *America's Families and Living Arrangements: 2003*, U.S. Census Bureau, November 2004, http://www.census.gov/prod/2004pubs/p20-553.pdf (accessed February 7, 2007)

FIGURE 1.4

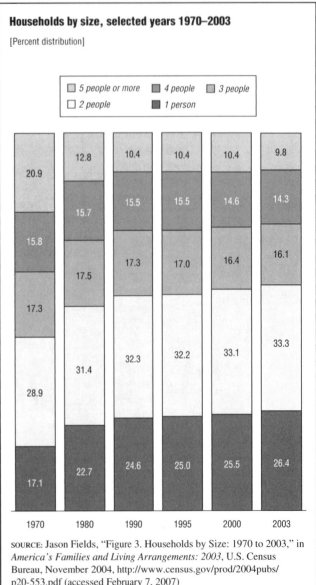

Households by size, selected years 1970–2003

[Percent distribution]

SOURCE: Jason Fields, "Figure 3. Households by Size: 1970 to 2003," in *America's Families and Living Arrangements: 2003*, U.S. Census Bureau, November 2004, http://www.census.gov/prod/2004pubs/p20-553.pdf (accessed February 7, 2007)

groups. African-American children were the least likely of all racial and ethnic groups to live in two-parent households throughout this period (37.6% in 2005). (See Table 1.3.)

The rise in single-parent families is the result of several factors, all pointing to a change in American lifestyles and values. Among these changes are an escalating divorce rate and an increase in the number of children born to unmarried women.

The Census Bureau reports in the 2005 American Community Survey (http://factfinder.census.gov) that 23.3 million individuals in the United States in 2005 were divorced and had not remarried. This was 3.6 times more than the 6.5 million divorced individuals in 1975, according to the bureau's *Number, Timing, and Duration of Marriages and Divorces in the United*

States: June 1975 (October 1976, http://www.census.gov/population/socdemo/marr-div/p20-297/p20-297.pdf).

The rise in the number of single-parent family households can also be attributed to the dramatic increase in the number of births to unmarried women. In 2004, 35.8% of births were to unmarried women. (See Table 1.4.) Nonmarital birthrates differed significantly by race and ethnicity. Hispanic women had the highest birthrate among unmarried mothers in 2004, at 95.7 births per 1,000 women of childbearing age. The birthrate for unmarried African-American women was 67.2 births per 1,000 women. The rate for unmarried, non-Hispanic white women was 29.4 births per 1,000 women. The rate of births to unmarried women was highest among women in their twenties; the birthrate for unmarried women aged twenty to twenty-four years was 72.5 births per 1,000 women, and the rate for women aged twenty-five to twenty-nine was 68.6 births per 1,000 women.

FIGURE 1.5

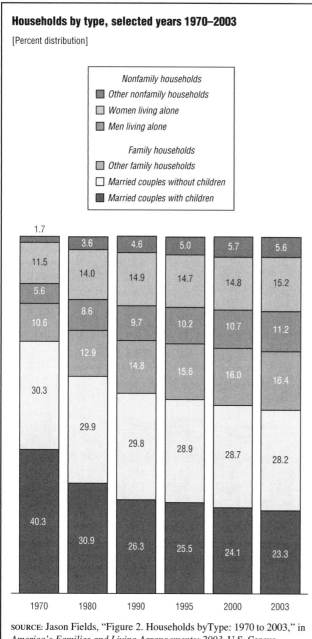

Households by type, selected years 1970–2003

[Percent distribution]

SOURCE: Jason Fields, "Figure 2. Households byType: 1970 to 2003," in *America's Families and Living Arrangements: 2003*, U.S. Census Bureau, November 2004, http://www.census.gov/prod/2004pubs/p20-553.pdf(accessed February 7, 2007)

LIVING ARRANGEMENTS OF CHILDREN
Single-Parent Families

Many children who live in single-parent households face significant challenges that can be exacerbated by racial and ethnic inequalities. In *America's Children in Brief* (http://www.childstats.gov/americaschildren/tables.asp), the Federal Interagency Forum on Child and Family Statistics indicates that in 2004 the poverty rate was 34% for African-American children and 29% for Hispanic children, but was only 11% for non-Hispanic white children. Children who live in minority families with a single parent are likely to have greatly reduced economic,

educational, and social opportunities. Single parents are more likely to have a low income and less education and are more likely to be unemployed and to be renting a home or apartment or living in public housing.

Nontraditional Families

Many single-parent families, however, are not single adult families; some single parents maintain a household with an unmarried partner. In 1990 the Census Bureau sought to reflect changing lifestyles in the United States by asking for the first time whether unmarried couples maintained households together. Although in 2000 a slight majority of U.S. households (52%) were headed by married couples, a significant number of unmarried couples also maintained households together. The Census Bureau notes in the 2005 American Community Survey that in 2005, 5.9 million unmarried couples cohabited in the United States. Most of these couples were opposite-sex couples, but over 776,000 of them were same-sex couples.

A significant portion of all coupled households in 2003 contained children under the age of eighteen. Fields notes that 45% of all married-couple households had children living within them, and almost as many unmarried-partner households, 41%, contained children. However, a sizeable percentage of same-sex partnered households also contained children; Tavia Simmons and Martin O'Connell note in *Married-Couple and Unmarried-Partner Households: 2000* (February 2003, http://www.census.gov/prod/2003pubs/censr-5.pdf) that in 2000, the latest year for which data are available, nearly a quarter (22.3%) of households headed by male partners and a third (34.3%) of households headed by female partners had children living with them.

Figure 1.6 shows the dramatic differences in the proportion of children living with single parents and cohabiting single parents by race and ethnic group. Children from all backgrounds were much more likely to be living with a single mother (23%) than a single father (5%). However, 33% of children living with single fathers also lived with cohabiting partners, compared with only 11% of children living with single mothers.

Grandparents

Grandparents sometimes provide housing for, and sometimes reside in, the homes of their children and grandchildren. According to the Child Trends Databank (2005, http://www.childtrendsdatabank.org/tables/59_Table_2.htm), in 2005, 5.6% of children under age eighteen (or 4.1 million children) lived in the homes of their grandparents; 2.2% (or 1.6 million children) lived with their grandparents without a parent present. This percentage remained fairly steady from 1970 to 2005, varying from a low of 1.3% in 1992 to a high of 2.2% in 2005. These caretaking grandparents are responsible for most of

TABLE 1.3

Family households by type, race, and Hispanic origin, selected years 1970–2005

[Numbers in thousands]

Year	Total with own children under 18	All family groups Two-parent	One parent Total	One parent Maintained by Mother	One parent Maintained by Father	Two-parent families as percent of total
All races						
2005	39,317	26,482	12,835	10,366	2,469	67.4
1970	29,626	25,823	3,803	3,410	393	87.2
White						
2005ᵃ	30,960	22,319	8,641	6,747	1,894	72.1
1970	26,115	23,477	2,638	2,330	307	89.9
Black						
2005ᵃ	5,495	2,065	3,430	3,037	393	37.6
1970	3,219	2,071	1,148	1,063	85	64.3
Hispanic originᵇ						
2002	6,752	4,346	2,406	1,964	442	64.5
1980	2,194	1,626	568	526	42	74.1
1970	(NA)	(NA)	(NA)	(NA)	(NA)	(NA)

ᵃHouseholder whose race was reported as only one race.
ᵇPersons of Hispanic origin may be of any race.

SOURCE: Adapted from "FM-2. All Parent/Child Situations, by Type, Race, and Hispanic Origin of Householder or Reference Person: 1970 to Present," in *Families and Living Arrangements*, U.S. Census Bureau, September 21, 2006, http://www.census.gov/population/socdemo/hh-fam/fm2.pdf (accessed February 7, 2007)

the basic needs (food, shelter, clothing) of one or more of the grandchildren living with them.

Living and caretaking arrangements of grandparents and grandchildren varied by race and ethnicity in 2000, the latest year for which detailed data are available. African-American, Native American, and Hispanic grandparents were four times more likely to live with their grandchildren than white grandparents. (See Table 1.5.) However, Hispanic grandparents (34.7%) were less likely than African-American (51.7%) or Native American (56.1%) grandparents to be the primary caregivers for those grandchildren. Asian grandparents (20%) were least likely of all groups to be the primary caretakers for the grandchildren with whom they resided.

The homes maintained by grandparents without parents present were more likely to experience economic hardship than families with a parent present, reflecting the often limited and fixed resources of senior citizens. According to Jason Fields, in *Children's Living Arrangements and Characteristics: March 2002* (June 2003, http://www.census .gov/prod/ 2003pubs/p20-547.pdf), of all grandchildren, 988,000 (18%) lived below the poverty line in 2002, 1.3 million (23%) were not covered by health insurance, and 506,000 (9%) received public assistance. Among children who lived with their grandparents with their parents absent, the numbers were much higher: 381,000 (30%) were below the poverty line, 457,000 (36%) were not covered by health insurance, and 215,000 (17%) received public assistance. These numbers suggest that children who live with their grandparents without

a parent present are at an economic disadvantage; grandchildren's presence in their grandparents' home without an economic contribution from the middle generation appears to severely tax the economic resources of grandparents.

Foster Care and Adoption

There is currently no comprehensive federal registry system for adoptions, which can be arranged by government agencies, private agencies, and through private arrangements between birth mothers and adoptive parents with the assistance of lawyers. The federally funded National Center for Social Statistics collected information on all finalized adoptions from 1957 to 1975, but with the dissolution of the center, limited statistical information is now available. With the passage of the Adoption and Safe Families Act of 1997, there was a renewed effort to improve the data available about adoption. The U.S. Department of Health and Human Services, through the Adoption and Foster Care Analysis and Reporting System (AFCARS), now tracks adoptions arranged through the foster care system, but this represents only some of the children adopted into American families each year.

According to *The AFCARS Report* (September 2006, http://www.acf.hhs.gov/programs/cb/stats_research/afcars/ tar/report10.htm), on September 30, 2003, 520,000 children lived in foster homes with foster parents. Foster parents are trained people supervised by local social service agencies who provide space in their homes and care for children who

TABLE 1.4

Number, birth rate, and percentage of births to unmarried women, by age, race, and Hispanic origin of mother, 2004

Measure and age of mother	All races[a]	White Total[b]	White Non-Hispanic	Black Total[b]	Black Non-Hispanic	American Indian or Alaska Native[b, c]	Asian or Pacific Islander[b]	Hispanic[d]
					Number			
All ages	1,470,189	983,459	562,539	423,950	400,980	27,376	35,404	439,541
Under 15 years	6,603	3,573	1,425	2,811	2,715	136	83	2,254
15–19 years	342,188	230,758	131,620	98,828	93,940	6,854	5,748	103,258
15 years	17,416	10,803	4,656	6,012	5,733	357	244	6,410
16 years	38,310	25,050	11,728	11,721	11,140	863	676	13,884
17 years	65,222	44,208	23,630	18,626	17,662	1,305	1,083	21,398
18 years	96,935	66,077	38,798	27,349	25,950	1,904	1,605	28,398
19 years	124,305	84,620	52,808	35,120	33,455	2,425	2,140	33,168
20–24 years	566,381	379,427	231,090	164,645	156,394	10,627	11,682	155,010
25–29 years	307,576	203,848	109,471	89,601	84,359	5,506	8,621	98,681
30–34 years	155,275	103,586	53,222	43,259	40,372	2,685	5,745	52,760
35–39 years	72,194	48,614	27,303	19,647	18,367	1,235	2,698	22,183
40 years and over	19,972	13,653	8,408	5,159	4,833	333	827	5,395
Rate per 1,000 unmarried women in specified group								
15–44 years[e]	46.1	41.6	29.4	67.2	—	—	23.6	95.7
15–19 years	34.7	30.1	21.2	61.7	—	—	13.3	67.9
15–17 years	20.1	17.1	10.7	37.0	—	—	7.7	43.3
18–19 years	57.7	50.4	37.5	100.9	—	—	21.6	110.1
20–24 years	72.5	64.1	48.0	119.8	—	—	27.9	138.6
25–29 years	68.6	63.9	43.3	91.8	—	—	33.2	143.4
30–34 years	47.0	45.7	29.6	52.0	—	—	35.4	109.6
35–39 years	23.5	22.6	15.6	25.8	—	—	20.7	56.8
40–44 years[f]	6.0	5.6	4.1	6.8	—	—	8.6	13.8
Percent of births to unmarried women								
All ages	35.8	30.5	24.5	68.8	69.3	62.3	15.5	46.4
Under 15 years	97.4	95.9	96.5	99.4	99.5	97.8	92.2	95.7
15–19 years	82.4	77.7	78.0	96.1	96.6	89.0	75.3	77.6
15 years	95.3	93.1	94.9	99.6	99.7	97.0	92.8	92.0
16 years	91.5	88.4	89.8	98.9	99.1	95.7	88.5	87.4
17 years	88.3	84.7	86.7	98.2	98.5	93.5	83.2	82.8
18 years	82.7	78.1	79.6	96.5	96.9	88.4	75.5	76.4
19 years	75.8	70.3	70.6	93.4	94.0	84.1	67.3	70.3
20–24 years	54.8	48.1	44.7	82.2	82.9	70.2	38.1	55.4
25–29 years	27.8	23.1	17.3	60.6	61.1	51.4	13.3	38.8
30–34 years	16.1	13.3	8.8	43.7	43.6	41.4	7.2	29.7
35–39 years	15.2	12.6	9.0	39.3	39.1	41.2	7.2	27.4
40 years and over	18.2	15.6	12.1	39.5	39.3	44.1	9.9	29.9

— Data not available.

[a]Includes races other than white and black and origin not stated.

[b]Race and Hispanic origin are reported separately on the birth certificate. Race categories are consistent with the 1977 Office of Management and Budget (OMB) standards. Data for persons of Hispanic origin are included in the data for each race group according to the mother's reported race. Fifteen states reported multiple-race data for 2004. The multiple-race data for these states were bridged to the single-race categories of the 1977 OMB standards for comparability with other states.

[c]Includes births to Aleuts and Eskimos.

[d]Includes all persons of Hispanic origin of any race.

[e]Birthrates computed by relating total births to unmarried mothers, regardless of age of mother, to unmarried women aged 15–44 years.

[f]Birthrates computed by relating births to unmarried mothers aged 40 years and over to unmarried women aged 40–44 years.

Notes: For the 48 states and the District of Columbia, marital status is reported in the birth registration process; for Michigan and New York, mother's marital status is inferred. Rates cannot be computed for unmarried non-Hispanic black women or for American Indian women because the necessary populations are not available.

SOURCE: Joyce A. Martin, et al., "Table 18. Number, Birth Rate, and Percent of Births to Unmarried Women by Age, Race, and Hispanic Origin of Mother: United States, 2004," in "Births: Final Data for 2004," *National Vital Statistics Reports*, vol. 55, no. 1, September 29, 2006, http://www.cdc.gov/nchs/data/nvsr/nvsr55/nvsr55_01.pdf (accessed February 6, 2007)

have been neglected, abused, or abandoned, or whose parents have surrendered them to public agencies because they are unable to care for them. According to the American Public Welfare Association, foster care is the most common type of substitute care, but children needing substitute care might also live in group homes, emergency shelters, child care facilities, hospitals, correctional institutions, or on their own. It is becoming more difficult to place children in foster care. The number of potential foster care families is down, due in part to the fact that women, the primary providers of foster care, are entering the paid labor force in greater numbers.

The AFCARS report estimates that in fiscal year 2003, 296,000 children younger than eighteen years old entered foster care, with an average age of 8.4 years. A disproportionate share of children entering foster care were African-American—27% of children entering foster care were

FIGURE 1.6

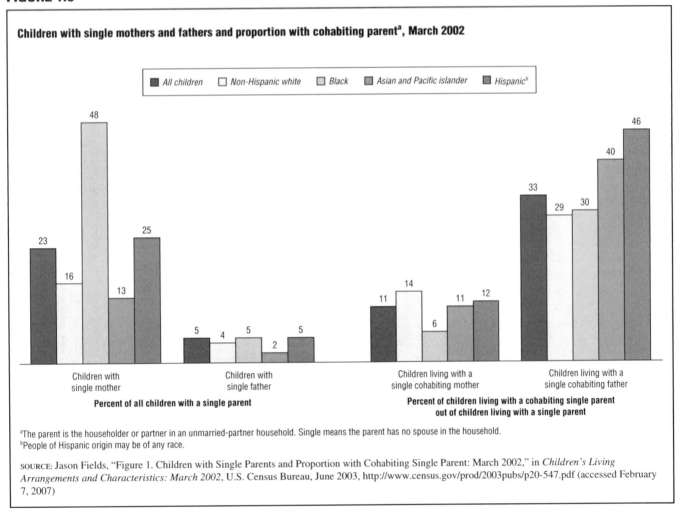

Children with single mothers and fathers and proportion with cohabiting parentᵃ, March 2002

■ All children □ Non-Hispanic white ▨ Black ▨ Asian and Pacific islander ▨ Hispanicᵇ

Children with single mother

23, 16, 48, 13, 25

Children with single father

5, 4, 5, 2, 5

Percent of all children with a single parent

Children living with a single cohabiting mother

11, 14, 6, 11, 12

Children living with a single cohabiting father

33, 29, 30, 40, 46

Percent of children living with a cohabiting single parent out of children living with a single parent

ᵃThe parent is the householder or partner in an unmarried-partner household. Single means the parent has no spouse in the household.
ᵇPeople of Hispanic origin may be of any race.

SOURCE: Jason Fields, "Figure 1. Children with Single Parents and Proportion with Cohabiting Single Parent: March 2002," in *Children's Living Arrangements and Characteristics: March 2002*, U.S. Census Bureau, June 2003, http://www.census.gov/prod/2003pubs/p20-547.pdf (accessed February 7, 2007)

African-American, but according to the Census Bureau's National Population Estimates—Characteristics (May 16, 2006, http://www.census.gov/popest/national/asrh/) only 15.5% of all Americans under age eighteen were African-American in that year. White children were underrepresented among those entering foster care—46% were white, non-Hispanic children, compared with the 59.4% of all white, non-Hispanic children under the age of eighteen. Hispanic and Native American or Alaskan Native children were more proportionally represented—17% entering foster care were Hispanic (compared with 18.7% of children in the general population), and 2% were Native American or Alaskan Native (compared with 0.4% of children in the general population).

A child's stay in foster care can vary from just a few days to many years. Almost one in five children (18%) who left foster care in fiscal year 2003 had been in care less than a month. (See Table 1.6.) Almost a third (32%) had been in care from one to eleven months, another one-fifth (20%) from one to two years, and 30% for more than two years.

More than half (55%) of the children who left foster care in fiscal year 2003 were reunited with their parents. (See Table 1.6.) Some of these children moved to a

relative's or guardian's home (15%). Eight percent were emancipated, or "aged out" of the system when they turned eighteen years old. Almost one out of five (18%) of the children who left foster care were adopted.

According to the AFCARS report, adopted children were on average younger (7 years old) than children still in foster care (10.2 years old), reflecting the preference of adoptive parents for younger children. Of those adopted children, 25,118 were male and 24,882 were female. Foster parents adopted 62% of these children, relatives other than parents adopted 23%, and nonrelatives who had not fostered the child previously adopted 15%. Even though traditional families—married couples—made up two-thirds (67%) of those who adopted children from foster care, a significant share were nontraditional families—28% of adopters were single women, 3% were single men, and 2% were unmarried couples.

In 1996 the federal government began to provide incentives to potential adoptive parents to move children into adoptive homes more quickly. The government provided a $5,000 tax credit for adoptive parents to cover adoption expenses; the credit was $6,000 if the adopted

TABLE 1.5

Grandparents living with grandchildren, responsible for coresident grandchildren, and duration of responsibility, by race and Hispanic origin, 2000

Characteristic	Total	Race							Hispanic origin		
		White alone	Black or African American alone	American Indian and Alaska Native alone	Asian alone	Native Hawaiian and other Pacific Islander alone	Some other race alone	Two or more races	Hispanic or Latino (of any race)	Not Hispanic or Latino	
										Total	White alone, not Hispanic or Latino
Population 30 years old and over	158,881,037	126,715,472	16,484,644	1,127,455	5,631,301	169,331	5,890,748	2,862,086	14,618,891	144,262,146	119,063,492
Grandparents living with grandchildren	5,771,671	3,219,409	1,358,699	90,524	359,709	17,014	567,486	158,830	1,221,661	4,550,010	2,654,788
Percent of population 30 and over	3.6	2.5	8.2	8.0	6.4	10.0	9.6	5.5	8.4	3.2	2.2
Responsible for grandchildren	2,426,730	1,340,809	702,595	50,765	71,791	6,587	191,107	63,076	424,304	2,002,426	1,142,006
Percent of coresident grandparents	42.0	41.6	51.7	56.1	20.0	38.7	33.7	39.7	34.7	44.0	43.0
By duration of care (percent)*											
Total	**100.0**	**100.0**	**100.0**	**100.0**	**100.0**	**100.0**	**100.0**	**100.0**	**100.0**	**100.0**	**100.0**
Less than 6 months	12.1	12.6	9.8	13.0	13.6	12.7	15.6	13.5	14.6	11.5	12.4
6 to 11 months	10.8	11.6	9.3	10.5	11.0	8.4	11.4	11.2	11.2	10.7	11.6
1 to 2 years	23.2	23.8	21.2	22.5	25.2	23.8	26.1	23.4	25.1	22.8	23.6
3 to 4 years	15.4	15.8	14.6	13.9	17.6	11.7	15.7	16.0	15.8	15.3	15.7
5 years to more	38.5	36.3	45.2	40.0	32.7	43.3	31.1	35.9	33.3	39.6	36.6

*Percent duration based on grandparents responsible for grandchildren. Percent distribution may not sum to 100 percent because of rounding.

SOURCE: Tavia Simmons and Jane Lawler Dye, "Table 1. Grandparents Living with Grandchildren, Responsible for Coresident Grandchildren, and Duration of Responsibility by Race and Hispanic Origin: 2000," in *Grandparents Living with Grandchildren: 2000*, U.S. Census Bureau, October 2003, http://www.census.gov/prod/2003pubs/c2kbr-31.pdf (accessed February 7, 2007)

child had special needs. Children with special needs were defined as those with physical, mental, or emotional problems; children needing to be adopted with siblings; or children who were difficult to place because of age, race, or ethnicity. In 2002 the tax credit was increased to $10,000 to cover adoption expenses for children without special needs; adoptive parents of special-needs children, including many children from foster care, received the full amount of the tax credit regardless of incurred expenses. That tax credit increased in subsequent years and was $10,960 in 2006.

In addition, Congress passed the Adoption and Safe Families Act in 1997, providing fiscal incentives to states to move children from foster care into adoptive families more quickly. States that increased the number of adoptions of foster children (in a given year over a base year) received a standard payment of $4,000 per adopted child and an additional $2,000 for the adoption of each special-needs child and an additional $4,000 for the adoption of each child aged nine or older.

Despite these incentives, many children who enter foster care will never have a permanent family but instead will age out of the system. On September 30, 2003, there were 120,000 foster children whose parents' rights had been terminated. (See Table 1.7.) These "waiting children"

were disproportionately African-American. Even though in 2003, 15.5% of all children under age eighteen were African-American and 27% of children entering foster care were African-American, 40% of waiting children were African-American. Fifty-five percent of waiting children lived in foster homes with nonrelatives while waiting to be adopted.

Living Arrangements of Young Adults

A young person's transition into adult independence does not necessarily occur at age eighteen. The marriage age has risen since the 1950s, and, because obtaining a college education has become the norm, young people have delayed finding employment that allows them to support themselves independently of their parents. A growing number of young adults older than eighteen continue to live in, or return to, their parents' home. Some young people live with their parents until their mid-twenties, and others are likely to return home at some point after moving out, especially after college or service in the military. Many young adults also share households with other people.

Socioeconomic experts attribute this phenomenon to the rising cost of living in the United States. Wages have not increased at the same rate as the cost of living; therefore, the same amount of money buys less than it did in

TABLE 1.6

Children who exited foster care, fiscal year 2003

[Data from both the regular and revised submissions received by June 2006 are included in the information below. Missing data are not used in the calculation of percentages.]

HOW MANY CHILDREN EXITED FOSTER CARE DURING FISCAL YEAR 2003? 282,000

WHAT WERE THE AGES OF THE CHILDREN WHO EXITED CARE DURING FISCAL YEAR 2003?

Mean years	10.0	
Median years	10.0	
Less than 1 year	4%	12,660
1 year	6%	17,269
2 years	6%	17,761
3 years	6%	16,339
4 years	5%	15,002
5 years	5%	13,682
6 years	4%	12,668
7 years	4%	12,038
8 years	4%	11,905
9 years	4%	11,781
10 years	4%	11,417
11 years	4%	11,540
12 years	4%	11,838
13 years	4%	12,560
14 years	5%	14,458
15 years	6%	16,713
16 years	6%	17,675
17 years	8%	23,530
18 years	5%	14,919
19 years	1%	3,512
20 years	1%	2,732

WHAT WERE THE OUTCOMES FOR THE CHILDREN EXITING FOSTER CARE DURING FISCAL YEAR 2003?

Reunification with parent(s) or primary caretaker(s)	55%	155,499
Living with other relative(s)	11%	31,572
Adoption	18%	50,355
Emancipation	8%	22,432
Guardianship	4%	10,959
Transfer to another agency	2%	6,439
Runaway	1%	4,158
Death of a child*	0%	586

*Deaths are attributed to a variety of causes including medical conditions, accidents, and homicide.

WHAT WERE THE LENGTHS OF STAY OF THE CHILDREN WHO EXITED FOSTER CARE DURING FISCAL YEAR 2003?

Mean months	21.7	
Median months	11.9	
Less than 1 month	18%	51,619
1 to 5 months	16%	45,811
6 to 11 months	16%	45,371
12 to 17 months	12%	33,985
18 to 23 months	8%	23,440
24 to 29 months	6%	16,872
30 to 35 months	5%	12,719
3 to 4 years	10%	27,973
5 years or more	9%	24,209

TABLE 1.6

Children who exited foster care, fiscal year 2003 [CONTINUED]

[Data from both the regular and revised submissions received by June 2006 are included in the information below. Missing data are not used in the calculation of percentages.]

HOW MANY CHILDREN EXITED FOSTER CARE DURING FISCAL YEAR 2003? 282,000

WHAT WAS THE RACE/ETHNICITY OF THE CHILDREN WHO EXITED CARE DURING FISCAL YEAR 2003?

American Indian/Alaska Native-non Hispanic	2%	5,733
Asian-non Hispanic	1%	2,633
Black-non Hispanic	29%	82,839
Hawaiian/Pacific Islander-non Hispanic	0%	972
Hispanic	16%	46,123
White-non Hispanic	45%	128,256
Unknown/unable to determine	3%	7,348
Two or more-non Hispanic	3%	8,097

SOURCE: Adapted from "How Many Children Exited Foster Care during FY 2003?" in *The AFCARS Report*, no. 10, U.S. Department of Health and Human Services, Administration for Children and Families, September 2006, http://www.acf.hhs.gov/programs/cb/stats_research/afcars/tar/report10.htm (accessed February 6, 2007)

college dormitories who were still counted as residing at their parents' residence. Males in this age group were more likely (54.8%) than females (45.7%) to live with their parents. This was primarily because men tend to marry at a later age than women do. Almost all men and women in this age group who lived with their parents had never been married. Table 1.9 shows that the percentage of both men and women aged twenty to twenty-four and twenty-five to twenty-nine that had never married rose dramatically between 1970 and 2003, but the percentage of men who had never married was consistently higher.

Young adults who live by themselves for any length of time are unlikely to return home after experiencing independence. By contrast, those who move in with roommates or who cohabit without marrying are more likely to return to the parental home if the living situation does not work out or the relationship fails. Some young people struggle on their own only to return home for respite from financial pressures, loneliness, or because they need emotional support or security.

Even if they do not settle into careers immediately, most young adults living at home work for wages. Those young people who lived away from home and then moved back were more likely to pay rent or make some financial contribution to the household than those who never lived on their own, even if they were employed.

HOW LONG DO THEY STAY? Young men are more likely than young women to stay with their parents indefinitely. This may be because young men typically lose less of their autonomy when they return home than young women do. Young women report that they have more responsibility to help around the house and more rules to obey than do their young male counterparts.

previous years. Real estate prices, particularly in the most populous states (New York, California, Florida, and Texas), have skyrocketed. This is good news for homeowners but bad news for renters and first-time homebuyers, a large percentage of whom are young adults.

In 2003, 13.8 million young adults between the ages of eighteen and twenty-four lived in their parents' home. (See Table 1.8.) This figure includes those who were living in

TABLE 1.7

Children waiting to be adopted on September 30, 2003

HOW MANY CHILDREN WERE WAITING TO BE ADOPTED ON SEPTEMBER 30, 2003?
120,000

WHAT IS THE GENDER DISTRIBUTION OF THE WAITING CHILDREN?

Male	53%	63,811
Female	47%	56,189

HOW MANY MONTHS HAVE THE WAITING CHILDREN BEEN IN CONTINUOUS FOSTER CARE?

Mean months	44.5	
Median months	34.0	
Less than 1 month	0%	446
1 through 5 months	3%	4,016
6 through 11 months	7%	8,349
12 through 17 months	11%	13,065
18 through 23 months	11%	13,623
24 through 29 months	11%	13,029
30 through 35 months	9%	10,587
36 through 59 months	23%	27,125
60 or more months	25%	29,760

WHAT IS THE RACIAL/ETHNIC DISTRIBUTION OF THE WAITING CHILDREN?

American Indian/Alaska Native-non Hispanic	2%	2,204
Asian-non Hispanic	0%	501
Black-non Hispanic	40%	48,305
Hawaiian/Pacific Islander-non Hispanic	0%	346
Hispanic	14%	16,307
White-non Hispanic	37%	44,346
Unknown/unable to determine	4%	4,218
Two or more-non Hispanic	3%	3,773

HOW OLD WERE THE WAITING CHILDREN WHEN THEY WERE REMOVED FROM THEIR PARENTS OR CARETAKERS?

Mean years	5.0	
Median years	4.4	
Less than 1 year	24%	28,568
1 year	8%	10,018
2 years	8%	9,113
3 years	7%	8,523
4 years	7%	8,146
5 years	7%	8,132
6 years	7%	8,067
7 years	6%	7,672
8 years	6%	6,982
9 years	5%	6,375
10 years	5%	5,497
11 years	4%	4,349
12 years	3%	3,336
13 years	2%	2,418
14 years	1%	1,530
15 years	1%	797
16 years	0%	362
17 years	0%	101
18 years	0%	10
19 years	0%	3
20 years	0%	0

WHERE WERE THE WAITING CHILDREN LIVING ON SEPTEMBER 30, 2003?

Pre-adoptive home	17%	19,938
Foster family home (relative)	16%	19,541
Foster family home (non-relative)	55%	65,629
Group home	4%	5,194
Institution	7%	8,376
Supervised independent living	0%	186
Runaway	1%	693
Trial home visit	0%	444

TABLE 1.7

Children waiting to be adopted on September 30, 2003 [CONTINUED]

HOW OLD WERE THE CHILDREN ON SEPTEMBER 30, 2003?

Mean years	8.7	
Median years	8.8	
Less than 1 year	3%	3,826
1 year	6%	7,731
2 years	7%	8,405
3 years	6%	7,767
4 years	6%	7,320
5 years	6%	6,990
6 years	5%	6,582
7 years	5%	6,382
8 years	5%	6,418
9 years	6%	6,860
10 years	6%	7,172
11 years	6%	7,512
12 years	6%	7,549
13 years	6%	7,317
14 years	6%	6,981
15 years	5%	6,456
16 years	4%	4,534
17 years	3%	3,031
18 years	1%	856
19 years	0%	220
20 years	06%	93

SOURCE: Adapted from "How Many Children Were Waiting to be Adopted on September 30, 2003?" in *The AFCARS Report*, no. 10, U.S. Department of Health and Human Services, Administration for Children and Families, September 2006, http://www.acf.hhs.gov/programs/cb/stats_research/afcars/tar/report10.htm (accessed February 6, 2007)

TABLE 1.8

Young adults living at home, selected years 1960–2003

[Numbers in thousands. Data based on Current Population Survey (CPS) unless otherwise specified.]

Age	Male			Female		
	Total	Child of householder	Percent	Total	Child of householder	Percent
18 to 24 years						
2003	13,811	7,569	54.8	13,592	6,215	45.7
2002	13,696	7,575	55.3	13,602	6,252	46.0
2001	13,412	7,385	55.1	13,361	6,068	45.4
2000	13,291	7,593	57.1	13,242	6,232	47.1
1999	12,936	7,440	57.5	13,031	6,389	49.0
1998	12,633	7,399	58.6	12,568	5,974	47.5
1997	12,534	7,501	59.8	12,452	6,006	48.2
1996	12,402	7,327	59.0	12,441	5,955	48.0
1995	12,545	7,328	58.4	12,613	5,896	46.7
1994	12,683	7,547	59.5	12,792	5,924	46.3
1993	12,049	7,145	59.3	12,260	5,746	46.9
1992	12,083	7,296	60.4	12,351	5,929	48.0
1991	12,275	7,385	60.2	12,627	6,163	48.8
1990	12,450	7,232	58.1	12,860	6,135	47.7
1989	12,574	7,308	58.1	13,055	6,141	47.0
1988	12,835	7,792	60.7	13,226	6,398	48.4
1987	13,029	7,981	61.3	13,433	6,375	47.5
1986	13,324	7,831	58.8	13,787	6,433	46.7
1985	13,695	8,172	59.7	14,149	6,758	47.8
1984	14,196	8,764	61.7	14,482	6,779	46.8
1983	14,344	8,803	61.4	14,702	7,001	47.6
1982	14,368	(NA)	(NA)	14,815	(NA)	(NA)
1981	14,367	(NA)	(NA)	14,848	(NA)	(NA)
1980 census	14,278	7,755	54.3	14,844	6,336	42.7
1970 census	10,398	5,641	54.3	11,959	4,941	41.3
1960 census	6,842	3,583	52.4	7,876	2,750	34.9
25 to 34 years						
2003	19,543	2,631	13.5	19,659	1,375	7.0
2002	19,220	2,610	13.6	19,428	1,618	8.3
2001	19,308	2,520	13.1	19,527	1,583	8.1
2000	18,563	2,387	12.9	19,222	1,602	8.3
1999	18,924	2,636	13.9	19,551	1,690	8.6
1998	19,526	2,845	14.6	19,828	1,680	8.5
1997	20,039	2,909	14.5	20,217	1,745	8.6
1996	20,390	3,213	16.0	20,528	1,810	9.0
1995	20,589	3,166	15.4	20,800	1,759	8.5
1994	20,873	3,261	15.6	21,073	1,859	8.8
1993	20,856	3,300	15.8	21,007	1,844	8.8
1992	21,125	3,225	15.3	21,368	1,874	8.8
1991	21,319	3,172	14.9	21,586	1,887	8.7
1990	21,462	3,213	15.0	21,779	1,774	8.1
1989	21,461	3,130	14.6	21,777	1,728	7.9
1988	21,320	3,207	15.0	21,649	1,791	8.3
1987	21,142	3,071	14.5	21,494	1,655	7.7
1986	20,956	2,981	14.2	21,097	1,686	8.0
1985	20,184	2,685	13.3	20,673	1,661	8.0
1984	19,876	2,626	13.2	20,297	1,548	7.6
1983	19,438	2,664	13.7	19,903	1,520	7.6
1982	19,090	(NA)	(NA)	19,614	(NA)	(NA)
1981	18,625	(NA)	(NA)	19,203	(NA)	(NA)
1980 census	18,107	1,894	10.5	18,689	1,300	7.0
1970 census	11,929	1,129	9.5	12,637	829	6.6
1960 census	10,896	1,185	10.9	11,587	853	7.4

Note: Unmarried college students living in dormitories are counted as living in their parent(s) home.
NA Not available.

SOURCE: "Table AD-1. Young Adults Living at Home: 1960 to Present," U.S. Census Bureau, September 15, 2004, http://www.census.gov/population/socdemo/hh-fam/tabAD-1.pdf (accessed February 7, 2007)

TABLE 1.9

Marital status of the population 15 years and over by sex and age, 1970 and 2003

[In thousands]

Sex and age	2003 Number							Percent never married	March 1970 percent never married*
	Total	Married spouse present	Married spouse absent	Separated	Divorced	Widowed	Never married		
Both sexes									
Total 15 years and over	225,057	117,172	3,139	4,723	21,649	13,995	64,380	28.6	24.9
15 to 19 years	20,176	257	43	70	39	16	19,751	97.9	93.9
20 to 24 years	19,856	3,181	177	213	243	16	16,026	80.7	44.5
25 to 29 years	18,696	8,158	308	476	832	50	8,872	47.5	14.7
30 to 34 years	20,505	12,268	317	515	1,606	80	5,720	27.9	7.8
35 to 44 years	44,025	28,633	759	1,461	5,567	407	7,197	16.3	5.9
45 to 54 years	40,196	27,299	606	1,056	6,478	842	3,914	9.7	6.1
55 to 64 years	27,387	18,949	393	550	4,157	1,779	1,558	5.7	7.2
65 years and over	34,217	18,427	535	382	2,725	10,806	1,341	3.9	7.6
Males									
Total 15 years and over	108,696	58,586	1,651	1,905	8,976	2,697	34,881	32.1	28.1
15 to 19 years	10,241	66	13	37	21	7	10,098	98.6	97.4
20 to 24 years	9,953	1,156	78	63	93	—	8,563	86.0	54.7
25 to 29 years	9,366	3,573	170	171	327	14	5,112	54.6	19.1
30 to 34 years	10,177	5,733	187	185	678	21	3,371	33.1	9.4
35 to 44 years	21,702	14,045	406	587	2,335	88	4,242	19.5	6.7
45 to 54 years	19,578	13,704	322	413	2,821	202	2,117	10.8	7.5
55 to 64 years	13,158	9,970	200	260	1,679	292	757	5.8	7.8
65 years and over	14,521	10,341	274	190	1,022	2,074	621	4.3	7.5
Females									
Total 15 years and over	116,361	58,586	1,488	2,817	12,673	11,297	29,499	25.4	22.1
15 to 19 years	9,935	193	30	32	18	9	9,652	97.2	90.3
20 to 24 years	9,903	2,025	99	150	150	16	7,463	75.4	35.8
25 to 29 years	9,330	4,585	138	305	505	36	3,760	40.3	10.5
30 to 34 years	10,329	6,535	130	330	928	58	2,349	22.7	6.2
35 to 44 years	22,322	14,588	353	875	3,233	319	2,955	13.2	5.2
45 to 54 years	20,617	13,595	283	643	3,658	640	1,797	8.7	4.9
55 to 64 years	14,229	8,980	193	290	2,478	1,487	801	5.6	6.8
65 years and over	19,696	8,086	261	192	1,704	8,732	720	3.7	7.7

—Represents zero or rounds to zero.
*The 1970 percentages include 14-year-olds, and thus are for 14+ and 14–19.

SOURCE: Jason Fields, "Table 6. Marital Status of the Population 15 Years and Over by Sex and Age: March 1970 and 2003," in *America's Families and Living Arrangements: 2003*, U.S. Census Bureau, November 2004, http://www.census.gov/prod/2004pubs/p20-553.pdf (accessed February 7, 2007)

CHAPTER 2
CHILDREN, TEENS, AND MONEY

FAMILY INCOME

Almost all children are financially dependent on their parents, with their financial condition directly dependent on how much their parents earn. In *Income, Poverty, and Health Insurance Coverage in the United States: 2005* (August 2006, http://www.census.gov/prod/2006pubs/ p60-231.pdf), Carmen DeNavas-Walt, Bernadette D. Proctor, and Cheryl Hill Lee report that real income rose throughout the 1990s and then declined in the early twenty-first century. The median (half were higher and half were lower) household income in 2005 was $46,326, up 1.1% from the previous year. For married-couple families the median household income was $66,067, not statistically different from the previous year.

DeNavas-Walt, Proctor, and Hill Lee find that single-parent families, particularly those headed by single mothers, fare worse than other households. Families with female heads-of-household and no husband present had a 2005 median income of $30,650, slightly down from the previous year, whereas male-headed households with no wife present had a median income of $46,756, slightly higher than the year before.

DeNavas-Walt, Proctor, and Hill Lee also find that median income varied greatly by race and ethnic group. They used three-year average medians to compare income between groups. Asians had the highest median income, at $59,877, followed by non-Hispanic whites, at $50,677. (See Table 2.1.) The median income for Hispanics was $35,467, whereas the median income for African-Americans, at $31,140, was the lowest of any race or ethnic group.

Cost of Raising a Child

Since the 1960s the Family Economics Research Group of the U.S. Department of Agriculture (USDA) has provided estimates on the cost of rearing a child to adulthood. The estimates are calculated per child in a household with two children and are categorized by the age of the child using different family income levels. Attorneys and judges use these estimates in determining child-support awards in divorce cases as well as in cases involving the wrongful death of a parent. Public officials use these estimates to determine payments for the support of children in foster care and for subsidies to adoptive families. Financial planners and consumer educators use them in helping people determine their life insurance needs.

INCOME LEVELS. Estimated annual family expenditures for a child vary widely depending on the income level of the household. The estimated amount a family spends on a child also tends to increase as the child ages. The USDA estimates that in 2005 married-couple households that earned less than $43,200 per year spent amounts ranging from $7,300 for young children to $8,290 for fifteen- to seventeen-year-olds. (See Table 2.2.) Estimates for middle-income, married-couple families ranged from $10,220 for infants and young toddlers to $11,290 for fifteen- to seventeen-year-olds. Estimates for married-couple families with incomes above $72,600 ranged from $15,190 to $16,390, depending on the age of the child.

Estimated annual expenditures for single-parent families that earned less than $43,200 per year were slightly less than those of two-parent families, most likely because their average incomes were lower ($18,100 for single-parent families and $26,900 for two-parent families). The USDA estimates that in 2005 these single parents spent an annual average of $6,080 to $8,440, depending on the age of the child. (See Table 2.3.) The single-parent families that earned $43,200 or more spent $14,000 to $16,670 per child, slightly more than the middle-income, two-parent families.

Although the USDA estimates that in 2005 the highest-income households spent about twice the amount on their

TABLE 2.1

Median household income by race and Hispanic origin, using 3-year average medians, 2003–05

[Income in 2005 dollars]

Race[a] and Hispanic origin	3-year-average median income[b] 2003–2005[c] (dollars) Estimate
All races	
White	48,399
White, not Hispanic	50,677
Black	31,140
American Indian and Alaska Native	33,627
Asian	59,877
Native Hawaiian and other Pacific Islander	54,318
Hispanic origin (any race)	35,467

[a]Federal surveys now give respondents the option of reporting more than one race. Therefore, two basic ways of defining a race group are possible. A group such as Asian may be defined as those who reported Asian and no other race (the race-alone or single-race concept) or as those who reported Asian regardless of whether they also reported another race (the race-alone-or-in-combination concept). This table shows data using the first approach (race alone). The use of the single-race population does not imply that it is the preferred method of presenting or analyzing data. The Census Bureau uses a variety of approaches. About 2.6 percent of people reported more than one race in Census 2000.
[b]The 3-year-average median is the sum of three inflation-adjusted single-year medians divided by 3.
[c]The 2004 data have been revised to reflect a correction to the weights in the 2005 ASEC.

SOURCE: Carmen DeNavas-Walt, Bernadette D. Proctor, and Cheryl Hill Lee, "Table 2. Income of Households by Race and Hispanic Origin Using 3-Year-Average Medians: 2003 to 2005," in *Income, Poverty, and Health Insurance Coverage in the United States: 2005*, U.S. Census Bureau, August 2006, http://www.census.gov/prod/2006pubs/p60-231.pdf (accessed February 1, 2007)

children than the lowest-income households, this difference varied by the type of expense. For example, the estimated food expenditure for children aged fifteen to seventeen in the highest-income husband-wife families was $2,790, compared with $1,960 in the lowest-income group. (See Table 2.2.) However, the estimated annual expense for education and child care for children aged fifteen to seventeen in these high-income families ($1,890) was nearly four times that for a child the same age in the lowest-income families ($510). These variations among income groups by type of expense hold true for single-parent households as well. (See Table 2.3.)

AGE OF CHILD. The 2005 estimates of family expenditures on a child generally increased with the child's age, except for housing, education, and child care. (See Table 2.2 and Table 2.3.) Households with young children are more likely to have recently purchased homes at higher prices and, until recently, with higher interest rates, explaining the higher housing estimates for young children. Estimates for education, child care, and related expenses were also highest for preschoolers (under the age of six) in all income groups. Many women with children this age are in the labor force and must pay for child care. Once children enter school, the child care costs decrease. As school-age children grow up, the need

for after-school and summer care also decreases. The estimates do not include expenses related to college attendance, which typically do not occur until the child is at least eighteen.

FUTURE COSTS. The USDA also estimates the total cost of raising a child born in 2005 who will reach the age of seventeen in 2022, incorporating an average annual inflation rate of 3.04% (the average annual inflation rate over the previous twenty years). Total family expenses for raising a child born in 2005 were estimated to be $182,920 for the lowest-income group, $250,530 for the middle-income group, and $366,020 for the highest-income group. (See Table 2.4.)

CHILDREN IN POVERTY

Children are the largest group of poor in the United States. In 1975 they replaced the elderly as the poorest age group. (See Figure 2.1.) In 2005 the poverty rate for all children younger than eighteen years of age was 17.6%, or about 12.9 million children, which was statistically unchanged from the previous year. In that year children under eighteen years old made up one-quarter (24.8%) of the population of the United States, but they made up over one-third (34.9%) of the people living below the poverty line. (For population estimates for July 1, 2005, by age, see the Census Bureau's National Population Estimates—Characteristics [May 10, 2006, http://www.census.gov/popest/national/asrh/NC-EST2005-sa.html]). DeNavas-Walt, Proctor, and Hill Lee note that children under the age of six are particularly vulnerable to poverty. In 2005 the poverty rate for families with children under age six was 20%, which was higher than the overall rate of child poverty. In addition, over half (52.9%) of children younger than the age of six living with a single mother were in poverty, over five times the rate of poverty for children younger than age six living in married-couple families (9.9%).

Overall, the child poverty rate declined between 1995 and 2000; however, the rate of children living in poverty (100% of the poverty line or below) and in low-income families (100% to 200% of the poverty line) began to rise again in 2000. (See Figure 2.2.) Even though Figure 2.3 shows that the largest group of low-income children in 2005 was white (39%), Hispanic and African-American children were disproportionately poor. Ayana Douglas-Hall, Michelle Chau, and Heather Koball of the National Center for Children in Poverty report in *Basic Facts about Low-Income Children: Birth to Age 18* (September 2006, http://www.nccp.org/media/lic06b_text.pdf) that the majority of both African-American children (61%) and Hispanic children (61%) lived in low-income or poor families in 2005. Another trend in child poverty emerged in the twenty-first century. The Children's Defense Fund notes in *The State of America's Children 2005* (2005,

TABLE 2.2

Estimated annual expenditures on a child by husband-wife families, 2005

Age of child	Total	Housing	Food	Transportation	Clothing	Health care	Child care and education	Miscellaneous*
Before-tax income: less than $43,200 (average=$26,900)								
0–2	$7,300	$2,770	$1,000	$880	$350	$550	$1,080	$670
3–5	7,480	2,740	1,120	850	340	520	1,220	690
6–8	7,510	2,640	1,440	990	380	600	730	730
9–11	7,480	2,390	1,720	1,080	420	660	440	770
12–14	8,310	2,660	1,810	1,210	700	660	310	960
15–17	8,290	2,150	1,960	1,630	620	710	510	710
Total	**$139,110**	**$46,050**	**$27,150**	**$19,920**	**$8,430**	**$11,100**	**$12,870**	**$13,590**
Before-tax income: $43,200 to $72,600 (average=$57,400)								
0–2	$10,220	$3,750	$1,200	$1,310	$410	$720	$1,780	$1,050
3–5	10,500	3,710	1,390	1,280	400	690	1,970	1,060
6–8	10,410	3,620	1,770	1,420	440	790	1,270	1,100
9–11	10,250	3,360	2,080	1,500	490	850	830	1,140
12–14	10,990	3,640	2,090	1,640	820	860	610	1,330
15–17	11,290	3,120	2,330	2,080	730	910	1,040	1,080
Total	**$190,980**	**$63,600**	**$32,580**	**$27,690**	**$9,870**	**$14,460**	**$22,500**	**$20,280**
Before-tax income: more than $72,600 (average=$108,700)								
0–2	$15,190	$5,960	$1,590	$1,830	$540	$830	$2,690	$1,750
3–5	15,550	5,920	1,800	1,800	530	800	2,930	1,770
6–8	15,250	5,830	2,170	1,940	570	910	2,020	1,810
9–11	14,970	5,570	2,520	2,030	620	980	1,400	1,850
12–14	15,800	5,850	2,650	2,160	1,040	980	1,080	2,040
15–17	16,390	5,330	2,790	2,620	940	1,040	1,890	1,780
Total	**$279,450**	**$103,380**	**$40,560**	**$37,140**	**$12,720**	**$16,620**	**$36,030**	**$33,000**

Notes: Estimates are based on 1990–92 consumer expenditure survey data updated to 2005 dollars using the consumer price index. For each age category, the expense estimates represent average child-rearing expenditures for each age (e.g., the expense for the 3–5 age category, on average, applies to the 3-year-old, the 4-year-old, or the 5-year-old). The figures represent estimated expenses on the younger child in a two-child family. Estimates are about the same for the older child, so to calculate expenses for two children, figures should be summed for the appropriate age categories. To estimate expenses for an only child, multiply the total expense for the appropriate age category by 1.24. To estimate expenses for each child in a family with three or more children, multiply the total expense for each appropriate age category by 0.77. For expenses on all children in a family, these totals should be summed.

*Miscellaneous expenses include personal care items, entertainment, and reading materials.

SOURCE: Mark Lino, "Table ES1. Estimated Annual Expenditures on a Child by Husband-Wife Families, Overall United States, 2005," in *Expenditures on Children by Families, 2005*, U.S. Department of Agriculture, Center for Nutrition Policy and Promotion, 2006, http://www.cnpp.usda.gov/Publications/CRC/crc2005.pdf (accessed February 16, 2007)

http://www.childrensdefense.org/site/DocServer/Greenbook_2005.pdf?docID=1741) that the number of children living in extreme poverty—below one-half of the poverty level—increased by 20% between 2000 and 2004, almost twice as fast as the number of children in poverty overall.

Government Aid to Children

Many programs exist in the United States to assist families and children living with economic hardship. Some of these programs are federally run, and others are run at the state level. In many cases the programs are mandated at the federal level and administered by the states, which can make tracking them complicated.

TEMPORARY ASSISTANCE FOR NEEDY FAMILIES. In 1996 Congress enacted the Personal Responsibility and Work Opportunity Reconciliation Act to reform the country's welfare system. The primary goal of the legislation was to get as many people as possible into the paid labor force and off welfare rolls. The law set limits on how long welfare recipients could receive assistance, encouraging them to seek gainful employment. Under Temporary Assistance for Needy Families (TANF), states

receive a fixed amount from the federal government with few federal constraints on how they manage the funds. According to the Administration for Children and Families of the U.S. Department of Health and Human Services (HHS), in *TANF Financial Data* (January 2007, http://www.acf.hhs.gov/programs/ofs/data/2005/tableA_spending_2005.html), the total federal funds spent on TANF expenditures for fiscal year (FY) 2005 were $20.7 billion.

Under TANF each state decides what categories of children receive aid. TANF requires that an adult recipient work in exchange for time-limited assistance. In *Temporary Assistance for Needy Families Program (TANF): Seventh Annual Report to Congress* (December 2006, http://www.acf.hhs.gov/programs/ofa/annualreport7/TANF_7th_Report_Final_101006.pdf), the HHS reports that in FY 2003, 22.9% of adult TANF recipients were employed, down from 25.3% the year before.

The size of families receiving public assistance is decreasing. According to the HHS report, the average number of people in a TANF family was 2.5 in 2003,

TABLE 2.3

Estimated annual expenditures on a child by single-parent families, 2005

Age of child	Total	Housing	Food	Transportation	Clothing	Health care	Child care and education	Miscellaneous*
Before-tax income: less than $43,200 (average=$18,100)								
0–2	$6,080	$2,480	$1,110	$820	$310	$270	$680	$410
3–5	6,880	2,820	1,170	720	330	390	920	530
6–8	7,720	3,000	1,470	840	390	460	840	720
9–11	7,140	2,880	1,710	600	390	580	400	580
12–14	7,650	2,890	1,710	690	670	620	510	560
15–17	8,440	3,060	1,860	1,090	780	610	390	650
Total	$131,730	$51,390	$27,090	$14,280	$8,610	$8,790	$11,220	$10,350
Before-tax income: $43,200 or more (average=$65,500)								
0–2	$14,000	$5,350	$1,720	$2,510	$450	$610	$1,670	$1,690
3–5	15,100	5,690	1,820	2,400	470	810	2,090	1,820
6–8	15,990	5,870	2,180	2,520	540	930	1,950	2,000
9–11	15,320	5,750	2,620	2,290	540	1,120	1,140	1,860
12–14	16,230	5,750	2,570	2,380	890	1,180	1,620	1,840
15–17	16,670	5,930	2,720	2,580	1,020	1,170	1,320	1,930
Total	$279,930	$103,020	$40,890	$44,040	$11,730	$17,460	$29,370	$33,420

Notes: Estimates are based on 1990–92 consumer expenditure survey data updated to 2005 dollars using the consumer price index. For each age category, the expense estimates represent average child-rearing expenditures for each age (e.g., the expense for the 3–5 age category, on average, applies to the 3-year-old, the 4-year-old, or the 5-year-old). The figures represent estimated expenses on the younger child in a single-parent, two-child family. For estimated expenses on the older child, multiply the total expense for the appropriate age category by 0.93. To estimate expenses for two children, the expenses on the younger child and older child after adjusting the expense on the older child downward should be summed for the appropriate age categories. To estimate expenses for an only child, multiply the total expense for the appropriate age category by 1.35. To estimate expenses for each child in a family with three or more children, multiply the total expense for each appropriate age category by 0.72 after adjusting the expenses on the older children downward. For expenses on all children in a family, these totals should be summed.
*Miscellaneous expenses include personal care items, entertainment, and reading materials.

SOURCE: Mark Lino, "Table 7. Estimated Annual Expenditures on a Child by Single-Parent Families, Overall United States, 2005," in *Expenditures on Children by Families, 2005*, U.S. Department of Agriculture, Center for Nutrition Policy and Promotion, 2006, http://www.cnpp.usda.gov/Publications/CRC/crc2005.pdf (accessed February 16, 2007)

down from an average of 2.8 in 1996. Half of TANF families in 2003 included only one child recipient, whereas only 10% had four or more children. More than a third (38.6%) of TANF families were child-only cases, including no adult recipients.

The amount of government assistance provided to individuals and families under current welfare regulations is down sharply. The average monthly benefit per TANF recipient in 2004 was $150, down from a high of $221 (in 2004 dollars) in 1978 under the AFDC program. (See Table 2.5.) The average monthly benefit per family was $360, down from a high of $793 (in 2004 dollars) in 1969. Benefits included cash and work-based assistance, child care, and transportation assistance.

The reduction in the welfare roles and expenditures may actually harm poor children. Olivia Golden, the assistant secretary for children and families in the HHS under President Bill Clinton, states in "Welfare Reform Mostly Worked" (*Orlando Sentinel*, July 24, 2005) that she believes the welfare-to-work model "mostly worked" in the sense that welfare caseloads had dropped and that most low-income parents were now working to support their families. However, this success brought about additional problems. She notes, "In less than a decade, welfare has faded as a means of support for impoverished families. Many of these families are working long hours despite low wages, shrinking health-insurance coverage and serious trade-offs between work and decent care for their children. Yet, neither our politics nor our policies have adjusted to our success at bringing more of these parents into the labor force."

FOOD STAMP PROGRAM. The Food Stamp Program, which is administered by the USDA, provides low-income households with electronic benefit cards that can be used at most grocery stores, much like debit cards, in place of cash. Food stamps are intended to ensure that recipients have access to a nutritious diet. They are available to households that have a gross monthly income of no more than 130% of the poverty line and a net monthly income at or below the poverty line. In *Characteristics of Food Stamp Households: Fiscal Year 2005* (September 2006, http://www.fns.usda.gov/oane/menu/Published/FSP/FILES/Participation/2005Characteristics.pdf), Allison Barrett indicates that almost nine out of ten (88%) of all households that received food stamp benefits in 2005 lived in poverty.

The amount of money a family receives on its benefit card is based on the USDA's estimate of how much it costs to provide households with nutritious, low-cost meals. This estimate changes yearly to reflect inflation.

TABLE 2.4

Estimated annual expenditures on children born in 2005, by income group

Year	Age	Income group		
		Lowest	Middle	Highest
2005	<1	$7,300	$10,220	$15,190
2006	1	7,520	10,530	15,650
2007	2	7,750	10,850	16,130
2008	3	8,180	11,490	17,010
2009	4	8,430	11,840	17,530
2010	5	8,690	12,200	18,060
2011	6	8,990	12,460	18,250
2012	7	9,260	12,840	18,810
2013	8	9,540	13,230	19,380
2014	9	9,790	13,420	19,600
2015	10	10,090	13,830	20,200
2016	11	10,400	14,250	20,810
2017	12	11,900	15,740	22,630
2018	13	12,270	16,220	23,320
2019	14	12,640	16,710	24,030
2020	15	12,990	17,690	25,680
2021	16	13,390	18,230	26,470
2022	17	13,790	18,780	27,270
Total		**$182,920**	**$250,530**	**$366,020**

Note: Estimates are for the younger child in husband-wife families with two children.

SOURCE: Mark Lino, "Table 12. Estimated Annual Expenditures on Children Born in 2005, by Income Group, Overall United States," in *Expenditures on Children by Families, 2005*, U.S. Department of Agriculture, Center for Nutrition Policy and Promotion, 2006, http://www.cnpp.usda.gov/Publications/CRC/crc2005.pdf (accessed February 16, 2007)

According to the USDA, in *Food Stamps Make America Stronger* (September 2006, http://www.fns.usda.gov/fsp/outreach/Translations/English/313Brochure-06.pdf), between October 1, 2006, and September 30, 2007, the maximum monthly benefit for a family of four was $518. The average monthly benefit for all households in FY 2005 was $209. (See Table 2.6.) Food stamp households containing children received an average of $300 in benefits per month, in part because households with children tended to be larger (3.3 people) than households in general (2.3 people).

Barrett mentions that most households that received food stamps in 2005 contained children—53.8%, or 5.8 million households. A third of all food stamp households (33.5%) were single-parent households, most of them headed by single mothers.

SPECIAL SUPPLEMENTAL NUTRITION PROGRAM FOR WOMEN, INFANTS, AND CHILDREN. The Special Supplemental Nutrition Program for Women, Infants, and Children (WIC) provides food assistance and nutritional screening for low-income pregnant and postpartum women and their infants and children under the age of five. This program can help women and young children with household incomes that are too high to receive food stamps. In "Frequently Asked Questions about WIC" (March 13, 2007, http://www.fns.usda.gov/wic/FAQs/

FAQ.HTM), the USDA's Food and Nutrition Service reports that income eligibility guidelines for the period July 1, 2006, to June 30, 2007, required applicants to have an income at or below 185% of the poverty level and be nutritionally "at risk," meaning that to be eligible, an individual must have diet- or medically based risks. The income eligibility guidelines stated that a family of one (in other words, a single, pregnant woman) could earn up to $1,511 per month and still qualify for WIC. A family of four could earn $3,084 per month and participate in WIC. Furthermore, Susan Bartlett et al., in *WIC Participant and Program Characteristics, 2004* (March 2006, http://www.fns.usda.gov/oane/MENU/Published/WIC/FILES/pc2004.pdf), note that two-thirds (66.9%) of WIC participants in 2004 had household incomes below the poverty line.

According to Bartlett et al., in April 2004 about 8.6 million women and their children participated in WIC, an increase of 7% since April 2002. Twenty-six percent of WIC participants were infants, another 49% were children aged one to four years old, and 25% were pregnant, postpartum, or breastfeeding women. Recipients receive food items or vouchers for purchases of certain items in retail stores. The WIC program is federally funded but administered by state and local health agencies. In "WIC Program Participation and Costs" (March 27, 2007, http://www.fns.usda.gov/pd/wisummary.htm), the Food and Nutrition Service notes that in FY 2006 the WIC program's estimated food cost was $3.6 billion and estimated administrative costs were $1.4 billion, for a total cost of $5 billion.

SCHOOL NUTRITION PROGRAMS. School nutrition programs continue food assistance to school-age children. The programs provide millions of children with nutritious food each day. Children whose families earn no more than 185% of the poverty level are eligible for reduced price school meals; children whose families earn no more than 130% of the poverty level are eligible for free school meals. The Food and Nutrition Service reports in "Federal Cost of School Food Programs" (March 27, 2007, http://www.fns.usda.gov/pd/cncosts.htm) that in FY 2006 the U.S. government spent $10.2 billion on school nutrition programs, including the National School Lunch Program, the School Breakfast Program, and the Special Milk Program. In that year 30.1 million children took part in the school lunch program, up from 28 million in 2002. (See Table 2.7.)

CHILD SUPPORT

Children living in single-parent families are far more likely to be poor than children living in two-parent households, and the number of children living with only one parent—usually the mother—is increasing. According to Timothy S. Grall, in *Custodial Mothers and Fathers and*

FIGURE 2.1

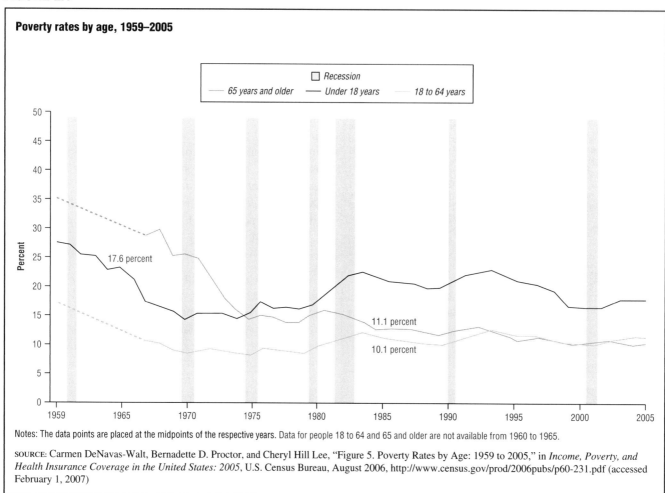

Poverty rates by age, 1959–2005

Notes: The data points are placed at the midpoints of the respective years. Data for people 18 to 64 and 65 and older are not available from 1960 to 1965.

SOURCE: Carmen DeNavas-Walt, Bernadette D. Proctor, and Cheryl Hill Lee, "Figure 5. Poverty Rates by Age: 1959 to 2005," in *Income, Poverty, and Health Insurance Coverage in the United States: 2005*, U.S. Census Bureau, August 2006, http://www.census.gov/prod/2006pubs/p60-231.pdf (accessed February 1, 2007)

Their Child Support: 2003 (July 2006, http://www.census .gov/prod/2006pubs/p60-230.pdf), in the spring of 2004, 14 million parents had custody of 21.6 million children under the age of twenty-one whose other parent lived elsewhere. Mothers accounted for 83.1% of all custodial parents; 16.9 % of custodial parents were fathers. These proportions have not changed significantly since 1994.

Grall notes that six out of ten (60%) of the fourteen million custodial parents in 2003 had a child support agreement with the other parent. Most of these agreements required child support payments from the noncustodial parent. In 2003, 76.4% of custodial parents due support received at least some payments. (See Figure 2.4.) Almost half (45.3%) received all the payments they were due, up from only a little more than a third (36.9%) in 1993. Grall also mentions that noncustodial parents who had either joint custody agreements or visitation rights to their children were more likely to pay child support (85.9% and 76.2%, respectively) than parents who did not have any visitation rights at all (62.5%).

Differences existed in the child support arrangements for custodial mothers and custodial fathers. Custodial mothers were much more likely than custodial fathers to

be awarded child support (64.2% and 39.8%, respectively). (See Table 2.8.) On average, custodial mothers were due $5,175 in child support in 2003 and received $3,579. Custodial fathers were due, on average, $4,471 and actually received $2,797. As noted earlier, fewer than half of all custodial parents actually receive the child support due them; in 2003 only 45.2% of custodial mothers and 46.2% of custodial fathers received the total amount due.

Grall notes that receipt of child support payments made a significant difference in the household incomes of single-parent families. In 2003 the average family income of custodial parents who received at least some of the child support due them was $28,600, and the child support represented 9.2% of the total household income. Child support represented 19.3% of the total household income for those parents who received all of the child support due them. In contrast, custodial parents who had child support agreements but received none of the child support due had an average income of only $23,400.

Government Assistance in Obtaining Child Support

As demonstrated earlier, inadequate financial support from noncustodial parents contributes to the high incidence

FIGURE 2.2

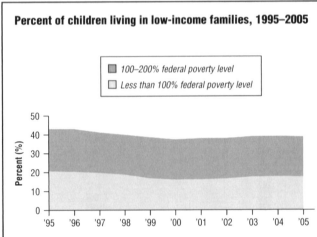

Percent of children living in low-income families, 1995–2005

☐ 100–200% federal poverty level
☐ Less than 100% federal poverty level

SOURCE: Ayana Douglas-Hall, Michelle Chau, and Heather Koball, "Children Living in Low-Income Families, 1995–2005," in *Basic Facts about Low-Income Children: Birth to Age 18*, National Center for Children in Poverty, Columbia University, Mailman School of Public Health, September 2006, http://www.nccp.org/media/lic06b_text.pdf (accessed February 16, 2007)

FIGURE 2.3

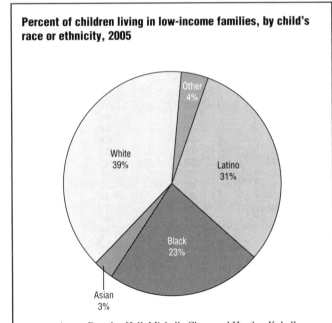

Percent of children living in low-income families, by child's race or ethnicity, 2005

Other 4%
White 39%
Latino 31%
Black 23%
Asian 3%

SOURCE: Ayana Douglas-Hall, Michelle Chau, and Heather Koball, "Children Living in Low-Income Families, by Race/Ethnicity, 2005," in *Basic Facts about Low-Income Children: Birth to Age 18*, National Center for Children in Poverty, Columbia University, Mailman School of Public Health, September 2006, http://www.nccp.org/media/lic06b_text.pdf (accessed February 16, 2007)

of poverty among children living in single-parent families. When custodial parents are not paid the child support due them, their families suffer financially and often must turn to public welfare. Government agencies, therefore, have an interest in recovering child support from delinquent parents.

In 1975 Congress established the Child Support Enforcement (CSE) Program, a collaborative effort among local, state, and federal agencies to ensure that children received financial support from both parents. Under the Child Support Recovery Act of 1992, noncustodial parents delinquent on child support due in another state can be prosecuted. CSE services are automatically provided to families receiving assistance under the TANF program; any support collected usually reimburses the state and federal governments for TANF payments made to the family. Child support services are also available for a small application fee to families not receiving TANF.

Provisions in the Personal Responsibility and Work Opportunity Reconciliation Act of 1996 strengthened and improved child support collection activities. The law established a National Directory of New Hires to track parents across state lines, made the process for establishing paternity faster and easier, and enacted tough new penalties for delinquent parents, including expanded wage garnishment and suspension or revocation of driver's licenses. The law also required single-mother TANF applicants to disclose the paternity of their children and to assign any child support payments to the state. According to the report *Child Support Enforcement, FY 2005: Preliminary Report* (May 2006, http://www.acf.hhs.gov/programs/cse/pubs/2006/reports/preliminary_report/) by the HHS's Administration for Children and Families, these efforts have paid off; in FY 2005 the CSE Program handled 15.9 million cases and collected more than $23 billion, up 5.2% from the previous year.

TEENS AND MONEY
Teen Employment

The U.S. Bureau of Labor Statistics (BLS) finds in *The Employment Situation: December 2006* (January 5, 2007, http://www.bls.gov/news.release/archives/empsit_01052007.pdf) that in December 2006, 7.3 million people aged sixteen to nineteen, or a little less then half of the population that age (43.4%), were employed or looking for work. The unemployment rate in this age group was 15.2%. Employment rates among young people are highest during the summer months, when many full-time students are out of school. For example, in the press release "Employment and Unemployment among Youth—Summer 2006" (August 25, 2006, http://www.bls.gov/news.release/pdf/youth.pdf), the BLS reports that employment of youth between the ages of sixteen and twenty-four increased by 2.5 million between April and July 2006.

Studies find that the rate of teens in the labor force is correlated with family income; as a household's income rises, the likelihood that a teen within the household will work also rises. In March 2002 only 17% of teens aged

TABLE 2.5

Trends in average monthly payment for Aid to Families with Dependent Children (AFDC) and Temporary Assistance for Needy Families (TANF), 1962–2004

Fiscal year	Monthly benefit per recipient		Average number of persons per family	Monthly benefit per family (not reduced by child support)		Weighted average[a] maximum benefit (per 3-person family)	
	Current dollars	2004 dollars		Current dollars	2004 dollars	Current dollars	2004 dollars
1962	$31	$168	3.9	$121	$654	NA	NA
1963	31	167	4.0	126	672	NA	NA
1964	32	168	4.1	131	692	NA	NA
1965	34	175	4.2	140	728	NA	NA
1966	35	178	4.2	146	741	NA	NA
1967	36	179	4.1	150	741	NA	NA
1968	40	189	4.1	162	772	NA	NA
1969	43	199	4.0	173	793	$186[b]	$856
1970	46	201	3.9	178	779	194[b]	850
1971	48	200	3.8	180	755	201[b]	842
1972	51	208	3.6	187	756	205[b]	830
1973	53	205	3.5	187	726	213[b]	827
1974	57	203	3.4	194	693	229[b]	818
1975	63	206	3.3	209	681	243	792
1976	71	216	3.2	226	688	257	783
1977	78	221	3.1	241	685	271	770
1978	83	221	3.0	250	667	284	758
1979	87	213	3.0	257	630	301	737
1980	94	208	2.9	274	604	320	707
1981	96	193	2.9	277	556	326	654
1982	103	193	2.9	300	565	331	622
1983	106	192	2.9	311	559	336	605
1984	110	191	2.9	322	557	352	609
1985	112	188	2.9	329	551	369	618
1986	115	189	2.9	339	554	383	627
1987	123	196	2.9	359	573	393	627
1988	127	195	2.9	370	569	403	619
1989	131	194	2.9	381	561	413	608
1990	135	190	2.9	389	548	420	592
1991	135	182	2.9	388	523	424	572
1992	136	179	2.9	389	512	419	551
1993	131	169	2.8	373	479	414	532
1994	134	168	2.8	376	473	416	522
1995	134	165	2.8	376	463	418	514
1996	135	161	2.8	374	448	419	502
1997[c]	130	152	2.8	362	423	418	489
1998	130	150	2.7	358	412	429	494
1999	133	150	2.7	357	404	450	509
2000	133	146	2.6	349	383	446	489
2001	137	146	2.6	351	373	448	476
2002	146	153	2.5	364	381	452	474
2003	140	148	2.5	354	362	449	460
2004	150	150	2.5	360	360	473	473

Note: AFDC benefit amounts have not been reduced by child support collections. Constant dollar adjustments to 2004 level were made using a Consumer Price Index Research Series Using Current Methods (CPI-U-RS) fiscal-year price index.

[a]The maximum benefit for a 3-person family in each state is weighted by that state's share of total AFDC families.

[b]Estimated based on the weighted average benefit for a 4-person family.

[c]The Personal Responsibility and Work Opportunity Reconciliation Act of 1996 repealed the AFDC program as of July 1, 1997 and replaced it with the TANF program. Beginning in 1997, average monthly benefits are calculated from case-level data rather than by dividing aggregate expenditures on cash assistance by aggregate caseloads, as in the past. This change was necessary due to uncertainty about the extent to which states may be reporting non-cash basic assistance as well as cash assistance in the expenditure data formerly used to calculate average cash benefits.

SOURCE: "Table TANF 6. Trends in AFDC/TANF Average Monthly Payments: 1962–2004," in *Indicators of Welfare Dependence, Annual Report to Congress, 2006*, U.S. Department of Health and Human Services, 2006, http://aspe.hhs.gov/hsp/indicators06/apa.pdf (accessed February 16, 2007)

fifteen to seventeen from families with a household income of less than $15,000 were in the labor force, compared with 28% of teens from families with a household income of more than $50,000. (See Figure 2.5.)

Most teens are employed as hourly workers, and they make low wages compared with other age groups. The BLS reports in *Characteristics of Minimum Wage Workers: 2005* (May 19, 2006, http://www.bls.gov/cps/minwage 2005tbls.htm#1) that in 2005, 8.9% of sixteen- to nineteen-year-olds earned the minimum hourly wage of $5.15 or less, compared with only 1.5% of workers aged twenty-five years and older.

HOW DOES WORKING AFFECT ACADEMIC ACHIEVEMENT? In "Employment during High School and Student Achievement" (*Journal of Educational Research*, September 2001), Kimberly J. Quirk, Timothy Z. Keith, and

TABLE 2.6

Average values of selected characteristics of food stamp households, 2005

Households with:	Average values			
	Gross monthly countable income (dollars)	Net monthly countable income (dollars)[a]	Monthly food stamp benefit (dollars)	Household size (persons)
Total	**648**	**319**	**209**	**2.3**
Children	768	397	300	3.3
Single-adult household	685	341	291	3.0
Male adult	688	334	263	2.8
Female adult	684	341	292	3.1
Multiple-adult household	1,068	617	349	4.4
Married head household	1,120	643	349	4.4
Other multiple-adult household	966	564	348	4.2
Children only	515	185	231	2.1
Elderly individuals	690	359	87	1.3
Living alone	625	292	70	1.0
Not living alone	926	569	151	2.4
Disabled nonelderly individuals[b]	802	445	145	2.0
Living alone	639	273	75	1.0
Not living alone	1,004	641	231	3.3
Other households[c]	205	60	146	1.1
Single-person household	174	44	138	1.0
Multi-person household	525	227	228	2.1
Single-person households	462	185	97	1.0

[a]Because net income is not used in their benefit determination, 36,040 households participating in the Minnesota Family Investment Program (MFIP) and 305,045 households participating in an Supplemental Security Income Combined Application Project (SSI-CAP) in Mississippi, New York, North Carolina, South Carolina, or Texas are excluded from this column.
[b]Due to changes in the food stamp program quality control (FSPQC) data, the definition of disabled changed in 2003. Beginning with the 2003 report, we are able to identify households that contain a disabled person. In previous reports, we had additional information that helped to identify which household member was disabled.
[c]Households not containing children, elderly individuals, or disabled individuals.

SOURCE: Allison Barrett, "Table 3.4. Average Values of Selected Characteristics by Household Composition, Fiscal Year 2005," in *Characteristics of Food Stamp Households: Fiscal Year 2005*, U.S. Department of Agriculture, Food and Nutrition Service, Office of Analysis, Nutrition and Evaluation, September 2006, http://www.fns.usda.gov/oane/menu/Published/FSP/FILES/Participation/2005Characteristics.pdf (accessed February 16, 2007)

Jeffrey T. Quirk present the results of a longitudinal study examining the effects of high school student employment on academic achievement. The researchers conclude that "working displayed a moderate, significant, and negative effect on high school grades." However, smaller amounts of work (twelve hours or less per week) seemed to slightly improve grades. Quirk, Keith, and Quirk also find that the lower a student's grades were, the more likely he or she was to get a job.

The U.S. Department of Labor, in "The Relationship of Youth Employment to Future Educational Attainment and Labor Market Experience" (*Report on the Youth Labor Force*, November 2000), finds a correlation between teen employment and future college education. Adults who had worked one to twenty hours per week as sixteen- and seventeen-year-olds were more likely than other adults to have completed at least some college education by age thirty. In contrast, less than half of adults who had not worked at all or who had worked more than twenty hours per week had completed some college education. The findings suggest that working a limited number of hours in the junior and senior years of high school has a positive effect on educational attainment.

Teens as Consumers

By the last decades of the twentieth century teens had a big influence on the economy—from affecting major family purchases to buying groceries. According to the Mintel International Group, in *Spending Power of the Teen Consumer* (September 2006, http://www.marketresearch.com), teens had an estimated spending power of $153 billion in 2006. However, the spending power of teens had declined 12% from 2003 to 2006, probably reflecting the economic downturn of the early twenty-first century. The report also examines teens' spending habits; although teens were attracted to the youthful image of retailers such as Abercrombie & Fitch, they actually spent their money in more affordable stores such as Old Navy and Target.

TABLE 2.7

Total participation by state/territory in the National School Lunch Program, fiscal years 2002–06

State/Territory	Fiscal year 2002	Fiscal year 2003	Fiscal year 2004	Fiscal year 2005	Fiscal year 2006
					Preliminary
Alabama	545,726	549,241	558,455	565,962	570,741
Alaska	52,807	52,962	52,069	52,091	52,908
Arizona	490,039	517,837	545,033	579,438	607,537
Arkansas	315,263	317,843	322,753	335,891	345,734
California	2,658,705	2,732,026	2,798,852	2,866,347	2,895,262
Colorado	325,715	327,775	335,266	336,565	348,066
Connecticut	280,212	283,625	291,886	301,665	307,156
Delaware	73,803	75,377	78,045	81,032	83,648
District of Columbia	50,350	47,961	46,536	46,976	45,229
Florida	1,369,013	1,397,558	1,463,971	1,523,754	1,523,536
Georgia	1,112,375	1,129,503	1,170,116	1,205,372	1,252,706
Guam	15,849	17,408	15,951	16,932	20,096
Hawaii	135,219	131,954	123,721	121,180	112,801
Idaho	147,115	148,798	152,570	155,700	160,644
Illinois	1,090,023	1,097,467	1,079,949	1,104,595	1,104,958
Indiana	643,464	663,592	679,283	700,742	723,583
Iowa	380,099	380,864	385,111	385,015	389,721
Kansas	316,260	317,481	323,008	326,805	332,884
Kentucky	508,526	511,470	528,271	534,807	542,704
Louisiana	632,139	626,153	629,541	615,880	571,269
Maine	107,618	103,847	106,097	107,743	109,153
Maryland	426,838	435,790	426,182	438,302	444,059
Massachusetts	541,981	541,767	548,522	558,107	557,524
Michigan	826,252	842,678	858,209	869,217	884,534
Minnesota	572,720	577,652	583,459	590,250	596,893
Mississippi	397,076	395,089	399,460	398,951	404,503
Missouri	622,416	603,434	610,807	624,385	634,282
Montana	77,649	77,464	78,651	79,664	82,879
Nebraska	221,491	222,865	225,506	228,681	232,825
Nevada	130,314	136,856	145,963	172,292	181,944
New Hampshire	107,514	109,815	111,863	113,074	112,654
New Jersey	599,548	604,595	616,759	629,815	638,688
New Mexico	198,166	201,272	208,453	211,793	213,064
New York	1,792,586	1,788,136	1,803,687	1,823,454	1,819,086
North Carolina	843,699	863,716	886,274	915,560	945,480
North Dakota	77,833	77,230	77,924	78,418	78,351
Ohio	1,019,361	1,028,227	1,046,593	1,059,942	1,085,030
Oklahoma	377,254	382,606	389,270	402,962	412,994
Oregon	267,595	275,713	284,467	291,326	300,498
Pennsylvania	1,041,166	1,057,774	1,086,661	1,121,383	1,135,239
Puerto Rico	399,236	392,900	379,940	369,889	362,119
Rhode Island	68,802	82,161	83,188	84,080	83,806
South Carolina	469,481	466,834	473,208	482,820	491,090
South Dakota	103,480	103,592	103,809	103,986	104,772
Tennessee	636,692	635,613	648,215	660,282	670,620
Texas	2,582,461	2,672,099	2,776,775	2,892,593	3,007,619
Utah	278,500	283,627	289,402	297,669	304,856
Vermont	53,713	54,356	54,808	55,363	55,363
Virginia	678,369	687,945	705,401	730,950	745,036
Virgin Islands	15,440	15,450	14,286	14,113	13,479
Washington	488,212	495,468	505,999	513,526	522,950
West Virginia	195,950	204,626	201,002	202,574	209,128
Wisconsin	552,561	561,155	569,648	583,358	590,872
Wyoming	49,889	49,485	49,449	51,187	52,274
Dept. of Defense	36,990	33,489	31,534	31,237	28,872
Total	**28,001,553**	**28,392,222**	**28,961,857**	**29,645,694**	**30,103,719**

Note: Participation data are nine-month averages; summer months (June–August) are excluded. Participation is based on average daily meals divided by an attendance factor of 0.927. Department of Defense activity represents children of armed forces personnel attending schools overseas. Data are subject to revision.

SOURCE: "National School Lunch Program: Total Participation," U.S. Department of Agriculture, Food and Nutrition Service, January 25, 2007, http://www .fns.usda.gov/pd/01slfypart.htm (accessed February 16, 2007)

FIGURE 2.4

Custodial parents receiving part or full child support payments due, by poverty status, selected years 1993–2003

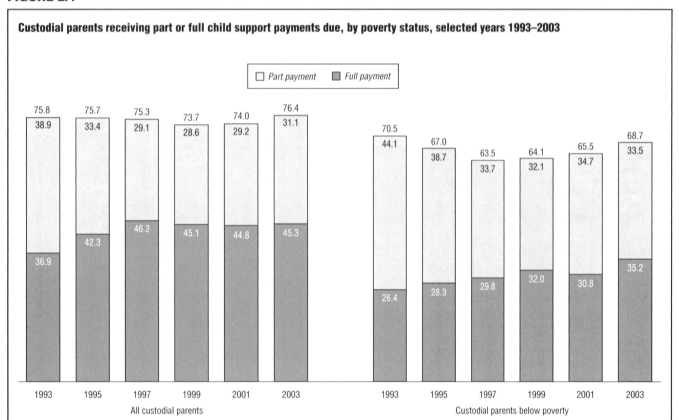

SOURCE: Timothy S. Grall, "Figure 4. Custodial Parents Receiving Part or Full Child Support Payments Due by Poverty Status: 1993–2003," in *Custodial Mothers and Fathers and Their Child Support: 2003*, U.S. Census Bureau, July 2006, http://www.census.gov/prod/2006pubs/p60-230.pdf (accessed February 16, 2007)

TABLE 2.8

Award status and child support recipiency for custodial parents due child support, by sex of custodial parent, selected years 1993–2003

[Numbers in thousands as of spring of the following year. Parents living with own children under 21 years of age whose other parent is not living in the home. Amounts in 2003 dollars.]

Award status and child support recipiency	1993	1995	1997	1999	2001	2003
All custodial parents	Number	Number	Number	Number	Number	Number
Total	**13,690**	**13,715**	**13,949**	**13,529**	**13,383**	**13,951**
Awarded child support	7,800	7,967	7,876	7,945	7,916	8,376
Percent	57.0	58.1	56.5	58.7	59.1	60.0
Due child support	6,688	6,958	7,018	6,791	6,924	7,256
Average child support due*	$4,489	$4,875	$4,741	$5,249	$5,242	$5,104
Average child support received*	$2,922	$3,212	$3,159	$3,081	$3,284	$3,499
Received any child support	5,070	5,269	5,282	5,005	5,119	5,548
Percent	75.8	75.7	75.3	73.7	73.9	76.5
Received full amount of child support	2,466	2,945	3,240	3,066	3,093	3,290
Percent	36.9	42.3	46.2	45.1	44.7	45.3
Not awarded child support	5,889	5,747	6,074	5,584	5,466	5,576
Custodial mothers						
Total	**11,505**	**11,607**	**11,872**	**11,499**	**11291**	**11,587**
Awarded child support	6,878	7,123	7,080	7,150	7110	7,436
Percent	59.8	61.4	59.6	62.2	63.0	64.2
Due child support	5,913	6,224	6,342	6,133	6,212	6,516
Average child support due*	$4,548	$4,958	$4,763	$5,301	$6,017	$5,176
Average child support received*	$2,984	$3,252	$3,178	$3,167	$3,494	$3,579
Received any child support	4,501	4,742	4,802	4,578	4,639	5,018
Percent	76.1	76.2	75.7	74.6	74.7	77.0
Received full amount of child support	2,178	2,674	2,945	2,818	2,815	2,948
Percent	36.8	43.0	46.4	45.9	45.3	45.2
Not awarded child support	4,627	4,484	4,792	4,349	4,181	4,151
Custodial fathers						
Total	**2,184**	**2,108**	**2,077**	**2,030**	**2,092**	**2,364**
Awarded child support	922	844	796	795	807	940
Percent	42.2	40.0	38.3	39.2	38.6	39.8
Due child support	775	733	676	658	712	740
Average child support due*	$4,043	$4,168	$4,531	$4,763	$4,386	$4,471
Average child support received*	$2,534	$2,883	$2,986	$2,276	$2,994	$2,797
Received any child support	569	527	479	427	480	530
Percent	73.4	71.9	70.9	64.9	67.4	71.6
Received full amount of child support	288	270	295	248	278	342
Percent	37.2	36.8	43.6	37.7	39.0	46.2
Not awarded child support	1,262	1,263	1,281	1,235	1,285	1,424

*All child support income amounts are adjusted to reflect 2003 dollars using the Consumer Price Index Research Series Using Current Methods (CPI-U-RS).

SOURCE: Timothy S. Grall, "Table 1. Award Status and Child Support Recipiency for Custodial Parents Due Child Support by Sex of Custodial Parent: 1993–2003," in *Custodial Mothers and Fathers and Their Child Support: 2003*, U. S. Census Bureau, July 2006, http://www.census.gov/prod/2006pubs/p60-230.pdf (accessed February 16, 2007)

FIGURE 2.5

Labor force status of children 15–17 years old, by family income, March 2002

[In percent]

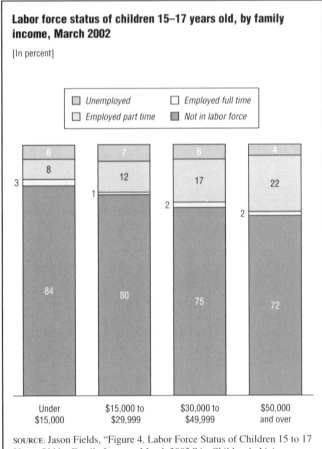

SOURCE: Jason Fields, "Figure 4. Labor Force Status of Children 15 to 17 Years Old by Family Income: March 2002," in *Children's Living Arrangements and Characteristics: March 2002*, U.S. Census Bureau, June 2003, http://www.census.gov/prod/2003pubs/p20-547.pdf (accessed February 16, 2007)

CHAPTER 3
CARING FOR CHILDREN

SOCIETAL CHANGES AND WORKING MOTHERS

In the early twenty-first century, women with young children were much more likely to work outside the home than they had been three decades previously. Jane Lawler Dye reports in *Fertility of American Women: June 2004* (December 2005, http://www.census.gov/prod/2005pubs/p20-555.pdf) that in 1976, 31% of women aged fifteen to forty-four with a child under twelve months old worked. By 2004 that percentage had increased to 55%, down from a high of 59% in 1998. Table 3.1 shows that in 2005, 62.8% of mothers with children under age six and 76.5% of mothers with school-age children were in the labor force.

Legislation passed in the late 1970s that made it more possible for women to return to work after the birth of a child. In 1976 tax code changes allowed families a tax credit on child care costs, making it more financially feasible for women to return to work. In 1978 the Pregnancy Discrimination Act was passed, making it illegal for employers to discriminate in hiring, firing, promoting, or establishing pay levels based on pregnancy or childbirth. And in 1993 the Family and Medical Leave Act (FMLA) was passed, requiring employers to give eligible employees up to twelve weeks of unpaid leave for childbearing or family care each year.

Societal changes also contributed to the greater number of women with young children participating in the labor force. In *Maternity Leave and Employment Patterns, 1961–1995* (November 2001, http://www.census.gov/prod/2001pubs/p70-79.pdf), Kristin Smith, Barbara Downs, and Martin O'Connell review the changing demographic profile of first-time mothers between the 1960s and 1990s to explain, in part, this increase. The researchers emphasize that during this period the incidence of first-time motherhood at age thirty or older tripled and that first-time mothers in the 1990s tended to be better educated than their 1960 counterparts. These older, well-educated mothers often viewed their jobs as long-term careers and believed time lost could adversely affect their ability to hold a position and earn promotions and could decrease contributions to retirement funds. This trend continued into the twenty-first century. Laura B. Shrestha, in *The Changing Demographic Profile of the United States* (May 5, 2006, http://fas.org/sgp/crs/misc/RL32701.pdf), notes that the mean age of first-time mothers reached 25.2 years in 2003, up from 21.4 years in 1970 and an all-time high for American women.

Furthermore, the increasing number of single mothers meant that more women had to work to support their families. In 1970, 3.4 million women maintained single-parent households; by 2005 that number had tripled, to 10.4 million. (See Table 1.3 in Chapter 1.) Changes in government programs that provided assistance to poor families also resulted in increasing numbers of single mothers entering the workforce. In 1996 the federal government placed a two-year time limit on receiving public assistance benefits while not working, requiring poor parents to work even if they had to place young children in day care. In 2005, 63.4% of single mothers with children under three years old were in the labor force, with a 15% unemployment rate. (See Table 3.2.)

Married women have also entered the workforce in larger numbers. A decline in men's real wages plus a rising cost of living has led some two-parent families to decide to maintain two incomes to meet financial obligations and pay for their children's future college expenses. According to the U.S. Census Bureau, in *The 2007 Statistical Abstract* (December 22, 2006, http://www.census.gov/compendia/statab/income_expenditures_wealth/), the median income in 2003 for married couples in which both husbands and wives worked was $77,899, which was significantly higher than the $51,303 median income for married-couple families in which the wife was not in the paid labor force. Table 3.1 shows that 68.2% of married women with children

TABLE 3.1

Employment status of population by sex, marital status, and presence and age of own children under 18, 2005

[Numbers in thousands]

Characteristic	2005 Total	Men	Women
With own children under 18 years			
Civilian noninstitutional population	64,482	28,065	36,417
Civilian labor force	52,056	26,399	25,657
Participation rate	80.7	94.1	70.5
Employed	49,882	25,587	24,294
Employment-population ratio	77.4	91.2	66.7
Full-time workers[a]	42,852	24,713	18,139
Part-time workers[b]	7,029	875	6,155
Unemployed	2,174	811	1,363
Unemployment rate	4.2	3.1	5.3
Married, spouse present			
Civilian noninstitutional population	51,519	25,578	25,942
Civilian labor force	41,905	24,215	17,690
Participation rate	81.3	94.7	68.2
Employed	40,614	23,556	17,058
Employment-population ratio	78.8	92.1	65.8
Full-time workers[a]	35,086	22,808	12,278
Part-time workers[b]	5,528	748	4,780
Unemployed	1,291	659	632
Unemployment rate	3.1	2.7	3.6
Other marital status[c]			
Civilian noninstitutional population	12,963	2,487	10,475
Civilian labor force	10,151	2,184	7,967
Participation rate	78.3	87.8	76.1
Employed	9,268	2,032	7,236
Employment-population ratio	71.5	81.7	69.1
Full-time workers[a]	7,766	1,905	5,861
Part-time workers[b]	1,502	127	1,375
Unemployed	883	152	731
Unemployment rate	8.7	7.0	9.2
With own children 6–17 years, none younger			
Civilian noninstitutional population	35,937	15,590	20,348
Civilian labor force	30,068	14,496	15,572
Participation rate	83.7	93.0	76.5
Employed	28,953	14,066	14,887
Employment-population ratio	80.6	90.2	73.2
Full-time workers[a]	25,074	13,606	11,468
Part-time workers[b]	3,880	460	3,419
Unemployed	1,115	430	684
Unemployment rate	3.7	3.0	4.4
With own children under 6 years			
Civilian noninstitutional population	28,545	12,475	16,070
Civilian labor force	21,988	11,903	10,085
Participation rate	77.0	95.4	62.8
Employed	20,928	11,521	9,407
Employment-population ratio	73.3	92.4	58.5
Full-time workers[a]	17,778	11,107	6,671
Part-time workers[b]	3,150	414	2,736
Unemployed	1,060	381	678
Unemployment rate	4.8	3.2	6.7

TABLE 3.1

Employment status of population by sex, marital status, and presence and age of own children under 18, 2005 [CONTINUED]

[Numbers in thousands]

Characteristic	2005 Total	Men	Women
With no own children under 18 years			
Civilian noninstitutional population	159,751	79,237	80,514
Civilian labor force	95,545	51,914	43,631
Participation rate	59.8	65.5	54.2
Employed	90,171	48,709	41,462
Employment-population ratio	56.4	61.5	51.5
Full-time workers[a]	72,515	41,496	31,019
Part-time workers[b]	17,657	7,213	10,444
Unemployed	5,374	3,205	2,169
Unemployment rate	5.6	6.2	5.0

[a]Usually work 35 hours or more a week at all jobs.
[b]Usually work less than 35 hours a week at all jobs.
[c]Includes never-married, divorced, separated, and widowed persons.

SOURCE: Adapted from "Table 5. Employment Status of the Population by Sex, Marital Status, and Presence and Age of Own Children under 18, 2004–05 Annual Averages," in *Employment Characteristics of Families in 2005*, U.S. Department of Labor, Bureau of Labor Statistics, April 27, 2006, http://www.bls.gov/news.release/pdf/famee.pdf (accessed February 20, 2007)

under the age of eighteen were in the labor force in 2005, and Table 3.2 shows that 56.7% of married women with children under age three were in the labor force in that year. Many families have come to depend on women's economic contributions to the household.

WHO CARES FOR AMERICA'S CHILDREN?
School-Age Children

Married parents who both work and single parents who work need reliable child care. The Federal Inter-agency Forum on Child and Family Statistics reports in *America's Children in Brief: Key National Indicators of Well-Being, 2006* (http://childstats.gov/americaschildren/pop.asp) that about half of children in kindergarten through eighth grade were cared for by someone other than their parents in 2005. (See Figure 3.1.) Of those who were cared for by someone other than parents, younger children were more likely to receive home- or center-based care for before- or after-school hours; children in grades four and up were less likely to receive these types of care and more likely to care for themselves. Only 2.6% of children in kindergarten through third grade cared for themselves regularly, whereas 22.2% of older children did. (See Table 3.3.)

SELF-CARE—LATCHKEY KIDS. The term *latchkey kids* is used to describe children left alone or unsupervised either during the day or before or after school. These are children five to fourteen years of age whose parents report "child cares for self" as either the primary or secondary child care arrangement. In 2002 approximately 6.1 million grade school-aged children cared for themselves regularly without adult supervision. (See Table 3.4.) Self-care was higher among children who lived with their father without their mother present (18.3%) than it was among children who lived with their mother, with or without their father present (14.8%). Most of these children were age twelve or older, but 1.9 million children eleven years of age and younger regularly took care of themselves. In *Who's Minding the Kids? Child Care Arrangements: Winter 2002* (October 2005, http://www.census.gov/prod/2005pubs/p70-101.pdf), Julia Overturf Johnson finds that the percentage of children

TABLE 3.2

Employment status of mothers with own children under three years old, by single year of age of youngest child and marital status, 2005

[Numbers in thousands]

	Civilian non-institutional population	Civilian labor force						Unemployed	
				Employed					
		Total	Percent of population	Total	Percent of population	Full-time workers[a]	Part-time workers[b]	Number	Percent of labor force
2005									
Total mothers									
With own children under 3 years old	9,365	5,470	58.4	5,077	54.2	3,501	1,576	393	7.2
2 years	2,845	1,773	62.3	1,654	58.1	1,162	492	119	6.7
1 year	3,287	1,958	59.6	1,823	55.5	1,247	576	135	6.9
Under 1 year	3,233	1,740	53.8	1,600	49.5	1,092	508	140	8.0
Married, spouse present									
With own children under 3 years old	6,951	3,939	56.7	3,776	54.3	2,588	1,188	164	4.2
2 years	2,118	1,268	59.9	1,214	57.3	840	374	55	4.3
1 year	2,435	1,389	57.0	1,337	54.9	901	436	52	3.7
Under 1 year	2,398	1,282	53.5	1,225	51.1	847	378	58	4.5
Other marital status[c]									
With own children under 3 years old	2,414	1,531	63.4	1,301	53.9	913	388	230	15.0
2 years	726	504	69.5	440	60.6	322	118	64	12.7
1 year	852	569	66.8	486	57.0	346	139	83	14.6
Under 1 year	836	457	54.7	375	44.9	245	130	82	18.0

[a]Usually work 35 hours or more a week at all jobs.
[b]Usually work less than 35 hours a week at all jobs.
[c]Includes never-married, divorced, separated, and widowed persons.

SOURCE: Adapted from "Table 6. Employment Status of Mothers with Own Children under 3 Years Old by Single Year of Age of Youngest Child and Marital Status, 2004–05 Annual Averages," in *Employment Characteristics of Families in 2005*, U.S. Department of Labor, Bureau of Labor Statistics, April 27, 2006, http://www.bls.gov/news.release/pdf/famee.pdf (accessed February 20, 2007)

FIGURE 3.1

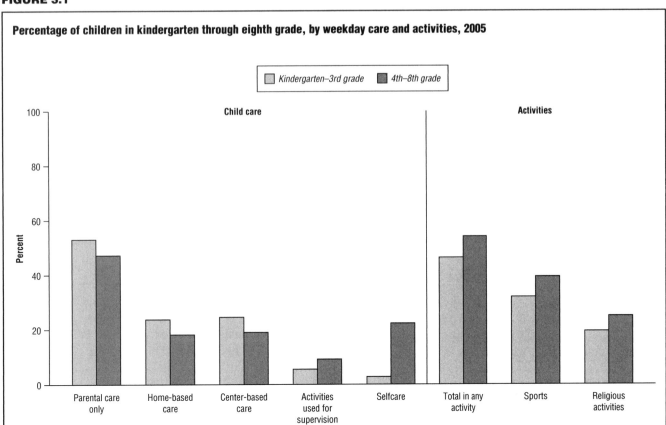

Percentage of children in kindergarten through eighth grade, by weekday care and activities, 2005

SOURCE: "Figure POP8C. Percentage of Children in Kindergarten through 8th Grade by Weekday Care and Activities, 2005," in *America's Children in Brief: Key National Indicators of Well-Being, 2006*, Federal Inter agency Forum on Child and Family Statistics, 2006, http://www.childstats.gov/americaschildren/pop8.asp#pop8c (accessed February 20, 2007)

TABLE 3.3

Percentage of children in kindergarten through eighth grade, by weekday care and before- and after-school activities, by grade level, poverty, race, and Hispanic origin, 2005

Grade level, care arrangement, and activity	Total	Poverty status			Race and Hispanic origin[a]			
		Below 100% poverty	100–199% poverty	200% poverty and above	White, non-Hispanic	Black, non-Hispanic	Asian	Hispanic
Kindergarten through 3rd grade								
Care arrangements								
Parental care only	53.1	52.0	54.5	53.0	58.3	34.6	49.9	55.3
Nonparental care[b]	46.9	48.0	45.5	47.0	41.7	65.4	50.1	44.7
Home-based care[c]	23.6	25.2	24.5	22.6	22.0	32.2	26.5	20.4
Center-based care	24.4	25.0	21.6	25.2	20.5	39.8	21.4	23.4
Activities used for supervision	5.2	3.1	5.3	6.0	4.8	5.8	13.4	3.2
Self care	2.6	5.1	3.6	1.3	1.6	4.1	3.6	4.2
Activities								
Any activity[b]	46.2	24.3	34.0	59.5	56.2	30.4	45.8	30.4
Sports	31.8	12.1	19.5	44.3	40.2	16.8	29.3	20.8
Religious activities	19.4	13.5	14.8	23.4	24.0	14.6	11.5	11.9
Arts[d]	17.2	6.0	10.8	24.1	21.8	8.3	27.1	8.2
Scouts	12.9	5.3	8.0	17.8	18.2	4.9	11.1	3.8
Academic activities[e]	4.7	3.8	3.8	5.3	5.1	4.4	7.4	3.5
Community services	4.2	1.9	3.0	5.5	5.3	3.3	2.6	1.7
Clubs	3.2	1.3	2.4	4.3	4.3	1.1	4.2	1.8
4th through 8th grade								
Care arrangements								
Parental care only	46.9	46.7	45.2	47.6	51.2	34.5	44.2	45.0
Nonparental care[b]	53.1	53.3	54.8	52.4	48.8	65.5	55.8	55.0
Home-based care[c]	18.1	15.0	20.0	18.4	16.4	24.1	17.5	18.6
Center-based care	19.0	21.3	21.3	17.4	14.2	28.9	21.9	25.4
Activities used for supervision	9.0	7.8	6.9	10.2	8.9	10.5	11.9	7.5
Self care	22.2	23.5	23.8	21.2	21.1	27.1	21.0	19.6
Activities								
Any activity[b]	53.7	30.4	40.5	65.9	63.3	39.7	51.2	35.4
Sports	39.3	18.6	26.1	50.8	47.8	24.2	37.2	26.7
Religious activities	24.9	12.5	20.0	30.7	29.7	20.9	18.3	14.8
Arts[d]	21.5	9.7	12.5	28.5	25.8	13.3	25.5	13.2
Community services	12.7	5.0	10.6	15.9	15.6	8.2	13.1	7.1
Scouts	10.1	4.8	6.4	13.2	13.3	5.6	7.7	5.4
Academic activities[e]	9.7	6.6	7.1	11.6	10.0	12.0	13.0	5.9
Clubs	8.7	3.7	4.6	11.8	11.0	4.9	8.9	4.1

[a]The 1997 Office of Management and Budget Standards for Data on Race and Ethnicity were used, allowing persons to select one or more of five racial groups: white, black or African American, American Indian or Alaska Native, Asian, and Native Hawaiian or other Pacific Islander. Included in the total, but not shown separately are American Indian/Alaskan Native and respondents with two or more races. Respondents who reported the child being Asian or Native Hawaiian or other Pacific Islander were combined. Data on race and Hispanic origin are collected separately. Persons of Hispanic origin may be of any race.
[b]Children may have multiple nonparental child care arrangements, as well as be involved in more than one activity; thus, the total of the four kinds of nonparental arrangements may not sum to the category "nonparental care"; likewise, the seven activities listed may not sum to the category "any activity." Activities include organized programs a child participates in outside of school hours that are not part of a before- or after-school program.
[c]Home-based care includes care that takes place in a relative's or nonrelative's private home.
[d]Arts include activities such as music, dance, and painting.
[e]Academic activities include activities such as tutoring or math lab.

SOURCE: "Table POP8C. Child Care and Activities: Percentage of Children in Kindergarten through 8th Grade by Weekday Care and Before- and After-School Activities by Grade Level, Poverty Status, Race, and Hispanic Origin, 2005," in *America's Children in Brief: Key National Indicators of Well-Being, 2006*, Federal Interagency Forum on Child and Family Statistics, 2006, http://www.childstats.gov/americaschildren/tables/pop8c.asp (accessed February 20, 2007)

in self-care held steady between 1997 and 2002 in both families with married parents and in families living with an unemployed single parent; however, the percentage of children of a single, employed parent in self-care actually declined from 24% in 1997 to 18% in 2002.

TWENTY-FIRST-CENTURY COMMUNITY LEARNING CENTERS. More than half of all families use after-school programs, and in many families parents rely on after-school care to provide a safe and nurturing place for their children while they are working. In response to concerns about the availability of quality after-school programs, the U.S. Department of Education initiated the Twenty-First-Century Community Learning Centers (21st CCLC), authorized under Title X, Part I, of the Elementary and Secondary Education Act and reauthorized under Title IV, Part B, of the No Child Left Behind Act. This initiative gives grants to low-performance middle and elementary schools in rural and urban areas to provide after-school opportunities for their students, both educational and recreational. In 1997 the 21st CCLC had a budget of only $1 million; by fiscal year 2006 the program's budget was $981 million. According to the Department of Education, in "21st CCLC Profile and Performance Information Collection System" (2007, http://ppics.learningpt.org/ppics/publicGrantSearch.asp), by 2007 the 21st CCLC supported after-school programs in 3,425 communities across the country.

However, Duncan Chaplin and Michael J. Puma, in *What "Extras" Do We Get with Extracurriculars? Technical Research Consideration* (September 30, 2003, http://www.urban.org/UploadedPDF/410862_what_extras.pdf), offer a cautionary note about claims that these programs may give disadvantaged students an academic boost. The researchers find that extracurricular activities included in after-school programs that do not specifically target academic outcomes (e.g., arts, music, drama, and language classes) had no affect on academic achievement. Chaplin and Puma suggest more rigorous evaluation of after-school programs that target disadvantaged youth be conducted before further money is spent on these programs, as that money might be spent on potentially more effective educational programs for disadvantaged youth. The MDRC states in "Evaluation of Academic Instruction in After-School Programs" (2007, http://www.mdrc.org/project_30_66.html) that the Department of Education is currently funding a study to evaluate whether children who receive academic instruction in these programs actually enjoy a better academic outcome than do other students.

Children Younger Than Five (Preschoolers)

In 2004 mothers with children under twelve months old were much less likely to be employed full time (thirty-five hours or more each week) than were mothers with children older than twelve months. Roughly a third of mothers whose youngest child was an infant (35%) were employed full time, compared with 39% of mothers whose youngest child was a one- to two-year-old, 47% of mothers whose youngest child was a three- to five-year-old, and 55% of mothers with only school-aged children. (See Figure 3.2.) Almost half the mothers with an infant were not in the labor force at all (45%), whereas only a quarter of mothers whose youngest child was aged six to eleven (25%) were not in the labor force. Unemployment and part-time employment were relatively equal across all groups of mothers.

In 2005, 50.7% of children under age two and 73.7% of children aged three to six were in nonparental care at least some of the time. (See Table 3.5.) Among the youngest children, home-based care by a relative was most common (22%), followed by care in a center-based program (19.6%), and home-based care by a nonrelative (15.6%). Among older preschoolers, center-based programs were by far the most common; 57.1% of three- to six-year-olds were enrolled in these programs, whereas 22.7% were cared for in a home by a relative and only 11.7% were cared for in a home by a nonrelative. These numbers reflect the fact that as their children grow from infancy to school age, working mothers often change

FIGURE 3.2

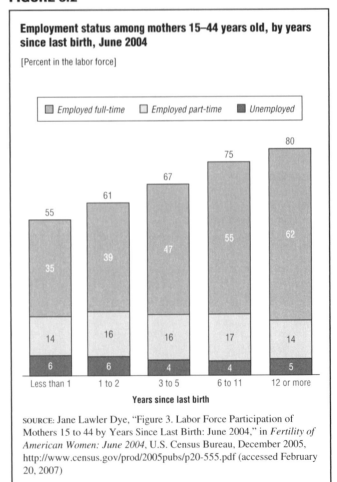

Employment status among mothers 15–44 years old, by years since last birth, June 2004

[Percent in the labor force]

Legend: Employed full-time ▫ Employed part-time ▪ Unemployed

Years since last birth	Employed full-time	Employed part-time	Unemployed	Total
Less than 1	35	14	6	55
1 to 2	39	16	6	61
3 to 5	47	16	4	67
6 to 11	55	17	4	75
12 or more	62	14	5	80

SOURCE: Jane Lawler Dye, "Figure 3. Labor Force Participation of Mothers 15 to 44 by Years Since Last Birth: June 2004," in *Fertility of American Women: June 2004*, U.S. Census Bureau, December 2005, http://www.census.gov/prod/2005pubs/p20-555.pdf (accessed February 20, 2007)

child care arrangements to meet the needs of their children, their families, and their employers. Making child care arrangements for infants and toddlers is often more difficult than for older children, because fewer organized child care facilities admit infants and young children, primarily because of the cost involved in hiring enough workers and adapting facilities to care adequately for babies. In addition, many parents prefer, if possible, to keep their infants in a home environment as long as possible. And many mothers view center-based programs, which often have an educational focus, as most appropriate for older preschoolers.

FACTORS THAT AFFECT CHILD CARE
Preschool Child Care

RACIAL AND ETHNIC DIFFERENCES. In 2005 African-American mothers of preschoolers relied more heavily on relatives to provide child care than did other mothers. More than one out of four (27.7%) African-American preschoolers were cared for by relatives in that year, compared with 21% of white, non-Hispanic preschoolers, 21.2% of Hispanic preschoolers, and 21.3% of Asian

TABLE 3.4

Prevalence of self-care among grade school-aged children, by selected characteristics for those living with mother, 2002

[Numbers in thousands]

Characteristic	Total	Age of child 5 to 11 years	12 to 14 years
Total children 5 to 14 years	40,624	28,276	12,348
Living with father[a]	1,676	1,084	592
Number in self-care	307	106	201
Percent in self-care	18.3	9.8	34.0
Living with mother	38,948	27,192	11,756
Number in self-care	5,766	1,862	3,904
Percent in self-care	14.8	7.0	33.3
Race and Hispanic origin of mother			
White	15.4	6.9	34.9
Non-Hispanic	17.5	8.0	38.7
Black	11.9	6.4	24.7
Asian and Pacific Islander	10.9	4.1	28.1
Hispanic (any race)	7.9	3.5	19.8
Marital status of mother			
Married[b]	14.7	6.8	32.7
Separated, divorced, widowed	18.1	7.9	37.5
Never married	10.0	5.4	27.3
Poverty status of family[c]			
Below poverty level	9.4	4.7	21.7
At or above poverty level	16.3	7.4	36.2
100 to 199 percent of poverty level	11.6	5.4	26.4
200 percent of poverty level or higher	18.2	8.3	39.9
Employment schedule of mother			
Not employed	7.1	3.7	17.2
Employed (all)	18.6	8.5	39.3
Self-employed	15.4	7.7	33.0
Not self-employed[d]	18.9	8.6	39.8
Full-time[e]	20.1	9.1	41.5
Part-time	16.1	7.5	35.6
Worked day shift	19.9	9.3	40.9
Worked non-day shift	16.6	7.1	37.2
Enrichment activities of child			
Participated in an activity	24.9	12.3	50.1
Did not participate in an activity	12.9	5.8	29.5
Average hours per week in self-care among children in self-care	6.3	5.2	6.9
Number of hours in self-care per week (Percent distribution)			
Total	100.0	100.0	100.0
Less than 2 hours	13.0	19.6	9.9
2 to 4 hours	33.3	39.4	30.4
5 to 9 hours	31.3	25.7	34.0
10 or more hours	22.4	15.4	25.7

[a]Mother not present in the household, so father is the designated parent.
[b]Includes married spouse present and spouse absent (excluding separated).
[c]Excludes those with missing income data.
[d]Includes mothers with wage and salary jobs and employment arrangements other than self-employed.
[e]Those who work 35 or more hours per week are considered working full-time.

SOURCE: Julia Overturf Johnson, "Table 5. Prevalence of Self-Care Among Grade School-Aged Children, by Selected Characteristics for Those Living with Mother: Winter 2002," in *Who's Minding the Kids? Child Care Arrangements: Winter 2002*, U.S. Census Bureau, October 2005, http://www.census.gov/prod/2005pubs/p70-101.pdf (accessed February 20, 2007)

to be cared for by nonrelatives or in center-based programs than were Hispanic preschoolers (35.6%).

POVERTY MAKES A DIFFERENCE. In 2005, 85.3% of preschoolers whose mothers worked full time and 69.7% of preschoolers whose mothers worked part time were regularly in nonparental care. (See Table 3.5.) However, the type of care varied by the income levels of those families. Jeffrey Capizzano and Gina Adams find in "Snapshots of America's Families III: Children in Low-Income Families Are Less Likely to Be in Center-Based Child Care" (November 2003, http://www.urban.org/UploadedPDF/310923_snapshots3_no16.pdf) that preschoolers from lower-income families (families with an income less than 200% of the poverty line) were less likely to be in center-based care (24.9%) than children from higher-income families (31.2%). Data from *America's Children in Brief* supports this conclusion. In 2005, 42.2% of preschoolers from families whose incomes were above 200% of the poverty line were in center-based care, compared with 29.4% of children from families with incomes 100% to 199% of the poverty line and 28.3% of children from families with incomes below the poverty line. (See Table 3.5.)

Capizzano and Adams suggest the lower percentage of low-income children in center care reflects the lower cost of home-based care. At the same time, they argue that there is evidence that quality, center-based care plays a big role in helping preschoolers make a successful transition to school and that low-income children are in large part missing this opportunity. In *Key Facts: Essential Information about Child Care, Early Education and School-Age Care* (2003), the Children's Defense Fund also stresses the importance of providing low-income families with child care assistance to help their children succeed.

FORMAL CHILD CARE FACILITIES

Even though no comprehensive data exist on the types or quality of child care facilities in the United States, the National Association for Regulatory Administration, in *The 2005 Child Care Licensing Study Executive Summary* (2006, http://www.nara.affiniscape.com/associations/4734/files/Executive%20Summary.pdf), estimates that in 2005 there were 335,520 licensed child care facilities in the United States, including 105,444 licensed child care centers and 213,966 licensed family child care homes. More than nine million children are taken care of in these licensed facilities, and over 70% of these children are in center-based programs. Many more unlicensed child care facilities exist, but because they are not regulated, no reliable statistics are collected.

In 2005 half of all children aged two and under and almost three-quarters of all children aged three to six spent time in nonparental care each week. (See Table 3.5.) Their care providers are major influences in their lives. Many

preschoolers. (See Table 3.5.) Non-Hispanic white preschoolers (54.8%), African-American preschoolers (54.1%), and Asian preschoolers (46%) were all more likely

TABLE 3.5

Percentage of preschool children by type of care arrangement and child and family characteristics, 2005

	Parental care only	Total in nonparental care[b]	Type of nonparental care arrangement		Center-based program[c]
			Care in a home[a]		
			By a relative	By a nonrelative	
Characteristic	2005	2005	2005	2005	2005
Total	39.2	60.8	22.3	13.9	36.1
Age					
Ages 0–2	49.3	50.7	22.0	15.6	19.6
Ages 3–6, not yet in kindergarten	23.6	73.7	22.7	11.7	57.1
Race and Hispanic origin[d]					
White, non-Hispanic	37.2	62.8	21.0	17.0	37.8
Black, non-Hispanic	30.1	69.9	27.7	10.2	43.9
Asian	43.5	56.5	21.3	9.0	37.0
Hispanic	50.5	49.5	21.2	10.4	25.2
Poverty status					
Below 100% poverty	49.2	50.8	23.3	8.0	28.3
100–199% poverty	47.2	52.8	23.5	9.3	29.4
200% poverty and above	31.6	68.4	21.4	18.3	42.2
Family type					
Two parents[e]	42.9	57.1	18.8	14.1	34.4
Two parents, married	41.8	58.2	18.6	14.2	35.8
Two parents, unmarried	53.0	47.0	20.4	13.0	21.7
One parent	24.9	75.1	36.0	13.4	42.3
No parents	33.1	66.9	28.3	10.0	43.6
Mother's highest level of education[f]					
Less than high school	63.7	36.3	16.1	5.5	18.9
High school diploma or equivalent	44.4	55.6	24.1	9.9	30.7
Some college, including vocational/technical/ associate's degree	36.5	63.5	25.8	14.5	35.2
Bachelor's degree or higher	30.5	69.5	19.1	19.2	45.8
Mother's employment status[f]					
35 hours or more per week	14.7	85.3	31.8	23.3	47.6
Less than 35 hours per week	30.3	69.7	30.5	18.0	37.8
Looking for work	53.3	46.7	20.7	7.5	23.3
Not in the labor force	66.1	33.9	7.8	3.6	25.8

—=Not available.

[a]Relative and nonrelative care can take place in either the child's own home or another home.

[b]Some children participate in more than one type of nonparental care arrangement. Thus, details do not sum to the total percentage of children in nonparental care.

[c]Center-based programs include day care centers, prekindergartens, nursery schools, head start programs, and other early childhood education programs.

[d]In 1995 and 2001, the 1977 Office of Management and Budget (OMB) Standards for Data on Race and Ethnicity were used to classify persons into one of the following four racial groups: white, black, American Indian or Alaskan Native, or Asian or Pacific Islander. For data from 2005, the revised 1997 OMB standards were used. Persons could select one or more of five racial groups: white, black or African American, American Indian or Alaska Native, Asian, and Native Hawaiian or other Pacific Islander. Included in the total, but not shown separately are American Indian/Alaskan Native and respondents with two or more races. For continuity purposes, in 2005 respondents who reported the child being Asian or Native Hawaiian or other Pacific Islander were combined. Data on race and Hispanic origin are collected separately. Persons of Hispanic origin may be of any race.

[e]Refers to adults' relationship to child and does not indicate marital status.

[f]Children without a mother in the home are excluded from estimates of mother's highest level of education and mother's employment status.

Notes: Some children participate in more than one type of arrangement, so the sum of all arrangement types exceeds the total percentage in nonparental care. Center-based programs include day care centers, prekindergartens, nursery schools, head start programs, and other early childhood education programs. Relative and nonrelative care can take place in either the child's own home or another home.

SOURCE: Adapted from "Table POP8A. Child Care: Percentage of Children Ages 0–6, Not Yet in Kindergarten by Type of Care Arrangement and Child and Family Characteristics, 1995, 2001, and 2005," in *America's Children in Brief: Key National Indicators of Well-Being, 2006*, Federal Interagency Forum on Child and Family Statistics, 2006, http://www.childstats.gov/americaschildren/tables/pop8a.asp (accessed February 20, 2007)

working parents discover that quality and affordable care is difficult to find. In some communities child care is hard to find at any cost. Shortages of child care for infants, sick children, children with special needs, and for school children before and after school pose problems for many parents.

Regulations and Quality of Care

Federal assistance to low-income families to pay for child care eroded in the late twentieth century at the same time that the government imposed requirements that more low-income parents work. The Personal Responsibility and Work Opportunity Reconciliation Act of 1996 eliminated the guarantee that families on welfare would receive subsidized child care and replaced it with the Child Care and Development Block Grant to states. Even though the legislation gave states wide discretion in the use of these funds, it also imposed penalties if states failed to meet criteria for getting low-income parents into the workforce.

TABLE 3.6

Full-time shift workers by reason for working a non-daytime schedule, May 2004

[Percent distribution]

Reason for working a non-daytime schedule	Total shift workers[a]	Evening shift	Night shift	Rotating shift	Split shift	Employer-arranged irregular schedule	Other shift
Number[b] (thousands)	14,805	4,736	3,221	2,526	497	3,064	715
Percent[b]	100.0	100.0	100.0	100.0	100.0	100.0	100.0
Better arrangements for family or child care	8.2	11.0	15.9	1.6	5.8	2.6	4.3
Better pay	6.8	7.1	10.1	6.5	6.0	3.5	6.1
Allows time for school	3.2	6.0	2.5	1.4	3.7	1.5	1.8
Could not get any other job	8.1	13.9	8.2	5.5	3.8	3.2	3.2
Nature of the job	54.6	37.8	32.8	76.7	70.3	80.4	68.3
Personal preference	11.5	15.9	21.0	3.0	5.9	3.6	8.0
Some other reason	5.6	6.2	7.0	3.8	3.9	4.6	7.1

[a]Includes persons who worked a non-daytime schedule, but did not report the shift worked.
[b]Includes persons who worked a non-daytime schedule, but did not report a reason.
Note: Data relate to the sole or principal job of full-time wage and salary workers and exclude all self-employed persons, regardless of whether or not their businesses were incorporated.

SOURCE: "Table 6. Full-Time Wage and Salary Shift Workers by Reason for Working a Non-Daytime Schedule, May 2004," in *Workers on Flexible and Shift Schedules in May 2004*, U.S. Department of Labor, Bureau of Labor Statistics, July 1, 2005, http://www.bls.gov/news.release/pdf/flex.pdf (accessed February 20, 2007)

This legislation pushed the issue of regulation of child care facilities to the forefront. In 1989 the National Institute of Child Health and Human Development initiated the Study of Early Child Care. This comprehensive ongoing longitudinal study was designed to answer many questions about the relationship between child care experiences and children's developmental outcomes. The 1999 phase of the study examined whether the amount of time children spent in child care affected their interactions with their mothers. Results showed that the number of hours infants and toddlers spent in child care was modestly linked to the sensitivity of the mother to her child, as well as to the engagement of the child with the mother in play activities. Children in consistent quality day care showed less problem behavior, whereas those who switched day care arrangements showed more problem behaviors. Children in quality care centers had higher cognitive and language development than those in lower-quality centers.

The second phase of the study, *The NICHD Study of Early Child Care and Youth Development: Findings for Children up to Age 4½ Years* (January 2006, http://www.nichd.nih.gov/publications/pubs/upload/seccyd_051206.pdf), found that the quality of child care had an impact on children's social and intellectual development. The study defined a better quality of care as care that met ideal adult-to-child ratios, maintained ideal group sizes, and had well-trained child care providers. It also focused on the quality of children's actual day-to-day experiences in child care, observing children's social interactions and their activities with toys.

The study found that children who were in higher-quality child care had better cognitive function and language development in the first three years of life, as well as greater school readiness by age four and a half. Children in higher-quality care were also more sensitive to

other children, more cooperative, and less aggressive and disobedient than were children in lower-quality care. Lastly, the study found that children who were cared for in child care centers rather than in home-based care had better cognitive and language development but also showed somewhat more behavior problems both in the child care setting and once they began kindergarten.

Child Care during Nonstandard Hours

Many parents choose to have one parent work non-standard hours to allow both parents to provide child care at different times of the day. According to the U.S. Bureau of Labor Statistics, in the press release "Workers on Flexible and Shift Schedules in May 2004" (July 1, 2005, http://www.bls.gov/news.release/pdf/flex.pdf), in 2004 twenty-seven million workers, or 27.5% of all full-time wage and salary workers, worked flexible hours and were able to vary their work hours to fit their schedules. That number was more than twice as many workers as in May 1985, but down from a high of 28.6% in May 2001. Flexible schedules were most common among management (44.7%) and professionals (31.5%), and were more common among non-Hispanic white (28.7%) and Asian (27.4%) workers than among African-American (19.7%) or Hispanic workers (18.4%).

By contrast, the percentage of those who worked an evening or overnight shift had fallen from 18% in 1991 to 14.8% in 2004. When asked why they worked a non-daytime schedule, 8.2% of shift workers answered they did so for better family or child care arrangements. (See Table 3.6.)

COST OF CHILD CARE

In February 2006 the National Association of Child Care Resource and Referral Agencies (NACCRRA) published

Breaking the Piggy Bank: Parents and the High Price of Child Care (http://www.naccrra.org/docs/policy/breaking_the_piggy_bank.pdf), which surveyed child care costs across the country. The survey shows that the average yearly cost for child care for a four-year-old ranged from $3,016 in Alabama to $9,628 in Massachusetts. For an infant, annual costs jumped to $3,803 in Alabama and $13,480 in Massachusetts. And child care in urban care centers was so expensive that it could cost more than public college tuition.

Low-Income Families

According to the NACCRRA, in 2007 a low-income family with two parents working full time, fifty-two weeks per year at the federal minimum wage earned $21,424 per year before taxes. These families spent an exorbitant proportion of their income on child care. For example, in New York, where the average annual cost of preschool care was $8,530, the median income for single-parent families was $21,128. This family would spend 40.4% of its annual income on preschool care. Even in Nevada, where the cost of child care averaged a relatively low $3,200, a single-parent family earning the median income of $22,429 would spend 14.3% of its annual income on child care.

Julia Overturf Johnson estimates that in 2002 the average family with a working mother with a preschool child spent 10% of its income on child care. Families in poverty in which the mother was employed paid an average of $67 per week in child care costs, compared with families not in poverty, who paid, on average, $98 per week. Although families below the poverty level paid less per week than higher income families, they spent more than three times the percentage of their income on child care as other families (25% compared with 7%). Many poor and low-income families were forced to enroll their children in low-cost, and often poor-quality, child care centers. As a result, these children spent much of their day in unstimulating and possibly unsafe environments.

Government Assistance with Child Care

BLOCK GRANTS. In some cases low-income and poor parents can receive government assistance in paying for child care. Recognizing that child care assistance helps contribute to a productive workforce, every state has a child care assistance program that subsidizes some child care using federal block grant money and state funds for those on welfare and for low-income working families. In some instances parents receive a voucher that they can use to pay for a portion of child care costs; in other states payments are made directly to the child care provider of the parents' choice. However, the NACCRRA notes that in early 2005 seventeen states had waiting lists for child care assistance, and Tennessee was no longer accepting applications even for their waiting list. Furthermore, the income cut-off to even be eligible for assistance was extremely low. In other

words, child care assistance is available to only a small percentage of those families who need it.

HEAD START. Perhaps the best-known and most successful government-funded child care program is Head Start, a federal program begun in 1965 under the Administration for Children and Families (ACF) of the U.S. Department of Health and Human Services. The free program provides early education, health care, social services, and free meals to preschool children in families whose incomes are below the poverty line or who receive public assistance. In the "Head Start Program Fact Sheet" (March 2006, http://www.acf.hhs.gov/programs/hsb/research/2006.htm), the ACF states that Head Start operates in every state, and in fiscal year 2005 it served 906,993 children. The Children's Defense Fund reports in *Head Start Basics: 2005* (April 2005, http://www.childrensdefense.org/site/DocServer/headstartbasics2005. pdf?docID=616) that the program provides many benefits, including a greater likelihood that children will do well in school and graduate from high school.

TAX CREDITS. The Federal Dependent Care Tax Credit helps families by allowing them to claim an income tax credit for part of their child care expenses for children under the age of thirteen that enabled parents to work outside the home. The credit is on a sliding scale, ranging from 20% to 35% of qualified expenses; therefore, lower-income families receive slightly larger credits. According to the U.S. Department of the Treasury, in "Child and Dependent Care Credit" (2007, http://www.irs.gov/publications/p17/ch32.html#d0e71607), in 2006 parents could claim up to $3,000 in qualified expenses for one child or $6,000 for two or more children.

FAMILY LEAVE. In 1993 Congress enacted the FMLA, requiring employers with fifty or more employees to give unpaid time off—twelve weeks in any twelve-month period—to employees to care for newborn or newly adopted children, sick family members, or for personal illness. The employee must be returned to the same position—or one equivalent in pay, benefits, and other terms of employment—and must receive uninterrupted health benefits. The U.S. Department of Labor reports that before this legislation fewer than a quarter of all U.S. workers received family leave benefits and that most of those who did worked in establishments of more than one hundred employees.

Jane Waldfogel notes in "Family and Medical Leave: Evidence from the 2000 Surveys" (*Monthly Labor Review*, September 2001) that in 2000, 17.9% percent of FMLA leave takers took their leave to care for a newborn, newly adopted, or newly placed foster child; 9.8% used it to care for a sick child; and 7.8% used it as maternity or disability time. Of all employees covered by the FMLA with children eighteen months or younger, 45.1% of men and 75.8% of women had taken an FMLA leave in the previous eighteen months.

Employer Involvement

Employers are increasingly providing family leave beyond the requirements of the FMLA as well as providing assistance to employees in finding child care. Employers find that providing such benefits can pay off in increased productivity, worker recruitment and retention, and community goodwill. According to the Bureau of Labor Statistics, in *Pilot Survey on the Incidence of Child Care Resource and Referral Services in June 2000* (November 2000, http://www.bls.gov/ncs/ocs/sp/ncrp0002.pdf), 13.8% of workers in private industry, as well as in state and local government, had access to child care resource and referral services. Most often these services were provided to employees by outside resources rather than directly by their employers. People working for large establishments (employing five thousand or more workers) fare best in access to child care resources.

CHAPTER 4
HEALTH AND SAFETY

FACTORS AFFECTING CHILDREN'S HEALTH

A variety of factors affect children's health. These range from prenatal influences; access to and quality of health care; poverty, homelessness, and hunger; childhood diseases; and diet and exercise. This chapter discusses these factors and looks at leading causes of death among infants, children, and adolescents.

Birth Defects

According to the Centers for Disease Control and Prevention (CDC), in "Birth Defects: Frequently Asked Questions" (December 12, 2006, http://www.cdc.gov/ncbddd/bd/faq1.htm), birth defects affect one out of every thirty-three babies born. Birth defects are the leading cause of infant deaths; in addition, these babies have a greater chance of illness and disability than do babies without birth defects. Two major birth defects, neural tube defects and fetal alcohol syndrome, are in large part preventable.

NEURAL TUBE DEFECTS. Major defects of the brain and spine are called neural tube defects. The CDC notes in "Medical Progress in the Prevention of Neural Tube Defects" (June 17, 2005, http://www.cdc.gov/ncbddd/bd/mp.htm) that each year as many as one out of every one thousand pregnancies is affected by a neural tube defect. Infants born with neural tube defects suffer from an incomplete closing of the spine and skull. The occurrence of these defects can be greatly reduced by adequate folic acid consumption before and during early pregnancy.

FETAL ALCOHOL SYNDROME. Alcohol consumption by pregnant women can cause fetal alcohol syndrome (FAS), a birth defect characterized by a low birth weight, facial abnormalities such as small eye openings, growth retardation, and central nervous system deficits, including learning and developmental disabilities. The condition is a lifelong, disabling condition that puts those children affected at risk for secondary conditions, such as mental health problems, criminal behavior, alcohol and drug abuse, and inappropriate sexual behavior. Not all children affected by prenatal alcohol use are born with the full syndrome, but they may have selected abnormalities.

According to the CDC, in "Fetal Alcohol Spectrum Disorders" (December 5, 2006, http://www.cdc.gov/ncbddd/fas/fassurv.htm), estimates of the prevalence of FAS vary from 0.2 to 1.5 per 1,000 births in different areas of the United States. Other alcohol-related birth defects are thought to occur three times as often as FAS. In "Alcohol Consumption among Women Who Are Pregnant or Who Might Become Pregnant—United States, 2002" (*Morbidity and Mortality Weekly Report*, December 24, 2004, http://www.cdc.gov/mmwr/preview/mmwrhtml/mm5350a4.htm), the CDC finds that in 2002, 10.1% of pregnant women drank alcohol, putting their babies at risk for FAS. As many as one out of fifty pregnant women (1.9%) frequently drank alcohol.

Health Care

IMMUNIZATIONS. The proportion of preschool-age children immunized against communicable and potentially dangerous childhood diseases—including diphtheria, tetanus, and pertussis (whooping cough), known collectively as DTP; polio; and measles—dropped during the 1980s but rose significantly during the 1990s. By 2004, 87% of all children had received four doses of DTP, 92% had received three doses of the poliovirus vaccine, 94% had received the *haemophilus influenzae* type b vaccine, 94% had received the measles vaccine, 93% had received three doses of the hepatitis B vaccine, and 88% had received the varicella (chickenpox) vaccine. (See Table 4.1.) More than four out of five of these children received the vaccinations in combined series. Children living below the poverty line and African-American children were slightly less likely than the general child population to be immunized.

TABLE 4.1

Percentage of children vaccinated for selected diseases, by poverty status[a], race, and Hispanic origin[b], 1996–2004

Characteristic	Total 1996	1997	1998	1999	2000	2001	2002	2003	2004	Below poverty 1996	1997	1998	1999	2000	2001	2002	2003	2004	At or above poverty 1996	1997	1998	1999	2000	2001	2002	2003	2004
Total																											
Combined series (4:3:1:3)[c]	76	76	79	78	76	77	78	81	83	69	71	74	73	71	72	72	76	78	80	79	82	81	78	79	79	83	85
Combined series (4:3:1)[d]	78	78	81	80	78	79	79	82	84	72	72	76	75	72	73	73	77	79	81	80	83	82	79	80	80	84	86
DTP (4 doses or more)[e]	81	82	84	83	82	82	82	85	86	74	76	80	79	76	77	75	80	81	84	84	86	85	82	84	84	87	87
Polio (3 doses or more)	91	91	91	90	90	89	90	92	92	88	89	90	87	87	87	88	89	90	92	92	92	91	90	90	91	93	92
Measles-containing (MCV)[f]	91	90	93	92	91	91	92	93	93	87	86	90	90	88	89	90	92	92	92	92	93	92	91	92	93	93	94
Hib (3 doses or more)[g]	91	93	93	94	93	93	93	94	94	87	90	91	91	90	90	90	91	92	93	94	95	95	95	95	94	95	94
Hepatitis B (3 doses or more)	82	84	87	88	90	89	90	92	92	78	81	85	87	87	86	88	91	91	83	85	88	89	91	90	90	93	93
Varicella[h]	12	26	43	58	68	76	81	85	88	5	17	41	55	64	74	79	84	86	15	29	44	58	69	77	81	85	88
PCV (3 doses or more)[i]	—	—	—	—	—	—	41	68	73	—	—	—	—	—	—	33	62	69	—	—	—	—	—	—	43	71	75
White, non-Hispanic																											
Combined series (4:3:1:3)[c]	79	79	82	81	79	79	80	84	85	68	72	77	76	73	71	72	79	78	80	82	83	82	80	80	81	85	86
Combined series (4:3:1)[d]	80	80	83	82	80	80	81	85	86	70	73	79	77	74	72	73	80	78	82	82	84	83	81	81	82	86	87
DTP (4 doses or more)[e]	83	84	87	86	84	84	84	88	88	72	76	82	81	78	75	75	82	81	85	84	88	86	85	85	86	88	89
Polio (3 doses or more)	92	92	92	90	91	90	91	93	92	88	90	91	88	88	87	88	91	88	93	92	93	91	91	91	92	93	93
Measles-containing (MCV)[f]	91	91	93	92	92	92	93	94	94	85	84	90	90	88	87	91	90	90	93	93	94	93	92	92	93	94	94
Hib (3 doses or more)[g]	93	94	95	95	95	94	94	95	95	87	90	92	92	88	89	91	91	92	94	95	96	95	95	95	95	96	95
Hepatitis B (3 doses or more)	82	85	88	89	91	90	91	93	93	76	80	87	88	88	86	86	91	92	83	85	88	89	92	90	92	94	93
Varicella[h]	15	28	42	56	66	75	79	84	87	6	17	38	51	58	67	75	80	84	16	29	43	57	68	76	80	85	87
PCV (3 doses or more)[i]	—	—	—	—	—	—	44	71	75	—	—	—	—	—	—	31	56	66	—	—	—	—	—	—	46	73	77
Black, non-Hispanic																											
Combined series (4:3:1:3)[c]	74	73	73	74	71	71	71	75	76	69	71	72	72	69	69	68	70	74	79	77	74	77	72	74	72	79	80
Combined series (4:3:1)[d]	77	74	74	75	72	73	72	77	78	73	72	74	74	70	71	69	72	76	81	78	76	78	73	75	73	80	81
DTP (4 doses or more)[e]	79	77	77	79	76	76	76	80	80	74	76	77	78	78	74	74	75	78	83	80	79	83	78	78	77	84	83
Polio (3 doses or more)	90	89	88	87	87	85	87	89	90	87	89	91	86	85	84	87	86	88	93	91	90	88	87	86	87	91	91
Measles-containing (MCV)[f]	90	89	89	90	88	89	90	92	91	86	87	90	90	88	88	87	90	90	91	94	90	91	87	91	90	93	91
Hib (3 doses or more)[g]	89	91	90	92	93	90	92	93	91	86	91	87	86	89	87	88	90	89	93	94	92	90	90	91	94	95	92
Hepatitis B (3 doses or more)	82	86	84	87	89	85	88	92	91	78	80	86	88	89	86	89	92	90	85	84	83	90	90	85	88	92	92
Varicella[h]	9	21	42	58	67	75	83	85	86	*	16	40	51	60	71	80	84	84	13	27	44	60	72	77	84	86	87
PCV (3 doses or more)[i]	—	—	—	—	—	—	34	62	68	—	—	—	—	—	—	30	61	67	—	—	—	—	—	—	38	64	70
American Indian and Alaska Native																											
Combined series (4:3:1:3)[c]	82	73	78	75	69	76	*	77	75	*	*	*	*	*	*	*	*	*	*	*	*	79	*	84	*	*	*
Combined series (4:3:1)[d]	83	78	79	78	70	76	*	79	76	*	*	*	*	*	*	*	*	*	*	*	*	81	*	84	*	*	*
DTP (4 doses or more)[e]	85	80	83	80	75	77	*	80	77	*	*	*	*	*	*	*	*	*	*	*	92	83	76	84	*	*	*
Polio (3 doses or more)	90	90	85	88	90	88	*	91	87	92	93	*	93	82	96	*	89	96	*	88	93	94	96	96	*	*	*
Measles-containing (MCV)[f]	89	92	91	92	87	94	84	92	89	87	94	*	93	83	*	84	93	96	*	*	96	92	93	90	92	89
Hib (3 doses or more)[g]	91	86	90	91	90	91	*	89	90	95	93	*	*	82	*	*	92	90	89	92	97	92	95	*	90	89
Hepatitis B (3 doses or more)	79	83	82	*	91	86	70	90	91	*	*	22	*	85	*	*	92	90	89	82	87	*	97	91	*	*	89
Varicella[h]	*	20	28	*	62	69	33	81	84	*	*	*	*	*	*	*	*	95	*	*	87	*	*	76	*	82	85
PCV (3 doses or more)[i]	—	—	—	—	—	—	—	60	75	—	—	—	—	—	—	—	—	*	—	—	—	—	—	—	*	*	*

TABLE 4.1

Percentage of children vaccinated for selected diseases, by poverty status[a], race, and Hispanic origin[b], 1996–2004 [CONTINUED]

Characteristic	Total									Below poverty									At or above poverty								
	1996	1997	1998	1999	2000	2001	2002	2003	2004	1996	1997	1998	1999	2000	2001	2002	2003	2004	1996	1997	1998	1999	2000	2001	2002	2003	2004
Asian																											
Combined series (4:3:1:3)[c]	78	71	79	77	75	77	83	81	84	*	*	*	*	*	*	*	*	*	77	70	81	80	77	77	84	80	83
Combined series (4:3:1)[d]	81	76	83	82	79	80	85	84	87	*	*	*	*	*	*	*	*	*	79	74	84	85	81	79	86	84	87
DTP (4 doses or more)[e]	85	80	89	87	85	84	88	89	90	*	*	80	*	*	85	*	*	91	84	79	91	90	87	85	90	90	89
Polio (3 doses or more)	90	89	93	90	93	90	92	91	93	*	90	85	*	*	90	93	92	92	89	88	93	91	93	90	91	90	92
Measles-containing (MCV)[f]	93	90	92	93	90	90	95	96	94	94	92	95	86	*	*	98	92	94	93	90	94	93	93	89	95	96	93
Hib (3 doses or more)[g]	92	89	92	90	92	92	95	91	92	*	94	*	*	84	95	93	93	96	94	90	94	88	92	92	95	90	90
Hepatitis B (3 doses or more)	85	88	89	88	91	90	94	94	93	*	94	*	84	*	95	95	93	96	86	86	90	66	80	89	94	93	92
Varicella[h]	18	36	53	64	77	82	87	91	91	*	*	*	*	*	90	*	93	91	20	41	55	66	80	81	87	90	90
PCV (3 doses or more)[i]	—	—	—	—	—	—	55	71	76	—	—	—	—	—	—	*	*	*	—	—	—	—	—	—	55	73	77
Hispanic																											
Combined series (4:3:1:3)[c]	71	73	75	75	73	77	76	79	81	68	70	73	73	70	73	75	78	80	73	77	79	78	74	79	76	81	84
Combined series (4:3:1)[d]	74	75	77	77	75	79	77	79	82	71	71	76	76	73	76	76	79	80	75	77	80	80	75	80	77	81	84
DTP (4 doses or more)[e]	77	78	81	80	79	83	79	82	84	74	75	79	78	76	79	78	81	83	78	81	83	82	80	83	80	84	86
Polio (3 doses or more)	89	90	89	89	88	91	90	90	91	88	88	90	89	88	90	89	89	90	90	90	90	90	87	91	91	92	92
Measles-containing (MCV)[f]	88	88	91	90	90	92	91	93	93	87	85	91	90	90	91	91	93	92	89	90	92	91	90	93	89	93	94
Hib (3 doses or more)[g]	89	90	92	92	91	93	92	93	93	87	89	92	91	88	91	93	93	92	90	90	94	95	93	94	92	95	94
Hepatitis B (3 doses or more)	81	81	86	89	88	90	89	91	92	80	79	83	87	88	88	89	91	91	81	84	88	88	90	91	89	93	93
Varicella[h]	8	22	47	61	70	80	82	86	89	6	18	44	59	70	81	82	86	88	11	25	49	62	70	82	81	85	89
PCV (3 doses or more)[i]	—	—	—	—	—	—	37	66	70	—	—	—	—	—	—	35	65	71	—	—	—	—	—	—	38	67	71

—=Not available.

*Estimates are considered unreliable.

[a]Based on family income and household size using US Bureau of Census poverty thresholds for the year prior to each year of data collection.

[b]From 1996 to 2000, the 1977 Office of Management and Budget (OMB) Standards for Data on Race and Ethnicity were used. From 2002 onward, the 1997 OMB Standards for Data on Race and Ethnicity were used. Persons of Hispanic origin may be of any race. Included in the total, but not shown separately, are Native Hawaiian and other Pacific Islanders, and two or more races.

[c]The 4:3:1:3 series consists of ≥ 4 doses of diphtheria, tetanus toxoids and pertussis vaccines, diphtheria and tetanus toxoids, and diphtheria, tetanus toxoids and any acellular pertussis vaccine (DTP/DT/DTaP); ≥ 3 doses of poliovirus vaccine; ≥ 1 doses of any measles-containing vaccine; and ≥ 3 doses of haemophilus influenzae type b (Hib) vaccine.

[d]The 4:3:1 series consists of ≥ 4 doses of diphtheria, tetanus toxoids and pertussis vaccines, diphtheria and tetanus toxoids, and diphtheria, tetanus toxoids and any acellular pertussis vaccine (DTP/DT/DTaP); ≥ 3 doses of poliovirus vaccine; and ≥ 1 doses of any measles-containing vaccine.

[e]Diphtheria, tetanus toxoids, and pertussis vaccine (≥ 4 doses of any diphtheria, tetanus toxoids and pertussis vaccines, including diphtheria and tetanus toxoids, and any acellular pertussis vaccine).

[f]Providers were asked about measles-containing vaccine, including MMR (measles-mumps-rubella) vaccines.

[g]Haemophilus influenzae type b (Hib) vaccine (three or more doses).

[h]Providers were asked about history of varicella illness (chicken pox). (One or more doses of varicella at or after child's first birthday, unadjusted for history of varicella illness). Recommended in July 1996. Administered on or after the first birthday, unadjusted for history of varicella illness.

[i]Pneumococcal conjugate vaccine (three or more doses); the percentage of children ages 19–35 months who received 3 (or more) doses of pneumococcal conjugate vaccine was low in 2002, because universal infant vaccination was not recommended until October 2000.

SOURCE: "Table HEALTH5. Childhood Immunization: Percentage of Children Ages 19–35 Months Vaccinated for Selected Diseases by Poverty Status, Race and Hispanic Origin, Selected Years 1996–2004," in *America's Children in Brief: Key National Indicators of Well-Being, 2006,* Federal Interagency Forum on Child and Family Statistics, 2006, http://childstats.gov/americaschildren/tables/health5.asp (accessed February 25, 2007)

In 1994 the U.S. Department of Health and Human Services (HHS) implemented the Vaccines for Children (VFC) program, which provides free or low-cost vaccines to children at participating private and public health care provider sites. Eligible children, including children on Medicaid, children without insurance or whose insurance does not cover vaccinations, and Native American or Alaskan Native children can receive the vaccinations through their primary care physician. Children not covered under the program but whose parents cannot afford vaccinations can receive free vaccines at public clinics under local programs. The HHS reports in *FY 2007 Budget in Brief: Centers for Disease Control and Prevention* (February 20, 2006, http://www.hhs.gov/budget/07budget/cdc.html#infectious) that the VFC program had a budget of $2.6 billion for fiscal year 2007. Vaccines provided through the program represented about 40% of all childhood vaccines purchased in the country.

The World Health Organization and the United Nations Children's Fund report in *Global Immunization Vision and Strategy, 2006–2015* (October 2005, http://www.who.int/vaccines-documents/DocsPDF05/GIVS_Final_EN.pdf) that developed nations, including the United States, generally have among the highest immunization rates in the world. The global immunization rate for DTP in 2003 was 78%, up from 72% in 1999. Immunization rates for the developed world for the same time period were ten to twenty percentage points higher than the global average, reflecting the low immunization rates in many developing nations. In 2003 only 28% of developing countries reported that their immunization rate for DTP was 80% or higher.

PHYSICIAN VISITS. Children's health depends on access to and usage of medical care. Based on household interviews of a sample of the civilian noninstitutionalized population, the CDC's National Center for Health Statistics (NCHS) finds that in 2004, 55.3% of children under age eighteen visited the doctor between one and three times, 26.2% saw the doctor between four and nine times, and 8% saw the doctor ten or more times. (See Table 4.2.) However, 10.6% of children did not see a doctor at all. Poor children have less access to health care than nonpoor children.

HEALTH INSURANCE. One reason some children do not have access to medical care is their lack of health insurance. According to Carmen DeNavas-Walt, Bernadette D. Proctor, and Cheryl Hill Lee of the U.S. Census Bureau, in *Income, Poverty, and Health Insurance Coverage in the United States: 2005* (August 2006, http://www.census.gov/prod/2006pubs/p60-231.pdf), 11.2% of American children (or 8.3 million) had no health insurance coverage in 2005. Factors affecting children's access to coverage included their age, race and ethnicity, and their family's economic status. Children between the ages of twelve and seventeen were more likely to be uninsured than those under age twelve (12.6% versus 10.5%). Poor children were proportionately more likely to be uninsured than all children (19% versus 11.2%) because of government programs such as Medicaid, and those of Hispanic origin were the least likely racial or ethnic group to receive health insurance coverage, with 21.9% of them being uninsured. Uninsured rates for other racial and ethnic groups were 7.2% for non-Hispanic white children, 12.2% for Asian-American children, and 12.5% for African-American children. Robin A. Cohen and Michael E. Martinez of the NCHS estimate in *Health Insurance Coverage: Early Release Estimates from the National Health Interview Survey, January–June 2006* (December 2006, http://www.cdc.gov/nchs/data/nhis/earlyrelease/insur200612.pdf) that 9.2% of all children were uninsured for at least part of 2006.

Child health insurance coverage increased slightly among all age groups, races, and ethnicities from 2000 to 2004, although the percent of children covered by private health insurance declined from 70% in 2000 to 66% in 2004. (See Table 4.3 and Figure 4.1.) In the press release "HHS Issues New Report Showing More American Children Received Health Insurance in Early 2002" (December 31, 2002, http://www.hhs.gov/news/press/2002pres/20021231.html), the HHS secretary Tommy G. Thompson attributes ongoing increases to a push to provide more government coverage, particularly under the State Children's Health Insurance Program. This trend, however, may be leveling off. Cohen and Martinez find that there was no significant change in the number of uninsured children between 2005 and 2006. (See Figure 4.1.)

DeNavas-Walt, Proctor, and Hill Lee note that in 2005 government programs, such as Medicare, Medicaid, and military insurance, covered a greater proportion of African-American children and Hispanic children than other children. Almost half (44.9%) of African-American children and 39.3% of Hispanic children had government insurance, compared with only 18% of non-Hispanic white children and 15.9% of Asian children.

To remain in the Medicaid program, families must have their eligibility reassessed at least every six months. If family income or other circumstances change even slightly, the family can lose its eligibility for the Medicaid program, disrupting health care coverage.

From the late 1980s through the mid-1990s the numbers of uninsured American children rose as coverage rates for employer-sponsored health insurance declined, even though the proportion of children covered by Medicaid also rose. In 1997, as part of the Balanced Budget Act, Congress created the State Children's Health Insurance Program (SCHIP) to expand health insurance to children whose families earned too much money to be eligible for Medicaid but not enough money to pay for private insurance. SCHIP provides funding to states to insure children, offering three alternatives: states may use SCHIP funds to

TABLE 4.2

Health care visits to doctor's offices, emergency departments, and home visits over a 12-month period, by selected characteristics, selected years 1997–2004

[Data are based on household interviews of a sample of the civilian noninstitutionalized population]

	Number of health care visits[a]											
	None			1–3 visits			4–9 visits			10 or more visits		
Characteristic	1997	2003	2004	1997	2003	2004	1997	2003	2004	1997	2003	2004
	Percent distribution											
All persons[b, c]	16.5	15.8	16.1	46.2	45.8	45.8	23.6	24.8	24.6	13.7	13.6	13.5
Age												
Under 18 years	11.8	11.3	10.6	54.1	54.5	55.3	25.2	26.7	26.2	8.9	7.5	8.0
Under 6 years	5.0	5.5	5.3	44.9	46.0	47.5	37.0	39.0	36.9	13.0	9.4	10.3
6–17 years	15.3	14.0	13.1	58.7	58.7	59.0	19.3	20.8	21.1	6.8	6.6	6.8
18–44 years	21.7	22.4	23.8	46.7	46.7	45.6	19.0	19.1	19.2	12.6	11.8	11.5
18–24 years	22.0	23.6	25.7	46.8	47.2	45.0	20.0	18.2	19.2	11.2	11.0	10.1
25–44 years	21.6	22.0	23.1	46.7	46.6	45.8	18.7	19.4	19.2	13.0	12.0	12.0
45–64 years	16.9	14.7	15.0	42.9	42.2	43.3	24.7	26.6	25.3	15.5	16.5	16.3
45–54 years	17.9	16.9	16.9	43.9	44.2	45.0	23.4	24.5	22.9	14.8	14.3	15.2
55–64 years	15.3	11.4	12.3	41.3	39.2	40.9	26.7	29.8	28.9	16.7	19.6	18.0
65 years and over	8.9	6.3	5.6	34.7	31.5	31.6	32.5	35.8	36.8	23.8	26.4	26.1
65–74 years	9.8	7.1	6.8	36.9	34.0	36.0	31.6	35.7	34.5	21.6	23.3	22.6
75 years and over	7.7	5.4	4.1	31.8	28.6	26.4	33.8	36.0	39.5	26.6	30.0	30.0
Sex[c]												
Male	21.3	20.6	20.9	47.1	46.8	46.6	20.6	21.9	21.6	11.0	10.7	10.9
Female	11.8	11.1	11.5	45.4	44.9	45.0	26.5	27.7	27.5	16.3	16.3	16.0
Race[c, d]												
White only	16.0	15.7	16.0	46.1	45.6	45.4	23.9	25.1	24.8	14.0	13.6	13.8
Black or African American only	16.8	14.7	15.8	46.1	45.8	47.0	23.2	25.2	24.6	13.9	14.3	12.6
American Indian or Alaska Native only	17.1	23.3	17.7	38.0	41.4	41.7	24.2	20.6	25.0	20.7	14.7	15.5
Asian only	22.8	22.6	20.8	49.1	47.8	51.5	19.7	20.7	19.7	8.3	8.9	8.1
Native Hawaiian or other Pacific Islander only	—			—			—			—		
2 or more races	—	11.1	13.6	—	44.9	42.9	—	23.0	26.2	—	21.0	17.3
Hispanic origin and race[c, d]												
Hispanic or Latino	24.9	25.3	26.7	42.3	42.9	41.8	20.3	20.3	20.6	12.5	11.5	10.9
Mexican	28.9	27.8	29.7	40.8	42.5	41.0	18.5	18.8	18.9	11.8	11.0	10.4
Not Hispanic or Latino	15.4	14.1	14.2	46.7	46.3	46.5	24.0	25.6	25.2	13.9	14.0	14.14
White only	14.7	13.5	13.5	46.6	46.2	46.1	24.4	26.1	25.7	14.3	14.2	14.7
Black or African American only	16.9	14.6	15.6	46.1	45.9	47.3	23.1	25.3	24.6	13.8	14.2	12.5
Respondent-assessed health status[c]												
Fair or poor	7.8	8.7	8.1	23.3	23.2	22.0	29.0	28.8	28.0	39.9	39.3	41.9
Good to excellent	17.2	16.4	16.9	48.4	48.1	48.0	23.3	24.5	24.4	11.1	10.9	10.7
Percent of poverty level[c, e]												
Below 100%	20.6	20.9	21.1	37.8	37.8	37.7	22.7	23.7	23.5	18.9	17.6	17.7
100%–less than 200%	20.1	19.8	20.9	43.3	41.5	42.5	21.7	23.6	22.3	14.9	15.1	14.4
200% or more	14.5	13.7	13.8	48.7	48.4	48.1	24.2	25.4	25.3	12.6	12.6	12.8
Hispanic origin and race and percent of poverty level[c, d, e]												
Hispanic or Latino:												
Below 100%	30.2	29.9	31.6	34.8	37.0	35.0	19.9	18.5	19.6	15.0	14.6	13.9
100%–less than 200%	28.7	28.6	30.5	39.7	40.2	39.3	20.4	20.6	19.4	11.2	10.5	10.9
200% or more	18.9	20.7	21.5	48.8	47.7	47.0	20.4	21.2	22.2	11.9	10.3	9.2
Not Hispanic or Latino:												
White only:												
Below 100%	17.0	17.0	16.2	38.3	37.5	37.5	23.9	25.9	25.4	20.9	19.5	20.9
100%–less than 200%	17.3	16.6	16.7	44.1	41.0	43.2	22.2	24.9	23.4	16.3	17.4	16.7
200% or more	13.8	12.5	12.7	48.2	48.1	47.4	24.9	26.3	26.1	13.1	13.1	13.8
Black or African American only:												
Below 100%	17.4	15.7	15.9	38.5	38.1	40.9	23.4	26.5	25.7	20.7	19.6	17.5
100%–less than 200%	18.8	15.4	18.1	43.7	44.2	44.5	22.9	25.9	23.8	14.5	14.5	13.7
200% or more	15.6	13.7	14.3	51.7	50.6	51.3	22.7	24.3	24.4	10.0	11.4	10.0

establish separate coverage programs, expand their Medicaid coverage, or use a combination of both. By September 1999 all fifty states had SCHIP plans in place. By September 4, 2003, the program had been expanded to enroll even more children at higher income levels. According to the Centers for Medicare and Medicaid Services, in *FY 2005 Annual Enrollment Report* (July 12, 2006, http://www.cms.hhs.gov/NationalSCHIPPolicy/downloads/FY2005AnnualEnrollmentReport.pdf), in fiscal year 2005, 6.1 million children were enrolled in SCHIP.

TABLE 4.2

Health care visits to doctor's offices, emergency departments, and home visits over a 12-month period, by selected characteristics, selected years 1997–2004 [CONTINUED]

[Data are based on household interviews of a sample of the civilian noninstitutionalized population]

	Number of health care visits[a]											
	None			1–3 visits			4–9 visits			10 or more visits		
Characteristic	1997	2003	2004	1997	2003	2004	1997	2003	2004	1997	2003	2004
Health insurance status at the time of interview[f, g]												
Under 65 years of age:												
Insured	14.3	12.8	13.4	49.0	49.1	49.1	23.6	25.2	24.6	13.1	12.9	12.8
Private	14.7	13.2	13.6	50.6	51.1	51.4	23.1	24.6	23.9	11.6	11.1	11.2
Medicaid	9.8	9.9	11.8	35.5	35.2	35.1	26.5	28.1	28.2	28.2	26.8	24.9
Uninsured	33.7	38.1	37.8	42.8	42.4	42.5	15.3	13.4	13.6	8.2	6.1	6.1
Health insurance status prior to interview[f, g]												
Under 65 years of age:												
Insured continuously all 12 months	14.1	12.7	13.4	49.2	49.3	49.4	23.6	25.2	24.6	13.0	12.8	12.7
Uninsured for any period up to 12 months	18.9	20.4	20.0	46.0	46.2	45.7	20.8	21.2	21.9	14.4	12.2	12.3
Uninsured more than 12 months	39.0	44.3	43.9	41.4	39.8	41.3	13.2	11.2	10.0	6.4	4.7	4.8
Percent of poverty level and insurance status prior to interview[e, f, g]												
Under 65 years of age:												
Below 100%:												
Insured continuously all 12 months	13.8	12.7	14.3	39.7	40.9	39.6	25.2	25.8	25.7	21.4	20.5	20.4
Uninsured for any period up to 12 months	19.7	18.4	17.6	37.6	43.9	42.0	21.9	21.6	24.6	20.9	16.1	15.7
Uninsured more than 12 months	41.2	47.7	47.1	39.9	35.7	38.6	12.2	11.7	9.4	6.6	4.9	5.0
100%–less than 200%:												
Insured continuously all 12 months	16.0	13.8	15.7	46.4	45.0	45.4	21.9	24.4	23.5	15.8	16.8	15.5
Uninsured for any period up to 12 months	18.8	20.2	21.7	45.1	42.0	45.1	21.0	24.8	22.1	15.0	12.9	11.1
Uninsured more than 12 months	38.7	43.4	45.0	41.0	39.1	39.4	14.0	12.1	9.9	6.3	5.4	5.7
200% or more:												
Insured continuously all 12 months	13.7	12.4	12.6	51.0	51.1	51.3	23.6	25.3	24.7	11.7	11.3	11.5
Uninsured for any period up to 12 months	17.8	20.4	20.3	50.3	49.6	47.5	20.4	19.1	20.4	11.5	10.9	11.9
Uninsured more than 12 months	36.6	41.8	39.7	43.8	44.7	45.4	13.2	9.6	10.9	6.4	4.0	4.1
Geographic region[c]												
Northeast	13.2	10.4	11.6	45.9	47.6	45.5	26.0	27.0	27.5	14.9	15.0	15.4
Midwest	15.9	14.2	13.9	47.7	47.2	47.5	22.8	25.4	25.1	13.6	13.2	13.5
South	17.2	16.5	16.7	46.1	45.1	46.2	23.3	24.8	23.8	13.5	13.6	13.3
West	19.1	21.0	21.3	44.8	44.2	43.8	22.8	22.2	22.7	13.3	12.6	12.2
Location of residence[c]												
Within MSA[h]	16.2	16.0	16.3	46.4	45.9	45.9	23.7	24.8	24.4	13.7	13.3	13.4
Outside MSA[h]	17.3	15.0	15.3	45.4	45.6	45.4	23.3	24.9	25.3	13.9	14.5	14.0

*Estimates are considered unreliable.

—Data not available.

[a]This table presents a summary measure of health care visits to doctor's offices, emergency departments, and home visits during a 12-month period.

[b]Includes all other races not shown separately and unknown health insurance status.

[c]Estimates are age adjusted to the year 2000 standard population using six age groups: Under 18 years, 18–44 years, 45–54 years, 55–64 years, 65–74 years, and 75 years and over.

[d]The race groups, white, black, American Indian or Alaska Native, Asian, Native Hawaiian or other Pacific Islander, and 2 or more races, include persons of Hispanic and non-Hispanic origin. Persons of Hispanic origin may be of any race. Starting with 1999 data, race-specific estimates are tabulated according to the 1997 Revisions to the Standards for the Classification of Federal Data on Race and Ethnicity and are not strictly comparable with estimates for earlier years. The five single race categories plus multiple race categories shown in the table conform to the 1997 standards. Starting with 1999 data, race-specific estimates are for persons who reported only one racial group; the category 2 or more races includes persons who reported more than one racial group. Prior to 1999, data were tabulated according to the 1977 Standards with four racial groups and the Asian only category included Native Hawaiian or other Pacific Islander. Estimates for single race categories prior to 1999 included persons who reported one race or, if they reported more than one race, identified one race as best representing their race. Starting with 2003 data, race responses of other race and unspecified multiple race were treated as missing, and then race was imputed if these were the only race responses. Almost all persons with a race response of other race were of Hispanic origin.

[e]Percent of poverty level is based on family income and family size and composition using U.S. Census Bureau poverty thresholds. Missing family income data were imputed for 25%–29% of persons in 1997–1998 and 32%–35% in 1999–2004.

[f]Estimates for persons under 65 years of age are age adjusted to the year 2000 standard population using four age groups: Under 18 years, 18–44 years, 45–54 years, and 55–64 years of age.

[g]Health insurance categories are mutually exclusive. Persons who reported both Medicaid and private coverage are classified as having private coverage. Starting in 1997 Medicaid includes state-sponsored health plans and State Children's Health Insurance Program (SCHIP).

[h]MSA is metropolitan statistical area.

SOURCE: "Table 80. Health Care Visits to Doctor's Offices, Emergency Departments, and Home Visits within the Past 12 Months, by Selected Characteristics, United States, Selected Years 1997–2004," in *Health, United States, 2006, with Chartbook on Trends in the Health of Americans*, Centers for Disease Control and Prevention, National Center for Health Statistics, 2006, http://0-www.cdc.gov.mill1.sjlibrary.org/nchs/data/hus/hus06.pdf (accessed February 6, 2007)

TABLE 4.3

Percentage of children under age 18 covered by health insurance, by type of insurance, age, race, and Hispanic origin, 1987–2004

Characteristic	1987	1988	1989	1990	1991	1992	1993	1994	1995	1996	1997	1998	1999	2000	2001	2002	2003	2004
All health insurance																		
Total	87	87	87	87	87	87	86	86	86	85	85	85	87	88	88	88	89	89
Gender																		
Male	87	87	87	87	87	88	87	86	86	85	85	85	87	88	88	88	89	89
Female	87	87	87	87	88	87	86	86	86	85	85	85	87	88	88	89	89	89
Age																		
Ages 0–5	88	87	87	89	89	89	88	86	87	86	86	84	87	89	89	89	90	90
Ages 6–11	87	87	87	87	88	88	87	87	87	85	86	85	88	88	89	89	89	89
Ages 12–17	86	86	86	85	85	85	83	85	86	84	83	84	87	87	87	87	87	88
Race and Hispanic origin[b]																		
White, non-Hispanic	90	90	90	90	90	90	89	89	90	89	89	89	92	93	93	92	93	92
Black	83	84	84	85	85	86	84	83	85	81	81	80	84	86	86	86	86	87
Hispanic[c]	72	71	70	72	73	75	74	72	73	71	71	70	74	75	76	77	79	79
Region																		
Northeast	92	93	91	92	92	91	90	88	89	88	88	89	92	92	92	91	91	91
Midwest	92	93	92	91	92	91	91	91	91	91	90	89	91	92	92	92	92	92
South	82	81	82	83	83	84	83	83	83	82	82	82	84	86	86	86	86	87
West	85	85	84	84	85	86	84	83	84	83	83	82	84	86	86	87	88	88
Private health insurance																		
Total	74	74	74	71	70	69	67	66	66	66	67	68	70	70	68	67	66	66
Gender																		
Male	73	74	74	71	70	69	68	66	66	67	67	68	70	70	69	67	66	65
Female	74	73	74	71	69	68	67	65	66	66	67	67	70	70	68	68	66	66
Age																		
Ages 0–5	72	71	71	68	66	65	63	60	60	62	63	64	66	66	64	63	62	61
Ages 6–11	74	74	75	73	71	71	70	67	67	67	68	68	70	70	69	68	66	67
Ages 12–17	75	76	76	73	72	71	69	70	71	70	69	70	73	73	72	71	69	69
Race and Hispanic origin[b]																		
White, non-Hispanic	83	83	83	81	80	80	78	77	78	78	78	79	81	81	80	79	78	77
Black	49	50	52	49	45	46	46	43	44	45	48	47	52	53	52	50	47	48
Hispanic[c]	48	48	48	45	43	42	42	38	38	40	42	43	46	45	44	43	42	43
Region																		
Northeast	79	78	78	77	75	73	71	70	71	69	69	70	73	74	72	71	71	71
Midwest	79	80	80	76	75	74	73	74	74	75	76	75	77	78	77	76	74	73
South	68	68	69	66	65	64	63	62	61	61	62	64	66	66	64	63	61	61
West	71	70	70	68	66	67	65	60	61	62	63	63	65	65	64	65	62	63
Government health insurance[d]																		
Total	19	19	19	22	24	25	27	26	26	25	23	23	23	24	26	27	29	30
Gender																		
Male	19	19	19	22	24	25	27	26	26	25	23	22	24	25	26	27	29	30
Female	19	19	19	22	24	26	27	27	27	25	24	23	23	24	26	27	29	29
Age																		
Ages 0–5	22	23	24	28	30	33	35	33	33	31	29	27	27	29	31	32	34	35
Ages 6–11	19	18	18	20	22	23	25	25	26	25	23	23	23	25	26	27	29	29
Ages 12–17	16	16	15	18	19	19	20	20	21	19	19	19	19	20	20	22	24	25
Race and Hispanic origin[b]																		
White, non-Hispanic	12	13	13	15	16	17	19	18	18	18	17	16	16	17	19	18	21	21
Black	42	42	41	45	48	49	50	48	49	45	40	42	40	42	42	44	47	48
Hispanic[c]	28	27	27	32	37	38	41	38	39	35	34	31	33	35	37	40	42	42

Homelessness

Under the McKinney-Vento Homeless Assistance Act, the U.S. Department of Education is required to file a report on homeless children served by the act. The Department of Education obtains the data from school districts; school districts use different methods of estimation. In the *Report to the President and Congress on the Implementation of the Education for Homeless Children and Youth Program under the McKinney-Vento Homeless Assistance Act* (2006, http://www.ed.gov/programs/homeless/rpt2006.doc), the Department of Education states that 602,568 children who experienced homelessness at some point during the year were enrolled in school during the 2003–04 school year. Of these children, about half (50.3%) lived doubled-up with relatives or friends; 25.3% lived in shelters, 10% stayed in hotels or motels, and 2.6% were unsheltered—in other words, sleeping outside, in vehicles, or in abandoned buildings. This number is almost certainly much lower than the number of children who actually experienced homelessness during that period, as the homeless status of children does not always come to the attention of school officials and many homeless children are not enrolled in school.

The U.S. Conference of Mayors, in the *Hunger and Homelessness Survey: A Status Report on Hunger and Homelessness in America's Cities, a 23-City Survey* (December

TABLE 4.3

Percentage of children under age 18 covered by health insurance, by type of insurance, age, race, and Hispanic origin, 1987–2004 [CONTINUED]

Characteristic	1987	1988	1989	1990	1991	1992	1993	1994	1995	1996	1997	1998	1999	2000	2001	2002	2003	2004
Region																		
Northeast	18	19	18	21	22	22	25	23	23	24	23	24	24	24	25	25	26	26
Midwest	18	17	17	20	22	23	24	24	23	21	19	19	20	19	21	22	25	26
South	20	19	20	23	25	28	29	29	28	27	25	24	24	26	29	30	32	32
West	20	22	22	23	27	27	28	29	30	27	25	24	25	27	27	28	31	32

[a]Children are considered to be covered by health insurance if they had government or private coverage at any time during the year. Some children are covered by both types of insurance; hence, the sum of government and private is greater than the total.

[b]For race and Hispanic-origin data in this table: From 1987 to 2002, following the 1977 Office of Management and Budget (OMB) standards for collecting and presenting data on race, the Current Population Survey (CPS) asked respondents to choose one race from the following: white, black, American Indian or Alaskan Native, or Asian or Pacific Islander. The Census Bureau also offered an "other" category. Beginning in 2003, following the 1997 OMB standards for collecting and presenting data on race, the CPS asked respondents to choose one or more races from the following: white, black, Asian, American Indian or Alaska Native, or Native Hawaiian or other Pacific Islander. All race groups discussed in this table from 2002 onward refer to people who indicated only one racial identity within the racial categories presented. People who responded to the question on race by indicating only one race are referred to as the race-alone population. The use of the race-alone population in this table does not imply that it is the preferred method of presenting or analyzing data. Data from 2002 onward are not directly comparable with data from earlier years. Data on race and Hispanic origin are collected separately; Hispanics may be any race.

[c]Persons of Hispanic origin may be of any race.

[d]Government health insurance for children consists mostly of Medicaid, but also includes Medicare, the State Children's Health Insurance Programs (SCHIP), and the Civilian Health and Medical Care Program of the Uniformed Services (CHAMPUS/Tricare).

Note: Estimates beginning in 1999 include follow-up questions to verify health insurance status and use the Census 2000-based weights. Estimates for 1999 through 2004 are not directly comparable with estimates for earlier years, before the verification questions were added.

SOURCE: "Table ECON5.A. Access to Health Care: Percentage of Children Ages 0–17 Covered by Health Insurance by Selected Characteristics, Selected Years 1987–2004," in *America's Children in Brief: Key National Indicators of Well-Being, 2006*, Federal Interagency Forum on Child and Family Statistics, 2006, http://childstats.gov/americaschildren/tables/econ5a.asp (accessed February 25, 2007)

2006, http://www.usmayors.org/uscm/hungersurvey/2006/report06.pdf), finds that 30% of homeless people were in families with children, 51% were single men, 17% were single women, and 2% were unaccompanied youth—usually runaways. Since 1994 the proportion of families among the homeless has generally declined, as has the proportion of unaccompanied youth among the homeless population. Data from the Conference of Mayors survey show city-by-city estimates of children as a percent of homeless family members. Values range from 20% of family members in Charleston, South Carolina, and Los Angeles, California, to 83% in Santa Monica, California, and Trenton, New Jersey.

The poverty and lack of stability that homelessness brings has a negative impact on children. An example of the poor educational achievement of homeless youths is shown in the *Homeless Census and Homeless Youth/Foster Teen Study* (2002, http://www.appliedsurveyresearch.org/www/products/MC_Homeless02_report.pdf), a study of unaccompanied homeless youths conducted in Monterey County, California. Twenty-one percent of sixteen-year-olds, 22% of seventeen-year-olds, 33% of eighteen-year-olds, 51% of nineteen-year-olds, 59% of twenty-year-olds, and 70% of twenty-one-year-olds were below grade level, according to its findings. Only 13% of the homeless youths in the study had a high school diploma or general equivalency diploma (GED). The remaining 87% were performing below grade level.

Homelessness also has a negative impact on children's health. Catherine Karr of the National Health Care for the Homeless Council, in *Homeless Children: What Every Health Care Provider Should Know* (2006, http://www.nhchc.org/Children/), argues that these children suffer from frequent health problems. They are seen in emergency rooms and hospitalized more often than other poor children. The often crowded and unsanitary conditions they live in lead to a higher rate of infectious diseases, such as upper respiratory infections, diarrhea, and scabies. Homeless children live in less structured and often unsafe environments, leaving them more vulnerable to accidents and injury. They tend not to have access to nutritious food and are often malnourished or obese. Homeless children tend to lag behind their housed peers developmentally, and school-age homeless children often have academic problems. The greater likelihood that homeless children come from families plagued by mental illness, drug use, and domestic violence negatively impacts their own mental health. Homelessness results in serious negative consequences for children's health.

Hunger

Food insecurity is defined as the lack of access to enough food to meet basic needs. Mark Nord, Margaret Andrews, and Steven Carlson of the U.S. Department of Agriculture report in *Household Food Security in the United States, 2005* (November 2006, http://www.ers.usda.gov/Publications/ERR29/ERR29.pdf), that in 2005, 89% of U.S. households were food secure. However, the remaining 11% (12.6 million U.S. households) experienced food insecurity at some time during the year. Most of these households used a variety of coping strategies to obtain adequate food, such as eating less varied diets, participating in food assistance programs, or getting food from community food pantries or soup kitchens. However, 3.9% of all households (4.4 million households) experienced very low food security—in other words, some household members reduced or otherwise altered their normal food intake because of a lack of money.

FIGURE 4.1

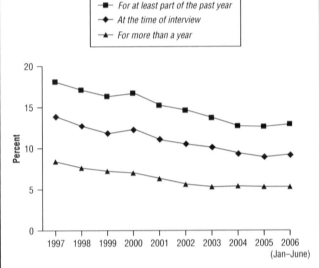

Percent of children under 18 years of age who lacked health insurance coverage when interviewed, for at least part of the past year, or for more than a year, 1997–2006

- ■ *For at least part of the past year*
- ◆ *At the time of interview*
- ▲ *For more than a year*

SOURCE: Robin A. Cohen and Michael E. Martinez, "Figure 1. Percentage of Children under 18 Years of Age Who Lacked Health Insurance Coverage at the Time of Interview, for at Least Part of the Past Year, or for More Than a Year: United States, 1997–June 2006," in *Health Insurance Coverage: Early Release of Estimates from the National Health Interview Survey, January–June 2006*, Centers for Disease Control and Prevention, National Center for Health Statistics, December 2006, http://www.cdc.gov/nchs/data/nhis/earlyrelease/insur200612.pdf (accessed February 25, 2007).

Nord, Andrews, and Carlson find that in 2005 a higher percentage of children than adults were food insecure (16.9% and 11%, respectively). Households that are experiencing food insecurity tend to go through a sequence of steps as food insecurity increases: first, families begin to worry about having enough food, then they begin to decrease other necessities, then they reduce the quality and quantity of all household members' diets, then they decrease the frequency of meals and quantity of adult members' food, and finally they decrease the frequency of meals and the quantity of children's food. Even though children are usually protected from being hungry, almost one out of every one hundred children (0.7%) experienced very low food security on one or more days during 2005. Households with incomes below the poverty line, households with children headed by a single woman, and African-American and Hispanic households were the most likely to experience food insecurity.

EMERGENCY FOOD ASSISTANCE. America's Second Harvest, the nation's largest charitable hunger-relief organization, reports in the *Hunger Study, 2006* (http://www.hungerinamerica.org/key_findings/) that in 2005, 25.3 million Americans sought emergency food assistance. In the *Hunger and Homelessness Survey*, the Conference of Mayors finds that requests for emergency food assistance increased by 7% in 2006, and requests for food assistance by families with children increased by an average of 5% in the surveyed cities. Almost half (48%) of those requesting assistance were members of families with children; 18% of requests by families were estimated to have gone unmet because of lack of resources. The most frequent reasons for hunger cited by city officials were unemployment and low-paying jobs. Other causes included high housing and medical costs, substance abuse, high utility and transportation costs, and a lack of education.

Exposure to Toxins

Another threat to children's health is exposure to environmental toxins. Two toxins that children are most frequently exposed to are lead and secondhand smoke.

LEAD POISONING. Lead exposure now comes primarily from leaded paints that have worn off or been scraped from older homes. Lead is also found in lead plumbing and emitted by factory smokestacks. Because they have smaller bodies and are growing, children suffer the effects of lead exposure more acutely than adults do. Lead poisoning causes nervous system disorders, reduction in intelligence, fatigue, inhibited infant growth, and hearing loss. Toxic levels of lead in a parent can also affect unborn children.

In "CDC Surveillance Data, 1997–2005" (February 16, 2007, http://www.cdc.gov/nceh/lead/surv/stats.htm), the CDC indicates that in 2005 approximately 46,770 children from age five and under had confirmed blood lead levels greater than the center's recommended level of ten micrograms per deciliter of blood. This was about 1.6% of all children tested. According to the U.S. Environmental Protection Agency (EPA), in *Children's Health and the Environment in North America, United States* (December 2005, http://www.cec.org/files/PDF/POLLUTANTS/CountryReport-US-CHE_en.pdf), this number has dropped substantially since the early 1970s, due largely to the phasing out of lead in gasoline between 1973 and 1995. Although children from all social and economic levels can be affected by lead poisoning, children in families with low incomes who live in older, deteriorated housing are at higher risk. Paint produced before 1978 frequently contains lead, so federal legislation now requires owners to disclose any information they may have about lead-based paint before renting or selling a home built earlier than 1978.

SECONDHAND SMOKE AND CHILDREN. In *Children's Health and the Environment in North America, United States*, the EPA reports that environmental tobacco smoke (ETS) is a major hazard for children, whose respiratory, immune, and other systems are not as well developed as those of adults. Secondhand or passive smoke—smoke produced by other people's cigarettes—increases the number of attacks and severity of symptoms in children with asthma and can even cause asthma in preschool-age children. As noted in the American Lung Association's *Secondhand Smoke and Children Fact Sheet* (August 2006), "Exposure to secondhand smoke causes 150,000 and 300,000 acute lower respiratory tract infections (pneumonia and bronchitis) annually in children 18 months and younger; these infections result in 7,500 to 15,000 hospitalizations each year." Passive smoking can also cause middle-ear disease and a reduction in lung function in children, and is considered a risk factor in sudden infant death syndrome. The EPA finds in *Children's Health and the Environment in North America, United States* that the percentage of children under age six who were regularly exposed to secondhand smoke in their homes decreased substantially from 27% in 1994 to 11% in 2003.

DISEASES OF CHILDHOOD

Overweight and Obese Children

The number of overweight and obese Americans has reached epidemic proportions and has become a national concern. The percentage of overweight children and adolescents has grown significantly since the 1970s. Between 1976 and 1980, 6.7% of boys and 6.4% of girls aged six to eleven years were overweight. (See Table 4.4.) In the 2003–04 period those percentages had almost tripled for boys (19.9%) and more than doubled for girls (17.6%). An even more alarming upward trend was seen in the rates of overweight adolescents; 4.5% of boys and 5.4% of girls aged twelve to seventeen were overweight in the 1976–80 period, but 18.3% of adolescent boys and 16% of adolescent girls were overweight in the 2003–04 period. The proportion of overweight children overall between the ages of six and eighteen more than tripled (from 5.7% to 18%) between 1976 and 2004.

Percentages of overweight children vary by race and ethnicity. In the 2003–04 period African-American adolescents (21.5%) were more likely to be overweight than white, non-Hispanic adolescents (16.9%) or Mexican-American adolescents (16.3%). (See Table 4.4.) Among children aged six to eleven, white, non-Hispanic children were the least likely to be overweight (17.7%), compared with African-American (22%) and Mexican-American (22.5%) children of the same age.

Medical professionals are concerned about this trend, because overweight children are at increased risk for premature death in adulthood, as well as for many chronic diseases, including coronary heart disease, hypertension, diabetes mellitus (type 2), gallbladder disease, respiratory disease, some cancers, and arthritis. Type 2 diabetes, previously considered an adult disease, has increased dramatically in children and adolescents. Being overweight or obese can also lead to poor self-esteem and depression in children. According to the CDC, in 2005, 15.7% of high school students were at risk for becoming overweight and 13.1% were already overweight. (See Table 4.5.)

Weight problems in children are thought to be caused by a lack of physical activity, unhealthy eating habits, or a combination of these factors, with genetics and lifestyle playing important roles in determining a child's weight. Television watching and playing computer and video games contribute to the inactive lifestyles of children. According to the CDC, in "Youth Risk Behavior Surveillance—United States, 2005" (*Morbidity and Mortality Weekly Report*, June 6, 2006), 21.1% of high school students spent three or more hours per school day on the computer, and 37.2% spent three or more hours per school day watching television, often not getting a sufficient amount of physical exercise as a consequence.

Physical activity patterns established during youth may extend into adulthood and affect the risk of illnesses such as coronary heart disease, diabetes, and cancer. Mental health experts correlate increased physical activity with improved mental health and overall improvement in life satisfaction. The CDC reports that less than half of students in high school participated in vigorous physical activity, exercise, and physical education classes, and this percentage was even lower for females than for males. (See Table 4.6.) Only 43.8% of male high school students engaged in sufficient vigorous physical activity, whereas only 27.8% of female high school students did. White students were somewhat more likely to meet recommended levels of physical activity (38.7%) than Hispanic (32.9%) or African-American (29.5%) students. Rigorous activity among high school students also generally declined with age.

Asthma

Another serious disease affecting children is asthma, a chronic respiratory disease that causes attacks of difficulty breathing. In *The State of Childhood Asthma, United States, 1980–2005* (December 12, 2006, http://www.cdc.gov/nchs/data/ad/ad381.pdf), Lara J. Akinbami of the CDC reports that millions of children in the United States have asthma. In 2005, 8.9% of children (6.5 million) were currently suffering from asthma, and 12.7% of children (9 million) had suffered with it at some point in their lifetime. Childhood asthma caused 27 hospitalizations per 10,000 children in 2004, and caused 12.8 million missed days of school in 2003. The American Lung Association (ALA) estimates that up to a million asthmatic children are exposed to secondhand smoke, worsening their condition.

Akinbami notes that African-American children suffer from asthma at a rate 60% higher than that of non-Hispanic white children, whereas Puerto Rican children

TABLE 4.4

Percentage of children 6–17 who are overweight, by gender, race, and Hispanic origin, selected years 1976–2004

	Total					Male					Female				
	1976–1980	1988–1994	1999–2000	2001–2002	2003–2004	1976–1980	1988–1994	1999–2000	2001–2002	2003–2004	1976–1980	1988–1994	1999–2000	2001–2002	2003–2004
Ages 6–17															
Total	**5.7**	**11.2**	**15.0**	**16.5**	**18.0**	**5.5**	**11.8**	**15.7**	**18.0**	**19.1**	**5.8**	**10.6**	**14.3**	**15.1**	**16.8**
Race and Hispanic origin[a]															
White, non-Hispanic	4.9	10.5	11.2	14.6	17.3	4.7	11.3	11.9	16.0	18.8	5.1	9.6	10.5	13.2	15.7
Black, non-Hispanic	8.2	14.0	21.1	20.4	21.7	5.8[b]	11.5	19.2	17.7	18.3	10.7	16.5	23.1	23.3	25.3
Mexican American	—	15.4	24.1	21.5	19.6	—	16.1	28.0	25.2	22.3	—	14.7	20.0	17.6	16.6
Ages 6–11															
Total	**6.5**	**11.3**	**15.1**	**16.3**	**18.8**	**6.7**	**11.6**	**15.7**	**17.5**	**19.9**	**6.4**	**11.0**	**14.3**	**14.9**	**17.6**
Race and Hispanic origin[a]															
White, non-Hispanic	5.7	10.2	11.7	14.8	17.7	6.1	10.7	11.9	15.5	18.5	5.2	9.8	11.6	14.1	16.9
Black, non-Hispanic	9.0	14.6	19.6	19.9	22.0	6.8[b]	12.3	17.1	16.9	17.5	11.2	17.0	22.4	23.1	26.5
Mexican American	—	16.4	23.4	20.1	22.5	—	17.5	26.7	26.0	25.3	—	15.3	19.8	13.6	19.4
Ages 12–17															
Total	**5.0**	**11.1**	**14.9**	**16.8**	**17.2**	**4.5**	**12.0**	**15.6**	**18.4**	**18.3**	**5.4**	**10.2**	**14.2**	**15.2**	**16.0**
Race and Hispanic origin[a]															
White, non-Hispanic	4.3	10.8	10.7	14.4	16.9	3.6	12.0	12.0	16.5	19.0	5.0	9.5	9.3	12.4	14.6
Black, non-Hispanic	7.5	13.3	22.7	21.0	21.5	*	10.7	21.6	18.6	19.1	10.3	16.0	23.5	23.4	24.1
Mexican American	—	14.2	24.9	23.1	16.3	—	14.4	29.8	24.2	18.8	—	14.0	20.3	22.0	13.4

— =Not available.

* Estimates are considered unreliable.

[a] From 1976 to 1994, the 1977 Office of Management and Budget (OMB) Standards for Data on Race and Ethnicity were used to classify persons into one of the following four racial groups: white, black, American Indian or Alaskan Native, or Asian or Pacific Islander. For data from 1999 to 2004, the revised 1997 OMB standards were used. Persons could select one or more of five racial groups: white, black or African American, American Indian or Alaska Native, Asian, and Native Hawaiian or other Pacific Islander. Data on race and Hispanic origin are collected separately but are combined for reporting. Persons of Mexican origin may be of any race. Included in the total but not shown separately are American Indian or Alaska Native, Asian, or Native Hawaiian or other Pacific Islander race due to the small sample size for each of these groups. Data from 1999 onward are not directly comparable with data from earlier years. The National Health and Nutrition Examination Survey (NHANES) sample was designed to provide estimates specifically for persons of Mexican-origin and not for all Hispanic-origin persons.

[b] Estimates are unstable because they are based on a small number of persons.

Notes: Overweight is defined as body mass index (BMI) at or above the 95th percentile of the 2000 Centers for Disease Control and Prevention BMI-for-age growth charts (http://www.cdc.gov/growthcharts). BMI is calculated as weight in kilograms divided by the square of height in meters.

SOURCE: "Table HEALTH4. Overweight: Percentage of Children Ages 6–17 Who Are Overweight by Gender, Race, and Hispanic Origin, 1976–1980, 1988–1994, 1999–2000, 2001–2002, and 2003–2004," in *America's Children in Brief: Key National Indicators of Well-Being, 2006*, Federal Interagency Forum on Child and Family Statistics, 2006, http://childstats.gov/americaschildren/tables/health4.asp (accessed February 25, 2007)

TABLE 4.5

Percentage of high school students who had or perceived they had a problem with weight, by sex, race/ethnicity, and grade, 2005

Category	At risk for becoming overweight[a]			Overweight[b]		
	Female	Male	Total	Female	Male	Total
	%	%	%	%	%	%
Race/ethnicity						
White[c]	13.8	15.2	14.5	8.2	15.2	11.8
Black[c]	22.6	16.7	19.8	16.1	15.9	16.0
Hispanic	16.8	16.5	16.7	12.1	21.3	16.8
Grade						
9	15.9	18.3	17.1	10.4	15.0	12.7
10	15.4	14.5	14.9	10.6	16.5	13.6
11	15.2	15.9	15.6	9.4	17.2	13.3
12	15.6	14.1	14.8	9.7	15.5	12.6
Total	**15.5**	**15.8**	**15.7**	**10.0**	**16.0**	**13.1**

Category	Described themselves as overweight			Were trying to lose weight		
	Female	Male	Total	Female	Male	Total
	%	%	%	%	%	%
Race/ethnicity						
White[c]	37.7	24.7	31.1	63.5	28.8	45.9
Black[c]	36.3	17.6	27.2	52.7	24.4	38.9
Hispanic	42.4	32.0	37.1	64.1	38.6	51.2
Grade						
9	36.2	24.3	30.2	60.1	31.9	45.8
10	36.2	24.5	30.2	61.5	28.2	44.4
11	39.1	26.0	32.6	61.7	30.5	46.2
12	41.8	25.6	33.7	64.0	28.7	46.4
Total	**38.1**	**25.1**	**31.5**	**61.7**	**29.9**	**45.6**

[a]Students who were ≥85th percentile but <95th percentile for body mass index, by age and sex, based on reference data.
[b]Students who were ≥95th percentile for body mass index, by age and sex, on the basis of reference data.
[c]Non-Hispanic.

SOURCE: Adapted from "Table 60. Percentage of High School Students Who Were at Risk for Becoming or Were Overweight, by Sex, Race/Ethnicity, and Grade," and "Table 62. Percentage of High School Students Who Described Themselves as Slightly or Very Overweight and Who Were Trying to Lose Weight, by Sex, Race/Ethnicity, and Grade," in "Youth Risk Behavior Surveillance—United States, 2005," *Morbidity and Mortality Weekly Report*, vol. 55, no. SS-5, June 9, 2006, http://www.cdc.gov/mmwr/PDF/SS/SS5505.pdf (accessed February 25, 2007)

TABLE 4.6

High school participation in physical activity by sex, race/ethnicity, and grade, 2005

Category	Met currently recommended levels of physical activity[a]			Met previously recommended levels of physical activity[b]			No vigorous or moderate physical activity[c]		
	Female	Male	Total	Female	Male	Total	Female	Male	Total
	%	%	%	%	%	%	%	%	%
Race/ethnicity									
White[d]	30.2	46.9	38.7	63.3	77.0	70.2	9.3	6.9	1.1
Black[d]	21.3	38.2	29.5	53.1	71.7	62.0	18.2	10.2	1.8
Hispanic	26.5	39.0	32.9	62.6	76.0	69.4	12.3	8.9	2.0
Grade									
9	30.8	42.8	36.9	68.4	78.4	73.5	8.2	7.2	1.4
10	30.0	46.8	38.5	63.0	77.8	70.5	10.3	7.5	1.4
11	25.1	43.8	34.4	60.7	74.2	67.4	12.4	8.4	1.7
12	24.0	41.9	32.9	51.7	71.9	61.8	15.2	8.4	2.0
Total	**27.8**	**43.8**	**35.8**	**61.5**	**75.8**	**68.7**	**11.3**	**7.9**	**0.9**

[a]Were physically active doing any kind of physical activity that increased their heart rate and made them breathe hard some of the time for a total of at least 60 minutes/day on ≥5 of the 7 days preceding the survey.
[b]Participated in at least 20 minutes of vigorous physical activity (i.e., physical activity that made them sweat and breathe hard) on ≥3 of the 7 days preceding the survey and/or at least 30 minutes of moderate physical activity (i.e., physical activity that did not make them sweat and breathe hard) on ≥5 of the 7 days preceding the survey.
[c]During the 7 days preceding the survey.
[d]Non-Hispanic.

SOURCE: "Table 52. Percentage of High School Students Who Met Currently Recommended Levels of Physical Activity, Who Met Previously Recommended Levels of Physical Activity, and Who Participated in No Vigorous or Moderate Physical Activity, by Sex, Race/Ethnicity, and Grade," in "Youth Risk Behavior Surveillance—United States, 2005," *Morbidity and Mortality Weekly Report*, vol. 55, no. SS-5, June 9, 2006, http://www.cdc.gov/mmwr/PDF/SS/SS5505.pdf (accessed February 25, 2007)

suffer from asthma at a rate 140% higher than non-Hispanic white children. Akinbami finds that besides their higher prevalence rates, African-American children's asthma is apparently much less well controlled than non-Hispanic white children's asthma. African-American children have a 260% higher emergency department visit rate, a 250% higher hospitalization rate, and a 500% higher death rate from asthma. She speculates that this is because of the lower level and quality of health care received by African-American children.

HIV/AIDS

Acquired immunodeficiency syndrome (AIDS) was identified as a new disease in 1981, and, according to the CDC, in the *HIV/AIDS Surveillance Report* (2006, http://www.cdc .gov/hiv/topics/surveillance/resources/reports/2005report/ pdf/2005SurveillanceReport.pdf), an estimated 988,376 cases had been diagnosed in the United States through 2005. AIDS is caused by the human immunodeficiency virus (HIV), which weakens the victim's immune system, making it vulnerable to other opportunistic infections. Young children with AIDS usually have the virus transmitted to them either by an infected parent or through contaminated transfusions of blood or blood products. Adolescents who are sexually active or experimenting with drugs are also vulnerable to HIV infection, which can be spread through sexual intercourse without the use of a condom or through shared hypodermic needles.

In adults the most common opportunistic infections of AIDS are Kaposi's sarcoma—a rare skin cancer—and *pneumocystis carinii* pneumonia. In infants and children a failure to thrive and unusually severe bacterial infections characterize the disease. Except for *pneumocystis carinii* pneumonia, children with symptomatic HIV infection seldom develop opportunistic infections as adults do. More often, they are plagued by recurrent bacterial infections, persistent oral thrush (a common fungal infection of the mouth or throat), and chronic and recurrent diarrhea. They may also suffer from enlarged lymph nodes, chronic pneumonia, developmental delays, and neurological abnormalities.

HOW MANY ARE INFECTED? By the end of 2005 the CDC reported a cumulative total of 9,078 AIDS cases in children under the age of thirteen since record keeping began in 1981. (See Table 4.7.) African-American children made up the overwhelming majority of these cases (5,614 cases), followed by Hispanic children (1,732 cases), non-Hispanic white children (1,613 cases), Asians and Pacific Islanders (54 cases), and Native Americans or Alaskan Natives (32 cases). By the end of 2005, 5,136 children aged fourteen and under had died from the disease.

MEANS OF TRANSMITTAL. Most babies of HIV-infected mothers do not develop HIV. HIV-positive mothers can reduce the risk of transmission by taking antire-

troviral drugs during the last two trimesters of pregnancy and during labor; giving birth by caesarean section; giving the infant a short course of antiretroviral drugs after birth; and not breastfeeding. With these interventions, the transmission rate can be reduced to as low as 2%.

Although interventions are effective in preventing HIV transmission from pregnant mothers to babies, the overwhelming majority of children with AIDS contracted it from mothers who were either infected with HIV or at risk for AIDS (8,438 of 9,078 cases, or 93%). (See Table 4.7.) Another way HIV/AIDS has been transmitted to children was through blood transfusions contaminated with the virus, although this means of transmission has been all but eliminated in the twenty-first century.

ADOLESCENTS WITH AIDS. The number of AIDS cases among adolescents is comparatively low. The CDC reports that by the end of 2005, 6,324 adolescents aged thirteen to nineteen had been diagnosed with AIDS since the beginning of the epidemic in the early 1980s. However, because of the long incubation period between the time of infection and the onset of symptoms, it is highly probable that many people who develop AIDS in their early twenties became infected with HIV during their adolescence; by 2005, 34,987 twenty- to twenty-four-year-olds had been diagnosed.

MENTAL HEALTH ISSUES IN YOUNG PEOPLE
Marital Conflict and Divorce

Marital conflict hurts children whether it results in the breakup of marriages or not. Nearly all the studies on children of divorce focus on the period after the parents separated. However, some recent studies suggest that the negative effects children experience may not come so much from divorce itself as from the marital discord between parents before divorce. In fact, some research suggests that many problems reported with troubled teens not only began during the marriage but may have contributed to the breakup of the marriage. According to the article "Children of Divorce" (*Journal of the American Board of Family Practice*, 2001), children raised in discord and marital instability often experience a variety of social, emotional, and psychological problems.

Divorce can cause stressful situations for children in several ways. One or both parents may have to move to a new home, removing the children from family and friends who can give them support. Custody issues can generate hostility between parents. If one or both parents remarry, children are faced with yet another adjustment in their living arrangements.

Eating Disorders

Even though young people who are overweight increase their risk for certain diseases in adulthood, an overemphasis on thinness during childhood may contribute to eating

TABLE 4.7

Diagnoses of AIDS in children younger than 13, by year of diagnosis, race/ethnicity, and transmission category, 2001–05

	Year of diagnosis					
	2001	2002	2003	2004	2005	Cumulative[a]
Race/ethnicity						
White, not Hispanic	12	14	11	7	8	1,613
Black, not Hispanic	83	72	43	29	39	5,614
Hispanic	22	16	10	9	9	1,732
Asian/Pacific Islander	1	1	0	1	1	54
American Indian/Alaska Native	0	1	0	1	0	32
Transmission category						
Hemophilia/coagulation disorder	0	0	0	0	0	226
Mother with documented HIV infection or 1 of the following						
risk factors	115	102	67	47	57	8,438
Injection drug use	13	11	7	6	4	3,196
Sex with injection drug user	10	4	6	2	1	1,388
Sex with bisexual male	3	2	0	2	1	202
Sex with person with hemophilia	1	0	0	0	0	36
Sex with HIV-infected transfusion recipient	0	0	0	0	0	22
Sex with HIV-infected person, risk factor not specified	39	36	19	19	25	1,501
Receipt of blood transfusion, blood components, or tissue	1	2	1	0	0	143
Has HIV infection, risk factor not specified	47	47	32	18	25	1,949
Receipt of blood transfusion, blood components, or tissue	0	2	0	0	0	372
Other/risk factor not reported or identified	3	0	0	0	0	42
Total[b]	**118**	**104**	**67**	**47**	**58**	**9,078**

Note: These numbers do not represent reported case counts. Rather, these numbers are point estimates, which result from adjustments of reported case counts. The reported case counts have been adjusted for reporting delays and for redistribution of cases in persons initially reported without an identified risk factor, but not for incomplete reporting.

[a]From the beginning of the epidemic through 2005.

[b]Includes children of unknown race or multiple races. Cumulative total includes 33 children of unknown race or multiple races. Because column totals were calculated independently of the values for the subpopulations, the values in each column may not sum to the column total.

SOURCE: "Table 4. Estimated Numbers of AIDS Cases in Children <13 Years of Age, by Year of Diagnosis and Selected Characteristics, 2001–2005 and Cumulative—50 States and the District of Columbia," in *HIV/AIDS Surveillance Report*, vol. 17, Centers for Disease Control and Prevention, 2006, http://www.cdc.gov/hiv/topics/surveillance/resources/reports/2005report/pdf/2005SurveillanceReport.pdf (accessed February 25, 2007)

disorders such as anorexia nervosa (extreme and often fatal weight loss) and bulimia ("binging and purging"). Girls are both more likely to have a distorted view of their weight and more likely to have eating disorders than boys.

The CDC reports that although 13.1% of students were overweight in 2005, a much higher proportion thought they were overweight (31.5%). (See Table 4.5.) Girls (38.1%) were much more likely than boys (25.1%) to believe they were overweight. Non-Hispanic white (31.1%) and especially Hispanic (37.1%) youths were more likely than African-American youths (27.2%) to think of themselves as overweight.

In 2005 nearly half (45.6%) of high school students nationwide were trying to lose weight by a variety of methods. (See Table 4.5.) Almost one out of twenty (4.5%) high school students had taken laxatives or induced vomiting to lose weight, 12.3% went without eating for twenty-four hours or more, and 6.3% took diet pills. (See Table 4.8.) Hispanic and non-Hispanic white students were more likely to resort to these unhealthy behaviors than were African-American students. Many more females than males engaged in risky weight-loss methods.

Many more high school students engaged in healthier methods of losing weight. Well over half of high school

females dieted or exercised to lose weight (54.8% and 67.4%, respectively); among males, only 26.8% dieted and 52.9% exercised to lose weight. (See Table 4.8.) Once again, among females these behaviors varied by race: Far more white and Hispanic female students engaged in these weight-loss activities than did African-American female students.

Hyperactivity

Attention deficit hyperactivity disorder (ADHD) is one of the most common psychiatric disorders to appear in childhood. No one knows what causes ADHD, although recent research reported by the National Institute of Mental Health finds a link between a person's ability to pay attention and the body's use of glucose in the brain. Symptoms include restlessness, inability to concentrate, aggressiveness, and impulsivity; lack of treatment can lead to problems in school, at work, and in making friends. In "Attention Deficit Hyperactivity Disorder" (2001, http://www.nimh.nih.gov/publicat/helpchild.cfm), the National Institute of Mental Health estimates that 4.1% of youths aged nine to seventeen are affected in any six-month period by ADHD. Boys are two to three times more likely to be affected by ADHD than girls. Methylphenidate, a stimulant, is frequently used to treat hyperactive children.

TABLE 4.8

Percentage of high school students who engaged in healthy and unhealthy behaviors associated with weight control[a], by sex, race/ethnicity, and grade, 2005

Category	Ate less food, fewer calories, or foods low in fat to lose weight or to keep from gaining weight			Exercised to lose weight or to keep from gaining weight			Went without eating for ≥24 hours to lose weight or to keep from gaining weight			Took diet pills, powders, or liquids to lose weight or to keep from gaining weight[c]			Vomited or took laxatives to lose weight or to keep from gaining weight		
	Female	Male	Total	Female	Male	Total	Female	Male	Total	Female	Male	Total	Female	Male	Total
	%	%	%	%	%	%	%	%	%	%	%	%	%	%	%
Race/ethnicity															
White[b]	58.8	26.4	42.4	69.8	51.2	17.6	7.5	12.5	9.2	4.2	6.6	6.7	2.3	4.4	3.4
Black[b]	39.6	22.0	31.1	56.5	51.6	54.1	14.0	8.6	11.4	4.9	5.1	5.0	4.0	2.8	
Hispanic	53.2	31.5	42.2	68.9	63.0	65.9	17.7	7.4	12.6	7.5	5.7	6.6	6.8	3.9	5.4
Grade															
9	50.8	27.1	38.8	68.3	57.7	62.9	18.4	8.1	13.3	6.0	4.3	5.2	5.5	2.7	4.1
10	55.3	25.7	40.1	69.0	52.1	60.3	16.2	7.4	11.7	7.7	4.4	6.0	7.2	3.0	5.1
11	55.6	26.8	41.4	66.3	49.4	58.0	17.2	6.8	12.1	9.2	4.8	7.0	6.1	2.5	4.3
12	58.4	27.6	43.0	65.5	51.2	58.3	16.0	7.8	11.9	10.2	4.4	7.3	5.9	2.6	4.3
Total	**54.8**	**26.8**	**40.7**	**67.4**	**52.9**	**60.0**	**17.0**	**7.6**	**12.3**	**8.1**	**4.6**	**6.3**	**6.2**	**2.8**	**4.5**

[a]During the 30 days preceding the survey.
[b]Non-Hispanic.
[c]Without a doctor's advice.

SOURCE: Adapted from "Table 64. Percentage of High School Students Who Engaged in Healthy Behaviors to Lose Weight or to Keep from Gaining Weight, by Sex, Race/Ethnicity, and Grade," and "Table 66. Percentage of High School Students Who Engaged in Unhealthy Behaviors to Lose Weight or to Keep from Gaining Weight, by Sex, Race/Ethnicity, and Grade," in "Youth Risk Behavior Surveillance—United States, 2005," *Morbidity and Mortality Weekly Report,* vol. 55, no. SS-5, June 9, 2006, http://www.cdc.gov/mmwr/PDF/SS/SS5505.pdf (accessed February 25, 2007)

Drug and Alcohol Use

Few factors negatively influence the health and well-being of young people more than the use of drugs, alcohol, and tobacco. Monitoring the Future, a long-term study on the use of drugs, alcohol, and tobacco conducted by the University of Michigan's Institute for Social Research, annually surveys eighth, tenth, and twelfth graders on their use of these substances. According to the *Monitoring the Future: National Results on Adolescent Drug Use, Overview of Key Findings, 2005* (April 2006, http://www.drugabuse.gov/PDF/overview2005.pdf), University of Michigan researchers Lloyd D. Johnston et al. indicate that the percentage of high school students who have ever tried any illicit drug either remained steady or decreased slightly from the mid-1990s to 2005. This plateau followed sharp increases during the early 1990s. Johnston et al. find that by the time they neared high school graduation, half (50%) of American students had tried an illicit drug. Between 1975 and 2005, 83% to 90% of high school seniors reported that they could easily obtain marijuana, more than any other illicit drug. A third of twelfth graders had used marijuana in the previous twelve months. The CDC finds that in 2005, 38.4% of high school students reported they had tried marijuana, and 20.2% reported they had used it at least once in the thirty days before the survey. (See Table 4.9.)

TOBACCO. Most states prohibit the sale of cigarettes to anyone under the age of eighteen, but the laws are often ignored and may carry no penalties for youths who buy cigarettes or smoke in public. The ALA reports in "Smoking and Teens Fact Sheet" (April 2006, http://www.lungusa.org/site/pp.asp?c=dvLUK9O0E&b=39871) that each day six thousand children smoke their first cigarette and that almost two thousand of them will become regular smokers. The CDC indicates that in 2005, 23% of high school students had smoked at least one cigarette in the month prior to being surveyed and 9.4% had smoked at least twenty days in the past month. (See Table 4.10.) Almost twice as many male students smoked heavily than did female students: 7.2% of female adolescents and 14.2% of male adolescents smoked more than ten cigarettes per day.

Teens say they smoke for a variety of reasons—they "just like it," "it's a social thing," and many young women who are worried about their weight report that they smoke because "it burns calories." Many of them note they have seen their parents smoke. The ALA indicates that youth who have two parents who smoke are more than twice as likely to become smokers than youth whose parents do not smoke. Children in smoking households are at risk not only from secondhand smoke but also from this greater likelihood to take up smoking themselves.

ALCOHOL. According to Johnston et al., alcohol remained the drug of choice for teenagers in 2005. (See Table 4.11.) Almost seven out of ten (68.6%) high school

seniors had used alcohol in the twelve months prior to the survey, and 47% had used alcohol in the previous thirty days. Although there was some decline in drinking among students in the 1980s, alcohol use remained generally stable among young people between 1995 and 2005. The CDC finds that in 2005, 74.3% of all high school students had had at least one alcoholic drink in their lifetime, 43.3% had taken a drink in the thirty days prior to being surveyed, and 25.5% had had five or more drinks on one occasion at least once in the previous thirty days. (See Table 4.9.) African-American youth were less likely than either non-Hispanic white or Hispanic high schoolers to have ever had a drink, to have had a drink in the previous thirty days, or to engage in episodic heavy drinking.

CHILDHOOD DEATHS
Infant Mortality

The NCHS defines the infant mortality rate as the number of deaths of babies younger than one year per 1,000 live births. Neonatal deaths occur within 28 days after birth and postneonatal deaths occur 28 to 365 days after birth. The U.S. infant mortality rate declined from 165 per 1,000 live births in 1900 to a low of 6.8 per 1,000 live births in 2003, after increasing in 2002 for the first time in decades. (See Table 4.12.) In *Health, United States, 2003* (http://www.cdc.gov/nchs/data/hus/hus03.pdf), the CDC notes that several factors—including improved access to health care, advances in neonatal medicine, and educational campaigns—contributed to the overall decline in infant mortality in the twentieth century.

Not all racial and ethnic groups have reached that record-low infant mortality rate. In 2003 the infant mortality rate for non-Hispanic white infants was 5.7 deaths per 1,000 live births, less than half the rate of 13.5 for African-American infants. (See Table 4.12.) Rates for Native American or Alaskan Native, Hispanic, and Asian and Pacific Islander babies were 8.7, 5.6, and 4.8, respectively.

The NCHS lists the ten leading causes of infant mortality in the United States in 2004. (See Table 4.13.) Birth defects (congenital malformations) were the primary cause of infant mortality (136.6 deaths per 100,000 live births). Premature delivery or low birth weight was the second-leading cause of infant mortality (113.8 per 100,000 live births). Sudden infant death syndrome (51.2), complications of pregnancy (41.4), complications in the placenta or umbilical cord (24.2), respiratory distress (21.3), bacterial sepsis (19.4), neonatal hemorrhage (14.4), and intrauterine hypoxia/birth asphyxia (12.2) completed the list.

SUDDEN INFANT DEATH SYNDROME. Sudden infant death syndrome (SIDS; sometimes called crib death), the unexplained death of a previously healthy infant, was the third-leading cause of infant mortality in the United States in 2004. Moreover, it was the leading cause of death for infants older than one month. In 1992 the

TABLE 4.9

Percentage of high school students who drank alcohol and used marijuana, by sex, race/ethnicity, and grade, 2005

Category	Lifetime alcohol use[a]			Current alcohol use[b]			Episodic heavy drinking[c]			Lifetime marijuana use[e]			Current marijuana use[f]		
	Female	Male	Total	Female	Male	Total	Female	Male	Total	Female	Male	Total	Female	Male	Total
	%	%	%	%	%	%	%	%	%	%	%	%	%	%	%
Race/ethnicity															
White[d]	75.7	75.0	75.3	45.9	47.0	46.4	28.1	31.8	29.9	36.0	40.0	38.0	19.2	21.3	20.3
Black[d]	71.4	66.5	69.0	32.5	29.6	31.2	10.4	11.9	11.1	37.8	43.8	40.7	18.8	22.1	20.4
Hispanic	79.0	79.9	79.4	44.8	48.9	46.8	21.9	28.7	25.3	37.5	47.7	42.6	18.0	28.1	23.0
Grade															
9	66.5	66.6	66.5	36.2	36.3	36.2	17.3	20.7	19.0	27.8	30.9	29.3	16.2	18.6	17.4
10	75.6	73.2	74.4	42.7	41.4	42.0	24.1	25.1	24.6	35.7	39.0	37.4	18.9	21.5	20.2
11	77.1	75.5	76.3	44.2	47.8	46.0	25.0	30.4	27.6	39.4	45.1	42.3	18.5	23.5	21.0
12	81.8	81.5	81.7	49.6	52.0	50.8	29.2	36.2	32.8	42.8	52.4	47.6	19.5	26.1	22.8
Total	**74.8**	**73.8**	**74.3**	**42.8**	**43.8**	**43.3**	**23.5**	**27.5**	**25.5**	**35.9**	**40.9**	**38.4**	**18.2**	**22.1**	**20.2**

[a]Had at least one drink of alcohol on ≥1 day during their life.
[b]Had at least one drink of alcohol on ≥1 of the 30 days preceding the survey.
[c]Had ≥5 drinks of alcohol in a row (i.e., within a couple of hours) on ≥1 of the 30 days preceding the survey.
[d]Non-Hispanic.
[e]Used marijuana one or more times during their life.
[f]Used marijuana one or more times during the 30 days preceding the survey.

SOURCE: Adapted from "Table 28. Percentage of High School Students Who Drank Alcohol, by Sex, Race/Ethnicity, and Grade," and "Table 30. Percentage of High School Students Who Used Marijuana, by Sex, Race/Ethnicity, and Grade," in "Youth Risk Behavior Surveillance—United States, 2005," *Morbidity and Mortality Weekly Report*, vol. 55, no. SS-5, June 9, 2006, http://www.cdc.gov/mmwr/PDF/SS/SS5505.pdf (accessed February 25, 2007)

TABLE 4.10

Percentage of high school students who used tobacco, by sex, race/ethnicity, and grade, 2005

Category	Lifetime cigarette use[a]			Lifetime daily cigarette use[b]			Current cigarette use[d]		
	Female	Male	Total	Female	Male	Total	Female	Male	Total
	%	%	%	%	%	%	%	%	%
Race/ethnicity									
White[c]	53.2	54.9	54.0	17.0	15.1	16.1	27.0	24.9	25.9
Black[c]	53.2	56.3	54.7	3.2	7.5	5.2	11.9	14.0	12.9
Hispanic	52.0	62.1	57.1	9.2	11.5	10.4	19.2	24.8	22.0
Grade									
9	47.7	49.8	48.7	10.2	9.9	10.0	20.5	18.9	19.7
10	50.8	54.1	52.5	11.5	11.6	11.5	21.9	21.1	21.4
11	55.3	59.6	57.5	16.0	14.5	15.3	24.3	24.2	24.3
12	58.3	62.2	60.3	17.4	18.1	17.8	26.0	29.1	27.6
Total	**52.7**	**55.9**	**54.3**	**13.5**	**13.3**	**13.4**	**23.0**	**22.9**	**23.0**

Category	Current frequent cigarette use[e]			Smoked >10 cigarettes/day[f]			Bought cigarettes in a store or gas station[g]		
	Female	Male	Total	Female	Male	Total	Female	Male	Total
	%	%	%	%	%	%	%	%	%
Race/ethnicity									
White[c]	11.7	10.6	11.2	7.5	16.2	11.7	11.1	17.4	14.1
Black[c]	2.4	5.1	3.7	2.5	4.4	3.5	18.6	24.6	21.6
Hispanic	4.7	8.1	6.5	6.1	10.4	8.5	12.2	21.3	17.4
Grade									
9	7.0	6.7	6.9	4.6	12.8	8.6	5.0	11.6	8.2
10	8.4	7.0	7.7	6.5	6.7	6.6	7.8	13.4	10.6
11	10.0	10.5	10.3	8.6	17.9	13.1	14.8	25.8	20.3
12	12.5	13.9	13.2	9.2	16.9	13.2	27.7	34.0	30.8
Total	9.3	9.3	9.4	7.2	14.2	10.7	11.7	18.8	15.2

[a]Ever tried cigarette smoking, even one or two puffs.
[b]Ever smoked at least one cigarette every day for 30 days.
[c]Non-Hispanic.
[d]Smoked cigarettes on ≥1 of the 30 days preceding the survey.
[e]Smoked cigarettes on ≥20 of the 30 days preceding the survey.
[f]On the days they smoked during the 30 days preceding the survey, among the 23.0% of students nation wide who reported current cigarette use.
[g]During the 30 days preceding the survey, among the 19.1% of students nationwide who were aged <18 years and who reported current cigarette use.

SOURCE: Adapted from "Table 20. Percentage of High School Students Who Ever Smoked Cigarettes, by Sex, Race/Ethnicity, and Grade," and "Table 22. Percentage of High School Students Who Currently Smoked Cigarettes, by Sex, Race/Ethnicity, and Grade," and "Table 24. Percentage of High School Students Who Tried to Quit Smoking Cigarettes, Who Usually Got Their Own Cigarettes by Buying Them in a Store or Gas Station, and Who Were Not Asked to Show Proof of Age When They Bought or Tried to Buy Cigarettes in a Store, by Sex, Race/Ethnicity, and Grade," in "Youth Risk Behavior Surveillance— United States, 2005," *Morbidity and Mortality Weekly Report*, vol. 55, no. SS-5, June 9, 2006, http://www.cdc.gov/mmwr/PDF/SS/SS5505.pdf (accessed February 25, 2007)

American Academy of Pediatrics recommended that babies sleep on their backs to reduce the risk of SIDS and launched its Back to Sleep campaign to educate parents. It had been a long-held belief that the best position for babies to sleep was on their stomachs. The American SIDS Institute (2005, http://www.sids.org/) reports that the Back to Sleep campaign has resulted in the reduction of SIDS cases by over 50% since 1983. Other risk factors for SIDS include maternal use of drugs or tobacco during pregnancy, low birth weight, and poor prenatal care. For reasons not yet understood, the CDC notes in "Sudden Infant Death Syndrome" (November 13, 2006, http://www.cdc.gov/SIDS/index.htm) that even though the overall rate of SIDS has declined since the beginning of the Back to Sleep campaign, it has declined less among African-Americans and Native Americans than among other groups.

A number of recent studies consider the possible causes of and risk factors for SIDS. One study, "SIDS Risk Prevention Research Begins to Define Physical Abnormalities in Brainstem, Points to Possible Diagnostic/Screening Tools" (PRNewswire, October 18, 1999), which has been ongoing since 1985 and is being conducted by Hannah Kinney of Harvard Medical School in Boston, Massachusetts, finds a brain defect believed to affect breathing in babies who die of SIDS. Researchers suggest that as carbon dioxide levels rise and oxygen levels fall during sleep, the brains of some babies do not get the signal to regulate breathing or blood pressure accordingly to make up for the change. This condition is particularly dangerous for infants sleeping on their stomachs or on soft bedding. According to the article "SIDS Infants Show Brain Abnormalities" (*NIH Research Matters*, November 10, 2006), the project finds that this brain

TABLE 4.11

Percent of high school seniors who reported drug and alcohol use during 12-month period and 30-day period, 2005

	Used in past 12 months	Used in past 30 days
Marijuana/hashish	33.6	19.8
Inhalants	5.0	2.0
PCP	1.3	0.7
MDMA (ecstasy)	3.0	1.0
Cocaine	5.1	2.3
Crack	1.9	1.0
Heroin	0.8	0.5
Other narcotics	9.0	3.9
Amphetamines	8.6	3.9
Methamphetamine	2.5	0.9
Sedatives (barbiturates)	7.2	3.3
Tranquilizers	6.8	2.9
Alcohol	68.6	47.0
Steroids	1.5	0.9

SOURCE: Adapted from Lloyd D. Johnston et al., "Table 2. Trends in Annual Prevalence of Use of Various Drugs for Eighth, Tenth, and Twelfth Graders," and "Table 3. Trends in 30-Day Prevalence of Use of Various Drugs for Eighth, Tenth, and Twelfth Graders," in *Monitoring the Future: National Results on Adolescent Drug Use, Overview of Key Findings, 2005,* U.S. Department of Health and Human Services, National Institutes of Health, National Institute on Drug Abuse, April 2006, http://www.drugabuse.gov/PDF/overview2005.pdf (accessed February 25, 2007)

abnormality might be linked to higher levels of serotonin in the brainstem. Duane Alexander, the director of the National Institute of Child Health and Human Development, states that "this finding lends credence to the view that SIDS risk may greatly increase when an underlying predisposition combines with an environmental risk—such as sleeping face down—at a developmentally sensitive time in early life."

Mortality among Older Children

In the second half of the twentieth century childhood death rates declined dramatically. Most childhood deaths are from injuries and violence. Even though death rates for all ages decreased, the largest declines were among children.

In 2004 three of the leading causes of childhood death were unintentional injuries, congenital anomalies (birth defects), and malignant neoplasms (cancers). (See Table 4.14.) The remaining deaths were spread across a variety of diseases, including heart disease, pneumonia, influenza, HIV/AIDS, homicide, and suicide.

MOTOR VEHICLE INJURIES. According to the National Highway Traffic Safety Administration (NHTSA), in "Determine Why There Are Fewer Young Alcohol-Impaired Drivers" (September 2001, http://www.nhtsa.dot.gov/people/injury/research/FewerYoungDrivers/), during the 1980s and early 1990s traffic fatalities linked to teenage drinking fell. This decline was due in large part to stricter enforcement of drinking age laws and driving while intoxicated or

driving under the influence laws. Nevertheless, motor vehicle crashes were the leading cause of death among fifteen- to nineteen-year-olds in 2003. In the fact sheet "Mortality: Adolescents and Young Adults" (2006, http://nahic.ucsf.edu/downloads/Mortality.pdf), the National Adolescent Health Information Center reports that 25.2 of every 100,000 teenagers in that age group were killed in traffic accidents in 2003. Many of those killed had been drinking alcohol and were not wearing their seatbelts. Timothy M. Pickrell of the U.S. Department of Transportation reports in "Driver Alcohol Involvement in Fatal Crashes by Age Group and Vehicle Type" (June 2006, http://www-nrd.nhtsa.dot.gov/pdf/nrd-30/NCSA/RNotes/2006/810598.pdf) that 20% of all young drivers aged fifteen to twenty who were killed in crashes were intoxicated.

The CDC's 2005 "Youth Risk Behavior Surveillance" finds that in the month before the survey 17.1% of high school seniors (those most likely to have their driver's licenses) reported they had driven a vehicle after drinking alcohol. (See Table 4.15.) Male seniors (19.2%) were more likely than female seniors (15%) to drive after drinking. Another 28.5% of high school students admitted they had ridden with a driver who had been drinking. Females were slightly more likely to ride with a driver who had been drinking (29.6%) than were males (27.2%).

SUICIDE. In 2004 suicide was the seventh-leading cause of death among five- to fourteen-year-olds and the third-leading cause of death in fifteen- to twenty-four-year-olds. (See Table 4.14.) The CDC reports in "Homicides and Suicides—National Violent Death Reporting System, United States, 2003–2004" (*Morbidity and Mortality Weekly Report,* July 7, 2006) that the male suicide rate is more than four times higher than the female suicide rate. Robert N. Anderson and Betty L. Smith of the CDC's Division of Vital Statistics note in "Deaths: Leading Causes for 2001" (*National Vital Statistics Reports,* November 7, 2003) that in 2001, the most recent year for which detailed statistics are available, white males aged fifteen to nineteen had twice the suicide rate (14 per 100,000) of African-American males (7.3 per 100,000) or Hispanic male youth (7.8 per 100,000). Among females aged fifteen to nineteen, the rate for whites (2.9 per 100,000) was considerably higher than that for Hispanics (2.5 per 100,000) or African-Americans (1.3 per 100,000).

The CDC's "Youth Risk Behavior Surveillance" questioned high school students regarding their thoughts about suicide. In 2005 almost one out of six students (16.9%) surveyed claimed that they had seriously thought about attempting suicide in the previous twelve months. (See Table 4.16.) Although the suicide death rate was much higher among males than among females, females (21.8%) were more likely to have considered suicide than males (12%). Of all students, 13% (16.2% of females and 9.9% of males) had made a specific plan to attempt

TABLE 4.12

Infant mortality rate among selected groups, by race and Hispanic origin of mother, selected years 1983–2003

[Data are based on linked birth and death certificates for infants]

Race and Hispanic origin of mother	1983[a]	1985[a]	1990[a]	1995[b]	1999[b]	2000[b]	2001[b]	2002[b]	2003[b]
	Infant[c] deaths per 1,000 live births								
All mothers	10.9	10.4	8.9	7.6	7.0	6.9	6.8	7.0	6.8
White	9.3	8.9	7.3	6.3	5.8	5.7	5.7	5.8	5.7
Black or African American	19.2	18.6	16.9	14.6	14.0	13.5	13.3	13.8	13.5
American Indian or Alaska Native	15.2	13.1	13.1	9.0	9.3	8.3	9.7	8.6	8.7
Asian or Pacific Islander[d]	8.3	7.8	6.6	5.3	4.8	4.9	4.7	4.8	4.8
Chinese	9.5	5.8	4.3	3.8	2.9	3.5	3.2	3.0	—
Japanese	5.6*	6.0*	5.5*	5.3*	3.5*	4.5*	4.0*	4.9*	—
Filipino	8.4	7.7	6.0	5.6	5.8	5.7	5.5	5.7	—
Hawaiian	11.2	9.9*	8.0*	6.5*	7.0*	9.0	7.3*	9.6	—
Other Asian or Pacific Islander	8.1	8.5	7.4	5.5	5.1	4.8	4.8	4.7	—
Hispanic or Latino[e, f]	9.5	8.8	7.5	6.3	5.7	5.6	5.4	5.6	5.6
Mexican	9.1	8.5	7.2	6.0	5.5	5.4	5.2	5.4	5.5
Puerto Rican	12.9	11.2	9.9	8.9	8.3	8.2	8.5	8.2	8.2
Cuban	7.5	8.5	7.2	5.3	4.6	4.6	4.2	3.7	4.6
Central and South American	8.5	8.0	6.8	5.5	4.7	4.6	5.0	5.1	5.0
Other and unknown Hispanic or Latino	10.6	9.5	8.0	7.4	7.2	6.9	6.0	7.1	6.7
Not Hispanic or Latino:									
White[f]	9.2	8.6	7.2	6.3	5.8	5.7	5.7	5.8	5.7
Black or African American[f]	19.1	18.3	16.9	14.7	14.1	13.6	13.5	13.9	13.6
	Neonatal[c] deaths per 1,000 live births								
All mothers	7.1	6.8	5.7	4.9	4.7	4.6	4.5	4.7	4.6
White	6.1	5.8	4.6	4.1	3.9	3.8	3.8	3.9	3.9
Black or African American	12.5	12.3	11.1	9.6	9.5	9.1	8.9	9.3	9.2
American Indian or Alaska Native	7.5	6.1	6.1	4.0	5.0	4.4	4.2	4.6	4.5
Asian or Pacific Islander[d]	5.2	4.8	3.9	3.4	3.2	3.4	3.1	3.4	3.4
Chinese	5.5	3.3	2.3	2.3	1.8	2.5	1.9	2.4	—
Japanese	3.7*	3.1*	3.5*	3.3*	2.8*	2.6*	2.5*	3.7*	—
Filipino	5.6	5.1	3.5	3.4	3.9	4.1	4.0	4.1	—
Hawaiian	7.0*	5.7*	4.3*	4.0*	4.9*	6.2*	3.6*	5.6*	—
Other Asian or Pacific Islander	5.0	5.4	4.4	3.7	3.3	3.4	3.2	3.3	—
Hispanic or Latino[e, f]	6.2	5.7	4.8	4.1	3.9	3.8	3.6	3.8	3.9
Mexican	5.9	5.4	4.5	3.9	3.7	3.6	3.5	3.6	3.8
Puerto Rican	8.7	7.6	6.9	6.1	5.9	5.8	6.0	5.8	5.7
Cuban	5.0*	6.2	5.3	3.6*	3.5*	3.2*	2.5*	3.2*	3.4
Central and South American	5.8	5.6	4.4	3.7	3.3	3.3	3.4	3.5	3.6
Other and unknown Hispanic or Latino	6.4	5.6	5.0	4.8	4.8	4.6	3.9	5.1	4.7
Not Hispanic or Latino:									
White[f]	5.9	5.6	4.5	4.0	3.8	3.8	3.8	3.9	3.8
Black or African American[f]	12.0	11.9	11.0	9.6	9.6	9.2	9.0	9.3	9.3

*Estimates are considered unreliable. Rates preceded by an asterisk are based on fewer than 50 deaths in the numerator. Rates not shown are based on fewer than 20 deaths in the numerator.

[a]Rates based on unweighted birth cohort data.

[b]Rates based on a period file using weighted data.

[c]Infant (under 1 year of age), neonatal (under 28 days), and postneonatal (28 days–11 months).

[d]Starting with 2003 data, estimates are not shown for Asian or Pacific Islander subgroups during the transition from single race to multiple race reporting.

[e]Persons of Hispanic origin may be of any race.

[f]Prior to 1995, data shown only for states with an Hispanic-origin item on their birth certificates.

Notes: The race groups white, black, American Indian or Alaska Native, and Asian or Pacific Islander include persons of Hispanic and non-Hispanic origin. Starting with 2003 data, some states reported multiple-race data. The multiple-race data for these states were bridged to the single race categories of the 1977 Office of Management and Budget standards for comparability with other states. National linked files do not exist for 1992–1994. Data for additional years are available.

SOURCE: Adapted from "Table 19. Infant, Neonatal, and Postneonatal Mortality Rates, by Detailed Race and Hispanic Origin of Mother: United States, Selected Years 1983–2003," in *Health: United States, 2006, with Chartbook on Trends in the Health of Americans*, Centers for Disease Control and Prevention, National Center for Health Statistics, 2006, http://www.cdc.gov/nchs/data/hus/hus06.pdf (accessed February 25, 2007)

suicide, 8.4% of students (10.8% of females and 6% of males) said they had attempted suicide in the previous year, and 2.3% of high school students (2.9% of females and 1.8% of males) said they had suffered injuries from the attempt that required medical attention. These numbers reflect the fact that females of all ages tend to choose less fatal methods of attempting suicide, such as overdosing and cutting veins, than males, who tend to choose more deadly methods, such as shooting or hanging.

In "Homicides and Suicides" the CDC reports that the likelihood that a child will commit suicide increases with the presence of certain risk factors. Among the factors whose presence may indicate heightened risk are depression, mental health problems, relationship conflicts, a history of previous suicide attempts, and alcohol dependence. In addition, the suicide rate among male homosexual teens is believed to be extremely high. Gary Remafedi of the University of Minnesota's Youth

TABLE 4.13

Ten leading causes of infant death by race and Hispanic origin, 2004

[Data are based on a continuous file of records received from the states. Rates are per 100,000 live births. Figures are based on weighted data rounded to the nearest individual, so categories may not add to totals or subtotals Rates for Hispanic origin should be interpreted with caution because of inconsistencies between reporting Hispanic origin on birth and death certificates]

Rank[a]	Cause of death and age	Number	Rate
	All races[b]		
—	All causes	27,835	676.3
1	Congenital malformations, deformations and chromosomal abnormalities	5,623	136.6
2	Disorders related to short gestation and low birth weight, not elsewhere classified	4,685	113.8
3	Sudden infant death syndrome	2,109	51.2
4	Newborn affected by maternal complications of pregnancy	1,705	41.4
5	Newborn affected by complications of placenta, cord and membranes	998	24.2
6	Accidents (unintentional injuries)	995	24.2
7	Respiratory distress of newborn	877	21.3
8	Bacterial sepsis of new born	798	19.4
9	Neonatal hemorrhage	593	14.4
10	Intrauterine hypoxia and birth asphyxia	502	12.2
—	All other causes	8,950	217.5
	Non-Hispanic white		
—	All causes	13,084	567.8
1	Congenital malformations, deformations and chromosomal abnormalities	3,002	130.3
2	Disorders related to short gestation and low birth weight, not elsewhere classified	1,895	82.3
3	Sudden infant death syndrome	1,123	48.8
4	Newborn affected by maternal complications of pregnancy	753	32.7
5	Accidents (unintentional injuries)	534	23.2
6	Newborn affected by complications of placenta, cord and membranes	482	20.9
7	Respiratory distress of newborn	398	17.3
8	Bacterial sepsis of new born	344	14.9
9	Neonatal hemorrhage	277	12.0
10	Intrauterine hypoxia and birth asphyxia	264	11.4
—	All other causes	4,013	174.2
	Total black[c]		
—	All causes	8,347	1,362.8
1	Disorders related to short gestation and low birth weight, not elsewhere classified	1,766	288.4
2	Congenital malformations, deformations and chromosomal abnormalities	1,049	171.3
3	Sudden infant death syndrome	683	111.5
4	Newborn affected by maternal complications of pregnancy	624	101.9
5	Newborn affected by complications of placenta, cord and membranes	306	49.9
6	Respiratory distress of newborn	302	49.4
7	Accidents (unintentional injuries)	300	49.0
8	Bacterial sepsis of new born	268	43.7
9	Neonatal hemorrhage	157	25.6
10	Necrotizing enterocolitis of newborn	151	24.6
—	All other causes	2,741	447.5

and AIDS Projects, in "Suicidality in a Venue-Based Sample of Young Men Who Have Sex with Men" (*Journal of Adolescent Health*, October 2002), corroborates previous estimates that 20% to 42% of teens and young men who have sex with other males attempt suicide.

TABLE 4.13

Ten leading causes of infant death by race and Hispanic origin, 2004 [CONTINUED]

[Data are based on a continuous file of records received from the states. Rates are per 100,000 live births. Figures are based on weighted data rounded to the nearest individuals, so categories may not add to totals or subtotals Rates for Hispanic origin should be interpreted with caution because of inconsistencies between reporting Hispanic origin on birth and death certificates]

Rank[a]	Cause of death and age	Number	Rate
	Hispanic[d]		
—	All causes	3,782	400.2
1	Congenital malformations, deformations and chromosomal abnormalities	1,288	136.3
2	Disorders related to short gestation and low birth weight, not elsewhere classified	828	87.7
3	Newborn affected by maternal complications of pregnancy	268	28.3
4	Sudden infant death syndrome	241	25.5
5	Newborn affected by complications of placenta, cord and membranes	174	18.4
6	Bacterial sepsis of new born	163	17.2
7	Respiratory distress of newborn	160	16.9
8	Accidents (unintentional injuries)	132	14.0
9	Neonatal hemorrhage	127	13.5
10	Atelectasis	108	11.4
—	All other causes	294	31.1

—Category not applicable.
[a]Rank based on number of deaths.
[b]Includes races other than black and white.
[c]Race and Hispanic origin are reported separately on both the birth and death certificate. Race categories are consistent with the 1977 Office of Management and Budget (OMB) standards. California, Hawaii, Idaho, Maine, Michigan, Minnesota, Montana, New Hampshire, New Jersey, New York, Oklahoma, South Dakota, Washington, Wisconsin, and Wyoming reported multiple-race data in 2004. The multiple-race data for these states were bridged to the single race categories of the 1977 OMB standards for comparability with other states. Data for persons of Hispanic origin are included in the data for each race group, according to the decedent's reported race.
[d]Includes all persons of Hispanic origin of any race.
Notes: For certain causes of death such as unintentional injuries, homicides, suicides, and respiratory diseases, preliminary and final data differ because of the truncated nature of the preliminary file. Data are subject to sampling and/or random variation. Although the infant mortality rate is the preferred indicator of the risk of dying during the first year of life, another measure of infant mortality, the infant death rate, is shown elsewhere in this report. The two measures typically are similar yet they can differ because the denominators used for these measures are different.

SOURCE: Adapted from Arialdi M. Miniño, Melonie P. Heron, and Betty L. Smith, "Table 8. Infant Deaths and Infant Mortality Rates for the 10 Leading Causes of Infant Death, by Race and Hispanic Origin: United States, Preliminary 2004," in "Deaths: Preliminary Data for 2004," *National Vital Statistics Reports*, vol. 54, no. 19, June 28, 2006, http://www.cdc.gov/nchs/data/nvsr54/nvsr54_19.pdf (accessed February 25, 2007)

TABLE 4.14

Leading causes of death and numbers of deaths, by age, 1980 and 2004

[Data are based on death certificates]

Age and rank order	1980 Cause of death	Deaths	2004 Cause of death	Deaths
Under 1 year				
—	All causes	45,526	All causes	27,936
1	Congenital anomalies	9,220	Congenital malformations, deformations and chromosomal abnormalities	5,622
2	Sudden infant death syndrome	5,510	Disorders related to short gestation and low birth weight, not elsewhere classified	4,642
3	Respiratory distress syndrome	4,989	Sudden infant death syndrome	2,246
4	Disorders relating to short gestation and unspecified low birth weight	3,648	Newborn affected by maternal complications of pregnancy	1,715
5	Newborn affected by maternal complications of pregnancy	1,572	Unintentional injuries	1,052
6	Intrauterine hypoxia and birth asphyxia	1,497	Newborn affected by complications of placenta, cord and membranes	1,042
7	Unintentional injuries	1,166	Respiratory distress of newborn	875
8	Birth trauma	1,058	Bacterial sepsis of newborn	827
9	Pneumonia and influenza	1,012	Neonatal hemorrhage	616
10	Newborn affected by complications of placenta, cord, and membranes	985	Diseases of circulatory system	593
1–4 years				
—	All causes	8,187	All causes	4,785
1	Unintentional injuries	3,313	Unintentional injuries	1,641
2	Congenital anomalies	1,026	Congenital malformations, deformations and chromosomal abnormalities	569
3	Malignant neoplasms	573	Malignant neoplasms	399
4	Diseases of heart	338	Homicide	377
5	Homicide	319	Diseases of heart	187
6	Pneumonia and influenza	267	Influenza and pneumonia	119
7	Meningitis	223	Septicemia	84
8	Meningococcal infection	110	Certain conditions originating in the perinatal period	61
9	Certain conditions originating in the perinatal period	84	In situ neoplasms, benign neoplasms and neoplasms of uncertain or unknown behavior	53
10	Septicemia	71	Chronic lower respiratory diseases	48
5–14 years				
—	All causes	10,689	All causes	6,834
1	Unintentional injuries	5,224	Unintentional injuries	2,666
2	Malignant neoplasms	1,497	Malignant neoplasms	1,019
3	Congenital anomalies	561	Congenital malformations, deformations and chromosomal abnormalities	389
4	Homicide	415	Homicide	329
5	Diseases of heart	330	Suicide	285
6	Pneumonia and influenza	194	Diseases of heart	245
7	Suicide	142	Chronic lower respiratory diseases	120
8	Benign neoplasms	104	In situ neoplasms, benign neoplasms and neoplasms of uncertain or unknown behavior	84
9	Cerebrovascular diseases	95	Influenza and pneumonia	82
10	Chronic obstructive pulmonary diseases	85	Cerebrovascular diseases	77

TABLE 4.14

Leading causes of death and numbers of deaths, by age, 1980 and 2004 [CONTINUED]

[Data are based on death certificates]

Age and rank order	1980		2004	
	Cause of death	Deaths	Cause of death	Deaths
15–24 years				
—	All causes	49,027	All causes	33,421
1	Unintentional injuries	26,206	Unintentional injuries	15,449
2	Homicide	6,537	Homicide	5,085
3	Suicide	5,239	Suicide	4,316
4	Malignant neoplasms	2,683	Malignant neoplasms	1,709
5	Diseases of heart	1,223	Diseases of heart	1,038
6	Congenital anomalies	600	Congenital malformations, deformations and chromosomal abnormalities	483
7	Cerebrovascular diseases	418	Cerebrovascular diseases	211
8	Pneumonia and influenza	348	Human immunodeficiency virus (HIV) disease	191
9	Chronic obstructive pulmonary diseases	141	Influenza and pneumonia	185
10	Anemias	133	Chronic lower respiratory diseases	179

— Category not applicable.

SOURCE: Adapted from "Table 32. Leading Causes of Death and Numbers of Deaths, by Age: United States, 1980 and 2004," in *Health: United States, 2006, with Chartbook on Trends in the Health of Americans*, Centers for Disease Control and Prevention, National Center for Health Statistics, 2006, http://www.cdc.gov/nchs/data/hus/hus06.pdf (accessed February 25, 2007)

TABLE 4.15

Percentage of high school students who rode with a driver who had been drinking alcohol and who drove when they had been drinking alcohol, by sex, race/ethnicity, and grade, 2005

Category	Rode with a driver who had been drinking alcohol[a]			Drove when drinking alcohol[a]		
	Female	Male	Total	Female	Male	Total
	%	%	%	%	%	%
Race/ethnicity						
White[b]	30.4	26.2	28.3	10.1	12.4	11.3
Black[b]	24.0	24.3	24.1	3.5	6.5	4.9
Hispanic	34.7	37.4	36.1	6.4	14.6	10.5
Grade						
9	30.1	25.8	27.9	4.5	6.5	5.5
10	29.5	26.2	27.8	4.8	8.3	6.6
11	28.1	27.7	28.0	9.5	14.7	12.1
12	30.7	29.5	30.1	15.0	19.2	17.1
Total	**29.6**	**27.2**	**28.5**	**8.1**	**11.7**	**9.9**

[a]One or more times during the 30 days preceding the survey.
[b]Non-Hispanic.

SOURCE: "Table 4. Percentage of High School Students Who Rode in a Car or Other Vehicle Driven by Someone Who Had Been Drinking Alcohol and Who Drove a Car or Other Vehicle When They Had Been Drinking Alcohol, by Sex, Race/Ethnicity, and Grade," in "Youth Risk Behavior Surveillance—United States, 2005," *Morbidity and Mortality Weekly Report*, vol. 55, no. SS-5, June 9, 2006, http://www.cdc.gov/mmwr/PDF/SS/SS5505.pdf (accessed February 25, 2007)

TABLE 4.16

Percentage of high school students who felt sad or hopeless, who seriously considered attempting suicide, who made a suicide plan, and who attempted suicide, by sex, race/ethnicity, and grade, 2005

Category	Felt sad or hopeless[a, b]			Seriously considered attempting suicide[b]			Made a suicide plan[b]			Attempted suicide[a, d]			Suicide attempt treated by a doctor or nurse[a]		
	Female	Male	Total	Female	Male	Total	Female	Male	Total	Female	Male	Total	Female	Male	Total
	%	%	%	%	%	%	%	%	%	%	%	%	%	%	%
Race/ethnicity															
White[c]	33.4	18.4	25.8	21.5	12.4	16.9	15.4	9.7	12.5	9.3	5.2	7.3	2.7	1.5	2.1
Black[c]	36.9	19.5	28.4	17.1	7.0	12.2	13.5	5.5	9.6	9.8	5.2	7.6	2.6	1.4	2.0
Hispanic	46.7	26.0	36.2	24.2	11.9	17.9	18.5	10.7	14.5	14.9	7.8	11.3	3.7	2.8	3.2
Grade															
9	38.5	19.9	29.0	23.9	12.2	17.9	17.6	10.2	13.9	14.1	6.8	10.4	4.0	2.1	3.0
10	37.0	21.3	28.9	23.0	11.9	17.3	18.1	10.3	14.1	10.8	7.6	9.1	2.4	2.2	2.3
11	38.0	19.4	28.8	21.6	11.9	16.8	16.3	9.5	12.9	11.0	4.5	7.8	2.9	1.4	2.2
12	32.6	20.2	26.4	18.0	11.6	14.8	12.0	9.0	10.5	6.5	4.3	5.4	2.2	1.0	1.6
Total	**36.7**	**20.4**	**28.5**	**21.8**	**12.0**	**16.9**	**16.2**	**9.9**	**13.0**	**10.8**	**6.0**	**8.4**	**2.9**	**1.8**	**2.3**

[a]Almost every day for ≥2 weeks in a row so that they stopped doing some usual activities.
[b]During the 12 months preceding the survey.
[c]Non-Hispanic.
[d]One or more times.

SOURCE: Adapted from "Table 16. Percentage of High School Students Who Felt Sad or Hopeless, Who Seriously Considered Attempting Suicide, and Who Made a Plan about How They Would Attempt Suicide, by Sex, Race/Ethnicity, and Grade," and "Table 18. Percentage of High School Students Who Actually Attempted Suicide and Whose Suicide Attempt Resulted in an Injury, Poisoning, or Overdose That Had to Be Treated by a Doctor or Nurse, by Sex, Race/Ethnicity, and Grade," in "Youth Risk Behavior Surveillance—United States, 2005," *Morbidity and Mortality Weekly Report*, vol. 55, no. SS-5, June 9, 2006, http://www.cdc.gov/mmwr/PDF/SS/SS5505.pdf (accessed February 25, 2007)

CHAPTER 5
TEEN SEXUALITY AND PREGNANCY

EARLY SEXUAL ACTIVITY

Many teenagers are sexually active. The Centers for Disease Control and Prevention (CDC) reports that in 2005 almost half of high school students (46.8%) had had sexual intercourse, down from the 54.1% who were reported as sexually active in 1991. (See Table 5.1.) One out of seven (14.3%) had had sex with four or more partners. Girls (45.7%) were slightly less likely than boys (47.9%) to have had intercourse. African-American students (67.6%) were more likely than Hispanic (51%) or non-Hispanic white students (43%) to be sexually active.

The proportion of students who had intercourse rose with age; 34.3% of ninth graders, 42.8% of tenth graders, 51.4% of eleventh graders, and 63.1% of twelfth graders had ever had intercourse at the time of the survey. (See Table 5.1.) A number of youth were sexually active before age thirteen; 6.2% had had intercourse at age twelve or younger. This early sexual activity is of concern, especially among young girls. Sonya S. Brady and Bonnie L. Halpern-Felsher of the University of California at San Francisco, in "Adolescents' Reported Consequences of Having Oral Sex versus Vaginal Sex" (*Pediatrics*, February 2007), find that among sexually active young teens, boys tend to feel good about themselves and experience popularity as a result of sexual activity, whereas girls are more likely to feel bad about themselves as well as feeling used. In addition, the article "Risky Adolescent Behavior Leads to Depression, Not Vice Versa" (*NeuroPsychiatry Reviews*, December 2005) notes that being sexually active puts adolescents, particularly girls, at risk for depression.

Risk Factors for Early Sexual Activity

In "Early Adolescent Sexual Activity: A Developmental Study" (*Journal of Marriage and the Family*, November 1999), Les B. Whitbeck et al. note that "the main predictors of early intercourse were age, association with delinquent peers, alcohol use, opportunity, and sexually permissive attitudes." Cami K. McBride et al. of the University of Illinois, in "Individual and Familial Influences on the Onset of Sexual Intercourse among Urban African American Adolescents" (*Journal of Consulting and Clinical Psychology*, February 2003), indicate that family conflict can also be linked to early sexual activity among poor urban African-American adolescents. In "Parental Influences on Adolescent Sexual Behavior in High Poverty Settings" (*Archives of Pediatrics and Adolescent Medicine*, 1999), another study of poor African-American children, Daniel Romer et al. of the University of Pennsylvania find that those who reported high levels of monitoring from parents were less likely to have sex before adolescence (at age ten or earlier) and had lower rates of sexual initiation in their teen years as well. John S. Santelli et al., in "Initiation of Sexual Intercourse among Middle School Adolescents: The Influence of Psychosocial Factors" (*Journal of Adolescent Health*, March 2004), a study of inner-city seventh graders, report that peer norms about refraining from sex were strongly correlated with seventh and eighth graders abstaining; on the contrary, drug or alcohol use increased the risk of early sexual activity.

Reasons Given for Not Delaying Sex

A number of studies report that both sexes consider social pressure the major factor in engaging in early sexual activity. Peer pressure and a belief that "everyone is doing it" are often cited as explanations. However, in "Adolescent Girls' Perceptions of the Timing of Their Sexual Initiation: 'Too Young' or 'Just Right'?" (*Journal of Adolescent Health*, May 2004), Sian Cotton et al. of the Children's Hospital Medical Center in Cincinnati, Ohio, indicate that most female adolescents (78% of the studied group) felt that they had been "too young" at their first sexual experience.

In addition, recent research challenges the theory that social pressure is the strongest influence on teenagers'

TABLE 5.1

Percentage of high school students who engaged in sexual behaviors and who used a condom and birth control pills, by sex, race/ethnicity, and grade, 2005

Category	Ever had sexual intercourse			Had first sexual intercourse before age 13 years			Had sexual intercourse with ≥4 persons during their life			Currently sexually active[b]			Condom use[c]			Birth control pill use[d]		
	Female	Male	Total	Female	Male	Total	Female	Male	Total	Female	Male	Total	Female	Male	Total	Female	Male	Total
	%	%	%	%	%	%	%	%	%	%	%	%	%	%	%	%	%	%
Race/ethnicity																		
White[a]	43.7	42.2	43.0	2.9	5.0	4.0	11.1	11.6	11.4	33.5	30.6	32.0	55.6	70.1	62.6	27.1	17.2	22.3
Black[a]	61.2	74.6	67.6	7.1	26.8	16.5	18.6	38.7	28.2	43.8	51.3	47.4	62.1	75.5	68.9	10.7	9.4	10.0
Hispanic	44.4	57.6	51.0	3.6	11.1	7.3	10.4	21.7	15.9	33.7	36.3	35.0	49.8	65.3	57.7	9.4	10.3	9.8
Grade																		
9	29.3	39.3	34.3	5.4	12.0	8.7	5.7	13.2	9.4	19.5	24.5	21.9	71.5	77.1	74.5	8.8	6.4	7.5
10	44.0	41.5	42.8	4.1	7.7	5.9	9.7	13.2	11.5	31.1	27.2	29.2	57.1	74.4	65.3	18.0	10.3	14.3
11	52.1	50.6	51.4	2.6	8.0	5.2	14.2	18.1	16.2	40.8	37.9	39.4	57.8	66.0	61.7	20.2	16.6	18.5
12	62.4	63.8	63.1	2.0	6.2	4.1	20.2	22.6	21.4	51.7	47.0	49.4	46.1	65.8	55.4	28.9	21.9	25.6
Total	**45.7**	**47.9**	**46.8**	**3.7**	**8.8**	**6.2**	**12.0**	**16.5**	**14.3**	**34.6**	**33.3**	**33.9**	**55.9**	**70.0**	**62.8**	**20.6**	**14.6**	**17.6**

[a]Non-Hispanic.
[b]Had sexual intercourse with ≥1 person during the 3 months preceding the survey.
[c]Among the 33.9% of students nationwide who were currently sexually active.
[d]To prevent pregnancy.

SOURCE: Adapted from "Table 44. Percentage of High School Students Who Engaged in Sexual Behaviors, by Sex, Race/Ethnicity, and Grade," and "Table 46. Percentage of High School Students Who Were Currently Sexually Active, Who Used a Condom during Last Sexual Intercourse, and Who Used Birth Control Pills before Last Sexual Intercourse, by Sex, Race/Ethnicity, and Grade," in "Youth Risk Behavior Surveillance—United States, 2005," *Morbidity and Mortality Weekly Report*, vol. 55, no. SS-5, June 9, 2006, http://www.cdc.gov/mmwr/PDF/SS/SS5505.pdf (accessed February 25, 2007)

sexual decisions. In *Teens Today* (October 29, 2002, http://www.sadd.org/teenstoday/teenstodaypdfs/study.pdf), a survey commissioned by Students Against Destructive Decisions and the Liberty Mutual Group, students in grades six through twelve were asked what factors had most influenced their decisions about sexuality. The most common reasons teenagers gave for engaging in sexual activity were boredom, curiosity, and to please one's partner. The most commonly mentioned reasons not to have sex were fear of pregnancy, fear of sexually transmitted diseases (STDs), and not being in a relationship or in love.

Media and Teen Concepts of Sexuality

In *Sex on TV 4* (November 2005, http://www.kff.org/entmedia/upload/Sex-on-TV-4-Executive-Summary.pdf), the Kaiser Family Foundation and Dale Kunkel et al. of the University of Arizona report the results of the latest biennial study of sexual messages on television. The report finds that the percent of shows with sexual content had increased from 56% in 1998 to 70% in 2005. In addition, in those shows that included sexual content, the number of sexual scenes per hour had risen from 3.2 in 1998 to 5 in 2005—and in the top teen programs, there were on average 6.7 sexual scenes per hour. Of the twenty shows most popular with teenagers, 70% included some sexual content, and 45% included sexual behavior. More than one out of ten episodes (11%) included scenes in which sexual intercourse was depicted or strongly implied. Only one out of ten shows most popular with teens that contained sexual content included a reference to sexual risk or responsibility.

The study's authors note that the portrayal of sex on television does not have wholly negative consequences.

In fact, even though references to sexual risk or responsibility are still low, they have increased in recent years, and these references can have a big impact. The study's authors state, "New research over the past several years has documented the powerful positive impact television can have on young people—whether it is learning about HIV from an episode of *Girlfriends* or about condom efficacy from an episode of *Friends*. Indeed ... for many young people, exposure to a higher proportion of shows referencing sexual risks or responsibilities can promote healthier decision-making."

Sexual Activity and Substance Use

Over the years, a number of studies have suggested a link between substance use and sexual activity. Researchers find that both sexual activity and a history of multiple partners correlate with some use of drugs, alcohol, and cigarettes. However, the CDC finds that among sexually active students in 2005, only one-fourth (23.3%) reported they had used alcohol or drugs at the time of their last sexual experience. (See Table 5.2.) Males (27.6%) were more likely than females (19%) to report this behavior; African-Americans (14.1%) were less likely than Hispanics (25.6%) or non-Hispanic whites (25%) to report using alcohol or drugs during sexual activity.

In "Developmental Relationships between Adolescent Substance Use and Risky Sexual Behavior in Young Adulthood" (*Journal of Adolescent Health*, October 2002), Jie Guo et al. of the University of Washington note a link between adolescent binge drinking and marijuana use and risky sexual behavior. Young people who used marijuana or binge drank in high school are more

TABLE 5.2

Percentage of high school students who drank alcohol or used drugs before last sexual intercourse, who were taught about AIDS/HIV in school, and who had been tested for HIV, by sex, race/ethnicity, and grade, 2005

Category	Alcohol or drug use before last sexual intercourse[a]			Taught in school about AIDS or HIV infection			Tested for HIV		
	Female	Male	Total	Female	Male	Total	Female	Male	Total
	%	%	%	%	%	%	%	%	%
Race/ethnicity									
White[b]	20.5	29.9	25.0	90.1	88.7	89.4	11.6	8.8	10.2
Black[b]	12.8	15.4	14.1	87.2	85.4	86.3	24.1	17.9	21.0
Hispanic	18.7	32.2	25.6	85.8	83.6	84.7	11.2	12.7	12.0
Grade									
9	22.7	29.0	26.2	85.5	84.4	85.0	7.9	9.8	8.9
10	18.9	23.6	21.1	89.4	87.3	88.4	13.2	10.2	11.6
11	16.8	29.0	22.5	89.7	89.5	89.6	14.1	10.2	12.2
12	19.2	27.6	23.1	90.1	88.7	89.4	19.3	12.3	15.8
Total	**19.0**	**27.6**	**23.3**	**88.5**	**87.2**	**87.9**	**13.2**	**10.6**	**11.9**

[a]Among the 33.9% of students nationwide who were currently sexually active.
[b]Non-Hispanic.

SOURCE: "Table 48. Percentage of High School Students Who Drank Alcohol or Used Drugs before Last Sexual Intercourse, Were Ever Taught in School about Acquired Immunodeficiency Syndrome (AIDS) or Human Immunodeficiency Virus (HIV) Infection, and Who Were Tested for HIV, by Sex, Race/Ethnicity, and Grade," in "Youth Risk Behavior Surveillance—United States, 2005," *Morbidity and Mortality Weekly Report*, vol. 55, no. SS-5, June 9, 2006, http://www.cdc.gov/mmwr/PDF/SS/SS5505.pdf (accessed February 25, 2007)

likely at age twenty-one to have more sexual partners and to use condoms inconsistently.

The Kaiser Family Foundation, in *Substance Abuse and Risky Sexual Behavior* (February 2002, http://www.kff.org/youthhivstds/loader.cfm?url=/commonspot/security/getfile.cfm&PageID=14907), reports on a survey of almost a thousand teens and young adults from November 2001 through January 2002. More than a quarter (29%) of sexually active fifteen- to seventeen-year-olds surveyed said that alcohol or drugs had influenced their sexual decisions. More than one out of ten (12%) sexually active fifteen- to seventeen-year-olds reported having had unprotected sex while under the influence of drugs or alcohol. Two out of five of these (41%) said their peers drank or used drugs before having sex "a lot" of the time.

Voluntary and Nonvoluntary Experiences

The 1995 and 2002 National Survey of Family Growth asked women whether their first sexual experience was voluntary. In "A Demographic Portrait of Statutory Rape" (2005, http://www.childtrends.org/Files/Conference onSexualExploitationofTeensPresentation.pdf), Kristin Moore and Jennifer Manlove find that 18% of girls whose first sexual experience occurred at age thirteen or under said it was nonvoluntary, compared with 10% of fifteen- and sixteen-year-olds and 5% of seventeen- to nineteen-year-olds. In addition, Elizabeth Terry-Humen, Jennifer Manlove, and Sarah Cottingham report in "Trends and Recent Estimates: Sexual Activity among U.S. Teens" (June 2006, http://www.childtrends.org/Files//Child_Trends-2006_06_01_RB_SexualActivity.pdf) that they asked survey respondents to state which of three statements most closely described how much they wanted their first sexual intercourse experience: "I really didn't want it to happen at the time," "I had mixed feelings—part of me wanted it to happen at the time and part of me didn't," and "I really wanted it to happen at the time." Only 34% of adolescent females said they really wanted it to happen at the time, compared with 62% of adolescent males who felt that way. More than one out of ten (13%) females, compared with 6% of males, reported that they really did not want their first sexual intercourse to happen at that time.

Additionally, Anita Raj et al. of Boston University find in "The Relationship between Sexual Abuse and Sexual Risk among High School Students: Findings from the 1997 Massachusetts Youth Risk Behavior Survey" (*Maternal and Child Health Journal*, June 2000), a study of four thousand high school students, that almost a third of the girls (30.2%) and a tenth of the boys (9.3%) reported having been sexually abused. Sexually abused females were twice as likely to engage in early sexual intercourse and other risky sexual behaviors than girls who had not been abused. Elizabeth M. Saewyc, Lara Leanne Magee, and Sandra E. Pettingell corroborate in

"Teenage Pregnancy and Associated Risk Behaviors among Sexually Abused Adolescents" (*Perspectives on Sexual and Reproductive Health*, May–June 2004) evidence of the increased sexual risks taken by sexually abused youth.

Moreover, according to Child Trends, a nonprofit research organization dedicated to improving the lives of children, early sexual initiation for teenage girls has been linked to a higher risk of becoming the victim of rape or sexual assault at some later time during their adolescence. The Child Trends publication *Facts at a Glance 1997* (January 1, 1997) indicates that more than half (54%) of females age fourteen or younger at first sexual intercourse reported experiencing nonvoluntary sex at some point during their teen years. Vaughn I. Rickert et al. note, in "The Relationship among Demographics, Reproductive Characteristics, and Intimate Partner Violence" (*American Journal of Obstetrics and Gynecology*, October 2002), that early sexual initiation is linked to domestic violence and verbal abuse later in life. Furthermore, in "The Effects of Forced Sexual Intercourse on White Female Adolescents" (*Child Abuse and Neglect*, October 1995), Brent C. Miller, Bruce H. Monson, and Maria C. Norton of Utah State University find that early sexual initiation can lead to depression and low self-esteem.

CONTRACEPTIVE USE

Too Few Use Contraceptives

The CDC finds that in 2005, 62.8% of sexually active teenagers reported that they or their partners used condoms during their last sexual intercourse, up from 46.2% in 1991, when the CDC began tracking condom use. (See Table 5.1.) Young African-Americans reported the highest condom use (68.9%) among sexually active youth. Hispanic students reported the lowest rate of condom use (57.7%). Males (70%) were significantly more likely than females (55.9%) to report condom use. However, the use of condoms decreased from the ninth grade (74.5%) to the twelfth grade (55.4%), a period during which the frequency of sexual intercourse increased, probably because older adolescents turned to alternative methods of birth control, such as oral contraception.

Among sexually active students nationwide in 2005, 17.6% reported they or their partners used oral contraceptives, or "the pill." (See Table 5.1.) Even though this form of contraception protects against pregnancy, it does not protect against STDs. More white students (22.3%) reported using birth control pills than either Hispanic (9.8%) or African-American students (10%). This disparity may be because of the need for a prescription for birth control pills; white students tend to have greater access to medical care than minority students do. Birth control pill use increased between the ninth (7.5%) and twelfth grades (25.6%).

REASONS FOR USE OR NONUSE. Research indicates that adolescents' attitudes and beliefs about their relationships with their partners influence whether they will use condoms. Celia M. Lescano et al. find, in "Condom Use with 'Casual' and 'Main' Partners: What's in a Name?" (*Journal of Adolescent Health*, 2006), that adolescents are more likely to use a condom with a partner that they perceive as a casual one. However, even when partners are casual ones, teens report using condoms only about half the time; therefore, teens are not adequately protecting themselves against STDs, even with partners they perceive as more risky. Condom use with partners perceived as main partners is even lower. Lescano et al. state, "Perhaps adolescents overestimate the safety of using condoms 'most of the time' with a casual partner and underestimate the risk of unprotected sex with a 'serious' partner."

The November 2000 Sexsmart (http://www.kff.org/entpartnerships/upload/SexSmarts-Survey-Safer-Sex-Condoms-and-the-Pill-Toplines.pdf), a survey of 519 adolescents aged twelve to seventeen by the Henry J. Kaiser Family Foundation and *Seventeen* magazine, also highlights teens' fairly casual attitude toward condom use. The survey shows that teens do not completely understand the importance of using condoms consistently to avoid STDs, including the human immunodeficiency virus (HIV) and the acquired immunodeficiency syndrome (AIDS). Eleven percent agreed with the statement "having sex without a condom every now and then is not that big of a deal," and 9% believed that "if you don't have a lot of partners you don't need to use condoms." One out of four teenage females (25%) agreed with the statement "condoms break so often they are not worth using."

SEXUALLY TRANSMITTED DISEASES

Adolescents and young adults have a higher risk of acquiring STDs than older adults. Female adolescents may have an increased susceptibility to chlamydia, a bacterial infection that can cause pelvic inflammatory disease and is a contributing factor in the transmission of HIV. In 2003 chlamydia was the most common STD among adolescents. According to the Maternal and Child Health Bureau of the U.S. Department of Health and Human Services (HHS), in *Child Health USA 2005* (2005, http://www.mchb.hrsa.gov/mchirc/chusa_05/pages/pdf/c05.pdf), it was also more common in adolescents than in any other age group, with 1,524 cases among every 100,000 fifteen-to nineteen-year-old girls. This group also had the highest rate of gonorrhea infection, at 443 per 100,000. Syphilis was far less common in teens, with only 1.6 cases per 100,000 reported in 2003. As Figure 5.1 shows, African-American non-Hispanic teens had much higher rates of STDs than non-Hispanic white teens.

FIGURE 5.1

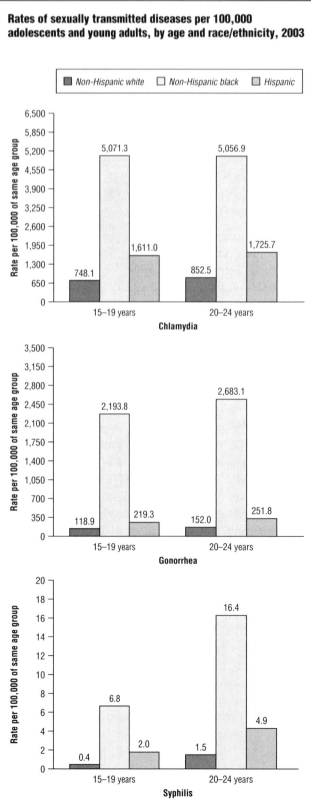

Rates of sexually transmitted diseases per 100,000 adolescents and young adults, by age and race/ethnicity, 2003

SOURCE: "Sexually Transmitted Infections among Adolescents and Young Adults, by Age and Race/Ethnicity: 2003," in *Child Health USA 2005*, U.S. Department of Health and Human Services, Maternal and Child Health Bureau, 2005, http://www.mchb.hrsa.gov/mchirc/chusa_05/pages/pdf/c05.pdf (accessed February 27, 2007)

The study "HIV Risk Behavior among Ethnically Diverse Adolescents Living in Low-Income Housing Developments" (*Journal of Adolescent Health*, August 2004) by Kathleen J. Sikkema et al. of Yale University emphasizes that half of all new HIV infections in the United States are diagnosed in people under twenty-five years old. Most of these young people become infected through sexual activity. Sikkema et al. find that the risk of HIV infection was highest among older adolescents who did not see a need to practice safer sex because they were with steady partners and among teens who abused drugs and alcohol. The researchers suggest that study results could be used to design prevention programs for those adolescents most at risk.

Furthermore, Julie A. Bettinger et al., in "Does Parental Involvement Predict New Sexually Transmitted Diseases in Female Adolescents?" (*Archives of Pediatrics and Adolescent Medicine*, 2004), examine whether parental involvement had any impact on rates of STDs among low-income African-American adolescent girls. They find that when these high-risk teens perceived their parents as exercising a high degree of supervision over their activities, they had lower rates of both gonorrhea and chlamydia infection.

HPV Vaccine

One STD, the human papillomavirus (HPV), can cause genital warts and cervical cancer in women. At least half of sexually active people will get HPV; most of the time, it resolves on its own. However, sometimes it lingers and causes cell changes that can lead to cervical cancer. The American Cancer Society estimates in *Cancer Facts and Figures 2005* (http://www.cancer.org/downloads/STT/CAFF2005f4PWSecured.pdf) that in 2005, 10,370 women were diagnosed with cervical cancer and 3,710 died from it. In "HPV Vaccine Questions and Answers" (August 2006, http://www.cdc.gov/std/hpv/hpv-vaccine.pdf), the CDC's Advisory Committee on Immunization Practices states that up to 70% of these cases are caused by HPV. Clinical trials for a new vaccine against certain strains of the virus, given in three doses over a six-month period, show that the vaccine was nearly 100% effective. The advisory committee recommends that the new vaccine be given to girls before they become sexually active, at around age twelve, to prevent the transmission of HPV.

However, such recommendations stirred up controversy, which heated up in February 2007 when Rick Perry, the governor of Texas, issued an executive order making the state the first to require that girls entering the sixth grade be vaccinated as a condition for enrolling in public school. Conservative groups feared that such a requirement undermined abstinence education and would condone premarital sex. Others argued for mandatory vaccination because young girls would not abstain from sexual activity due to fear of cervical cancer; HPV cannot be prevented by condom use; and 70% of cases of cervical cancer could be prevented by this vaccine.

TEEN CHILDBEARING TRENDS

Joyce A. Martin et al. of the CDC report in "Births: Final Data for 2004" (*National Vital Statistics Reports*, September 29, 2006) that even though birthrates for unmarried women had risen in recent years, the birthrates among unmarried teens had dropped from a high of 45.8 per 1,000 women in 1994 to 34.7 per 1,000 women in 2004. Among girls aged fifteen to seventeen, the birthrate dropped from a high of 31.7 per 1,000 women in 1994 to 20.1 per 1,000 women in 2004. (See Figure 5.2.) Among young women aged eighteen to nineteen years, the birthrate dropped from a high of 69.1 per 1,000 in 1994 to 57.7 in 2004. In "Can Changes in Sexual Behaviors among High School Students Explain the Decline in Teen Pregnancy Rates in the 1990s?" (*Journal of Adolescent Health*, August 2004), John S. Santelli et al. find that both later ages at first intercourse and improved contraceptive practice contributed equally to the decline in pregnancy rates over the period.

According to Martin et al., available data by race show that the greatest percentage decline in births between 1991 and 2004 was among African-American

FIGURE 5.2

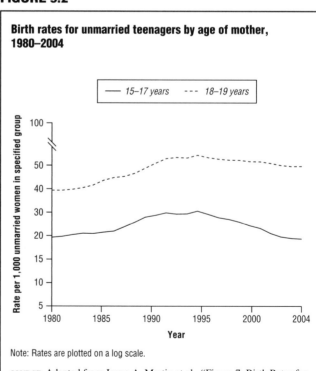

Birth rates for unmarried teenagers by age of mother, 1980–2004

Note: Rates are plotted on a log scale.

SOURCE: Adapted from Joyce A. Martin et al., "Figure 7. Birth Rates for Unmarried Women, by Age of Mother: United States, 1980–2004," in "Births: Final Data for 2004," *National Vital Statistics Reports*, vol. 55, no. 1, September 29, 2006, http://www.cdc.gov/nchs/data/nvsr/nvsr55/nvsr55_01.pdf(accessed February 6, 2007)

TABLE 5.3

Birth rates for teenagers by age, race, and Hispanic origin of mother, 1991, 2002, 2003, and 2004

[Rates per 1,000 women in specified group]

Age and race and Hispanic origin of mother	2004	2003	2002	1991	Percent change, 2003–04	Percent change, 1991–2004
10–14 years						
All races and origins[a]	0.7	0.6	0.7	1.4	17	−50
Non-Hispanic white	0.2	0.2	0.2	0.5	0	−60
Non-Hispanic black	1.6	1.6	1.9	4.9	0	−67
American Indian total[b, c]	0.9	1.0	0.9	1.6	−10	−44
Asian or Pacific Islander total[c]	0.2	0.2	0.3	0.8	0	−75
Hispanic[d]	1.3	1.3	1.4	2.4	0	−46
15–19 years						
All races and origins[a]	41.1	41.6	43.0	61.8	−1	−33
Non-Hispanic white	26.7	27.4	28.5	43.4	−3	−38
Non-Hispanic black	63.1	64.7	68.3	118.2	−2	−47
American Indian total[b, c]	52.5	53.1	53.8	84.1	−1	−38
Asian or Pacific Islander total[c]	17.3	17.4	18.3	27.3	−1	−37
Hispanic[d]	82.6	82.3	83.4	104.6	0	−21
15–17 years						
All races and origins[a]	22.1	22.4	23.2	38.6	−1	−43
Non-Hispanic white	12.0	12.4	13.1	23.6	−3	−49
Non-Hispanic black	37.1	38.7	41.0	86.1	−4	−57
American Indian total[b, c]	30.0	30.6	30.7	51.9	−2	−42
Asian or Pacific Islander total[c]	8.9	8.8	9.0	16.3	1	−45
Hispanic[d]	49.7	49.7	50.7	69.2	0	−28
18–19 years						
All races and origins[a]	70.0	70.7	72.8	94.0	−1	−26
Non-Hispanic white	48.7	50.0	51.9	70.6	−3	−31
Non-Hispanic black	103.9	105.3	110.3	162.2	−1	−36
American Indian total[b, c]	87.0	87.3	89.2	134.2	0	−35
Asian or Pacific Islander total[c]	29.6	29.8	31.5	42.2	−1	−30
Hispanic[d]	133.5	132.0	133.0	155.5	1	−14

[a]Includes origin not stated.
[b]Includes births to Aleuts and Eskimos.
[c]Data for persons of Hispanic origin are included in the data for each race group according to the mother's reported race.
[d]Includes all persons of Hispanic origin of any race.
Notes: Race and Hispanic origin are reported separately on birth certificates. Persons of Hispanic origin may be of any race. Race categories are consistent with the 1977 Office of Management and Budget (OMB) standards. Fifteen states reported multiple race data for 2004. The multiple race data for these states were bridged to the single-race categories of the 1977 OMB standards for comparability with other states.

SOURCE: Joyce A. Martin et al., "Table A. Birth Rates for Women Aged 10–19 Years, by Age and Race and Hispanic Origin of Mother: United States, 1991, 2002, 2003, and 2004, and Percentage Change in Rates, 1991–2004 and 2003–04," in "Births: Final Data for 2004," *National Vital Statistics Reports*, vol. 55, no. 1, September 29, 2006, http://www.cdc.gov/nchs/data/nvsr/nvsr55/nvsr55_01.pdf (accessed February 6, 2007).

teens aged fifteen to nineteen, down from 118.2 births per 1,000 in 1991 to 63.1 in 2004. (See Table 5.3.) The Hispanic rate in this age group in 2004 was higher, at 82.6 births per 1,000, even though it had declined from the 1991 rate of 104.6. Non-Hispanic white teens fifteen to nineteen years old had a birthrate of 26.7 in 2004, down from 43.4 in 1991. The rate for Native American teens dropped from 84.1 in 1991 to 52.5 in 2004, and for Asian and Pacific Islander teens, from 27.3 in 1991 to 17.3 in 2004.

Consequences for Teen Mothers and Their Children

Teenage mothers and their babies face more health risks than older women and their children. Teenagers who become pregnant are more likely than older women to suffer from pregnancy-induced hypertension and eclampsia (a life-threatening condition that sometimes results in convulsions and/or coma). Teenagers are more likely to

have their labor induced, and an immature pelvis can cause prolonged or difficult labor, possibly resulting in bladder or bowel damage to the mother, infant brain damage, or even death of the mother and/or child.

Even though most health risks are similar for children born to teenage and older mothers, teenage mothers may have a higher prevalence of certain risk factors. For example, in *Health, United States, 2006* (http://www.cdc.gov/nchs/data/hus/hus06.pdf), the CDC notes that teenagers had high rates of smoking during pregnancy (10.5% for fifteen- to seventeen-year-olds and 16% for eighteen- to nineteen-year-olds) in 2004 and that smokers are nearly twice as likely to have low birth weight babies as nonsmokers. The HHS finds in the fact sheet "Preventing Infant Mortality" (January 13, 2006, http://www.hhs.gov/news/factsheet/infant.html) that teenagers in general are at a higher risk of having low birth weight babies. Furthermore, in "Youngest Mothers' Infants Have Greatly Elevated Risk of Dying by Age One" (*Perspectives on Sexual and Reproductive Health*, January–February 2003), Michael Klitsch indicates that babies born to adolescents have a greater risk of dying between one and twelve months after birth.

Few teenage mothers are ready for the emotional, psychological, and financial responsibilities and challenges of parenthood. Becoming a parent at a young age usually cuts short a teenage mother's education, limiting her ability to support herself and her child. According to Sandra L. Hofferth, Lori Reid, and Frank L. Mottj, in "The Effects of Early Childbearing on Schooling over Time" (*Family Planning Perspectives*, November–December 2001), women who gave birth as teens in the early 1990s had only a 65% probability of graduating from high school, and only a 29% probability of completing some college. Additionally, Susheela Singh et al., in "Socioeconomic Disadvantage and Adolescent Women's Sexual and Reproductive Behavior: The Case of Five Developed Countries" (*Family Planning Perspectives*, November–December 2001), note that 40% of American women aged twenty to twenty-four who gave birth before age twenty had an income of less than 149% of the federal poverty guideline.

The children of teen mothers face consequences as well. In *Playing Catch-Up: How Children Born to Teen Mothers Fare* (January 2005, http://www.teenpregnancy.org/works/pdf/PlayingCatchUp.pdf), Elizabeth Terry-Humen, Jennifer Manlove, and Kristin Moore examine data on kindergarteners to determine the relationship between the age a woman has a child and how her child does in several key areas: cognition and knowledge, language and communication skills, approaches to learning, emotional well-being and social skills, and physical well-being and motor development. The researchers find that children born to mothers aged seventeen or younger had lower general knowledge scores and language and communication skills, compared with children born to mothers aged twenty or older. Children's approaches to learning, physical well-being, and emotional development, as well as their social skills and emotional well-being, were relatively unaffected by maternal age. In sum, Terry-Humen, Manlove, and Moore state, "Children born to mothers aged 17 and younger began kindergarten with lower levels of school readiness.... The children born to mothers in their 20s clearly outperformed those whose mothers were still teenagers at time of birth, and the most consistent and pronounced differences were observed when comparing children born to mothers aged 17 and younger to those children born to mothers aged 22–29."

In 1996 President Bill Clinton signed into law the Personal Responsibility and Work Opportunity Reconci-liation Act, which abolished the sixty-year-old Aid to Families with Dependent Children program and created the Temporary Assistance for Needy Families (TANF) block grant program. To be eligible for TANF benefits, unmarried minor parents are required to remain in high school or its equivalent and to live with a parent or in an adult-supervised setting. One provision in the law allows for the creation of second-chance homes for teen parents and their children. These homes require that all residents either enroll in school or participate in a job-training program. They also provide parenting and life-skills classes, as well as counseling and support services.

Adolescent Fathers

According to the Child Trends Databank, in "Teen Births" (January 2007, http://www.childtrendsdatabank .org/pdf/13_PDF.pdf), in 2004 fifteen- to nineteen-year-old males had a birthrate of 17 per 1,000, down from a high of 24.7 in 1991. This rate was substantially lower than the 2004 rate for teenage girls of 41.1 per 1,000. The rate was higher for African-American male teens (32.7) than for white male teens (14.3); data for Hispanic male teens was unavailable. The difference between male adolescent and female adolescent birthrates is due in part to the fact that many teen mothers have older partners, as well as to the underreporting of information about fathers on birth certificates. In *2003 Facts at a Glance* (November 2003, http://www.childtrends.org/Files/FAAG2003 .pdf), Child Trends reports that 38% of births to mothers aged eighteen and younger were to fathers four or more years older than the mother. In some cases teen mothers have been sexually abused by their older partners.

Such studies alert officials who design programs for the prevention of pregnancy and STDs to the need to pay attention not only to preadolescent and adolescent males but also to older males who are partners of teenage girls. Because these men are typically out of the public school system, officials agree that programs must be broader in scope.

TEEN ABORTION

The CDC reports that in 2003, 848,000 abortions were performed; the year before, 854,000 had been performed. (See Table 5.4.) The Alan Guttmacher Institute conducted a survey and estimated that a much higher number of abortions had been performed in 2003—almost 1.3 million. As Table 5.4 shows, the rate of abortions per 100 live births has decreased from a high of 35.9 in 1980 to 24.1 in 2003. Girls under fifteen years old have the highest rate of abortions (83 per 100 live births) followed by teens aged fifteen to nineteen (37.4 per 100 live births). All other age groups have lower rates of abortion. For all age groups, African-Americans have the highest abortion rate of any race or ethnic group (49.1 per 100 live births), followed by Hispanics (22.8 per 100

TABLE 5.4

Legal abortions and legal abortion ratios, by selected patient characteristics, selected years 1973–2003

Characteristic	1973	1975	1980	1985	1990	1995	1999[a]	2000[b]	2001[b]	2002[b]	2003[c]
						Number of legal abortions reported in thousands					
Centers for Disease Control and Prevention (CDC)	616	855	1,298	1,329	1,429	1,211	862	857	853	854	848
Alan Guttmacher Institute[d]	745	1,034	1,554	1,589	1,609	1,359	1,315	1,313	1,303	1,293	—
						Abortions per 100 live births[e]					
Total	**19.6**	**27.2**	**35.9**	**35.4**	**34.4**	**31.1**	**25.6**	**24.5**	**24.6**	**24.6**	**24.1**
Age											
Under 15 years	123.7	119.3	139.7	137.6	81.8	66.4	70.9	70.8	74.4	75.3	83.0
15–19 years	53.9	54.2	71.4	68.8	51.1	39.9	37.5	36.1	36.6	36.8	37.4
20–24 years	29.4	28.9	39.5	38.6	37.8	34.8	31.6	30.0	30.4	30.3	30.0
25–29 years	20.7	19.2	23.7	21.7	21.8	22.0	20.8	19.8	20.0	20.0	19.5
30–34 years	28.0	25.0	23.7	19.9	19.0	16.4	15.2	14.5	14.7	14.8	14.4
35–39 years	45.1	42.2	41.0	33.6	27.3	22.3	19.3	18.1	18.0	18.0	17.3
40 years and over	68.4	66.8	80.7	62.3	50.6	38.5	32.9	30.1	30.4	31.0	29.3
Race											
White[f]	32.6	27.7	33.2	27.7	25.8	20.3	17.7	16.7	16.5	16.4	16.5
Black or African American[g]	42.0	47.6	54.3	47.2	53.7	53.1	52.9	50.3	49.1	49.5	49.1
Hispanic origin[h]											
Hispanic or Latino	—	—	—	—	—	27.1	26.1	22.5	23.0	23.3	22.8
Not Hispanic or Latino	—	—	—	—	—	27.9	25.2	23.3	23.2	23.7	23.4
Marital status											
Married	7.6	9.6	10.5	8.0	8.7	7.6	7.0	6.5	6.5	6.5	6.3
Unmarried	139.8	161.0	147.6	117.4	86.3	64.5	60.4	57.0	57.2	57.0	53.8
Previous live births[i]											
0	43.7	38.4	45.7	45.1	36.0	28.6	24.3	22.6	26.4	23.3	22.7
1	23.5	22.0	20.2	21.6	22.7	22.0	20.6	19.4	18.0	19.4	19.0
2	36.8	36.8	29.5	29.9	31.5	30.6	29.0	27.4	25.5	27.9	27.1
3	46.9	47.7	29.8	18.2	30.1	30.7	29.8	28.5	26.4	29.1	28.3
4 or more[j]	44.7	43.5	24.3	21.5	26.6	23.7	24.2	23.7	21.9	23.6	23.4
						Percent distribution[k]					
Total	**100.0**	**100.0**	**100.0**	**100.0**	**100.0**	**100.0**	**100.0**	**100.0**	**100.0**	**100.0**	**100.0**
Period of gestation											
Under 9 weeks	36.1	44.6	51.7	50.3	51.6	54.0	57.6	58.1	59.1	60.5	60.5
9–10 weeks	29.4	28.4	26.2	26.6	25.3	23.1	20.2	19.8	19.0	18.4	18.0
11–12 weeks	17.9	14.9	12.2	12.5	11.7	10.9	10.2	10.2	10.0	9.6	9.7
13–15 weeks	6.9	5.0	5.1	5.9	6.4	6.3	6.2	6.2	6.2	6.0	6.2
16–20 weeks	8.0	6.1	3.9	3.9	4.0	4.3	4.3	4.3	4.3	4.1	4.2
21 weeks and over	1.7	1.0	0.9	0.8	1.0	1.4	1.5	1.4	1.4	1.4	1.4
Previous induced abortions											
0	—	81.9	67.6	60.1	57.1	55.1	53.7	54.7	55.5	55.3	55.3
1	—	14.9	23.5	25.7	26.9	26.9	27.1	26.4	25.8	25.8	25.7
2	—	2.5	6.6	9.8	10.1	10.9	11.5	11.3	11.0	11.3	11.2
3 or more	—	0.7	2.3	4.4	5.9	7.1	7.7	7.6	7.7	7.6	7.8

— Data not available.

[a]In 1998 and 1999, Alaska, California, New Hampshire, and Oklahoma did not report abortion data to CDC. For comparison, in 1997, the 48 corresponding reporting areas reported about 900,000 legal abortions.

[b]In 2000, 2001, and 2002, Alaska, California, and New Hampshire did not report abortion data to CDC.

[c]In 2003, California, New Hampshire, and West Virginia did not report abortion data to CDC.

[d]No surveys were conducted in 1983, 1986, 1989, 1990, 1993, 1994, 1997, 1998, 2001, or 2002. Data for these years were estimated by interpolation.

[e]For calculation of ratios by each characteristic, abortions with characteristic unknown were distributed in proportion to abortions with characteristic known.

[f]For 1989 and later years, white race includes women of Hispanic ethnicity.

[g]Before 1989, black race includes races other than white.

[h]Reporting area increased from 20–22 states, the District of Columbia (DC), and New York City (NYC) in 1991–1995 to 27 states, DC and NYC, with 12 additional states reporting to CDC, but with more than 15% unknowns, and thus excluded from analysis, for 2002 and 2003. California, Florida, Illinois, and Arizona, states with large Hispanic populations, do not report Hispanic ethnicity.

[i]For 1973–1975, data indicate number of living children.

[j]For 1975, data refer to four previous live births, not four or more. For five or more previous live births, the ratio is 47.3.

[k]For calculation of percent distribution by each characteristic, abortions with characteristic unknown were excluded.

Notes: The number of areas reporting adequate data (less than or equal to 15% missing) for each characteristic varies from year to year.

SOURCE: "Table 16. Legal Abortions and Legal Abortion Ratios, by Selected Patient Characteristics: United States, Selected Years 1973–2003," in *Health: United States, 2006, with Chartbook on Trends in the Health of Americans*, Centers for Disease Control and Prevention, National Center for Health Statistics, 2006, http://www.cdc.gov/nchs/data/hus/hus06.pdf (accessed February 25, 2007)

FIGURE 5.3

Pregnancy, birth, and abortion rates for teenagers 15–17 years old, 1976–2005

Rate per 1,000 women aged 15–17

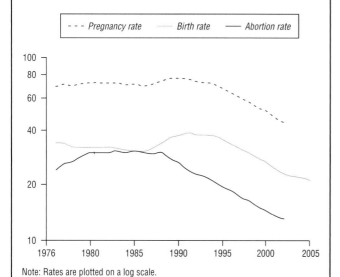

Note: Rates are plotted on a log scale.

SOURCE: Stephanie J. Ventura et al., "Figure 1. Pregnancy, Birth, and Abortion Rates for Teenagers 15–17 Years," in *Recent Trends in Teenage Pregnancy in the United States, 1990–2002*, Centers for Disease Control and Prevention, National Center for Health Statistics, Feburary 2007, http://www.cdc.gov/nchs/products/pubs/pubd/hestats/teenpreg1990-2002/teenpreg1990-2002.htm (accessed February 27, 2007)

FIGURE 5.4

Pregnancy, birth, and abortion rates for teenagers 18–19 years old, 1976–2005

Rate per 1,000 women aged 18–19

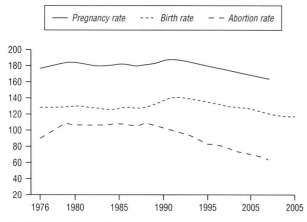

Note: Rates are plotted on a log scale.

SOURCE: Stephanie J. Ventura et al., "Figure 2. Pregnancy, Birth, and Abortion Rates for Teenagers 18–19 Years," in *Recent Trends in Teenage Pregnancy in the United States, 1990–2002*, Centers for Disease Control and Prevention, National Center for Health Statistics, Feburary 2007, http://www.cdc.gov/nchs/products/pubs/pubd/hestats/teenpreg1990-2002/teenpreg1990-2002.htm (accessed February 27, 2007)

live births) and whites (16.5 per 100 live births). As Figure 5.3 and Figure 5.4 show, the abortion rates for teens have declined dramatically since the late 1980s, as have the pregnancy and birthrates.

States have varying laws on parental involvement in minors' abortion decisions. In "An Overview of Abortion Laws" (April 1, 2007, http://www.guttmacher.org/statecenter/spibs/spib_OAL.pdf), the Alan Guttmacher Institute reports that sixteen states and the District of Columbia require no parental involvement in minors' abortions. Thirty-five states require some parental involvement: twenty-four require parental consent, and thirteen require parental notification (Oklahoma and Utah require both parental involvement and consent).

HOMOSEXUALITY

Just the Facts about Sexual Orientation and Youth: A Primer for Principals, Educators, and School Personnel (2007, http://www.apa.org/pi/lgbc/publications/justthefacts.html), a pamphlet for school personnel put together by several organizations, including the American Academy of Pediatrics, the American Psychological Association, and the National Education Association, stresses that sexual orientation is one aspect of the identity of adolescents—not a mental disorder. According to the publication, sexual orientation is developed across a lifetime and along a continuum; in other words, teens are not necessarily simply homosexual or heterosexual, but may feel varying degrees of attraction to people of both genders. The pamphlet emphasizes that gay, lesbian, and bisexual adolescents face prejudice and discrimination that negatively affect their educational experiences and emotional and physical health. Their legitimate fear of being hurt as a result of disclosing their sexuality often leads to a feeling of isolation. All these factors account for lesbian, gay, and bisexual adolescents' higher rates of emotional distress, suicide attempts, risky sexual behavior, and substance use. The publication underscores the need for school personnel to be as open and accepting as possible to support these adolescents.

STD AND PREGNANCY PREVENTION PROGRAMS FOR TEENS
Abstinence

In response to the growing concern about out-of-wedlock births and the threat of AIDS, several national youth organizations and religious groups began campaigns in the early and mid-1990s to encourage teens to sign an abstinence pledge—a promise to abstain from sexual activity until marriage. According to the National Institutes of Health news release "Virginity Pledge Helps Teens Delay Sexual Activity" (January 5, 2001, http://www.nichd.nih.gov/news/releases/virginity.cfm), by 1995, 2.5 million teens had taken the "virginity pledge." Debra Hauser, the vice president of Advocates for Youth, indicates in *Five Years of Abstinence-Only-until-Marriage Education: Assessing the Impact* (2004, http://www.advocatesforyouth .org/publications/stateevaluations.pdf) that in 1996 the federal government committed $250 million over the next five years to fund state initiatives to promote abstinence as Title V of the Social Security Act. Even though only eleven states made results of their evaluations of the effectiveness of these programs public, Hauser states that Advocates for Youth examined these evaluations and found that the programs "showed few short-term benefits and no lasting, positive impact.... No program was able to demonstrate a positive impact on sexual behavior over time."

The Bush administration placed a new stress on abstinence among teens. According to the White House report *Working toward Independence* (February 2002, http://www.whitehouse .gov/news/releases/2002/02/welfare-reform-announcement-book.pdf), an overview of President George W. Bush's suggested plan for welfare reform, "the goal of Federal policy should be to emphasize abstinence as the only certain way to avoid both unintended pregnancies and STDs." According to the HHS's *2008 Budget in Brief* (2007, http:// www.hhs.gov/budget/08budget/2008BudgetInBrief.pdf), $191 million was allocated for abstinence education in fiscal year 2008, an increase of $28 million over fiscal year 2007.

Regardless, the CDC finds that in 2005 approximately one-third of high school students (33.9%) were sexually active at the time of being surveyed—34.6% of females and 33.3% of males. (See Table 5.1.) Younger students were less likely to be currently sexually active than were older students. However, almost half of all students (46.8%) had ever had sexual intercourse; 63.1% of high school seniors had.

In this context, abstinence-only education will do little to prevent teen pregnancy or the spread of STDs. As John S. Santelli et al. state, in "Abstinence and Abstinence-Only Education: A Review of U.S. Policies and Program" (*Journal of Adolescent Health*, January 2006), "Although abstinence is a healthy behavioral option for teens, abstinence as a sole option for adolescents is scientifically and ethically problematic.... We believe that abstinence-only education programs, as defined by federal funding requirements, are morally problematic, by withholding information and promoting questionable and inaccurate opinions. Abstinence-only programs threaten fundamental human rights to health, information, and life."

Sex and STD/HIV Education in Schools

As of July 2007, thirty-five states and the District of Columbia required schools to provide education on HIV/ AIDS and other STDs, although in all cases parents were allowed to remove their children from sex education classes. (See Table 5.5.) Twenty-two states required schools to stress the importance of abstinence in STD and HIV/AIDS education, and ten states required abstinence to be covered. Fourteen states required schools to teach students about contraception, but none required that it be stressed.

According to the CDC, in "Youth Risk Behavior Surveillance—United States, 2005" (*Morbidity and Mortality Weekly Report*, June 9, 2006), 87.9% of all students were taught about AIDS or HIV in school in 2005, compared with 91.5% in 1997. As HIV/AIDS is increasingly common among young people, the declining percentages of students who learn about the disease in school is problematic.

TABLE 5.5

State sex and STD/HIV education policy, July 2004

State	Sex education			STD/HIV education			Parental role	
	Mandated	If taught, content required		Mandated	If taught, content required		Consent required	Opt-out permitted
		Abstinence	Contraception		Abstinence	Contraception		
Alabama		Stress	Cover	X	Stress	Cover		X[a]
Arizona		Stress			Stress		X[b]	X[b]
Arkansas		Stress			Stress			
California		Cover	Cover	X	Cover	Cover		
Colorado								X
Connecticut		Cover		X				X
Delaware	X	Cover	Cover	X	Cover	Cover		
Dist. of Columbia	X		Cover	X				X
Florida	X	Cover		X				X
Georgia	X	Cover		X	Cover			X
Hawaii	X	Stress	Cover	X	Stress	Cover		
Idaho								X
Illinois		Stress[c]			Stress[c]	Cover[c]		X
Indiana		Stress		X	Stress			
Iowa	X			X				X
Kansas	X			X				X
Kentucky	X	Cover		X	Cover			
Louisiana		Stress			Stress			X
Maine	X	Stress	Cover	X	Stress	Cover		X
Maryland	X	Cover	Cover	X	Cover	Cover		X
Massachusetts								X[b]
Michigan		Stress		X	Stress			X
Minnesota	X			X	Cover			X
Mississippi[d]		Stress			Stress			X
Missouri		Stress	Cover	X	Stress	Cover		X
Montana	X	Cover		X	Cover			X[b]
Nevada	X			X			X	
New Hampshire				X	Cover			
New Jersey	X			X				X[a]
New Mexico				X	Stress	Cover		
New York				X	Stress	Cover		X[b]
North Carolina	X	Stress		X	Stress			
Ohio				X	Stress			X
Oklahoma		Stress		X	Cover	Cover		X
Oregon		Stress	Cover	X	Stress	Cover		X
Pennsylvania				X	Stress			X[a, b]
Rhode Island	X	Stress	Cover	X	Stress	Cover		X
South Carolina	X	Stress	Cover	X	Stress	Cover		X
South Dakota[e]								
Tennessee	X	Stress		X	Stress			X
Texas		Stress			Stress			X
Utah[f]	X	Stress		X	Stress		X	
Vermont	X	Cover	Cover	X	Cover	Cover		X[a]
Virginia		Cover	Cover		Cover	Cover		
Washington		Stress	Cover	X	Stress	Cover		X
West Virginia		Stress	Cover	X	Stress	Cover		X
Wisconsin		Stress		X	Stress			X
Total	**19+DC**			**35+DC**			**3**	**35+DC**

[a] Parents' removal of student must be based on religious or moral beliefs.

[b] In AZ, MT, NY and PA, opt-out is only permitted for STD education, including instruction on HIV; in AZ, parental consent is required only for sex education.

[c] IL has a broad set of law mandating general health education, including abstinence; a more specific second law requires a school district that provides sex education to stress abstinence and to provide statistics on the efficacy of condoms as HIV/STD prevention.

[d] Localities may override state requirements for sex education topics, including abstinence; state prohibits including material that "contradicts the required components."

[e] Abstinence is taught within state-mandated character education.

[f] State prohibits teachers from responding to students' spontaneous questions in ways that conflict with the law's requirements.

SOURCE: Guttmacher Institute, "Sex and STD/HIV Education," in *State Policies in Brief*, New York: Guttmacher, 2007, http://guttmacher.org/statecenter/spibs/spib_SE.pdf (accessed May 12, 2007).

CHAPTER 6
GETTING AN EDUCATION

Despite the controversies surrounding the quality and direction of the U.S. education system, the United States remains one of the most highly educated nations in the world. According to the U.S. Department of Education's *Digest of Education Statistics, 2005* (June 2006, http://nces.ed.gov/programs/digest/d05/), 72.1 million Americans were enrolled students in elementary and secondary schools and colleges in the fall of 2005. (See Table 6.1.) An additional 4.4 million people were teachers and faculty at these institutions, and 5 million people were employed as administrative and support staff.

NO CHILD LEFT BEHIND ACT

However, in the 1980s concern grew that American youth were falling behind the educational achievements of young people in other industrialized countries. In response, the National Education Goals Panel was created in 1989 to further the achievement of several national goals, including increasing the high school graduation rate and student competency in English, mathematics, science, history, and geography. Although a task force recommended the panel's reauthorization in 1999, the passage of sweeping educational reform legislation, the No Child Left Behind Act (NCLB), shut down the panel in 2002.

The NCLB made huge changes to the laws defining and regulating the federal government's role in kindergarten through twelfth-grade education. According to the Department of Education (March 6, 2007, http://www.ed.gov/policy/elsec/guid/states/index.html), the law is based on four basic education reform principles:

• Stronger accountability for results

• Increased flexibility and local control

• Expanded options for parents

• Improved budget

Accountability

Under the NCLB, schools are required to demonstrate "adequate yearly progress" toward statewide proficiency goals, including closing the achievement gap between advantaged and disadvantaged students. Those schools that do not demonstrate progress face corrective action and restructuring measures. Progress reports are public, so parents can stay informed about their school and school district. Schools that are making or exceeding adequate yearly progress are eligible for awards.

The accountability outlined under the NCLB is measured through standards testing. States are required to establish strong academic standards and test students annually to see how they are meeting them. The requirement for annual testing was phased in over a six-year period. During the 2002–03 school year, students in grades three to five, six to nine, and ten to twelve were tested in math and reading. Beginning in the 2005–06 school year, testing expanded to all students in grades three to eight. General science achievement testing was scheduled to be fully implemented two years later, in the 2007–08 school year. The NCLB linked federal financing of schools to the results of these mandated tests.

The testing provisions of the NCLB are the subject of much debate. Martin R. West of the Brookings Institution notes in "No Child Left Behind: How to Give It a Passing Grade" (December 2005, http://www3.brookings.edu/comm/policybriefs/pb149.pdf) that advocates see testing as a means of raising expectations and helping guarantee that all children are held to the same high standards. They argue that many young people have passed through school without acquiring the basic reading and math skills needed in society and especially in the information-oriented economy. Critics of testing say classroom experiences become limited to the need to teach students with the test in mind—and what is tested is only a sample of what children should know. Furthermore, critics

TABLE 6.1

Estimated number of participants in elementary and secondary education and in higher education, fall 2005

[In millions]

Participants	All levels (elementary, secondary, and postsecondary degree-granting)	Elementary and secondary schools			Postsecondary degree-granting institutions		
		Total	Public	Private	Total	Public	Private
Total	81.4	61.6	54.5	6.9	19.9	15.0	4.9
Enrollment	72.1	54.7	48.4	6.3	17.4	13.3	4.1
Teachers and faculty	4.4	3.5	3.1	0.4	0.8	0.6	0.3
Other professional, administrative and support staff	5.0	3.2	3.0	0.3	1.7	1.2	0.6

Notes: Includes enrollments in local public school systems and in most private schools (religiously affiliated and nonsectarian). Excludes federal schools. Excludes private preprimary enrollment in schools that do not offer first grade or above. Data for enrollment in degree-granting institutions include full-time and part-time students enrolled in universities, other 4-year colleges, and 2-year colleges that participated in Title IV federal financial aid programs. Data for teachers and other staff in public and private elementary and secondary schools and colleges and universities are reported in terms of full-time equivalents. Detail may not sum to totals because of rounding.

SOURCE: "Table 1. Projected Number of Participants in Educational Institutions, by Level and Control of Institution: Fall 2005," in *Digest of Education Statistics, 2005*, U.S. Department of Education, National Center for Education Statistics, July 2006, http://nces.ed.gov/pubs2006/2006030_1.pdf (accessed February 28, 2007)

claim that standard exams tend to test for those things most easily measured and not the critical thinking skills students need to develop. In addition, the tests measure only how students perform on the tests at one point in time, not their progress over time.

Proficiency Testing

The testing requirements of the NCLB will be debated for some time to come as states grapple with the best means of implementing them. Standardized tests have, however, been around for years. A look at the changes in proficiency test scores over time is one way to gauge the performance of the education system.

In the *Condition of Education, 2006* (June 2006, http://nces.ed.gov/pubs2006/2006071.pdf), the National Center for Education Statistics (NCES) lists test results for a series of years. The percentage of both fourth and eighth graders who tested at or above proficient (indicating solid academic achievement) in reading rose from about 29% of both groups in 1992 to 31.5% of fourth graders in 2005 and 30.8% of eighth graders in 2005. The percentage of fourth graders at or above proficiency in mathematics rose from 17.9% in 1992 to 36.3% in 2005; the percentage of eighth graders at or above proficiency rose from 20.9% in 1992 to 29.8% in 2005. Despite improvements, especially in mathematics, only about one out of three fourth and eighth graders had achieved proficiency in each area.

The public's opinion of school performance is low. In the *Digest of Education Statistics: 2005*, the NCES presents data on the grades that the public gives to schools nationally. Based on a scale of A = 4, B = 3, C = 2, D = 1, and F = 0, the average grade given by adults to the nation's schools hit a high of 2.18—slightly better than a C—in 1987. By 2005 the average grade had dropped to 1.99, lower than it had been in 2002 when the NCLB was passed. When adults with children in the school system were asked to rate their local schools, they consistently gave them higher grades than the nation's schools in general (2.43 and 2.07, respectively), but still only about a C+.

Another way to evaluate the education system in the United States is to compare it to the systems of other industrialized countries. In February 2005 the NCES published *Comparative Indicators of Education in the United States and Other G-8 Countries: 2004* (http://nces.ed.gov/pubs2005/2005021.pdf). The study was designed to compare the U.S. education system with the systems in eight other highly industrialized nations: Canada, France, Germany, Italy, Japan, the Russian Federation, Scotland, and the United Kingdom. The United States compared poorly with the other countries in reading proficiency of primary and secondary school students. In 2001 U.S. fourth-grade students had a mean literacy achievement score of 542, below that of England (553) and Canada (544), but higher than that of the other countries. By age fifteen, however, U.S. students had average scores lower than any other country measured.

Flexibility

The NCLB gave states and local school districts more control over the federal funding they receive for education. Up to half of all non-Title I federal education funding can be allocated by states to whichever programs they wish. Federal programs were also simplified and consolidated under the law, so receiving funding is easier.

Parental Options

The NCLB provided that parents of students attending failing schools would be provided with the opportunity and transportation to send their child to an alternative public or charter school. If the parents chose to keep their child in a failing school, federal Title I funds would be available for supplemental services such as tutoring and summer school, run by either nonsectarian or faith-based organizations. The creation and use of charter schools were expanded under the NCLB.

Proven Educational Methods

The NCLB attached federal funding to programs that had already been shown to help children learn. According to the Department of Education (2007, http://www.gpoaccess.gov/usbudget/fy08/pdf/budget/education.pdf), emphasis was placed on the Reading First initiative, more than tripling funding for reading programs from $300 million in fiscal year (FY) 2001 to a proposed $1.1 billion in FY 2008. Included in this funding was an Early Reading First program, which was established to support literacy skills among preschool-age children to try to meet President George W. Bush's goal of every child being able to read by the third grade. The FY 2008 budget included a proposed $2.8 billion to be used for teacher quality programs, including funding to hire new teachers, increase teacher salaries, and improve teacher training and development.

Voucher Controversy

Many people believe that problems such as large class sizes, poor teacher training, and lack of computers and supplies in many public schools are unsolvable within the current public school system. One solution proposed in the early 1990s was the school voucher system: The government would provide a certain amount of money each year to parents in the form of a voucher to enroll their children at the school of their choice, either public or private. School vouchers became a highly polarized issue, with strong opinions both for and against the idea.

The National Education Association (NEA), a union of teachers and one of the largest unions in the country, immediately objected to school vouchers, arguing that voucher programs would divert money from the public education system and make the current problems worse. The NEA also argued that giving money to parents who choose to send their child to a religious or parochial school is unconstitutional. Little evidence exists to support the idea that voucher programs will lead to better educational outcomes. For example, in "Study Finds D.C. Voucher Schools More Racially Integrated, but No Change in Student Performance" (February 3, 2006, http://ielp.rutgers.edu/developments/020306101356), the Institute on Education Law and Policy finds that the

program had no effect on student performance in public schools. Furthermore, the NEA, in "Cleveland Vouchers Produce No Gains" (2006, http://www.nea.org/vouchers/resources-vouchers.html), notes that the Cleveland voucher program found no difference in the academic achievement of voucher-eligible students who used them to attend private school and those who chose to remain in public school.

Supporters of vouchers claim that parents should be able to choose the best educational environment for their children. They also argue that vouchers will give all people, not just the wealthy or middle class, the opportunity for a better education for their children in private schools. More important, supporters believe that making the educational system a free-market enterprise, in which parents can choose which school their children will attend, will force the public educational system to provide a higher standard of education to compete.

During the legislative process of getting the NCLB through Congress, President Bush agreed to drop the voucher provisions from the legislation, recognizing that debate on the voucher issue could prevent the bill from being passed. On January 8, 2002, the NCLB became law without specific provisions for a nationwide voucher program.

Frustrated at the national level, supporters of vouchers turned to state and local governments. Programs launched in Wisconsin, Florida, and Ohio provided students in some overcrowded or poorly performing schools with vouchers that could be used for private tuition. All these programs were met with court challenges. A landmark decision came on June 27, 2002, when the U.S. Supreme Court upheld, in *Zelman v. Simmons-Harris* (536 U.S. 639 [2002]), the use of public money for religious school tuition in Cleveland, Ohio, calling the city's voucher plan "a program of true private choice."

Public School Choice—The NCLB and Charter Schools

In lieu of a voucher program, the NCLB offered a public school choice program. Parents of students enrolled in failing public schools were allowed to move their children to a better-performing public or charter school. Local school districts were required to provide this choice and provide students with transportation to the alternative school.

Public charter schools are funded by government money and run by a group under an agreement, or charter, with the state that exempts it from many state or local regulations that govern most public schools. In return for these exemptions and funding, the school must meet certain standards. The Department of Education reports in "Helping Families by Supporting and Expanding School Choice" (March 2007, http://www.ed.gov/nclb/choice/schools/choicefacts.html) that by 2007 forty states and the District of Columbia had thirty-four hundred charter schools, in which more than a million students were enrolled. The FY 2008 budget provided $214.8 million to help fund new and ongoing charter schools.

COST OF PUBLIC EDUCATION

The average annual expenditure per student in the public school system in constant 2004–05 dollars more than doubled between 1970 and 2003, from $3,812 per pupil in 1969–70 to $8,468 per pupil during the 2002–03 school year. (See Figure 6.1.) Each year, when the federal budget is determined in Washington, D.C., the battle over the education budget is fierce. Public school officials and teachers stress the importance of investing in the public education system, arguing that more money will provide more teachers, educational materials, and—eventually—a better education to students. They point to school buildings in need of repair and classes that meet in hallways and other cramped areas because of a lack of space. Opponents of increasing public school funding say that more money does not create a better education—better teachers do. To support their argument, they point to the increase in spending per pupil while some measurements of academic achievement remain low.

PREPRIMARY SCHOOL

Preprimary Growth

Participating in early childhood programs such as nursery school, Head Start, prekindergarten, and kindergarten helps prepare children for the academic challenges of first grade. In contrast to the declining elementary and secondary school enrollments between 1970 and 1980, preprimary enrollment showed substantial growth, increasing from 4.1 million in 1970 to 4.9 million in 1980. (See Table 6.2 and Figure 6.2.) According to the Department of Education, enrollment had grown to eight million by 2004.

Not only did the numbers of children enrolled in early childhood programs increase but also the percentage of all three- to five-year-olds enrolled increased substantially between 1965 and 2004. In 1965, 27.1% of three- to five-year-olds were enrolled in nursery school or kindergarten; by 2004, 64.5% were enrolled. (See Table 6.2.)

Although programs such as Head Start and other locally funded preschool programs are available to children in low-income families, preprimary school attendance is still generally linked to parental income and educational achievement levels. According to data presented by the NCES, 47% of three- to five-year-olds from households with an income below the poverty level in 2005 were enrolled in preprimary programs. (See Table 6.3.) That same year, 60% of children aged three to five

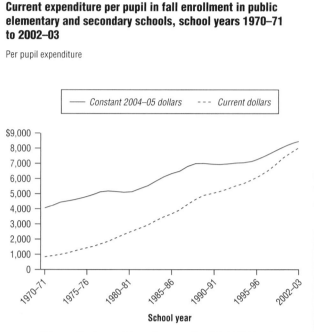

FIGURE 6.1

Current expenditure per pupil in fall enrollment in public elementary and secondary schools, school years 1970–71 to 2002–03

SOURCE: "Figure 10. Current Expenditure per Pupil in Fall Enrollment in Public Elementary and Secondary Schools: 1970–71 through 2002–2003," in *Digest of Education Statistics, 2005*, U.S. Department of Education, National Center for Education Statistics, July 2006, http://nces.ed.gov/pubs2006/2006030_2a.pdf (accessed February 28, 2007)

whose families were at or above the poverty level were enrolled in preprimary programs.

Preschool enrollment rates were even more strongly correlated with a mother's educational level. In 2005 the enrollment rate of children whose mothers had not earned a high school diploma was only 35%. (See Table 6.3.) The enrollment rate of children whose mothers had a high school diploma or equivalent was 49%. Most three- to five-year-olds whose mothers had attended some college were enrolled in preprimary programs; 56% of children whose mothers had attended some college were enrolled, and 73% of children whose mothers had a bachelor's degree or higher were enrolled. These numbers likely reflect three things: Women with higher educational levels are more likely to continue working after becoming mothers, they are better able to pay for these programs, and they value the educational benefits of preprimary programs for their children.

HEAD START. The Head Start program, which was established as part of the Economic Opportunity Act of 1964, is one of the most durable and successful federal programs for low-income and at-risk children. Directed by the Administration for Children and Families, Head Start is designed to help improve the social competence, learning skills, health, and nutrition of low-income children so they can begin school on a more level footing with children from higher-income families. Regulations

TABLE 6.2

Enrollment of 3- to 5-year-old children in preprimary programs, by level and control of program and by attendance, 1965–2004

[In thousands]

Year	Total population 3 to 5 years old	Enrollment by level and control						Enrollment by attendance		
		Total	Percent enrolled	Nursery school		Kindergarten		Full-day	Part-day	Percent full-day
				Public	Private	Public	Private			
1965	12,549	3,407	27.1	127	393	2,291	596	— (†)	— (†)	— (†)
1970	10,949	4,104	37.5	332	762	2,498	511	698	3,405	17.0
1975	10,185	4,955	48.7	570	1,174	2,682	528	1,295	3,659	26.1
1980	9,284	4,878	52.5	628	1,353	2,438	459	1,551	3,327	31.8
1985	10,733	5,865	54.6	846	1,631	2,847	541	2,144	3,722	36.6
1989	11,039	6,026	54.6	930	1,894	2,704	497	2,238	3,789	37.1
1990	11,207	6,659	59.4	1,199	2,180	2,772	509	2,577	4,082	38.7
1991	11,370	6,334	55.7	996	1,828	2,967	543	2,408	3,926	38.0
1992	11,545	6,402	55.5	1,073	1,783	2,995	550	2,410	3,992	37.6
1993	11,954	6,581	55.1	1,205	1,779	3,020	577	2,642	3,939	40.1
1994*	12,328	7,514	61.0	1,848	2,314	2,819	534	3,468	4,046	46.2
1995*	12,518	7,739	61.8	1,950	2,381	2,800	608	3,689	4,051	47.7
1996*	12,378	7,580	61.2	1,830	2,317	2,853	580	3,562	4,019	47.0
1997*	12,121	7,860	64.9	2,207	2,231	2,847	575	3,922	3,939	49.9
1998*	12,078	7,788	64.5	2,213	2,299	2,674	602	3,959	3,829	50.8
1999*	11,920	7,844	65.8	2,209	2,298	2,777	560	4,154	3,690	53.0
2000*	11,858	7,592	64.0	2,146	2,180	2,701	565	4,008	3,584	52.8
2001*	11,899	7,602	63.9	2,164	2,201	2,724	512	3,940	3,662	51.8
2002*	11,524	7,697	66.8	2,376	2,179	2,621	521	4,191	3,507	54.4
2003*	12,204	7,921	64.9	2,512	2,347	2,539	523	4,429	3,492	55.9
2004*	12,362	7,969	64.5	2,428	2,243	2,812	484	4,507	3,461	56.6

—Not available.

†Not applicable.

*Data collected using new procedures. May not be comparable with figures prior to 1994.

Notes: Data are based on sample surveys of the civilian noninstitutional population. Some data have been revised from previously published figures. Detail may not sum to totals because of rounding.

SOURCE: Adapted from "Table 40. Enrollment of 3-, 4-, and 5-Year-Old Children in Preprimary Programs, by Level and Control of Program and by Attendance Status: Selected Years, 1965 through 2004," in *Digest of Education Statistics, 2005*, U.S. Department of Education, National Center for Education Statistics, July 2006, http://nces.ed.gov/pubs2006/2006030_2a.pdf (accessed February 28, 2007)

FIGURE 6.2

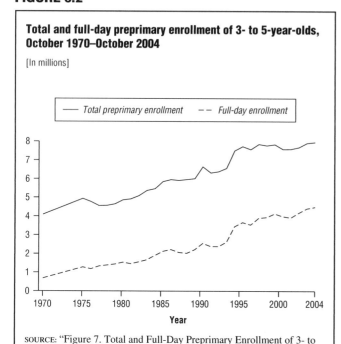

Total and full-day preprimary enrollment of 3- to 5-year-olds, October 1970–October 2004

[In millions]

SOURCE: "Figure 7. Total and Full-Day Preprimary Enrollment of 3- to 5-Year-Olds: October 1970 through October 2004," in *Digest of Education Statistics, 2005*, U.S. Department of Education, National Center for Education Statistics, July 2006, http://nces.ed.gov/pubs2006/2006030_2a.pdf (accessed February 28, 2007)

require that 90% of children enrolled in Head Start be from low-income households.

The U.S. Department of Health and Human Services reports in "Head Start Program Fact Sheet" (2006, http://www.acf.hhs.gov/programs/hsb/research/2006.htm) that in 2005, 906,993 children were served by Head Start programs. Of these children, 35% were non-Hispanic white, 32.9% were Hispanic, 31.1% were African-American, 5.2% were Native American and Alaskan Native, and 2.7% were Asian or Pacific Islander. Most participating children were three to four years old (34% and 52%, respectively). A significant portion (12.5%) were disabled—children with mental retardation, health impairments, visual handicaps, hearing impairments, emotional disturbance, speech and language impairments, orthopedic handicaps, and learning disabilities.

According to the Department of Health and Human Services, the average cost per child for Head Start in 2005 was $7,287. Between its inception in 1965 and 2005, Head Start provided services to more than twenty-three million children and their families. The National Conference of State Legislatures (2007, http://www.ncsl.org/statefed/humserv/HumServFY08.htm) indicates that the proposed budget for Head Start in FY 2008 was $6.8 billion. Despite these expenditures, the Children's Defense

TABLE 6.3

Percent of children ages 3–5 years old enrolled in center-based early childhood care and education programs, by child and family characteristics, 1995 and 2005

Characteristic	1995	2005
Total	55	57
Age		
3	41	43
4	65	69
5	75	69
Sex		
Male	55	60
Female	55	55
Race/ethnicity[a]		
White	57	59
Black	60	66
Hispanic	37	43
Poverty status[b]		
Poor	45	47
Nonpoor	59	60
Poverty status and race/ethnicity		
Poor		
White	43	45
Black	55	65
Hispanic	30	36
Nonpoor		
White	60	61
Black	66	68
Hispanic	44	48
Family type		
Two-parent household	55	57
One-parent or guardian-only household	56	58
Mother's education		
Less than high school	35	35
High school diploma or equivalent	48	49
Some college, including vocational/technical	57	56
Bachelor's degree or higher	75	73
Mother's employment		
35 hours or more per week	60	64
Less than 35 hours per week	62	61
Looking for work	52	42
Not in labor force	47	50

[a]Black includes African American and Hispanic includes Latino. Race categories exclude Hispanic origin unless specified. Included in the total, but not shown separately, are children from other racial/ethnic groups.
[b]"Poor" is defined to include those families below the poverty threshold; "nonpoor" is defined to include those families whose incomes are at or above the poverty threshold.
Notes: Estimates are based on children who have yet to enter kindergarten. Center-based programs include day care centers, head start programs, preschool, nursery school, prekindergarten, and other early childhood programs. Children without mothers in the home are not included in estimates for mother's education or mother's employment status.

SOURCE: Adapted from "Table 2-1. Percentage of Prekindergarten Children Ages 3–5 Who Were Enrolled in Center-Based Early Childhood Care and Education Programs, by Child and Family Characteristics: Various Years 1991–2005," in *The Condition of Education 2006*, U.S. Department of Education, National Center for Education Statistics, June 2006, http://nces.ed.gov/pubs2006/2006071.pdf (accessed February 28, 2007)

Fund notes in "Head Start Basics" (2005, http://www.childrensdefense.org/site/DocServer/headstartbasics2005.pdf?docID=616) that only about half of eligible children are served by the program because it continues to be underfunded.

Head Start faced more drastic budget cuts beginning in the mid-2000s, with its budget declining by more than 10% between 2005 and 2008. As a result of cuts in 2006, the National Head Start Association reports in *Special Report: Quality of Head Start Programs Imperiled by Steady Erosion of Funding* (February 7, 2007, http://www.nhsa.org/download/announcements/NHSA2007_Budge_Report.pdf) that 56% of programs reported having cut their services to children—including reducing hours; cutting instructional time, classroom materials, activities, and resources to children; and reducing extra services such as mental health, medical, and dental, the English as a second language program, and services for children with disabilities. Almost half (46%) of programs had to cut transportation services for children, and another 47% had to cut extra services to families. Over two-thirds (69%) of Head Start programs were forced to cut staff positions and hours and eliminated salary increases and benefits, leading to higher turnover rates.

ELEMENTARY AND SECONDARY SCHOOL
Compulsory Attendance

In 2002 all U.S. states required students to attend school through at least age sixteen. Most industrialized Western nations require children to attend school for about ten years.

Enrollment

Preprimary, elementary, and secondary school enrollments reflect the number of births over a specified period. Because of the baby boom following World War II, school enrollment grew rapidly during the 1950s and 1960s, when those children reached school age. Elementary enrollment reached a then-record high in 1969, as did high school enrollment in 1971.

In the late 1960s the birthrate began to decline, resulting in a steadily falling school enrollment. An echo effect occurred in the late 1970s and early 1980s, when those born during the baby boom began their own families. This echo effect triggered an increase in school enrollment starting in the mid-1980s. In 1985 public elementary and secondary school enrollment increased for the first time since 1971 and continued to increase, reaching 55 million in 2003. It is projected to reach 58.1 million by 2015. (See Figure 6.3.) In 2003, 39.3 million students were enrolled in kindergarten through eighth grade and 15.7 million were enrolled in high school.

Private Schools

The NCES reports in the *Digest of Education Statistics, 2005* that enrollment in public schools far surpasses enrollment in private schools; in 2005 only 11.6% of all primary and secondary school students were enrolled in private schools. Private school enrollment has risen more slowly than school enrollment overall, and as a result the proportion of students enrolled in private schools declined slightly between 1985 and 2005.

FIGURE 6.3

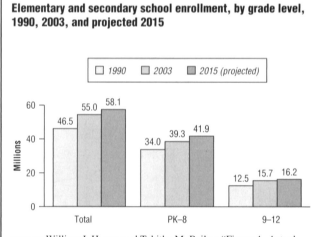

Elementary and secondary school enrollment, by grade level, 1990, 2003, and projected 2015

□ 1990   ☐ 2003   ■ 2015 (projected)

SOURCE: William J. Hussar and Tabitha M. Bailey, "Figure A. Actual and Projected Numbers for Elementary and Secondary School Enrollment, Total and by Grade Level: Selected Years, 1990–2015," in *Projections of Education Statistics to 2015*, 34th ed., U.S. Department of Education, National Center for Education Statistics, September 2006, http://nces.ed.gov/programs/projections/sec1b.asp#a (accessed February 28, 2007)

CATHOLIC SCHOOLS. According to Stephen P. Broughman and Nancy L. Swaim, in *Characteristics of Private Schools in the United States: Results from the 2003–2004 Private School Universe Survey* (March 2006, http://nces .ed.gov/pubs2006/2006319.pdf), 27.9% of all private schools were Catholic, and 46.2% of private school students attended Catholic schools. Economic and social changes have caused a decline in Catholic school enrollment and in the number of Catholic schools. In 1985 there were 9,220 Catholic schools in the United States; by 2004 there were only 7,919.

OTHER RELIGIOUS AND NONRELIGIOUS PRIVATE SCHOOLS. The other types of private schools are non-Catholic religious schools and nonreligious (nonsectarian) schools. According to Broughman and Swaim, non-Catholic religious schools made up 48.1% of all private schools in the 2003–04 school year and enrolled 35.8% of all private school students. Nonsectarian schools enrolled only 18% of private school students in 24% of private schools.

Dropping Out

DROPOUT RATES. Status dropouts are sixteen- to twenty-four-year-olds who have not finished high school and are not enrolled in school. The Department of Education reports in *Digest of Education Statistics: 2005* that status dropout rates decreased from 1972 (14.6%) through 2004 (10.3%). In 2004 the Hispanic status dropout rate was considerably higher, at 23.8%, than that of non-Hispanic African-Americans (11.8%) or non-Hispanic whites (6.8%).

Dropout rates also fluctuate greatly according to family income. In 2004, 17.7% of people aged sixteen to twenty-four from families who had the lowest incomes (bottom 25%) had dropped out of school, which was five times the dropout rate of sixteen- to twenty-four-year-olds whose families had the highest incomes (3.5%). (See Figure 6.4.)

Status dropout rates are consistently lower for women than for men regardless of race or ethnicity. This has been the case since 1977. (See Table 6.4.) In 2004 the status dropout rate for young women aged sixteen to twenty-four was 9%. Males of the same age in 2004 had a status dropout rate of 11.6%.

RETURNING TO SCHOOL OR GETTING AN ALTERNATIVE DIPLOMA. The decision to drop out of high school does not necessarily mean the end of a young person's education. Many former students return to school to get their diploma or take the test necessary to obtain an alternative credential or degree, such as a general equivalency diploma (GED). According to the Department of Education's *Digest of Education Statistics: 2005*, in 2003, 387,000 GEDs were issued. Many young people who earn their GED pursue a college education.

Special Populations

STUDENTS WITH DISABILITIES. In 1976 Congress passed the Education of the Handicapped Act, which required schools to develop programs for disabled children. Formerly, parents of many disabled students had few options other than institutionalization or nursing care. This act required that disabled children be put in the "least restrictive environment," which led to increased efforts to educate them in regular classrooms (known as mainstreaming).

The law defined *handicapped children* as those who were mentally retarded, hard of hearing or deaf, orthopedically impaired, speech and language impaired, visually impaired, seriously emotionally disturbed, or otherwise health impaired. It also included children with specific learning disabilities who require special education and related services.

In 1990 the Individuals with Disabilities Education Act was passed. This was a reauthorization and expansion of the earlier Education of the Handicapped Act. It added autism and traumatic brain injury to the list of disabilities covered by the law, and amendments added in 1992 and 1997 increased coverage for infants and toddlers and for children with attention deficit disorder and attention deficit hyperactivity disorder. The law required public school systems to develop an Individualized Education Program for each disabled child, reflecting the needs of individual students. In 2004 the Individuals with Disabilities Education Improvement Act was signed into law by President Bush, reauthorizing the Individuals

FIGURE 6.4

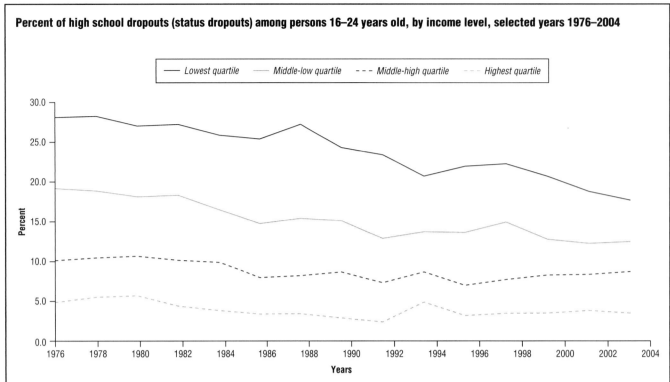

Percent of high school dropouts (status dropouts) among persons 16–24 years old, by income level, selected years 1976–2004

SOURCE: Adapted from "Table 106. Percentage of High School Dropouts (Status Dropouts) among Persons 16 to 24 Years Old, by Income Level, and Percentage Distribution of Dropouts, by Labor Force Status and Educational Attainment: 1970 through 2004, "in *Digest of Education Statistics: 2005*, U.S. Department of Education, National Center for Education Statistics, July 2006, http://nces.ed.gov/programs/digest/d05/tables/dt05_106.asp (accessed February 28, 2007)

with Disabilities Education Act and bringing it in line with the provisions of the NCLB.

As a result of legislation that enforces their rights, increased numbers of disabled children have been served in public schools. Between 1976 and 2004 the proportion of all students who participated in federal education programs for children with disabilities increased from 8.3% to 13.7%. (See Table 6.5.) In the 2003–04 school year the highest proportion of students needed services for specific learning disabilities (5.8%), followed by students who needed help with speech or language impairments (3%) and students who were mentally retarded (1.2%). According to the *Twenty-Sixth Annual Report to Congress on the Implementation of the Individuals with Disabilities Education Act, 2004* (April 2006, http://www.ed.gov/about/reports/annual/osep/2004/26th-vol-1-sec-1.pdf), the Office of Special Education and Rehabilitative Services reports that 268,331 infants and toddlers and 647,420 preschoolers aged three through five received early intervention services in 2002. Another 5.9 million children aged six through twenty-one received special education services.

HOMELESS CHILDREN. Homelessness harms children in many ways, including hindering their ability to attend and succeed in school. Homeless children have difficulty with transportation to school, maintaining necessary docu-

ments, and attaining privacy needed for homework, sleep, and interaction with parents in a shelter. Experts report that homeless children—when compared with children who are poor but housed—miss more days of school, more often repeat a grade, and are more often put into special education classes.

The McKinney-Vento Homeless Assistance Act of 1987 required in Title VII, subtitle B, that each state provide "free, appropriate, public education" to homeless youth. The law further required that all states develop a plan to address the denial of access to education to homeless children.

The McKinney-Vento Homeless Education Assistance Improvements Act of 2001 went further to address inequities that affect homeless children in the public school system. New guidance for states and school systems released by the Department of Education in April 2003 noted the main differences between the old and new programs:

- Homeless children may no longer be segregated in a separate program on the basis of their homeless status.

- Schools must immediately enroll homeless students even if they are missing some of the documentation normally required.

TABLE 6.4

Percentage of high school dropouts (status dropouts) among persons 16–24 years old, by sex, race, and ethnicity, 1960–2004

	Total				Male				Female			
Year	All races[a]	White, non-Hispanic	Black, non-Hispanic	Hispanic origin	All races[a]	White, non-Hispanic	Black, non-Hispanic	Hispanic origin	All races[a]	White, non-Hispanic	Black, non-Hispanic	Hispanic origin
1960[b]	27.2	—	—	—	27.8	—	—	—	26.7	—	—	—
1967[c]	17.0	15.4	28.6	—	16.5	14.7	30.6	—	17.3	16.1	26.9	—
1968[c]	16.2	14.7	27.4	—	15.8	14.4	27.1	—	16.5	15.0	27.6	—
1969[c]	15.2	13.6	26.7	—	14.3	12.6	26.9	—	16.0	14.6	26.7	—
1970[c]	15.0	13.2	27.9	—	14.2	12.2	29.4	—	15.7	14.1	26.6	—
1971[c]	14.7	13.4	24.0	—	14.2	12.6	25.5	—	15.2	14.2	22.6	—
1972	14.6	12.3	21.3	34.3	14.1	11.6	22.3	33.7	15.1	12.8	20.5	34.8
1973	14.1	11.6	22.2	33.5	13.7	11.5	21.5	30.4	14.5	11.8	22.8	36.4
1974	14.3	11.9	21.2	33.0	14.2	12.0	20.1	33.8	14.3	11.8	22.1	32.2
1975	13.9	11.4	22.9	29.2	13.3	11.0	23.0	26.7	14.5	11.8	22.9	31.6
1976	14.1	12.0	20.5	31.4	14.1	12.1	21.2	30.3	14.2	11.8	19.9	32.3
1977	14.1	11.9	19.8	33.0	14.5	12.6	19.5	31.6	13.8	11.2	20.0	34.3
1978	14.2	11.9	20.2	33.3	14.6	12.2	22.5	33.6	13.9	11.6	18.3	33.1
1979	14.6	12.0	21.1	33.8	15.0	12.6	22.4	33.0	14.2	11.5	20.0	34.5
1980	14.1	11.4	19.1	35.2	15.1	12.3	20.8	37.2	13.1	10.5	17.7	33.2
1981	13.9	11.3	18.4	33.2	15.1	12.5	19.9	36.0	12.8	10.2	17.1	30.4
1982	13.9	11.4	18.4	31.7	14.5	12.0	21.2	30.5	13.3	10.8	15.9	32.8
1983	13.7	11.1	18.0	31.6	14.9	12.2	19.9	34.3	12.5	10.1	16.2	29.1
1984	13.1	11.0	15.5	29.8	14.0	11.9	16.8	30.6	12.3	10.1	14.3	29.0
1985	12.6	10.4	15.2	27.6	13.4	11.1	16.1	29.9	11.8	9.8	14.3	25.2
1986	12.2	9.7	14.2	30.1	13.1	10.3	15.0	32.8	11.4	9.1	13.5	27.2
1987	12.6	10.4	14.1	28.6	13.2	10.8	15.0	29.1	12.1	10.0	13.3	28.1
1988	12.9	9.6	14.5	35.8	13.5	10.3	15.0	36.0	12.2	8.9	14.0	35.4
1989	12.6	9.4	13.9	33.0	13.6	10.3	14.9	34.4	11.7	8.5	13.0	31.6
1990	12.1	9.0	13.2	32.4	12.3	9.3	11.9	34.3	11.8	8.7	14.4	30.3
1991	12.5	8.9	13.6	35.3	13.0	8.9	13.5	39.2	11.9	8.9	13.7	31.1
1992[d]	11.0	7.7	13.7	29.4	11.3	8.0	12.5	32.1	10.7	7.4	14.8	26.6
1993[d]	11.0	7.9	13.6	27.5	11.2	8.2	12.6	28.1	10.9	7.6	14.4	26.9
1994[d]	11.4	7.7	12.6	30.0	12.3	8.0	14.1	31.6	10.6	7.5	11.3	28.1
1995[d]	12.0	8.6	12.1	30.0	12.2	9.0	11.1	30.0	11.7	8.2	12.9	30.0
1996[d]	11.1	7.3	13.0	29.4	11.4	7.3	13.5	30.3	10.9	7.3	12.5	28.3
1997[d]	11.0	7.6	13.4	25.3	11.9	8.5	13.3	27.0	10.1	6.7	13.5	23.4
1998[d]	11.8	7.7	13.8	29.5	13.3	8.6	15.5	33.5	10.3	6.9	12.2	25.0
1999[d]	11.2	7.3	12.6	28.6	11.9	7.7	12.1	31.0	10.5	6.9	13.0	26.0
2000[d]	10.9	6.9	13.1	27.8	12.0	7.0	15.3	31.8	9.9	6.9	11.1	23.5
2001[d]	10.7	7.3	10.9	27.0	12.2	7.9	13.0	31.6	9.3	6.7	9.0	22.1
2002[d]	10.5	6.5	11.3	25.7	11.8	6.7	12.8	29.6	9.2	6.3	9.9	21.2
2003[d, e]	9.9	6.3	10.9	23.5	11.3	7.1	12.5	26.7	8.4	5.6	9.5	20.1
2004[d, e]	10.3	6.8	11.8	23.8	11.6	7.1	13.5	28.5	9.0	6.4	10.2	18.5

—Not available.

[a]Includes other racial/ethnic categories not separately shown.

[b]Based on the April 1960 decennial census.

[c]White and black include persons of Hispanic origin.

[d]Because of changes in data collection procedures, data may not be comparable with figures for years prior to 1992.

[e]White, non-Hispanic and black, non-Hispanic categories exclude persons identifying themselves as more than one race.

Notes: "Status" dropouts are 16- to 24-year-olds who are not enrolled in school and who have not completed a high school program regardless of when they left school. People who have received GED credentials are counted as high school completers. All data except for 1960 are based on October counts. Data are based on sample surveys of the civilian noninstitutionalized population.

SOURCE: "Table 105. Percentage of High School Dropouts (Status Dropouts) among Persons 16 to 24 Years Old, by Sex and Race/Ethnicity: 1960 through 2004," in *Digest of Education Statistics, 2005*, U.S. Department of Education, National Center for Education Statistics, July 2006, http://nces.ed.gov/pubs2006/2006030_2b.pdf (accessed February 28, 2007)

• Upon parental request, states and school districts must provide transportation for homeless children to the school they attended before they became homeless.

• School districts must designate a local liaison for homeless children and youths.

HOMESCHOOLED CHILDREN. A number of parents, unhappy with public schools, teach their children at home. According to data from *Homeschooling in the United States: 2003* (February 2006, http://nces.ed.gov/pubs2006/2006042.pdf), the NCES estimates that approximately 850,000, or 1.7% of school-age children, were being homeschooled in the spring of 1999. By 2003 that number had risen to 1.1 million students, or 2.2% of school-age children.

Parents choose to homeschool their children for a variety of reasons. Almost a third (31%) of the homeschooling parents surveyed in the 2003 NCES National Household Education Survey said the most important reason they chose to homeschool was concern about the environment of the other schools. (See Figure 6.5.) Another 30% said they chose to homeschool to provide religious or moral instruction. The third most common

TABLE 6.5

Number of children with disabilities who were served by federal programs, as a percentage of total public K–12 enrollment, by type of disability, selected school years 1976–77 to 2003–04

Type of disability	Number served as a percent of total enrollment[a]														
	1976–77	1980–81	1990–91	1992–93	1993–94	1994–95	1995–96	1996–97	1997–98	1998–99	1999–2000	2000–01	2001–02	2002–03	2003–04
All disabilities	8.3	10.1	11.4	11.8	12.0	12.2	12.4	12.6	12.8	13.0	13.2	13.3	13.4	13.5	13.7
Specific learning disabilities	1.8	3.6	5.2	5.5	5.5	5.6	5.8	5.8	5.9	6.0	6.0	6.0	6.0	5.9	5.8
Speech or language impairments	2.9	2.9	2.4	2.3	2.3	2.3	2.3	2.3	2.3	2.3	2.3	2.3	2.3	2.9	3.0
Mental retardation	2.2	2.0	1.3	1.2	1.2	1.3	1.3	1.3	1.3	1.3	1.3	1.3	1.2	1.2	1.2
Emotional disturbance	0.6	0.8	0.9	0.9	1.0	1.0	1.0	1.0	1.0	1.0	1.0	1.0	1.0	1.0	1.0
Hearing impairments	0.2	0.2	0.1	0.1	0.1	0.1	0.1	0.1	0.1	0.2	0.1	0.1	0.1	0.2	0.2
Orthopedic impairments	0.2	0.1	0.1	0.1	0.2	0.2	0.1	0.1	0.1	0.1	0.2	0.2	0.2	0.2	0.2
Other health impairments	0.3	0.2	0.1	0.2	0.2	0.2	0.3	0.4	0.4	0.5	0.5	0.6	0.7	0.8	1.0
Visual impairments	0.1	0.1	0.1	0.1	0.1	0.1	0.1	0.1	0.1	0.1	0.1	0.1	0.1	0.1	0.1
Multiple disabilities	—	0.2	0.2	0.2	0.2	0.2	0.2	0.2	0.2	0.2	0.2	0.3	0.3	0.3	0.3
Deaf-blindness	—	#	#	#	#	#	#	#	#	#	#	#	#	#	#
Autism and traumatic brain injury	—	—	—	#	0.1	0.1	0.1	0.1	0.1	0.1	0.2	0.2	0.2	0.3	0.4
Developmental delay	—	—	—	—	—	—	—	—	#	#	#	0.1	0.1	0.6	0.6
Preschool disabled[b]	—	—	0.9	1.1	1.1	1.2	1.2	1.2	1.2	1.2	1.2	1.3	1.3	†	†

—Not available.
†Not applicable.
#Rounds to zero.

[a]Based on the total enrollment in public schools, prekindergarten through 12th grade.

[b]Includes preschool children ages 3–5 served under Chapter 1 and IDEA, Part B. Prior to 1987–88, these students were included in the counts by disability condition. Beginning in 1987–88, states were no longer required to report preschool children (ages 0–5) by disability condition. Beginning in 2002–03, preschool children were again identified by disability condition.

Notes: Includes students served under Chapter 1 and Individuals with Disabilities Education Act (IDEA), formerly the Education of the Handicapped Act. Prior to October 1994, children and youth with disabilities were served under the Individuals with Disabilities Education Act, Part B, and Chapter 1 of the Elementary and Secondary Education Act. In October 1994, Congress passed the Improving America's Schools Act, in which funding for children and youth with disabilities was consolidated under IDEA, Part B. Data reported in this table for years prior to 1993–94 include children ages 0–21 served under Chapter 1. Counts are based on reports from the 50 states and the District of Columbia only (i.e., figures from other jurisdictions are not included). Increases since 1987–88 are due in part to new legislation enacted in fall 1986, which mandates public school special education services for all disabled children ages 3 through 5, in addition to age groups previously mandated. Some data have been revised from previously published figures. Detail may not sum to totals because of rounding.

SOURCE: Adapted from "Table 50. Children 3 to 21 Years Old Served in Federally Supported Programs for the Disabled, by Type of Disability: Selected Years, 1976–77 through 2003–04," in *Digest of Education Statistics, 2005*, U.S. Department of Education, National Center for Education Statistics, July 2006, http://nces.ed.gov/pubs2006/2006030_2a.pdf (accessed February 28, 2007)

FIGURE 6.5

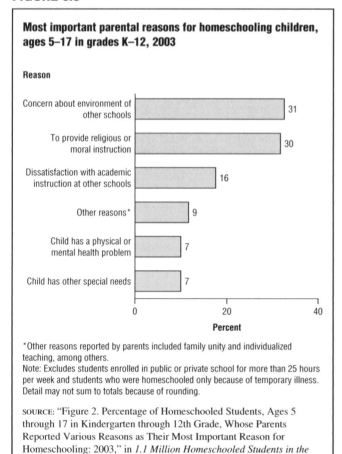

Most important parental reasons for homeschooling children, ages 5–17 in grades K–12, 2003

*Other reasons reported by parents included family unity and individualized teaching, among others.

Note: Excludes students enrolled in public or private school for more than 25 hours per week and students who were homeschooled only because of temporary illness. Detail may not sum to totals because of rounding.

SOURCE: "Figure 2. Percentage of Homeschooled Students, Ages 5 through 17 in Kindergarten through 12th Grade, Whose Parents Reported Various Reasons as Their Most Important Reason for Homeschooling: 2003," in *1.1 Million Homeschooled Students in the United States in 2003,* U.S. Department of Education, National Center for Education Statistics, July 2004, http://nces.ed.gov/pubs2004/2004115.pdf (accessed March 12, 2007)

reason parents gave for homeschooling was dissatisfaction with the academic instruction available at other schools (16%).

States have differing requirements for parents who teach their children at home. According to the Home School Legal Defense Association, some states, such as Idaho and New Jersey, give parents the right to educate their children as they see fit and impose only minor controls or none at all. Other states have more strict regulations. Highly regulated states, such as New York, Vermont, Pennsylvania, and a few others, require parents to get curriculum approved, send achievement test scores, or meet qualification requirements. Opponents of homeschooling argue that parents may not be qualified to be teachers, but proponents believe that parents can gain teaching skills through experience, just as other teachers do.

HIGHER EDUCATION—OFF TO COLLEGE

Formal schooling beyond high school is increasingly being viewed as a necessity, not only to a young person's development but also to his or her economic success. Many parents consider helping their children attend college to be an important financial responsibility.

College Entrance Examinations

Most students who wish to enter colleges and universities in the United States must take either the SAT (once known as the Scholastic Aptitude Test, then the Scholastic Assessment Test, now simply the SAT I) or the American College Test (ACT) as part of their admission requirements. The ACT is a curriculum-based achievement test that measures proficiency in reading, math, English, and science, whereas the SAT is a primary admissions test that measures a student's mathematical and verbal reasoning ability in a way intended to assess readiness for college. Students who take these tests usually plan to continue their education beyond high school; therefore, these tests do not profile all high school students.

MORE ARE TAKING SAT AND ACT EXAMS, WITH MIXED RESULTS. The number of students who take both the SAT and the ACT has grown steadily. The College Board notes in *2006 College-Bound Seniors* (2006, http://www.collegeboard.com/prod_downloads/about/news_info/cbsenior/yr2006/national-report.pdf) that in 2006 nearly 1.5 million students took the SAT. This represents an increase of 50% over the number who took the test in 1975 (996,000). According to ACT, Inc. (2007, http://www.act.org/news/aapfacts.html), the number of students taking the ACT increased over the same period, from 714,000 in 1975 to 1.2 million in 2006, an increase of 68%. In *State of College Admission 2006, Executive Summary* (May 2006, http://www.nacacnet.org/NR/rdonlyres/78BCFBFB-6871-4FCA-B1BF-50E330735706/0/06SOCA_Executive Summarypdf.pdf), the National Association for College Admission Counseling indicates that 73% of colleges reported significant increases in the number of applicants in 2005 over the previous year, as well. Students are either applying to a larger number of schools or, as the increased numbers taking the SAT and ACT suggest, more high school graduates are pursuing a college education.

Performance on the SAT is measured on a scale of two hundred to eight hundred for each of three sections, with the established average score being around five hundred for each. According to *2006 College-Bound Seniors*, over the period from 1972 to 2006, the average critical reading scores on the SAT declined from 530 to 503. The results for the math portion of the SAT, however, dropped and then rebounded over the same period, from 509 in 1972 to 518 in 2006. Writing was tested for the first time in 2006; test takers received an average score of 497. The average ACT scores also improved; in 1970 the average composite ACT score was 19.9, and in 2006 the average composite score was 21.1.

CHARACTERISTICS OF TEST TAKERS. *2006 College-Bound Seniors* notes that more women than men took the tests in 2006—53.6% of those who took the SAT were women. More women than men have taken the SAT since the 1970s as well. Men, on average, scored higher on both the critical reading and the math portions of the SAT test in 2006 (average scores of 505 and 536, respectively) compared with women (502 in each section). However, women scored higher on the writing section than men did (502 and 491, respectively).

According to the *2006 College-Bound Seniors*, the favorite intended areas of study or future career choice among those who took the SAT in order of preference were health related (18%), business (15%), and social science/history (9%). Areas in which students taking the ACT hoped to pursue future studies were similar to those reported for takers of the SAT. However, the ACT notes in "2006 ACT National Score Report News Release" (August 16, 2006, http://www.act.org/news/releases/2006/ndr.html) that even though the top planned college major was health sciences, only 27% of ACT test takers reached the college readiness benchmark on the science test.

Despite improvements in the scores of minority students, most lagged behind those of non-Hispanic white students. According to *2006 College-Bound Seniors*, in 2006 white students scored a mean of 527 on critical reading, 536 on math, and 519 on writing on the SAT. African-Americans scored an average of 434 on critical reading, 429 on math, and 428 on writing, the lowest average scores of any racial or ethnic group. Mexican-Americans scored an average of 454 on critical reading, 465 on math, and 452 on writing; Puerto Ricans scored 459 on critical reading, 456 on math, and 448 on writing; and other Hispanics scored 458 on critical reading, 463 on math, and 450 on writing. Native Americans and Alaskan Natives scored 487 on critical reading, 494 on math, and 474 on writing. Asians and Pacific Islanders scored an average of 510 on critical reading, 578 on math, and 512 on writing.

According to the 2006 *ACT High School Profile Report* (2006, http://www.act.org/news/data/06/pdf/National2006.pdf), results on the ACT in 2006 show that Asian-Americans and Pacific Islanders scored an average of 22.3, non-Hispanic whites scored an average of 22, Native Americans and Alaskan Natives scored an average of 18.8, Hispanics scored an average of 18.6, and African-American students scored an average of 17.1. Even though scores for all groups were up since 2002, in "ACT Scores Hold Steady in 2003" (http://www.act.org/activity/autumn2003/scores.html), Richard L. Ferguson notes, "Our research has shown that far too many African American students are not being adequately prepared for college. They are less likely than others to take rigorous, college-preparatory courses, and they often don't receive the information and guidance they need to properly plan for college." ACT data for 2006 show that fewer minority test takers had taken the core college-preparatory coursework and that groups that had taken more core coursework, such as non-Hispanic whites and Asian-Americans, tended to score higher on the ACT.

FIGURE 6.6

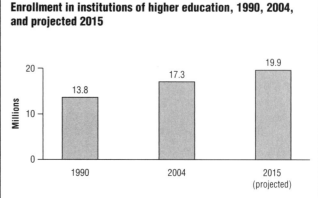

Enrollment in institutions of higher education, 1990, 2004, and projected 2015

SOURCE: William J. Hussar and Tabitha M. Bailey, "Figure C. Actual and Middle Alternative Projected Numbers for Total Enrollment in Degree-Granting Institutions: Selected Years, 1990–2015," in *Projections of Education Statistics to 2015*, 34th ed., U.S. Department of Education, National Center for Education Statistics, September 2006, http://nces.ed.gov/pubs2006/2006084.pdf (accessed February 28, 2007)

Projected Enrollment

Enrollment in institutions of higher education is expected to rise through 2015, due not only to large numbers of children of baby boomers approaching college age but also to the increasing numbers of people of all ages seeking advanced learning. Enrollment in degree-granting postsecondary institutions stood at 17.3 million in 2004 and is expected to reach 19.9 million by 2015. (See Figure 6.6.)

College Costs

Paying for a college education, even at public four-year institutions, now ranks as one of the most costly investments for American families. The NCES reports in *Digest of Education Statistics, 2005* that in the 2004–05 school year the average annual in-state cost at a four-year public college, including tuition and room and board, was $11,441. For one year at a private four-year college, the average cost for tuition and room and board was $26,489. Public college tuition varied widely among states, from $2,070 in the District of Columbia to $8,771 in Vermont. Most states with the highest tuition were in the Northeast and most with the lowest tuition were in the South and West.

FINANCIAL ASSISTANCE FOR STUDENTS. According to the NCES, during the 2003–04 academic year almost two-thirds (63.2%) of nineteen million undergraduates enrolled in postsecondary institutions received some type of financial aid from federal, state, institutional, or other sources to meet their educational expenses. About half (48%) of undergraduates received some form of federal aid. More than half (50.7%) of all students received grants (which do not have to be paid back), about a third (35.2%) took out loans (which do have to be paid back), and 7.5% were on work-study programs. Federal assistance that goes directly to students includes Pell Grants (the annual maximum was increased to $4,310 for the 2007–08 award year), the Stafford Student Loan Program (a maximum loan of $19,000 for four years of study for dependent undergraduate students), and Supplemental Education Opportunity Grants (which can range from $100 to $4,000 per year).

The NCES indicates that during the 2003–04 school year 62.7% of dependent undergraduate students whose families earned less than $20,000 per year and 77.8% of students whose families earned between $20,000 and $39,999 per year received financial aid. However, because of the high cost of college, students even in high income brackets received financial aid to help pay for college; 60.5% of dependent undergraduate students whose families earned $100,000 or more received some form of financial aid.

EDUCATIONAL ATTAINMENT AND EARNINGS

The educational attainment of the U.S. population has risen steadily since the 1940s. In 2003, 84.6% of adults older than the age of twenty-five had graduated from high school—the highest number ever. (See Figure 6.7.) More than one in four (27.2%) had earned a bachelor's degree or more.

The level of educational attainment has traditionally been higher for men than for women. In 2003, however, for the second year in a row, the high school graduation rate for women aged twenty-five and over (85%) exceeded that of men (84.1%). (See Table 6.6.) The 2002 difference was the first statistically significant one in high school graduation rates between men and women since 1989. In 2003, 28.9% of men and 25.7% of women had obtained bachelor's degrees or higher. Although college attainment had increased since 1990 for both men and women, women are narrowing the gap and making faster gains then men.

Educational attainment also varies by race and ethnic origin. In 2003 non-Hispanic whites were most likely to complete high school (89.4%), followed by Asians (87.6%), African-Americans (80%), and Hispanics (57%). (See Table 6.6.) Asians were by far the most likely to be college graduates (49.8%), followed by non-Hispanic whites (30%), African-Americans (17.3%), and Hispanics (11.4%).

Education is a good investment, because earning levels rise with increased education. For people aged eighteen or older who had not finished high school, the average annual income in 2002 (the latest year for which data were available) was $18,826. (See Table 6.7.) High school graduates earned an average income of $27,280 in

2002, and people with some college or an associate degree earned an average income of $31,046. The incomes of college graduates increased with the level of the degree earned. People with a bachelor's degree had mean annual earnings of $51,194, whereas holders of advanced degrees earned an average of $72,824 in 2002.

These averages differed considerably by gender and race or ethnicity. On average, for all educational attainment levels, women earned $27,271, or $0.62 for every dollar men earned. (See Table 6.7.) Compared with their male counterparts, the most highly educated women earned $50,756, or $0.56 for every dollar the men earned. The disparity between races and ethnic groups was not as pronounced. Annual earnings for high school graduates ranged from $28,756 for non-Hispanic whites to $22,823 for African-Americans. For college graduates, earnings ranged from $40,949 for Hispanics to $53,185 for non-Hispanic whites.

FIGURE 6.7

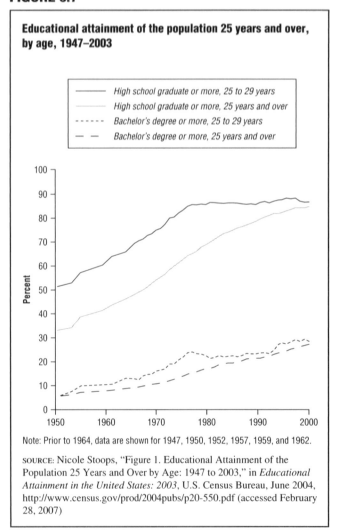

Educational attainment of the population 25 years and over, by age, 1947–2003

Note: Prior to 1964, data are shown for 1947, 1950, 1952, 1957, 1959, and 1962.

SOURCE: Nicole Stoops, "Figure 1. Educational Attainment of the Population 25 Years and Over by Age: 1947 to 2003," in *Educational Attainment in the United States: 2003*, U.S. Census Bureau, June 2004, http://www.census.gov/prod/2004pubs/p20-550.pdf (accessed February 28, 2007)

TABLE 6.6

Educational attainment of the population 25 years and over by demographic characteristics, 2003

Characteristic	Number of people (in thousands)	High school graduate or more — Percent	Some college or more — Percent	Bachelor's degree or more — Percent
Population 25 years and over	185,183	84.6	52.5	27.2
Age group:				
25 to 29 years	18,721	86.5	57.4	28.4
30 to 34 years	20,521	87.6	58.6	31.5
35 to 39 years	21,284	87.6	56.5	29.8
40 to 44 years	22,790	88.4	56.5	29.1
45 to 49 years	21,420	89.3	57.4	29.9
50 to 54 years	18,814	88.7	58.9	31.1
55 to 59 years	15,470	86.9	55.1	29.0
60 to 64 years	11,930	83.0	47.3	24.5
65 to 69 years	9,438	76.9	39.1	19.6
70 to 74 years	8,673	72.8	36.4	18.5
75 years and over	16,123	67.5	32.4	15.4
Sex:				
Men	88,597	84.1	53.2	28.9
Women	96,586	85.0	51.9	25.7
Race and origin:				
White alone	153,188	85.1	52.9	27.6
Non-Hispanic white alone	133,488	89.4	56.4	30.0
Black alone	20,527	80.0	44.7	17.3
Asian alone	7,691	87.6	67.4	49.8
Hispanic (of any race)	21,189	57.0	29.6	11.4
Nativity:				
Native	158,128	87.5	54.2	27.2
Foreign born	27,055	67.2	42.7	27.2
Marital status:				
Never married	28,694	84.9	54.8	29.0
Married spouse present	113,748	87.0	55.9	30.5
Married spouse absent	7,389	72.5	38.2	16.1
Separated	4,447	74.5	38.6	13.8
Widowed	13,970	67.2	30.3	12.5
Divorced	21,382	86.5	50.9	21.0
Region:				
Northeast	36,182	85.7	50.7	30.3
Midwest	41,728	87.8	52.5	26.0
South	66,071	82.2	50.1	25.3
West	41,202	84.0	58.1	28.7

SOURCE: Nicole Stoops, "Table A. Summary Measures of the Educational Attainment of the Population 25 Years and Over: 2003," in *Educational Attainment in the United States: 2003*, U.S. Census Bureau, June 2004, http://www.census.gov/prod/2004pubs/p20-550.pdf (accessed February 28, 2007)

TABLE 6.7

Average earnings by educational attainment, sex, race, and Hispanic origin for all workers, age 18 and over, 2002

Characteristic	Total	Not a high school graduate	High school graduate	Some college or associate's degree	Bachelor's degree	Advanced degree
Total	$36,308	$18,826	$27,280	$31,046	$51,194	$72,824
Men	$44,310	$22,091	$32,673	$38,377	$63,503	$90,761
Women	$27,271	$13,459	$21,141	$23,905	$37,909	$50,756
White alone	$37,376	$19,264	$28,145	$31,878	$52,479	$73,870
Non-Hispanic white alone	$39,220	$19,423	$28,756	$32,318	$53,185	$74,122
Black alone	$28,179	$16,516	$22,823	$27,626	$42,285	$59,944
Asian alone	$40,793	$16,746	$24,900	$27,340	$46,628	$72,852
Hispanic (of any race)	$25,824	$18,981	$24,163	$27,757	$40,949	$67,679

SOURCE: Nicole Stoops, "Table C. Average Earnings in 2002 by Educational Attainment, Sex, Race, and Hispanic Origin for All Workers, 18 Years and Over," in *Educational Attainment in the United States: 2003*, U.S. Census Bureau, June 2004, http://www.census.gov/prod/2004pubs/p20-550.pdf (accessed February 28, 2007)

CHAPTER 7
JUVENILE CRIME AND VICTIMIZATION

THE UNIFORM CRIME REPORTS AND THE NATIONAL CRIME VICTIMIZATION SURVEY

Two main government sources collect crime statistics. The Federal Bureau of Investigation (FBI) compiles the Uniform Crime Reports (UCR) annually. The FBI reports in *Crime in the United States 2005* (September 2006, http://www.fbi.gov/ucr/05cius/index.html) that the UCR, which was begun in 1930, now collects data from nearly seventeen thousand city, county, and state law enforcement agencies.

The second set of crime statistics is the National Crime Victimization Survey (NCVS), which is prepared by the Bureau of Justice Statistics (BJS). Established in 1972, the survey is an annual federal statistical study that measures the levels of victimization resulting from criminal activity in the United States. The BJS notes in "BJS Criminal Victimization Data Collections" (December 10, 2006, http://www.ojp.usdoj.gov/bjs/cvict.htm#Programs) that the survey collects data from a nationally representative sample of 77,200 households each year, which contain about 134,000 people, on the "frequency, characteristics and consequences of criminal victimization." The survey was previously known as the National Crime Survey, but it was renamed and redesigned in 1992 to emphasize the measurement of victimization experienced by citizens. The survey was created because of a concern that the UCR did not fully portray the true volume of crime. The UCR provides data on crimes reported to law enforcement authorities, but it does not estimate how many crimes went unreported.

The NCVS is designed to complement the UCR. It measures the levels of criminal victimization of people and households for the crimes of rape, robbery, assault, burglary, motor vehicle theft, and larceny. Murder is not included because the NCVS data are gathered through interviews with victims. Definitions for these crimes are the same as those established by the UCR.

Some observers believe the NCVS is a better indicator of the volume of crime in the United States than the UCR. Nonetheless, like all surveys, it is subject to error. The survey depends on people's memories of incidents that happened up to six months earlier. Many times, a victim is not sure what happened, even moments after the crime occurred. In addition, the NCVS limits the data to victims aged twelve and older, an admittedly arbitrary age selection.

CRIME TRENDS
Violent and Property Crimes

Shannan M. Catalano of the NCVS reports in *Criminal Victimization, 2005* (September 2006, http://www.ojp.usdoj.gov/bjs/pub/pdf/cv05.pdf) that in 2005 U.S. residents experienced about 23 million violent and property victimizations. Of these crimes, 18 million were property crimes (burglary, motor vehicle theft, and theft), 5.2 million were violent crimes (rape or sexual assault, robbery, aggravated assault, and simple assault), and 227,000 were personal thefts (pocket picking and purse snatching). The rate of theft was down from the year before, but the rate of every other type of crime remained unchanged.

Catalano notes that between 2002 and 2003 and between 2004 and 2005 the average yearly rate of violent crimes per 1,000 people aged twelve or older remained essentially unchanged for all age groups except for sixteen- to nineteen-year-olds. Among this age group, 55.6 per 1,000 people were victims of violent crimes between 2002 and 2003; this rate declined to 45 per 1,000 people between 2004 and 2005, a 19% decrease. Even though violent crimes for the most part remained stable between 2004 and 2005, between 1993 and 2005 the violent crime rate was down 58%.

The UCR reports that most violent crimes—including murder, nonnegligent manslaughter, forcible rape, robbery, and aggravated assault—remained fairly steady between 2004 and 2005, except for forcible rape, which decreased 1.2% between 2004 and 2005. The UCR also records decreasing violent crime rates over time. The violent crime rate had decreased from 620.1 per 100,000 people in 1986 to 469.2 per 100,000 in 2005.

According to the UCR, there were an estimated 10.2 million property crimes, including burglary, larceny-theft, and motor vehicle theft, in 2005. Property crime rates decreased by 1.5% between 2004 and 2005. This decline continued a long-term trend; property crime rates in 2005 were down 13.9% from 1996. In 2005 the property crime rate was 3,429.8 per 100,000 people, compared with a rate of 4,881.8 per 100,000 in 1986.

Trends in Juvenile Crime

According to the FBI, from the mid-1980s through the mid-1990s youth violence and crime grew at rapid rates. In *Juvenile Offenders and Victims: 2006 National Report* (March 2006, http://www.ojjdp.ncjrs.gov/ojstatbb/nr2006/downloads/NR2006.pdf), Howard N. Snyder and Melissa Sickmund of the National Center for Juvenile Justice examine juvenile homicide trends. They find that between 1980 and 1997 murders by juveniles were highest in 1993 and 1994. In murders involving juvenile offenders during this eighteen-year span, most involved a lone offender, but 39% featured two or more offenders.

The surge in youth crime and violence caused much concern in society. Various groups—both public and private—undertook the mission of trying to uncover the reasons juvenile crime was on the rise. Lawmakers responded by toughening existing laws and finding ways to try more juveniles as adults. Courts levied stricter sentences, and parents and educators looked into various programs and methods geared to help their children and students deal with the situation.

However, the rise in juvenile crime did not last. Snyder and Sickmund note that in the ten-year period between 1994 and 2003, juvenile arrests decreased by 18%, compared with a 1% increase in arrests of adults during the same period. The arrest rate of juveniles for murder in 2003 was the lowest since at least 1980. Snyder and Sickmund state that "the juvenile violent crime wave predicted by some in the mid-1990s has not occurred."

JUVENILE OFFENDERS

For some young people, their teenage and young adult years are difficult and challenging times. Even though their peers are playing baseball, going to proms, singing in the school choir, heading to college, and making plans for the future, some juveniles and youths are, for whatever reason, committing crimes. When dealing with young offenders, each state has its own definition of

the term *juvenile*: Most states put the upper age limit at seventeen years old, although some states set it as low as fourteen years old. When reporting its national crime statistics, the FBI considers those under the age of eighteen to be juveniles. The FBI often breaks its juvenile crime statistics into age-based subcategories, such as age sixteen or older and age fifteen or younger, to demonstrate how juvenile offenses vary with age. The FBI does the same with youth, who are often defined as ages eighteen to twenty-four. However, some organizations and studies classify youth age ranges differently, citing youths as those ages eighteen to twenty-one or ages eighteen to twenty-five.

The U.S. Department of Justice defines crime as all behaviors and acts for which society provides formally approved punishments. Written law, both federal and state, defines which behaviors are criminal and which are not. Some behaviors—murder, robbery, and burglary—have always been considered criminal. Other actions, such as domestic violence or driving under the influence of drugs or alcohol, became classified as criminal actions more recently. Other changes in society have also influenced crime. For example, the widespread use of computers provides new opportunities for white-collar cybercrime, including identity theft and the malicious spread of computer viruses and worms.

Crime can range from actions as simple as taking a candy bar from a store without paying for it, to those as severe and violent as murder. Most people have broken some law, wittingly or unwittingly, at some time in their lives. Therefore, the true extent of criminality is impossible to measure. Researchers can only keep records of what is reported by victims or known to the police.

Risk Factors for Youth Violence

Various government entities, schools, student and parent organizations, and research groups have devoted countless hours to the issue of youth violence. One of their goals is to find ways to recognize the potential for violent behavior in youth before it becomes a serious problem. They work individually and sometimes collectively to outline trends in youth violence and to determine what factors lead to violent behavior.

The Centers for Disease Control and Prevention, in "Youth Violence: Fact Sheet" (April 19, 2007, http://www.cdc.gov/ncipc/factsheets/yvfacts.htm), outlines risk factors that increase the likelihood that a young person will become violent. These factors include individual risk factors, such as a history of violent victimization, certain mental health problems, substance abuse, emotional distress, and exposure to violence within the family; family risk factors, including parenting styles that are authoritarian, harsh, inconsistent, lax, or parental substance abuse or criminality; peer/school risk factors, including involvement in gangs or with delinquent peers, social rejection, and poor school performance; and community risk factors, including a high concentration of poverty, family disruption, transiency, and social disorganization. Factors that make it less likely that a young person will engage in criminal or violent behavior (protective factors) include intelligence, positive social interactions, connectedness to family and other adults, consistent parental involvement, and a commitment to school.

In "Warning Signs of Youth Violence" (2004, http://www.apahelpcenter.org/featuredtopics/feature.php?id=38&ch=3), the American Psychological Association lists immediate signs that youth violence is a serious possibility as well as signs over a period of time that indicate a potential for violence. Signs that violence may be imminent include a frequent loss of temper or physical fighting, vandalism, an increase in substance use or risk-taking behavior, development of plans to commit violence, enjoying hurting animals, or carrying a weapon. The potential for violence exists when a young person has a history of aggressive behavior or substance abuse, has a strong desire to be in a gang or gang membership, has a fascination with weapons, begins to withdraw from friends and usual activities, performs poorly in school, fails to respect the feelings or rights of others, or has a history of discipline problems.

In response to the Columbine High School shootings in 1999, the U.S. Surgeon General began a comprehensive study of the status of youth and violence in the nation. Issued in 2001, *Youth Violence: A Report of the Surgeon General* (http://www.surgeongeneral.gov/library/youthviolence/) addresses many aspects of crime and violence, including risk factors for violence among youth aged fifteen to eighteen. The report contains detailed information on early onset factors (ages six to eleven), which include exposure to violence on television and substance abuse, as well as late onset factors (ages twelve to fourteen), which include aggression in general, antisocial attitudes, and abusive parents.

Those involved in the study of youth violence are quick to point out, however, that people need to be cautious when reacting to someone exhibiting warning signs. Although it is important to provide help to youth with violent tendencies, harm could be caused by mislabeling a student as being violent or by overreacting to a set of circumstances.

Juvenile violent behavior is more likely to occur at certain times of day than at other times. Snyder and Sickmund find that violent crime, including murder, violent sexual assault, robbery, aggravated assault, and simple assault, is most likely to be committed in the after school hours on school days for juvenile offenders, peaking around 3 p.m. In comparison, adult offenders are most likely to commit violent crimes between 9 p.m. and midnight. (See Figure 7.1.) These findings point out the relative ineffectiveness of some measures meant to curtail youth violence, especially the adoption of curfews. (See Chapter 10.)

FIGURE 7.1

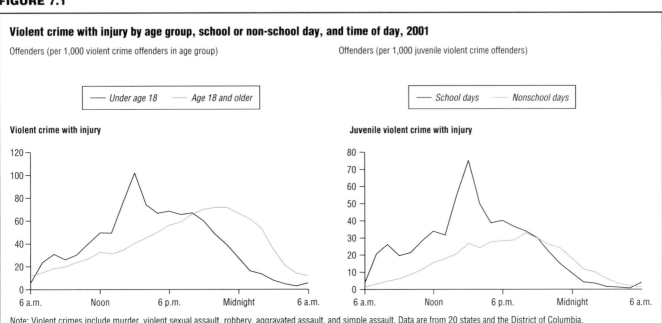

Violent crime with injury by age group, school or non-school day, and time of day, 2001

Note: Violent crimes include murder, violent sexual assault, robbery, aggravated assault, and simple assault. Data are from 20 states and the District of Columbia.

SOURCE: Howard N. Snyder and Melissa Sickmund, "Violent Crime that Results in Injury to the Victim is Most Likely in the Afterschool Hours on School Days for Juvenile Offenders, Between 9 p.m. and Midnight for Adult Offenders," in *Juvenile Offenders and Victims: 2006 National Report*, U.S. Department of Justice, Office of Justice Programs, Office of Juvenile Justice and Delinquency Prevention, March 2006, http://www.ojjdp.ncjrs.gov/ojstatbb/nr2006/downloads/NR2006.pdf (accessed March 2, 2007)

Homicide

The UCR defines murder and nonnegligent manslaughter as "the willful (nonnegligent) killing of one human being by another." The figures do not include "deaths caused by negligence, suicide, or accident; justifiable homicides; and attempts to murder or assaults to murder, which are scored as aggravated assaults." According to the UCR, approximately 16,692 murders occurred in 2005. Although this represented a 3.4% increase from 2004, murders were down about 15% in the United States since 1996.

Over 17,000 people were identified as murder offenders in 2005, including 866 males and 76 females under the age of eighteen, and 3,322 males and 284 females under the age of twenty-two. (See Table 7.1.) Because the identity of all murder offenders is not known, such figures are lower than they would be if all offenders had been identified. Those under age eighteen represented only 6% of all murder offenders in that year, whereas those under age twenty-two represented 21% of all murder offenders. Fewer than one out of ten of all known murderers were female; 92% of all murder offenders under age eighteen and 92% of all murder offenders under age twenty-two were males. Arrests of youth under age eighteen for murder rose 19.9% between 2004 and 2005.

In 2005, 32% of all murderers were known to be white, over 37% were African-American, and almost 29% were of unknown race. (See Table 7.1.) These proportions were similar for juvenile murderers. Among youth under age eighteen, 552 murder offenders were African-American (58%), 356 were white (38%), and 5 were unknown (0.5%). Among youth under age twenty-two, 2,084 were African-American (58%), 1,382 were white (38%), and 30 were unknown (0.8%).

LAW ENFORCEMENT OFFICERS KILLED. In *Law Enforcement Officers Killed and Assaulted, 2005* (October 2006, http://www.fbi.gov/ucr/killed/2005/), the UCR provides statistics on the number of law enforcement officers feloniously killed between 1996 and 2005. During this ten-year period 662 officers were killed—the highest number (85) occurred in 1996. In 2005, 57 officers were feloniously killed. Youth under age eighteen were responsible for 6% of the officers killed in the decade, whereas young adults aged eighteen to twenty-four were responsible for over a third (38.9%) of the murders.

TABLE 7.1

Murder offenders by age, sex, and race, 2005

Age	Total	Sex			Race			
		Male	Female	Unknown	White	Black	Other	Unknown
Total	17,029	11,117	1,246	4,666	5,452	6,379	299	4,899
Percent distribution[a]	100	65.3	7.3	27.4	32	37.6	2	28.8
Under 18[b]	944	866	76	2	356	552	31	5
Under 22[b]	3,611	3,322	284	5	1,382	2,084	115	30
18 and over[b]	10,354	9,195	1,141	18	4,911	5,046	258	139
Infant (under 1)	0	0	0	0	0	0	0	0
1 to 4	0	0	0	0	0	0	0	0
5 to 8	0	0	0	0	0	0	0	0
9 to 12	11	7	4	0	6	5	0	0
13 to 16	467	426	41	0	176	272	17	2
17 to 19	1,801	1,676	123	2	654	1,075	59	13
20 to 24	3,016	2,751	262	3	1,243	1,657	80	36
25 to 29	1,935	1,727	206	2	859	1,005	44	27
30 to 34	1,090	933	156	1	531	518	26	15
35 to 39	873	750	123	0	491	348	20	14
40 to 44	700	605	95	0	404	270	12	14
45 to 49	586	486	97	3	361	206	13	6
50 to 54	330	286	41	3	197	114	11	8
55 to 59	200	170	30	0	129	65	5	1
60 to 64	100	82	18	0	72	27	0	1
65 to 69	78	70	8	0	61	15	2	0
70 to 74	43	35	8	0	33	10	0	0
75 and over	68	57	5	6	50	11	0	7
Unknown	5,731	1,056	29	4,646	185	781	10	4,755

[a]Because of rounding, the percentages may not add to 100.0.
[b]Does not include unknown ages.

SOURCE: "Expanded Homicide Data Table 3. Murder Offenders by Age, Sex, and Race, 2005," in *Crime in the United States 2005*, U.S. Department of Justice, Federal Bureau of Investigation, September 2006, http://www.fbi.gov/ucr/05cius/offenses/expanded_information/data/shrtable_03.html (accessed March 2, 2007)

Rape

The UCR reports in *Crime in the United States 2005* that even though there were an estimated 93,934 forcible rapes reported in 2005, only 18,733 people were arrested for rape in that year. Rape is one of the most underreported crimes, and the low arrest rate demonstrates how few perpetrators are caught. Of those arrested for rape, 5.6% were under age fifteen, 15.4% were under age eighteen, and 29.8% were under age twenty-one.

Aggravated and Simple Assault

The UCR defines aggravated assault as "an unlawful attack by one person upon another for the purpose of inflicting severe or aggravated bodily injury.... This type of assault is usually accompanied by the use of a weapon or by other means likely to produce death or great bodily harm. Attempted aggravated assault that involves the display of—or threat to use—a gun, knife, or other weapon is included in this crime category because serious personal injury would likely result if the assault were completed." In 2005 an estimated 862,947 aggravated assaults were reported. In its arrest reports, the UCR notes that 331,469 people were arrested for aggravated assault in that year. Of that number, 4.7% were under age fifteen, 13.6% were under age eighteen, and 24.8% were under age twenty-one.

By contrast, simple assaults are assaults or attempted assaults not involving a weapon and not resulting in serious injury to the victim. These include acts such as assault and battery, resisting or obstructing the police, hazing, and so on. In its arrest reports, the UCR lists a category called "other assaults" (to differentiate between these types of assaults and aggravated assaults). The UCR notes that 958,477 people were arrested for other assaults in 2005. Of that number, 7.8% were under age fifteen, 19% were under age eighteen, and 28.7% were under age twenty-one.

Robbery, Burglary, and Theft

Robbery, burglary, and larceny-theft are different crimes under the UCR. Robbery is the taking of something from a person or people with force, the threat of force, or by instilling fear in a victim. Burglary involves the unlawful entry, not requiring force, into a building to commit a felony or theft. Larceny-theft is the unlawful taking of property without using force, including crimes such as shoplifting, pocket picking, purse snatching, thefts from motor vehicles, thefts of motor vehicle parts and accessories, bicycle thefts, and so on. These offenses, taken together, are disproportionately committed by young people.

In 2005 the UCR estimates that 417,122 robbery offenses had been committed, an increase of 3.9% over the previous year. However, robbery offenses had decreased by 22.1% from ten years earlier. In 2005,

85,309 people were arrested for robbery; those arrested were disproportionately young people. Of that number, 5.8% were under age fifteen, 25.2% were under age eighteen, and 46.3% were under age twenty-one.

In 2005 the UCR recorded 2,154,126 burglary offenses, an increase of 0.5% from the previous year but a 14.1% decline from ten years earlier. Burglary has a particularly low arrest rate. The UCR notes that 220,391 people were arrested for burglary in 2005. Of that number, 8.7% of perpetrators were under age fifteen, 26.1% were under age eighteen, and 43.9% were under age twenty-one.

In 2005 the UCR recorded 6.8 million larceny-theft offenses, a decrease of 2.3% from 2004 and a 14.3% decline from ten years earlier. In its arrest reports, the UCR notes that 854,856 people were arrested for larceny-theft in 2005. Of that number, 9% of perpetrators were under age fifteen, 25.7% were under age eighteen, and 40.2% were under age twenty-one.

Motor-vehicle theft is also disproportionately perpetrated by young people, usually in urban areas. In 2005 there were an estimated 1.2 million motor vehicle thefts nationwide. More than nine out of ten (93.3%) motor vehicle thefts occurred in metropolitan areas. In its arrest reports, the UCR notes that 108,301 people were arrested for motor-vehicle theft in 2005. Of those arrested, 5.9% were under age fifteen, 25.5% were under age eighteen, and 42.8% were under age twenty-one.

Computer Crime

Illegally accessing a computer, known as hacking, is a crime committed frequently by juveniles. When it is followed by manipulation of the information of private, corporate, or government databases and networks, it can be quite costly. Another means of computer hacking involves creation of what is known as a virus program. The virus program is one that resides inside another program and then is activated by some predetermined code to create havoc in the host computer. Virus programs can be spread either through the sharing of disks and programs or through e-mail.

Cases of juvenile hacking have been reported since the 1980s. In 1998 the U.S. Secret Service filed the first criminal case against a juvenile for a computer crime. The unnamed hacker shut down the Worcester, Massachusetts, airport in 1997 for six hours. The airport was integrated into the Federal Aviation Administration traffic system by telephone lines. The accused gained access to the communication system and disabled it by sending a series of computer commands that changed the data carried on the system. As a result, the airport could not function. (No accidents occurred during that time, however.) According to the Department of Justice, the juvenile pled guilty in return for two years' probation, a fine, and community service.

Other types of computer crime typically perpetrated by juveniles include trading stolen credit card numbers and pirating of computer software to be sold. Because of computer networks, juveniles and other perpetrators can commit these types of crimes on a large scale. In "It's Not Just Fun and 'War Games'—Juveniles and Computer Crime" (April 26, 2005, http://www.cybercrime.gov/usamay2001_7.htm), Joseph V. DeMarco, the assistant U.S. attorney in the Southern District of New York, states that "the enormous computing power of today's PCs make it possible for minors to commit offenses which are disproportionately serious to their age." Teens can commit property offenses on a large scale using computers, can portray themselves as adults in an online world, and "appear to have an ethical 'deficit' when it comes to computer crimes." He points out that children and teens who would never commit robbery, burglary, or assault may in fact commit online crimes.

Illegal Drug Use

Various studies show that many violent offenders are substance abusers. For some people, drugs and alcohol may cause violent tendencies to surface. In *Monitoring the Future: National Results on Adolescent Drug Use, Overview of Key Findings, 2005* (April 2006, http://www.drugabuse.gov/PDF/overview2005.pdf), University of Michigan researchers Lloyd D. Johnston et al. find that in 2005, 38.4% of twelfth graders, 29.8% of tenth graders, and 15.5% of eighth graders had used an illicit drug in the past year. Among twelfth graders, marijuana/hashish use was highest (33.6%), followed by narcotics (9%), amphetamines (8.6%), barbiturates (7.2%), and tranquilizers (6.8%). (See Table 4.11 in Chapter 4.) More than two-thirds (68.6%) had used alcohol in the past twelve months.

Other drugs gaining popularity in recent years included so-called club drugs, such as ecstasy (MDMA), flunitrazepam (known as the date-rape drug), GHB, and ketamine. These drugs have been popular among teenagers at dance clubs and raves. Because each of these club drugs is scheduled under the Controlled Substances Act (Title II of the Comprehensive Drug Abuse Prevention and Control Act of 1970), they are illegal and their use constitutes a criminal offense. In 2005, 3% of high school seniors had used MDMA in the previous twelve months. (See Table 4.11 in Chapter 4.)

In its arrest reports, the UCR notes that nearly 1.4 million people were arrested on drug abuse violations in 2005. Of that number, 1.7% were under age fifteen, 10.4% were under age eighteen, and 27.7% were under age twenty-one.

JUVENILE VICTIMS OF CRIME

Figure 7.2 and Figure 7.3 outline the trends in nonfatal violent victimizations and homicides by select age groups from about the mid-1970s to the mid-2000s.

FIGURE 7.2

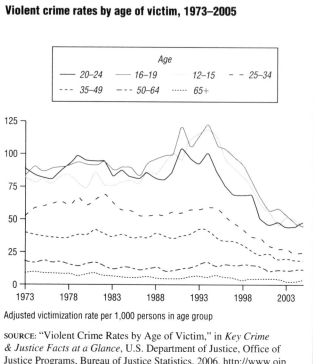

Violent crime rates by age of victim, 1973–2005

Adjusted victimization rate per 1,000 persons in age group

SOURCE: "Violent Crime Rates by Age of Victim," in *Key Crime & Justice Facts at a Glance*, U.S. Department of Justice, Office of Justice Programs, Bureau of Justice Statistics, 2006, http://www.ojp.usdoj.gov/bjs/glance/vage.htm (accessed March 2, 2007)

FIGURE 7.3

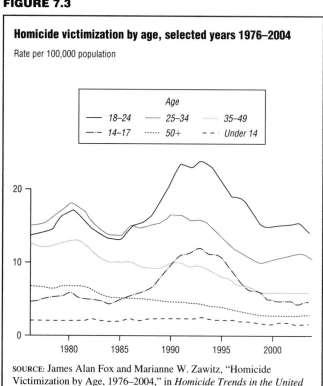

Homicide victimization by age, selected years 1976–2004

Rate per 100,000 population

SOURCE: James Alan Fox and Marianne W. Zawitz, "Homicide Victimization by Age, 1976–2004," in *Homicide Trends in the United States*, U.S. Department of Justice, Office of Justice Programs, Bureau of Justice Statistics, June 2006, http://www.ojp.usdoj.gov/bjs/homicide/teens.htm (accessed March 2, 2007)

Between 1973 and 2005 the rate of violent victimizations dropped in all age categories, but especially among young people. In 1973 the violent victimization rate for those aged twelve to fifteen was 81.8 per 1,000 people in that age group. The rate peaked in 1994 at 118.6 per 1,000, then dropped steadily to 44 per 1,000 in 2005, its lowest point in the thirty-two years recorded. For those ages sixteen to nineteen, the rate in 1973 was 81.7. That group also reached its zenith in 1994 at 123.9 and then decreased steadily to 44.3 in 2005. The highest nonfatal violent victimization rate in 1973 was among twenty- to twenty-four-year-olds (87.6). This age group reached its highest point in 1991 at 103.6 and then fluctuated before dropping to 43.2 in 2004; however, it had risen again to 47.1 in 2005.

According to James Alan Fox and Marianne W. Zawitz, in *Homicide Trends in the United States* (June 2006, http://www.ojp.usdoj.gov/bjs/homicide/teens.htm), violent crime rates are highest for young people aged twenty-four and younger; after age twenty-five the violent victimization rate declines steadily. In 1973 sixteen- to nineteen-year-olds were about twice as likely to be victimized by violent crime as people thirty-five to forty-nine years of age; in 2005, they were about two and a half times as likely.

The Office of Juvenile Justice and Delinquency Prevention (OJJDP) notes that when someone is victimized as an adolescent, long-term consequences result. When compared with adults who were not victimized as adolescents, adults who were adolescent victims are most likely to have drug problems and more likely to perpetrate violence. (See Figure 7.4.) They are also more likely to commit acts of domestic violence and become victims of domestic violence than are adults who were not victimized as adolescents. In addition, they are nearly twice as likely to become victims of violent crime and nearly three times as likely to commit property offenses. Their risk of developing posttraumatic stress disorder is also twice as great.

Becoming a victim of crime can have serious consequences—outcomes that the victim neither asks for nor deserves. A victim rarely expects to be victimized and seldom knows where to turn for help. Victims may end up in the hospital to be treated and released, or they may be confined to bed for days, weeks, or longer. Injuries may be temporary, or they may be permanent and forever change the way the victim lives his or her life. Victims may lose money or property, or in the case of homicide may lose their lives. In many cases they lose their confidence, self-esteem, and feelings of security.

The effects of crime are not limited to the victim, however. A victim's family is frequently devastated, and the psychological trauma may affect everyone connected to a victim. Victims and their families may experience

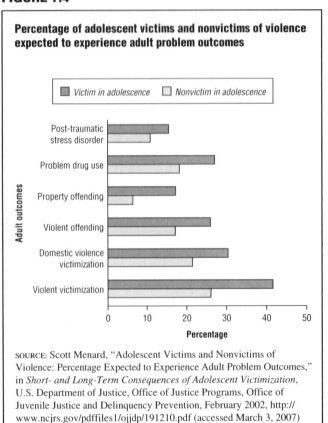

FIGURE 7.4

Percentage of adolescent victims and nonvictims of violence expected to experience adult problem outcomes

SOURCE: Scott Menard, "Adolescent Victims and Nonvictims of Violence: Percentage Expected to Experience Adult Problem Outcomes," in *Short- and Long-Term Consequences of Adolescent Victimization*, U.S. Department of Justice, Office of Justice Programs, Office of Juvenile Justice and Delinquency Prevention, February 2002, http://www.ncjrs.gov/pdffiles1/ojjdp/191210.pdf (accessed March 3, 2007)

feelings of fear, anger, shame, self-blame, helplessness, and depression—emotions that can scar life and health for years after the event. Those who were attacked in their home or whose home was entered illegally may no longer feel secure anywhere. They often blame themselves, feeling that they could have handled themselves better, or done something differently to prevent being victimized.

In the aftermath of crime, when victims most need support and comfort, there is often no one available who understands. Parents or spouses may be dealing with their own feelings of guilt and anger for not being able to protect their loved ones. Friends may withdraw, not knowing what to say or do. As a result, victims may lose their sense of self-esteem and no longer trust other people. These effects of violent victimization can be particularly devastating when the victim is a young person.

Child Abuse and Neglect

It is impossible to determine how many children suffer abuse. All observers can do is count the number of reported cases—which include only those known to public authorities—or they can survey families, in which case parents may deny or downplay abuse. As a result, estimates of child abuse are generally considered low. The National Child Abuse and Neglect Data System and its annual report, *Child Maltreatment*, is the primary source of

FIGURE 7.5

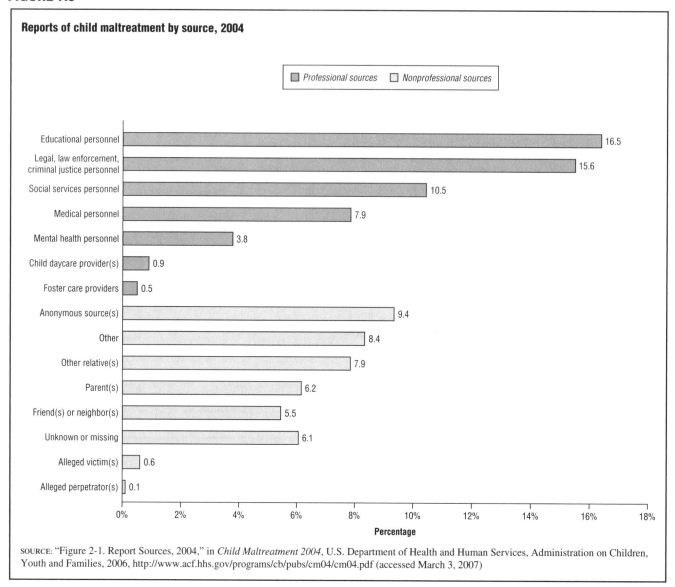

Reports of child maltreatment by source, 2004

■ Professional sources □ Nonprofessional sources

Source	Percentage
Educational personnel	16.5
Legal, law enforcement, criminal justice personnel	15.6
Social services personnel	10.5
Medical personnel	7.9
Mental health personnel	3.8
Child daycare provider(s)	0.9
Foster care providers	0.5
Anonymous source(s)	9.4
Other	8.4
Other relative(s)	7.9
Parent(s)	6.2
Friend(s) or neighbor(s)	5.5
Unknown or missing	6.1
Alleged victim(s)	0.6
Alleged perpetrator(s)	0.1

SOURCE: "Figure 2-1. Report Sources, 2004," in *Child Maltreatment 2004*, U.S. Department of Health and Human Services, Administration on Children, Youth and Families, 2006, http://www.acf.hhs.gov/programs/cb/pubs/cm04/cm04.pdf (accessed March 3, 2007)

national information on abused and neglected children that has been reported to state child protective services agencies.

Child Maltreatment 2004 (2006, http://www.acf.hhs.gov/programs/cb/pubs/cm04/cm04.pdf) reports that in 2004 an estimated three million children were alleged to have been abused or neglected and approximately 872,000 children were found to be victims of child maltreatment. Reports most often came from professional sources (such as educators), the legal system, social service employees, and medical professionals, and less often from nonprofessional sources, such as relatives, friends, neighbors, parents, the victims themselves, and a small percentage of perpetrators. (See Figure 7.5.)

In 2004, 62.4% of reported victims suffered neglect; 17.5% were physically abused; 9.7% were sexually abused; and 7% were emotionally or psychologically maltreated. (Figure 7.6 shows victimization rates for each group per 1,000 children.) The highest rate of victimization was among children three years of age or younger

(16.1 per 1,000), followed by children four to seven years of age (13.4 per 1,000). (See Figure 7.7.) The rate of occurrence decreased as the child's age increased.

The most tragic result of child maltreatment is death. In 2004 an estimated 1,490 children died as a result of abuse or neglect. Children in the youngest age groups were most likely to die of maltreatment; 81% of the children who died were three years old or younger.

The largest group of abusers were mothers acting alone (38.8%), followed by fathers acting alone (18.3%). (See Figure 7.8.) Abuse of children was overwhelmingly perpetrated by parents; only 10.1% of perpetrators were not parents. Parental abuse is probably the most devastating of all abuse, as child victims have absolutely no place to turn for help or support.

Missing Children

In the 1980s, as a result of several high-profile abductions and tragedies, the media focused public attention on

FIGURE 7.6

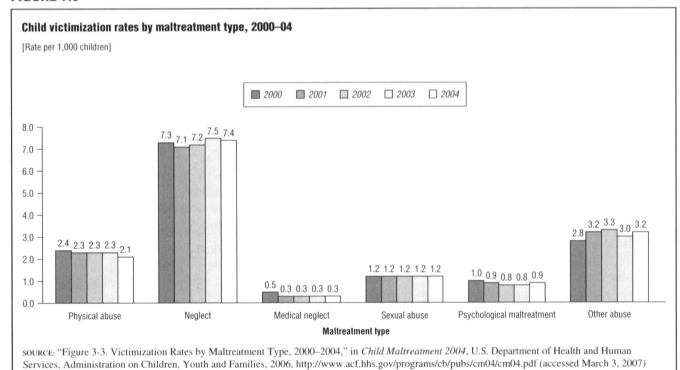

Child victimization rates by maltreatment type, 2000–04

[Rate per 1,000 children]

■ *2000* ■ *2001* ■ *2002* □ *2003* □ *2004*

SOURCE: "Figure 3-3. Victimization Rates by Maltreatment Type, 2000–2004," in *Child Maltreatment 2004*, U.S. Department of Health and Human Services, Administration on Children, Youth and Families, 2006, http://www.acf.hhs.gov/programs/cb/pubs/cm04/cm04.pdf (accessed March 3, 2007)

FIGURE 7.7

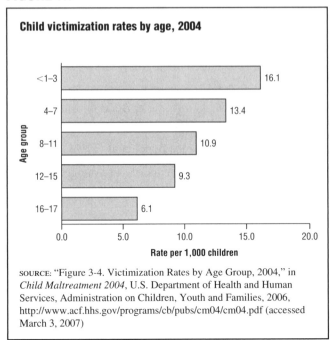

Child victimization rates by age, 2004

SOURCE: "Figure 3-4. Victimization Rates by Age Group, 2004," in *Child Maltreatment 2004*, U.S. Department of Health and Human Services, Administration on Children, Youth and Families, 2006, http://www.acf.hhs.gov/programs/cb/pubs/cm04/cm04.pdf (accessed March 3, 2007)

FIGURE 7.8

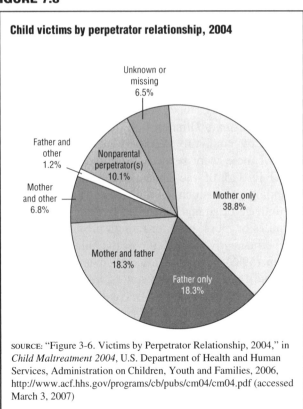

Child victims by perpetrator relationship, 2004

SOURCE: "Figure 3-6. Victims by Perpetrator Relationship, 2004," in *Child Maltreatment 2004*, U.S. Department of Health and Human Services, Administration on Children, Youth and Families, 2006, http://www.acf.hhs.gov/programs/cb/pubs/cm04/cm04.pdf (accessed March 3, 2007)

the problem of missing children. Citizens became concerned and demanded action to address what appeared to be a national crisis. Attempting to discover the nature and dimension of the problem, Congress passed the 1984 Missing Children's Assistance Act. The legislation mandated the OJJDP to conduct national incidence studies to determine the number of juveniles who were "victims of abduction by strangers" and the number of children who were

victims of "parental kidnapping." The result was the National Incidence Studies of Missing, Abducted, Runaway, and Thrownaway Children (NISMART), the first of which was conducted in 1988, with the results published in 1990. The second, more recent NISMART was conducted mainly in 1999, with most of the data published in a series of October 2002 reports.

FAMILY ABDUCTIONS. According to Heather Hammer, David Finkelhor, and Andrea J. Sedlak, in *Children Abducted by Family Members: National Estimates and Characteristics* (October 2002, http://www.ncjrs.gov/html/ojjdp/nismart/02/index.html), a family abduction is "the taking or keeping of a child by a family member in violation of a custody order, a decree, or other legitimate custodial rights, where the taking or keeping involved some element of concealment, flight, or intent to deprive a lawful custodian indefinitely of custodial privileges." In 1999, 203,900 children were victims of a family abduction. About half of these (53%) were abducted by biological fathers, and 25% by biological mothers. Most family abducted children were not missing for long— 46% were gone less than a week, and only 21% were away a month or more. Nearly half (42%) were abducted from a single-parent family. At the time the survey was done, 91% of the children had been returned, 6% had been located but not returned, and less than 1% had not been located or returned (there was no information on outcomes for 2% of cases).

NONFAMILY ABDUCTIONS. Although far fewer children are abducted by strangers than by family members, the consequences are often far worse. Violence, the use of force or weapons, sexual assault, and murder are more prevalent in nonfamily abductions. According to David Finkelhor, Heather Hammer, and Andrea J. Sedlak, in *Nonfamily Abducted Children: National Estimates and Characteristics* (October 2002, http://www.ncjrs.gov/html/ojjdp/nismart/03/index.html), 58,200 children were abducted by nonfamily members in 1999. Nearly half (46%) of these were sexually assaulted by their abductors. Only 115 of the abductions were "stereotypical kidnappings," in which a child was abducted by a slight acquaintance or stranger, detained overnight, transported fifty miles or more, held for ransom or with intention to keep permanently, or killed. Most nonfamily abducted children (59%) were fifteen to seventeen years old and 65% were female. The perpetrators were strangers 37% of the time and were three times as likely to be male as female. Most perpetrators (67%) were aged thirteen to twenty-nine. Most nonfamily abducted children (91%) were away for twenty-four hours or less, and 99% returned alive. The remaining 1% were either killed or had not been located at the time of the survey.

RUNAWAYS AND THROWNAWAYS. Heather Hammer, David Finkelhor, and Andrea J. Sedlak note in *Runaway/Thrownaway Children: National Estimates and Characteristics* (October 2002, http://www.ncjrs.gov/html/ojjdp/nismart/04/) that runaways are children who meet at least one of the following criteria:

- A child who leaves home without permission and stays away overnight

- A child fourteen years old (or older and mentally incompetent) who is away from home who chooses not to come home when expected to and who stays away overnight

- A child fifteen years old or older who is away from home who chooses not to come home and stays away two nights

In the 1970s the term *throwaways* or *thrownaways* was used by researchers for juveniles who were made to leave home or were abandoned. A thrownaway child meets one of the following criteria:

- A child who is asked or told to leave home by a parent or other household adult, with no adequate alternative care arranged for the child by a household adult, and who is out of the household overnight

- A child who is away from home who is prevented from returning home by a parent or other household adult, with no adequate alternative care arranged for by a household adult, and who is out of the household overnight

The OJJDP now combines its estimates of runaways and thrownaways. According to Hammer, Finkelhor, and Sedlak in *Runaway/Thrownaway Children*, in 1999, 1.7 million youths had a runaway/thrownaway episode. The runaway episode was thought to indicate that 1.2 million of these children were endangered in the following ways:

- The child had been physically or sexually abused at home in the year before the episode or was afraid of abuse upon return (21%).

- The child was substance dependent (19%).

- The child was thirteen years old or younger (18%).

- The child was in the company of someone known to be abusing drugs (18%).

- The child was using hard drugs (17%).

Most runaway/thrownaway youth (68%) were fifteen years old or older; half were females and half were males. Most runaways (77%) were away less than one week, and more than 99% returned. An estimated 38,600 of the runaways were at risk of sexual endangerment—assault, attempted assault, or prostitution—while away from home.

Murder Victims

According to the BJS, homicide rates for all age groups have been declining since the mid-1990s. (See Figure 7.3.) Although violent crime has diminished, it still plays a significant role as a cause of death for youth. In 2003, however, the leading cause of death among both males and females under the age of twenty-four was accidents. Of the leading causes of death, homicides and suicides accounted for many abbreviated lives as well, and these deaths increase in number among older youth. (See Table 7.2.)

In 2003 the homicide death rate for infants under age one was quite high at 8.5 per 100,000. After that age, the homicide death rate declined to 2.4 per 100,000 among one- to four-year-olds and 0.8 per 100,000 five- to fourteen-year-olds. The homicide death rate rose again after age fourteen; the homicide death rate was 13 per 100,000 for fifteen- to twenty-four-year-olds, higher than any other age group. (See Table 7.2.)

UCR data confirm that murder victims are disproportionately young people. Out of 14,860 murder victims in 2005, 1,446 victims were under age eighteen, including 1,019 males and 422 females. (See Table 7.3.) The number of murder victims more than doubled for those under age twenty-two. Of the 3,605 murder victims in this age range, 2,912 were male and 688 were female. Even though nearly one out of ten (9.7%) murder victims was under age eighteen, almost a quarter (24.3%) was under age twenty-two.

African-Americans are also disproportionately victims of homicide. Nearly equal numbers of whites

(7,133) and African-Americans (7,125) were murdered in 2005, even though whites far outnumber African-Americans in the general population. (See Table 7.3.) Of victims under age eighteen, 716 were white and 670 were African-American. Of victims under age twenty-two, 1,599 were white and 1,860 were African-American. African-American and white murder victims under age eighteen each represented approximately 10% of the total, whereas white victims under age twenty-two encompassed 22.4% of the total white victims and African-American victims under age twenty-two were 26.1% of the total African-American victims. Homicide has been and is the leading cause of death for African-American teenagers, both male and female, although victimization rates for African-American teens declined dramatically between the early 1990s and 2000.

VICTIM-OFFENDER RELATIONSHIP. Table 7.4 shows that between 1980 and 2002 the most frequent killers of children under age six were their parents, whereas parents were rarely involved in the murder of teens aged fifteen to seventeen, although this varied by gender of the child. Almost two-thirds (61%) of all female juveniles killed were murdered by a parent or stepparent, compared with only 26% of male juveniles. Half of all male juveniles killed (50%) were murdered by an acquaintance, compared with only 29% of female juveniles. Females were

TABLE 7.2

Death rates by age for the 15 leading causes of death, 2003

[Rates on an annual basis per 100,000 population in specified group; age-adjusted rates per 100,000 U.S. standard population. Rates are based on populations enumerated as of April 1 for 2000 and estimated as of July 1 for all other years.]

Cause of death	All ages[a]	Under 1 year[b]	1–4 years	5–14 years	15–24 years	25–34 years	35–44 years	45–54 years	55–64 years	65–74 years	75–84 years	85 years and over	Age-adjusted rate[c]
All causes	841.9	700.0	31.5	17.0	81.5	103.6	201.6	433.2	940.9	2,255.0	5,463.1	14,593.3	832.7
Diseases of heart	235.6	11.0	1.2	0.6	2.7	8.2	30.7	92.5	233.2	585.0	1,611.1	5,278.4	232.3
Malignant neoplasms	191.5	1.9	2.5	2.6	4.0	9.4	35.0	122.2	343.0	770.3	1,302.5	1,698.2	190.1
Cerebrovascular diseases	54.2	2.5	0.3	0.2	0.5	1.5	5.5	15.0	35.6	112.9	410.7	1,370.1	53.5
Chronic lower respiratory diseases	43.5	0.8	0.3	0.3	0.5	0.7	2.1	8.7	43.3	163.2	383.0	635.1	43.3
Accidents (unintentional injuries)	37.6	23.6	10.9	6.4	37.1	31.5	37.8	38.8	32.9	44.1	101.9	278.9	37.3
Diabetes mellitus	25.5	*	*	0.1	0.4	1.6	4.6	13.9	38.5	90.8	181.1	317.5	25.3
Influenza and pneumonia	22.4	8.0	1.0	0.4	0.5	0.9	2.2	5.2	11.2	37.3	151.1	666.1	22.0
Alzheimer's disease	21.8	*	*	*	*	*	*	0.2	2.0	20.9	164.4	802.4	21.4
Nephritis, nephrotic syndrome and nephrosis	14.6	4.5	*	0.1	0.2	0.7	1.8	4.9	13.6	40.1	109.5	293.1	14.4
Septicemia	11.7	6.9	0.5	0.2	0.4	0.8	2.1	5.3	13.1	32.6	85.0	202.5	11.6
Intentional self-harm (suicide)	10.8	—	—	0.6	9.7	12.7	14.9	15.9	13.8	12.7	16.4	16.9	10.8
Chronic liver disease and cirrhosis	9.5	*	*	*	*	0.9	6.8	18.3	23.0	29.5	30.0	20.1	9.3
Essential (primary) hypertension and hypertensive renal disease	7.5	*	*	*	0.1	0.2	0.8	2.5	6.3	16.9	51.7	188.9	7.4
Parkinson's disease	6.2	*	*	*	*	*	*	0.2	1.3	12.7	67.8	138.2	6.2
Assault (homicide)	6.1	8.5	2.4	0.8	13.0	11.3	7.0	4.9	2.8	2.4	2.5	2.2	6.0

*Figure does not meet standards of reliability or precision.
—Category not applicable.
[a]Figures for age not stated included in "all ages" but not distributed among age groups.
[b]Death rates for "under 1 year" (based on population estimates) differ from infant mortality rates (based on live births).
[c]For method of computation.

SOURCE: Adapted from Donna L. Hoyert et al., "Table 9. Death Rates by Age and Age-Adjusted Death Rates for the 15 Leading Causes of Death in 2003: United States, 1999–2003," in "Deaths: Final Data for 2003," *National Vital Statistics Reports*, vol. 54, no. 3, April 19, 2006, http://www.cdc.gov/nchs/data/nvsr/nvsr54/nvsr54_13.pdf (accessed March 3, 2007)

TABLE 7.3

Murder victims by age, sex, and race, 2004

Age	Total	Sex			Race			
		Male	Female	Unknown	White	Black	Other	Unknown
Total	14,860	11,683	3,155	22	7,133	7,125	390	212
Percent distribution[a]	100	78.6	21.2	0.1	48	47.9	2.6	1.4
Under 18[b]	1,446	1,019	422	5	716	670	35	25
Under 22[b]	3,605	2,912	688	5	1,599	1,860	96	50
18 and over[b]	13,153	10,474	2,677	2	6,302	6,370	350	131
Infant (under 1)	182	104	73	5	115	53	4	10
1 to 4	328	186	142	0	175	140	5	8
5 to 8	75	38	37	0	38	32	4	1
9 to 12	78	38	40	0	39	36	2	1
13 to 16	456	365	91	0	208	237	10	1
17 to 19	1,349	1,184	165	0	555	751	32	11
20 to 24	2,834	2,460	374	0	1,110	1,606	93	25
25 to 29	2,262	1,920	342	0	951	1,247	48	16
30 to 34	1,649	1,341	308	0	736	860	36	17
35 to 39	1,257	930	326	1	625	586	32	14
40 to 44	1,194	874	320	0	636	504	38	16
45 to 49	938	705	233	0	528	373	25	12
50 to 54	708	543	164	1	403	277	19	9
55 to 59	384	275	109	0	259	108	13	4
60 to 64	272	192	80	0	175	81	11	5
65 to 69	183	108	75	0	125	51	6	1
70 to 74	159	96	63	0	117	38	4	0
75 and over	291	134	157	0	223	60	3	5
Unknown	261	190	56	15	115	85	5	56

[a]Because of rounding, the percentages may not add to 100.0.
[b]Does not include unknown ages.

SOURCE: "Expanded Homicide Data Table 2. Murder Victims by Age, Sex, and Race, 2005," in *Crime in the United States 2005*, U.S. Department of Justice, Federal Bureau of Investigation, September 2006, http://www.fbi.gov/ucr/05cius/offenses/expanded_information/data/shrtable_02.html (accessed March 3, 2007)

TABLE 7.4

Offender relationship to juvenile homicide victims, by age and gender of victims, 1980–2002

Offender relationship to victim	Age of Victim					Victim ages 0–17	
	0–17	0–5	6–11	12–14	15–17	Males	Females
Offender known	74%	88%	81%	72%	64%	72%	88%
Total	100%	100%	100%	100%	100%	100%	100%
Parent/stepparent	31%	62%	40%	11%	3%	26%	61%
Other family member	7%	7%	15%	11%	5%	6%	7%
Acquaintance	47%	28%	30%	58%	66%	50%	29%
Stranger	15%	3%	15%	20%	25%	18%	3%
Offender unknown	26%	12%	19%	28%	36%	28%	12%

Note: Detail may not total 100% due to rounding.

SOURCE: "Victim-Offender Relationship in Juvenile Homicides by Age of Victim, 1980–2002," in *OJJDP Statistical Briefing Book*, U.S. Department of Justice, Office of Justice Programs, Office of Juvenile Justice and Delinquency Prevention, March 27, 2006, http://ojjdp.ncjrs.org/ojstatbb/victims/qa02302.asp?qaDate=2002 (acccessed March 2, 2007)

also less likely than males to be murdered by a stranger (3% and 18%, respectively.)

The risk of being killed by a parent decreases with age. Sixty-two percent of murder victims aged five and younger were killed by a parent or stepparent, compared with 40% of children aged six to eleven, 11% of children aged twelve to fourteen, and 3% of children aged fifteen to seventeen. (See Table 7.4.) The risk of being killed by an acquaintance or a stranger, however, increased with

age. About a quarter of children under age six (28%) were killed by an acquaintance, compared with 66% of fifteen- to seventeen-year-olds; only 3% of the youngest children were killed by strangers, compared with 25% of fifteen- to seventeen-year-olds.

WEAPONS USED IN MURDERS OF JUVENILES. Snyder and Sickmund report that the number of youths dying as a result of firearms increased 152% between 1985 and 1993 before beginning to decline. Even though the number of homicides involving no firearm declined little between 1993 and 2002, a huge drop in the number of homicides involving a firearm resulted in the overall number of homicides of juveniles falling to the lowest level since 1984 in 2002. Nonetheless, almost half of all juveniles murdered in 2002 (48%) were killed with a firearm. Another 22% were beaten/kicked to death or strangled, and 11% were killed with a knife or blunt object. The remaining 19% were killed with another type of weapon, or the type of weapon used was unknown.

The FBI reports that these trends continued in 2005; firearms were used in most murders of juveniles and young adults in that year. Of 1,446 murder victims under the age of eighteen, 720 (49.8%) were killed with firearms. (See Table 7.5.) Of 3,605 murder victims who were under the age of twenty-two, 9,244 (70.3%) were killed with firearms. A low proportion of the youngest murder victims were killed by firearms, but that proportion rose with age. The most firearm-related murders were in the twenty to twenty-four age group (2,269 deaths). However, the greatest percentage of firearm-related murders was among those aged seventeen to nineteen (83.7%). Other weapons most frequently used to kill juveniles included "personal" weapons—hands, feet, fists, and so on—and knives.

Rape

For several reasons, the statistics on rape are incomplete. The crime often goes unreported. The BJS estimates that only about one-third of the cases of completed or attempted rape are ever reported to police; other organizations estimate that the proportion of reported rapes is even lower. Because its data are collected through interviews, the BJS recognizes an underreporting in its statistics as well. Acquaintance rape is far more common than stranger rape. Most experts conclude that in 80% to 85% of all rape cases the victim knows the rapist.

In *Crime in the United States 2005*, the UCR defines forcible rape as "the carnal knowledge of a female forcibly and against her will. Assaults and attempts to commit rape by force or threat of force are also included; however, statutory rape (without force) [sex with a consenting minor] and other sex offenses are excluded." Rape is a crime of violence in which the victim may suffer serious physical injury and long-term psychological pain. The UCR indicates that in 2005 there were 93,934 reported rape offenses, a decrease of 1.2% from the year before. The rate of forcible rapes was reported at a rate of 62.5 offenses per 100,000 females.

Rape victims are disproportionately young. Catalano reports that rape/sexual assault in 2005 occurred at a rate of 1.2 per 1,000 twelve- to fifteen-year-olds and 3.2 per 1,000 sixteen- to nineteen-year-olds. NCVS data also include rapes committed against males. (See Table 7.6.) Females aged sixteen to nineteen experienced the highest rates (5.7 per 1,000). (See Table 7.7.)

The NCVS finds that in 2005 only 33.1% of those aged twelve to nineteen who acknowledged being victims of rape/sexual assault reported the incident to police. (See Table 7.8.)

Aggravated and Simple Assault

Catalano notes that in 2005 aggravated assault was most common among young people. It occurred at a rate of 8.7 per 1,000 twelve- to fifteen-year-olds, 9.7 per 1,000 sixteen- to nineteen-year-olds, and 10 per 1,000 twenty- to twenty-four-year-olds. After that age the rate began to decline. Among white males, those aged twenty to twenty-four experienced the highest rate (15.7 per 1,000), whereas among African-American males, sixteen- to nineteen-year-olds experienced the highest rate (16.3 per 1,000). The same pattern held among females; African-American women in the sixteen to nineteen age group experienced the highest rate (17.7 per 1,000), whereas white women in the twenty to twenty-four age group experienced the highest rate (4.9 per 1,000). (See Table 7.9.)

According to Catalano, in 2005 simple assault occurred at a rate of 30.6 per 1,000 twelve- to fifteen-year-olds, 24.2 per 1,000 sixteen- to nineteen-year-olds, and 30.3 per 1,000 twenty- to twenty-four-year-olds, after which the rate began to decline. Males had a higher rate of simple assault than females. White and African-American males had a similar rate of simple assault victimization. By contrast, young African-American females between the ages of twelve and fifteen had a significantly higher simple assault victimization rate than did white females in the same age group (34.3 per 1,000 and 21 per 1,000, respectively). (See Table 7.9.)

Robbery and Theft

Catalano reports that in 2005 robbery occurred at a rate of 3.5 per 1,000 twelve- to fifteen-year-olds, 7 per 1,000 sixteen- to nineteen-year-olds, and 5.5 per 1,000 twenty- to twenty-four-year-olds, after which age the rates began to decline. Young males, particularly young African-American males, had a high rate of robbery victimization. Among white males, those aged sixteen to twenty-four had a victimization rate of 8.8 per 1,000. Among African-American males aged sixteen to nineteen, the victimization rate was 29.5 per 1,000. (See Table 7.9.)

TABLE 7.5

Murder victims by age and weapon, 2005

Age	Total murder victims	Weapons										
		Firearms	Knives or cutting instruments	Blunt objects (clubs, hammers, etc.)	Personal weapons (hands, fists, feet, etc.)[a]	Poison	Explosives	Fire	Narcotics	Strangulation	Asphyxiation	Other weapon or weapon not stated[b]
Total	**14,860**	**10,100**	**1,914**	**597**	**892**	**9**	**2**	**123**	**44**	**120**	**96**	**963**
Percent distribution[c]	100.0	68.0	12.9	4.0	6.0	0.1	*	0.8	0.3	0.8	0.6	6.5
Under 18[d]	1,446	720	115	63	297	7	0	39	7	13	33	152
Under 22[d]	3,605	2,476	345	92	335	7	0	44	13	27	39	227
18 and over[d]	13,153	9,244	1,778	524	573	2	2	81	35	104	59	751
Infant (under 1)	182	5	4	11	103	2	0	4	5	2	13	33
1 to 4	328	32	14	32	150	1	0	15	0	4	14	66
5 to 8	75	20	9	3	16	3	0	12	1	1	0	10
9 to 12	78	33	11	3	9	1	0	5	0	4	1	11
13 to 16	456	361	47	9	11	0	0	1	1	0	3	23
17 to 19	1,349	1,129	118	18	24	0	0	3	1	11	3	42
20 to 24	2,834	2,269	315	43	64	0	0	11	6	11	9	106
25 to 29	2,262	1,802	231	49	65	0	0	9	6	10	7	83
30 to 34	1,649	1,263	176	40	63	0	1	4	4	6	3	89
35 to 39	1,257	861	184	60	47	0	0	9	1	11	7	77
40 to 44	1,194	748	191	73	79	0	0	6	1	13	4	79
45 to 49	938	528	185	50	65	1	0	9	3	17	4	76
50 to 54	708	351	148	60	60	0	0	12	4	8	2	63
55 to 59	384	189	78	41	22	0	0	6	0	3	5	40
60 to 64	272	130	52	21	26	0	1	4	1	2	3	32
65 to 69	183	92	46	18	9	0	0	2	1	2	2	11
70 to 74	159	58	38	20	13	0	0	1	1	1	4	23
75 and over	291	93	46	36	44	1	0	7	6	1	8	39
Unknown	261	136	21	10	22	0	0	3	2	3	4	60

[a]Pushed is included in personal weapons.
[b]Includes drowning.
[c]Because of rounding, the percentages may not add to 100.0.
[d]Does not include unknown ages.
*Less than one-tenth of 1 percent.

SOURCE: "Expanded Homicide Data Table 8. Murder Victims by Age, by Weapon, 2005," in *Crime in the United States 2005*, U.S. Department of Justice, Federal Bureau of Investigation, September 2006, http://www.fbi.gov/ucr/05cius/offenses/expanded_information/data/shrtable_08.html (accessed March 3, 2007)

TABLE 7.6

Rates of violent crime and personal theft, by gender, age, race, and Hispanic origin, 2005

Demographic characteristic of victim	Population	Victimizations per 1,000 persons age 12 or older						Personal theft
		Violent crimes						
					Assault			
		All	Rape/sexual assault	Robbery	Total	Aggravated	Simple	
Gender								
Male	118,937,730	25.5	0.1*	3.8	21.5	5.6	15.9	0.8
Female	125,555,710	17.1	1.4	1.4	14.3	3.1	11.2	1.0
Race								
White	200,263,410	20.1	0.6	2.2	17.2	3.8	13.4	0.9
Black	29,477,880	27.0	1.8	4.6	20.6	7.6	13.0	1.7
Other race	12,522,090	13.9	0.5*	3.0	10.4	2.5*	7.9	0.2*
Two or more races	2,230,050	83.6	3.8*	1.8*	78.0	16.6	61.5	0.0*
Hispanic origin								
Hispanic	31,812,270	25.0	1.1*	4.0	19.9	5.9	14.0	1.0*
Non-Hispanic	211,629,880	20.6	0.7	2.4	17.5	4.1	13.4	0.9
Age								
12–15	17,061,940	44.0	1.2*	3.5	39.3	8.7	30.6	1.3*
16–19	16,524,940	44.2	3.2	7.0	33.9	9.7	24.2	1.6*
20–24	20,363,570	46.9	1.1*	5.5	40.3	10.0	30.3	1.5*
25–34	39,607,310	23.6	0.7*	3.1	19.9	4.7	15.2	1.0
35–49	65,707,720	17.5	0.6*	1.9	15.0	3.2	11.8	1.0
50–64	50,164,650	11.4	0.6*	1.4	9.3	2.4	7.0	0.6*
65 or older	35,063,310	2.4	0.0*	0.6*	1.9	0.8*	1.1	0.4*

Note: The National Crime Victimization Survey (NCVS) includes as violent crime rape, sexual assault robbery, and assault. Because the NCVS interviews persons about their victimizations, murder and manslaughter cannot be included. Racial and ethnic categories in 2005 are not comparable to categories used prior to 2003.
*Based on 10 or fewer sample cases.

SOURCE: Shannan M. Catalano, "Table 6. Rates of Violent Crime and Personal Theft, by Gender, Race, Hispanic Origin, and Age, 2005," in *Criminal Victimization, 2005*, U.S. Department of Justice, Bureau of Justice Statistics, September 2006, http://www.ojp.usdoj.gov/bjs/pub/pdf/cv05.pdf (accessed March 3, 2007)

TABLE 7.7

Victimization rates for persons age 12 and over, by gender and age of victims and type of crime, 2005

Gender and age	Total population	Rate per 1,000 persons in each age group										
		Crimes of violence	Completed violence	Attempted/ threatened violence	Rape/ sexual assault[a]	**Robbery**			**Assault**			Purse snatching/ pocket picking
						Total	With injury	Without injury	Total	Aggravated	Simple	
Male												
12–15	8,762,340	53.1	18.1	35.0	0.0*	4.2	2.0*	2.2*	48.9	12.5	36.4	1.5*
16–19	8,400,350	54.0	23.4	30.6	0.8*	11.3	3.0*	8.3	41.8	12.5	29.3	1.9*
20–24	10,242,480	58.8	17.9	40.9	0.0*	8.1	2.3*	5.7	50.8	13.6	37.1	1.9*
25–34	19,870,640	26.4	8.4	18.0	0.1*	4.6	0.9*	3.7	21.7	5.0	16.6	1.0*
35–49	32,445,050	18.6	5.6	13.0	0.2*	2.5	1.2*	1.4	15.9	3.7	12.2	0.5*
50–64	24,293,640	13.4	3.1	10.3	0.0*	2.1	1.2*	0.9*	11.3	2.8	8.5	0.4*
65 and over	14,923,220	3.5	0.5*	3.0	0.0*	0.9*	0.2*	0.7*	2.6	1.5*	1.1*	0.2*
Female												
12–15	8,299,600	34.4	11.1	23.3	2.4*	2.8*	0.7*	2.1*	29.2	4.7	24.5	1.0*
16–19	8,124,580	34.0	12.0	22.0	5.7	2.6*	0.6*	1.9*	25.7	6.8	18.9	1.3*
20–24	10,121,090	34.8	11.4	23.4	2.2*	2.9*	0.6*	2.3*	29.7	6.3	23.4	1.2*
25–34	19,736,670	20.9	6.6	14.3	1.3*	1.5*	0.5*	1.0*	18.1	4.4	13.8	1.0*
35–49	33,262,670	16.3	5.0	11.3	0.9*	1.3	0.4*	0.9*	14.0	2.6	11.4	1.4
50–64	25,871,010	9.4	2.8	6.6	1.2*	0.7*	0.2*	0.5*	7.5	2.0	5.5	0.9*
65 and over	20,140,090	1.6*	0.6*	1.1*	0.0*	0.3*	0.3*	0.0*	1.3*	0.2*	1.1*	0.5*

Note: Detail may not add to total shown because of rounding.
*Estimate is based on about 10 or fewer sample cases.
[a]Includes verbal threats of rape and threats of sexual assault.

SOURCE: "Table 4. Personal Crimes, 2005: Victimization Rates for Persons Age 12 and Over, by Gender and Age of Victims and Type of Crime," in *Criminal Victimization in the United States, 2005 Statistical Tables*, U.S. Department of Justice, Bureau of Justice Statistics, December 2006, http://www.ojp.usdoj.gov/bjs/pub/pdf/cvus05.pdf (accessed March 3, 2007)

TABLE 7.8

Percent of victimizations reported to police by type of crime and age of victims, 2005

Type of crime	Percent of victimizations reported to the police, by age of victim				
	12–19	20–34	35–49	50–64	65 and over
All personal crimes	34.5%	47.5%	58.9%	49.4%	66.1%
Crimes of violence	35.6	48.0	59.3	49.2	68.2
Completed violence	44.4	69.4	74.1	57.6	100.0*
Attempted/threatened violence	30.6	38.2	52.8	46.2	58.8
Rape/sexual assault[a]	33.1*	29.7*	62.0*	37.0*	0.0*
Robbery	30.9	52.8	72.0	68.8	57.7*
Completed/property taken	26.8*	66.5	85.3	85.9*	100.0*
With injury	40.3*	80.5*	100.0	86.4*	100.0*
Without injury	18.9*	63.3	74.2	85.4*	100.0*
Attempted to take property	44.5*	33.5*	39.1*	42.3*	0.0*
With injury	100.0*	43.2*	0.0*	52.9*	0.0*
Without injury	38.8*	28.5*	62.3*	30.5*	0.0*
Assault	36.5	47.9	57.6	47.1	71.5
Aggravated	57.1	61.5	71.7	56.4	89.9*
With injury	69.9	86.9	71.5	57.1*	100.0*
Threatened with weapon	51.4	47.8	71.8	56.2	88.9*
Simple	29.6	43.6	53.8	43.9	58.2*
With minor injury	44.8	64.7	71.1	51.2*	100.0*
Without injury	23.8	36.6	48.8	42.5	51.2*
Purse snatching/pocket picking	0.0*	32.5*	52.3*	54.2*	52.2*

*Estimate is based on about 10 or fewer sample cases.
[a]Includes verbal threats of rape and threats of sexual assault.

SOURCE: "Table 96. Personal Crimes, 2005: Percent of Victimizations Reported to the Police, by Type of Crime and Age of Victims," in *Criminal Victimization in the United States, 2005 Statistical Tables*, U.S. Department of Justice, Bureau of Justice Statistics, December 2006, http://www.ojp.usdoj.gov/bjs/pub/pdf/cvus05.pdf (accessed March 3, 2007)

TABLE 7.9

Violent victimization rates for persons age 12 and over, by race and age of victims and type of crime, 2005

Race, gender, and age	Total population	Rate per 1,000 persons in each age group							
		Crimes of violence[a]		Robbery		Aggravated assault		Simple assault	
		Number	Rate	Number	Rate	Number	Rate	Number	Rate
White only									
Male									
12–15	6,702,090	335,520	50.1	19,640*	2.9*	84,170	12.6	231,710	34.6
16–19	6,525,180	355,260	54.4	57,370	8.8	84,210	12.9	206,660	31.7
20–24	8,316,230	539,540	64.9	73,490	8.8	130,630	15.7	335,420	40.3
25–34	15,903,200	393,230	24.7	46,590	2.9	64,140	4.0	282,510	17.8
35–49	26,845,900	483,400	18.0	66,290	2.5	87,840	3.3	323,850	12.1
50–64	20,799,270	270,610	13.0	43,410	2.1	46,960	2.3	180,240	8.7
65 and over	13,146,140	42,190	3.2	13,800*	1.0*	22,420*	1.7*	5,970*	0.5*
Female									
12–15	6,380,710	186,580	29.2	17,440*	2.7*	22,480*	3.5*	133,980	21.0
16–19	6,263,590	185,720	29.7	11,900*	1.9*	20,350*	3.2*	126,220	20.2
20–24	7,891,320	254,580	32.3	20,920*	2.7*	38,810	4.9	175,130	22.2
25–34	15,432,730	309,920	20.1	27,400*	1.8*	42,130	2.7	229,470	14.9
35–49	26,885,550	449,140	16.7	27,760*	1.0*	66,610	2.5	326,860	12.2
50–64	21,633,960	179,430	8.3	14,790*	0.7*	42,450	2.0	108,170	5.0
65 and over	17,537,540	30,790*	1.8*	6,230*	0.4*	4,740*	0.3*	19,820*	1.1*
Black only									
Male									
12–15	1,423,280	90,900	63.9	17,080*	12.0*	21,520*	15.1*	52,300	36.7
16–19	1,279,320	95,320	74.5	37,750*	29.5	20,840*	16.3*	36,730	28.7
20–24	1,199,560	54,800	45.7	9,240*	7.7*	4,900*	4.1*	40,670	33.9
25–34	2,390,860	55,750	23.3	17,610*	7.4*	26,510*	11.1*	8,930*	3.7*
35–49	3,658,110	80,430	22.0	13,030*	3.6*	30,240*	8.3*	37,160	10.2
50–64	2,334,400	39,960	17.1	3,610*	1.5*	18,220*	7.8*	18,130*	7.8*
65 and over	1,137,310	6,400*	5.6*	0*	0.0*	0*	0.0*	6,400*	5.6*
Female									
12–15	1,320,950	72,300	54.7	6,010*	4.5*	13,750*	10.4*	45,300	34.3
16–19	1,287,460	65,370	50.8	4,890*	3.8*	22,820*	17.7*	18,380*	14.3*
20–24	1,478,900	67,920	45.9	8,010*	5.4*	21,400*	14.5*	38,510	26.0
25–34	2,859,550	59,080	20.7	2,670*	0.9*	31,750*	11.1*	16,410*	5.7*
35–49	4,404,500	63,950	14.5	13,160*	3.0*	7,530*	1.7*	43,260	9.8
50–64	2,874,400	44,620	15.5	3,250*	1.1*	6,020*	2.1*	20,840*	7.3*
65 and over	1,829,280	0*	0.0*	0*	0.0*	0*	0.0*	0*	0.0*

Note: Excludes data on persons of "other" races and persons indicating two or more races.
*Estimate is based on about 10 or fewer sample cases.
[a]Includes data on rape and sexual assault, not shown separately.

SOURCE: "Table 10. Violent Crimes, 2005: Number of Victimizations and Victimization Rates for Persons Age 12 and Over, by Race, Gender, and Age of Victims and Type of Crime," in *Criminal Victimization in the United States, 2005 Statistical Tables*, U.S. Department of Justice, Bureau of Justice Statistics, December 2006, http://www.ojp.usdoj.gov/bjs/pub/pdf/cvus05.pdf (accessed March 3, 2007)

CHAPTER 8
VIOLENCE AND GANGS

SCOPE OF THE GANG PROBLEM

Gangs have a long history in the United States, dating back to the 1800s. As the United States became the "great melting pot" in the nineteenth century when people of diverse ethnicities and religions entered the country, some immigrants joined gangs to help them gain a group identity, defend themselves against other groups, and establish a unified presence. Although people feared street gangs of the nineteenth century, the gangs of today pose a greater threat to public safety than in years past.

Most criminal activities of the street gangs of the early twentieth century involved delinquent acts or petty crimes, such as brawls with rival gangs. As the twentieth century progressed, however, gangs became involved in more serious crimes. Toward the end of the century law enforcement officials came to regard gang members in general as serious criminals who used intimidation tactics, engaged in the illegal trafficking of drugs and weapons, and employed violence to pursue their goals. Respondents in the National Youth Gang Survey (NYGS) emphasized that a gang was defined by involvement in group criminal activity along with some degree of definition of a group as a separate entity, such as having a name, displaying distinct colors or symbols, or engaging in activities to protect the group's territory. Law enforcement officers noted that in the 1980s and 1990s more and more gang members began to support themselves through dealing drugs, such as crack cocaine and heroin. Many were said to have easy access to high-powered weapons. In addition, the proliferation of gangs in the late twentieth century meant that groups moved beyond city boundaries into suburban and rural areas as well. This movement into new territories occurred about the same time that youth violence surged in the 1980s and early 1990s.

Researchers noted various reasons for the growth of gangs during the end of the twentieth century. According to *Preventing Adolescent Gang Involvement* (September 2000, http://www.ncjrs.gov/pdffiles1/ojjdp/182210.pdf), Finn-Aage Esbensen of the University of Nebraska at Omaha notes that "American society witnessed a reemergence of youth gang activity and media interest in this phenomenon in the 1980's and 1990's. 'Colors,' 'Boyz in the Hood,' other Hollywood productions, and MTV brought Los Angeles gang life to suburban and rural America." These media portrayals might further entice youth to become involved in gangs.

In an effort to track the growth and activities of gangs, the National Youth Gang Center of the Office of Juvenile Justice and Delinquency Prevention (OJJDP) began conducting the NYGS in 1996. According to the *National Youth Gang Survey Analysis* (2006, http://www.iir.com/nygc/nygsa/methodology.htm), the National Youth Gang Center indicates that for purposes of the survey, researchers annually query all police and sheriff departments serving cities and counties with populations of fifty thousand or more (twenty-five thousand or more before 2002), as well as all suburban county police and sheriff's departments. Because gang membership has moved beyond large metropolitan areas, the NYGS also queries a random sample of law enforcement agencies in cities with populations between twenty-five hundred and twenty-five thousand and in rural counties. Not all jurisdictions that receive the survey respond, but a solid majority do. Survey participants are instructed to provide information on youth gangs within their jurisdictions. Motorcycle gangs, prison gangs, adult gangs, and hate or ideology-based groups are not included in the sample.

Statistics about gang membership show that the increased concern about gangs had its basis in the growth of gangs during the 1990s. According to Walter B. Miller of the OJJDP, in *The Growth of Youth Gang Problems in the United States: 1970–1998* (April 2001, http://www.ncjrs.gov/html/ojjdp/ojjdprpt_yth_gng_prob_2001/contents.html), during the 1970s about 1% of U.S. cities and about

40% of the states reported having problems with youth gangs. By the late 1990s the percentage of U.S. cities with gang problems grew to 7%, and youth gangs were reported in all fifty states and the District of Columbia. Gang growth in cities soared in the 1980s and 1990s, with the number of gangs reportedly increasing by 281%. During the period from 1995 to 1998 gang activity was recorded in 1,550 cities and 450 counties where it had not been reported previously. In the *1998 National Youth Gang Survey* (November 2000, http://www.gangsorus.com/survey .pdf), the OJJDP reports that in 1998 the West had the highest percentage of law enforcement agencies reporting active youth gangs, especially in the Pacific region.

At first, gangs tended to be big-city problems—the NYGS noted that most cities with populations over one hundred thousand reported that the proliferation of gangs became a problem between 1985 and the early 1990s. After that time, however, gangs spread to smaller areas. It is true that the larger the population, the greater the likelihood of the existence of gangs in that area. However, gangs can also be found in small towns, villages, and rural areas, some of which do not even have their own police departments.

The huge growth in gangs and gang membership slowed in the late 1990s. Comparing statistics between the 1996 and 2000 surveys, Arlen Egley Jr. of the NYGS, in the fact sheet "National Youth Gang Survey Trends from 1996 to 2000" (February 2002, http://www.ncjrs.gov/pdffiles1/ojjdp/fs200203.pdf), finds that "the proportion of respondents that reported youth gangs in their jurisdiction decreased over the survey years, from 53 percent in 1996 to 40 percent in 2000." In the *National Youth Gang Survey, 1999–2001* (July 2006, http://www.ncjrs.gov/pdffiles1/ojjdp/209392.pdf), Arlen Egley Jr., James C. Howell, and Aline K. Major of the NYGS estimate that there were approximately 21,500 gangs present in the United States in 2002. (See Figure 8.1.) Most of these (85%) were active in cities, but a substantial number—about six thousand—were present in non-urban counties. Between about 1997 and 2002 there was a general pattern of a reduction in the estimated number of gangs. Much of the decrease in the number of gangs and gang members occurred in jurisdictions with populations between 100,000 and 249,999 people. Egley, Howell, and Major note that all participating jurisdictions with 250,000 or more residents acknowledged having persistent gang activity during each survey year. These larger jurisdictions also experienced a drop in the average number of gang members but not in the average number of gangs.

As Figure 8.2 shows, gang membership generally decreased between 1996 and 2002, from an estimated 846,000 gang members in 1996 to 731,500 gang members in 2002. Gang membership in cities had decreased slightly between 1999 and 2002, from about 600,000 to about 550,000; in counties gang membership had decreased from about 250,000 to 225,000. Egley, Howell, and Major indicate that cities with a population of 25,000 or fewer

FIGURE 8.1

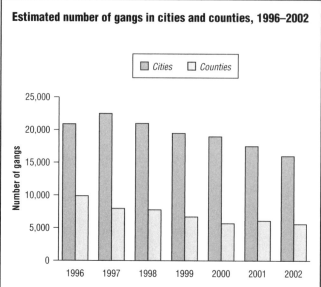

Estimated number of gangs in cities and counties, 1996–2002

SOURCE: Arlen Egley, Jr., James C. Howell, and Aline K. Major, "Figure 11. Estimated Number of Gangs Based on Reports by City and County Law Enforcement Agencies, 1996–2002," in *National Youth Gang Survey, 1999–2001*, U.S. Department of Justice, Office of Juvenile Justice and Delinquency Prevention, July 2006, http://www .ncjrs.gov/pdffiles1/ojjdp/209392.pdf (accessed March 4, 2007)

FIGURE 8.2

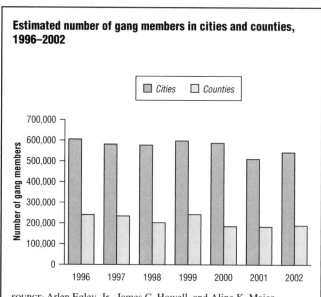

Estimated number of gang members in cities and counties, 1996–2002

SOURCE: Arlen Egley, Jr., James C. Howell, and Aline K. Major, "Figure 10. Estimated Number of Gang Members Based on Reports by City and County Law Enforcement Agencies, 1996–2002," in *National Youth Gang Survey, 1999–2001*, U.S. Department of Justice, Office of Juvenile Justice and Delinquency Prevention, July 2006, http://www .ncjrs.gov/pdffiles1/ojjdp/209392.pdf (accessed March 4, 2007)

reported a 43% reduction in gang members between 1998 and 2001, whereas larger cities and suburban counties reported 5% fewer gang members in 2001. Every city with a population of 250,000 or more reported that youth gangs were active in their cities in 2002.

In "Highlights of the 2004 National Youth Gang Survey" (April 2006, http://www.iir.com/nygc/publications/fs200601.pdf), Arlen Egley Jr. and Christina E. Ritz of the NYGS note that by 2004 there were an estimated 24,000 active gangs in the United States. Although this represented an overall decline of 2% from 2000 levels, a higher percentage of cities reported gang problems in the 2002–04 period than they did in the 1999–2001 period, after large declines in the late 1990s. Almost four out of five (79.8%) larger cities (population 50,000 or more), 40% of suburban counties, 28.4% of smaller cities (population 2,500 to 49,999), and 12.3% of rural counties reported gang problems in the 2002–04 period.

According to Egley and Ritz, in 2004 approximately 760,000 gang members were active in the United States. These numbers had held steady for about two years, after declines in the late 1990s. Approximately 85% of the estimated gang members lived in larger cities and suburban counties in 2004.

CHARACTERISTICS OF GANGS

According to the *2005 National Gang Threat Assessment* (2005, http://www.ojp.usdoj.gov/BJA/what/2005_threat_assesment.pdf), by the U.S. Department of Justice, the Bureau of Justice Assistance, and the National Alliance of Gang Investigators Associations, the modern street gang, or youth gang as it is often called, takes many forms. Individual members, gang cliques, or entire gang organizations engage in trafficking in drugs; operating car theft rings; committing shootings, assaults, robbery, extortion, and other felonies; and terrorizing neighborhoods. Some of the most ambitious gangs spread out from their home jurisdictions to other cities and states. Yet, some of the movement occurs simply because the gang members' families move to other areas, especially during times of economic growth. However, many gang members come from impoverished, immigrant, or transitional neighborhoods, where children are born into or must contend with second- and third-generation street gangs.

David Starbuck, James C. Howell, and Donna J. Lindquist, in *Hybrid and Other Modern Gangs* (December 2001, http://www.ncjrs.gov/html/ojjdp/jjbul2001_12_1/contents.html), examine survey data and current research to offer a portrait of the modern youth gang. Various stereotypes exist about gangs. For example, the stereotypical view holds that youth gangs are tightly organized groups made up of African-American or Hispanic inner-city males operating under strict codes of conduct with explicit punishments for infractions of the rules. However, the new hybrid gang can have members from both genders and from different racial groups as well as members having radically opposing viewpoints.

Starbuck, Howell, and Lindquist suggest that a modern gang might be made up of African-Americans, white supremacists, and females. The gangs are found in schools and the military and in territories as small as shopping malls. Rules or codes of conduct may be unclear. Hybrid gangs sometimes borrow the symbols, graffiti, and even the names of established organizations, such as those based in Los Angeles or Chicago (for example, Bloods, Crips, or Latin Kings), but are actually locally based and have no connection to those organizations. Rival gangs may cooperate in criminal activities, and mergers of small gangs are common.

Starbuck, Howell, and Lindquist note that in places where gangs are a fairly recent phenomenon, drug sales and distribution are less likely to be major problems. Gang member involvement in drug sales is most prevalent in areas where gangs emerged between 1981 and 1985, at the height of the crack cocaine epidemic. Highly organized, entrepreneurial, gang control of drug distribution across wide areas—and the violent crime that goes with it—are mainly associated with the gangs that emerged in the 1960s and 1970s in Los Angeles and Chicago.

Specific Gang Characteristics

Researchers, law enforcement, and community groups devote time to learning more about gangs and the types of characteristics they share. Much study has gone into gang slang, graffiti, hand signs, colors, and initiations, among other characteristics. The goal is to learn more about how gangs communicate and interact, both internally and externally, as well as test themselves and each other. If educators, law enforcement officials, and other concerned adults know how to recognize signs that young people may be involved in gangs, they will be better able to intervene.

GANG SLANG. Various gang members create their own slang language. Although some terms are used in gangs throughout the country, others are only used regionally and within certain gangs. Various terms originated with the infamous Crips and Bloods of Los Angeles, who have been adversaries for many years. Examples include "banging" (involved in gang activities), "colors" (clothing of a particular color, such as jackets, shoes, or bandanas, worn by gang members to identify themselves as part of the gang), "O.G." ("original gangster," meaning a gang member who has killed someone, or a founding member or leader of a gang), "tagging" (marking a territory with graffiti), and "turf" (territory).

GRAFFITI. Graffiti has been a form of communication since ancient times. Meaning "little scratches" in Italian, graffiti appeared in cave dwellings, Egyptian temples, and on other natural and human-made objects. Today, there are several categories of graffiti; each type is used to get the artists' message out to anyone who can read it.

Among the various types are personal musings, political messages, tagging, piecing or bombing, and gang graffiti.

The most common type of graffiti is that of personal musings—thoughts written down quickly in public places, such as restrooms and phone booths. Sometimes humorous, this type of graffiti might be of a sexual context, or might include memorable quotes. Oftentimes, it concerns race relations.

Political graffiti usually appears in places accessible to the general public—on the sides of buildings, freeway overpasses, and so on. The political message is generally against the establishment or authorities and may contain statements regarding labor conditions, civil rights, and religious thought.

Tagging is another type of graffiti. A tag is a signature, or moniker, which may incorporate the artist's physical features or symbolize his or her personality. Tags are found usually on exterior building walls in urban areas. They may also appear on mass transit systems (buses and trains), freeway overpasses, and other areas for all to see and wonder how it got there. Tagging first appeared on the East Coast in the late 1960s, making its way to the West Coast by the 1980s. Taggers feel a sense of power and fame as more and more surfaces contain their tags.

Mural-type graffiti is known as piecing or bombing. The piece usually contains elaborate depictions or a montage of images. Oftentimes, slogans appear within the piece. Whereas tags can be done quickly, piecing may take up to several hours and require many cans of spray paint in many colors.

Gang graffiti employs all the aforementioned types. Gangs use graffiti for many purposes. In some instances it may be a way of communicating messages to other gang members, functioning like a newsletter. Tags or monikers may be used to show a gang's hierarchy. Pieces may memorialize a dead gang member or pay tribute to the crimes committed by gang members. Some pieces may enumerate rules in the gang's society—it is often a means to advertise a gang's presence in the neighborhood. Gang graffiti may also serve as a threatening message to rival gangs—as if to say, "Stay away from our turf."

In today's society all types of graffiti are perceived as vandalism and a public nuisance and are punishable by law in the United States.

HAND SIGNS. Hand signs are a way of communicating concepts or ideas without using words. However, only those individuals who are familiar with the gesture's meaning are able to understand the message being conveyed. The rise of gang hand signs began in the Los Angeles area during the 1950s. Since that time many gangs have developed hand signs for use between members of the group.

Gang members "throw" or "flash" hand signs as a way of communicating among themselves, sending secret messages to other members within the group. For example, placing a clenched fist over the heart means "I'll die for you."

In *Recognize the Signs* (November 2005, http://www.nj.gov/oag/gang-signs-bro.pdf), the New Jersey Office of the Attorney General and the Juvenile Justice Commission explain that each gang usually has a hand sign that symbolizes affiliation with the gang. For example, the Los Angeles Bloods use the B sign (creating a circle with the thumb and index finger, with the other fingers raised) to signify membership in the gang. Crips use a sign that represents the letter C. Although this is a good way for gang members to recognize other members or affiliates, it can be used against them as well. A gang might use gestures created by a rival gang in an act called false flagging. When this occurs, a gang member will flash a rival gang's hand sign as a way to infiltrate the opposing gang or to lure an unsuspecting adversary into a bad situation.

Most gangs recognize many universal hand signals. One such ubiquitous sign dates back to World War II (1939–45)—the sign for "victory," made by raising the index and middle fingers in the shape of a V. Gangs use many universal gestures to intimidate or "dis" (disrespect) rival gangs. A raised fist means "power." Raising the index finger shows that the gang is "number one" and can beat all rivals. Gang hand signs may also appear prominently in gang graffiti.

FLYING THE COLORS. The idea of wearing different colors to identify opposing sides is not new. For example, during wartime opposing armies use different colors to symbolize their cause or protect their territory. Flags, uniforms, and the like were made in the color chosen to represent the nation or army at war. By donning the color of the army, soldiers were easily identified as being on one side or the other—the enemy could be spotted easily. During the American Revolution most of the British forces wore red uniforms; thus, they were called the Redcoats. To distinguish themselves from the British, the American colonists chose blue uniforms.

This is also true of gangs. *Recognize the Signs* notes that for many years they have used color to distinguish themselves from rival gangs, while protecting their turf. Gang members often show support for the gang by wearing "uniforms." Sporting clothes in the gang's colors, such as bandanas, shoes, jackets, jewelry, and other articles of clothing shows a person's membership in one gang over another. For example, the two largest gangs in the Los Angeles area are the Bloods and the Crips. The Bloods use red; the Crips use blue. The colors are a way to symbolize the gang's unity, power, and pride.

However, "flying the colors" can be a disadvantage to gangs. The *2005 National Gang Threat Assessment* indicates that although colors make it easier for other gangs to identify rival members, they also help law enforcement and school officials recognize gang members. Law enforcement officials have been able to crack down on gang-related criminal activities, rounding up juveniles and youths wearing gang colors. In response to this new threat, many gangs have opted to forego their traditional colors and are developing new methods of identification. Like the modern-day army, gang members are beginning to camouflage themselves from their rivals, making their uniforms less conspicuous. Wearing a hat tilted to the left may show membership in a gang whose rivals are those who wear their pant legs rolled up. Gang members also use hand signs to identify their affiliation to certain groups.

RECRUITMENT AND INITIATION. People tend to organize themselves into groups of like-minded individuals to meet and participate in group-related activities. Groups offer fellowship—a way to bond with others who share similar interests or goals. For today's youth, scouting, athletics, or debate clubs offer ways for kids to meet new friends and participate in various group activities, such as camping, learning crafts, and so on. The group organizers recruit members by offering experiences that a boy or girl might not have unless they are members of the group.

Although their activities are often criminal and their recruitment tactics highly aggressive, gangs operate in a similar fashion. Gang recruiters offer prospective members a chance to be a part of something—to gain a sense of belonging that might be lacking in their life. Through the use of graffiti, the wearing of colors or tattoos, or intimidation tactics, the gang recruits new members to increase its power. In turn, some juveniles see this power in the schools or on the sides of buildings and may feel pressured into joining a gang. In some instances gang members threaten the child or members of his or her family into joining, offering protection from bullies or rival gangs. Others might be eager to join a gang because they think it is cool and exciting to be part of a clique that engages in criminal activity.

In response to gang recruitment activities, some states and localities have changed their laws to make any kind of gang recruitment, even if it does not involve criminal behavior, illegal. For example, in 2007 the state of Illinois proposed to amend the criminal code by making street gang recruitment on school grounds or public property a felony, even if it did not involve the use or threat of physical force. In April 2004 Senator Charles Schumer of New York proposed a new law, the Criminal Street Gang Abatement Act, that would make gang recruitment punishable by up to ten years in jail.

As is common in some social clubs, many prospective gang inductees must undergo an initiation to show the members that they are worthy enough to be accepted into the group. "Jumping in" or "clicking in" to a gang usually involves some type of criminal activity for the inductee to perform. This may include stealing or damaging property, assaulting someone, or carrying and selling drugs. More radical forms of gang initiations may involve drive-by shootings or rape. In some instances the inductee is "beatdown" by gang members using baseball bats or brass knuckles. In rare instances a new member may be "blessed in"—not having to prove his or her worth—because a brother or sister is already a member of the gang. Some have difficulty trying to leave a gang. In these cases the youth might be pressured to remain in the clique or might be hesitant to leave because his or her friends and family (including parents) are in the gang.

Studies show that in many cases the modern adolescent may refuse to join a gang or leave it without fear of reprisal, even though gangs try to maintain the illusion that leaving is impossible. Terence P. Thornberry, David Huizinga, and Rolf Leober report in "The Causes and Correlates Studies: Findings and Policy Implications" (*Juvenile Justice*, September 2004) that this was borne out by OJJDP-supported longitudinal studies in Denver, Colorado (1988–99) and Rochester, New York (1986–97), as well as by the Seattle Social Development Project in Washington (1985–2001), all of which show that more than half (54% to 69%) of youths who joined gangs in those cities remained for one year or less, whereas only 9% to 21% stayed for three or more years. However, Egley, Howell, and Major find that gang membership appears to be getting older, which indicates that youth living in highly disadvantaged areas, where there is an absence of economic opportunity, may remain in gangs to later ages.

INDICATORS OF GANG INVOLVEMENT. Groups and researchers, such as the California Attorney General's Office, Crime and Violence Prevention Center, in *Gangs: A Community Response* (June 2003, http://safestate.org/shop/files/Gangs_Comm.resp.pdf), and Phelan A. Wyrick and James C. Howell, in "Strategic Risk-Based Response to Youth Gangs" (*Juvenile Justice*, September 2004), compile lists to aid parents, siblings, educators, and others in looking for signs that a youth has joined a gang. Even though a youth may present several warning signs that might indicate he or she is a gang member, these signs are not foolproof—that is, the youth may actually not be a gang member or even be a "wannabe" or "gonnabe" (at-risk youth). However, the more signs that a youth exhibits increases the likelihood that he or she is headed for gang involvement. The following are a few of the warning signs:

- Experiences sudden drop in school grades
- Lacks interest in school and other activities that were once important
- Becomes truant (skips school)

- Comes home late

- Acts more outwardly aggressive or outright defiant

- Develops a new circle of friends who seem more rough and tough

- Behaves more secretively and is less forthcoming

- Changes clothing style; begins wearing some colors exclusively or wears clothes in a unique way consistently (such as rolling up pant legs)

- Exhibits more antisocial tendencies; becomes withdrawn or uninterested in family activities

- Suddenly acquires costly material possessions (CDs, DVDs, electronics equipment, etc.) or large amounts of cash, and the source of the funds cannot be explained

- Starts using a new nickname (or street name)

- Becomes fascinated with weapons, particularly guns

- Has new cuts and bruises, indicating evidence of being in a fight, and is unable to provide a reasonable explanation

- Sports new unusual tattoos

- Writes gang graffiti on notebooks, schoolbooks, and posters

- Develops increased interest in gangsta rap music

- Hides stash of spray paint, permanent markers, and other graffiti supplies

- Has encounters with law enforcement

- Shows dependency on drugs or alcohol

Characteristics of Gang Members

GENDER. An overwhelming majority of gang members are reported by law enforcement agencies to be male; this fact changed little over the NYGS survey years. According to Egley, Howell, and Major, an estimated 10% of gang members are female. The larger the population size, the lower the proportion of gang members that are reported to be female; still, in the smallest population areas (fewer than twenty-five thousand), only 17% of gang members are female. However, 84% of survey respondents said that there were female gang members in their communities.

Other researchers who survey gang members themselves find higher proportions of female members. For example, Finn-Aage Esbensen and L. Thomas Winfree report in "Race and Gender Differences between Gang and Nongang Youths: Results from a Multisite Survey" (*Justice Quarterly*, September 1998) that 38% of self-identified middle-school gang members were female. Egley, Howell, and Major state that other studies find that 10% to 20% of all female survey participants in gang-problem areas are gang members. Some differences have been found to exist, however, between female and male gang members. Females involved in gangs are believed to join and leave gangs at an earlier age and at a faster rate than males. Female gang members are also believed to be not as involved in serious or violent crimes as are male gang members. As a result, this lower rate of serious criminal behavior may not bring female gang members to the attention of law enforcement officials.

AGE. Gang members are not always juveniles; in fact, over time law enforcement agencies have reported that a larger percentage of gang members are adults. In 1996 half of all gang members were reported to be age eighteen or older; by 2001 two-thirds (67%) of all gang members were reported to be adults. (See Figure 8.3.) However, Egley, Howell, and Major note that this proportion varies by the size of the community; in the largest cities adults make up a larger proportion of gang members, compared with the smallest population groups, where juveniles predominate. Still, in 2001, 51% of all reporting law enforcement agencies said that half or more of the gang members active in their communities were juveniles.

Gangs have a particular appeal to some youth. Gangs sometimes serve as families for children whose own families may be dysfunctional. Gang members say there

FIGURE 8.3

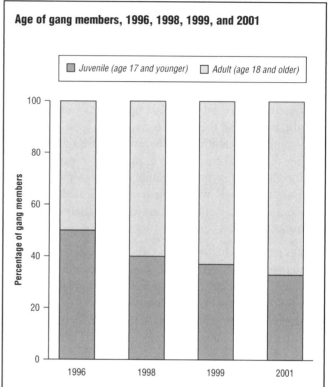

Age of gang members, 1996, 1998, 1999, and 2001

SOURCE: Arlen Egley, Jr., James C. Howell, Aline K. Major, "Figure 12. Age of Gang Members, 1996, 1998, 1999, and 2001," in *National Youth Gang Survey, 1999–2001*, U.S. Department of Justice, Office of Juvenile Justice and Delinquency Prevention, July 2006, http://www.ncjrs.gov/pdffiles1/ojjdp/209392.pdf (accessed March 4, 2007)

is often little need to intimidate youngsters to recruit them because they know what youth need and are willing to provide it in return for the child's commitment. Gangs provide emotional support, shelter, and clothing—in essence, just what the child's family may not be providing. However, some children are intimidated into joining gangs either out of fear or for protection from other gangs.

Egley, Howell, and Major also comment on the age ranges of members of youth gangs by area type where gangs operated in 2001. Large cities and suburban counties with populations of 250,000 or more reported the highest proportions of adult gang members; juveniles made up only about 30% of gang membership in these areas. By contrast, small cities and rural counties with populations less than 25,000 reported the highest proportions of juveniles by far (about 70%).

RACE AND ETHNICITY. According to Egley, Howell, and Major, law enforcement agencies reported in 2001 that approximately half of all gang members were Hispanic, whereas about one-third were African-American and one out of ten gang members was non-Hispanic white. Another 5% were Asian. Minorities are overrepresented among gang members because gangs arise and persist in economically disadvantaged and socially disorganized areas, and minority communities are overrepresented in these communities. As the Bureau of Justice Assistance notes, "It is not necessarily race that explains gang life, for gang members usually come from socially and economically disadvantaged communities." In addition, Egley, Howell, and Major explain that 29% of the 2001 NYGS respondents reported that the racial/ethnic groups other than African-American and/or Hispanic are the majority of gang members in their area; in other words, gang membership tends to reflect the demographics of the disadvantaged community from which it arises.

The *2005 National Gang Threat Assessment* also notes the connection between recent immigrant communities and gangs. New immigrant communities are often isolated by language barriers and difficulties in finding employment. Gangs are attractive to many in Hispanic immigrant communities because they provide support and protection. By contrast, Asian communities are less likely than other communities to report criminal activity to law enforcement agencies. As a result, gangs often victimize these communities.

Gang Types and Activities

The *2005 National Gang Threat Assessment* indicates that gangs remain the primary drug traffickers in the United States. In addition, gangs are thought to be increasingly associating themselves with organized crime groups, such as Mexican drug organizations and Asian and Russian organized crime. Imprisoning gang members is thought to do little to curb their activities, and the return of previously imprisoned gang members to communities is believed to intensify criminal activity, drug trafficking, and violence in those communities. In addition, California-style gangs have been found throughout the United States. Furthermore, gang members are becoming increasingly able to use technology and computers to engage in criminal activity.

Several Hispanic gangs originated in California but have since spread throughout the nation. Southern California gang members who moved out of the state united under the name Sureño (or Sur 13). According to the *2005 National Gang Threat Assessment*, in 2001 Sur 13 was present in thirty-five states across the nation. This group has connections to the Mexican mafia. Norteños are gang members who originated in Northern California; they are believed to have an alliance with an outlaw motorcycle gang that allows them to acquire drugs and aids them in defending against Hispanic gangs from Southern California. Mara Salvatrucha (MS-13) is an El Salvadoran street gang aligned with the Mexican mafia that originated in Los Angeles but spread to Virginia, Maryland, North Carolina, and New York. The Hispanic gang 18th Street is open to individuals of any racial background that reportedly has spread across the country and recruits in elementary and middle schools. The Latin Kings is a powerful gang that has split into three primary factions; its membership is primarily Puerto Rican males, but it does include individuals of other ethnicities. It is particularly active in New York, New Jersey, and Connecticut, where it engages in drug-related crime and bitter wars with other gangs over territory. Law enforcement officials report that they are seeing an increasing effort of some Hispanic gangs to align with one another to organize a criminal network.

A gang subculture has also emerged on Native American reservations. These gangs are primarily composed of youth. They engage in less criminal behavior than other gangs; according to the *2005 National Gang Threat Assessment*, "gang behavior is more about group cohesiveness, predatory activities, and a party atmosphere than it is about organized criminal behavior with a profit motive." Gangs on reservations tend to be small and unaligned with large, national gang networks. Even though violent crime is on the increase, most gang activity on reservations is associated with graffiti, vandalism, and drug sales.

In an effort to learn more about Native American gangs, the National Youth Gang Center conducted a survey, and Aline K. Major et al. reported the findings in "Youth Gangs in Indian Country" (*Juvenile Justice Bulletin*, March 2004). Major et al. note that the survey included "persons of American Indian, Alaska Native, or Aleut heritage who reside within the limits of Indian reservations, pueblos, rancherias, villages, dependent Indian communities, or Indian allotments, and who together comprise a federally recognized tribe or community." Major et al. report that youth gangs were active in 23% of Indian communities. Fifty-nine percent of communities reporting active gangs estimated the number of gangs between one and five, 19% estimated the number to be between six and ten, and 6% estimated more than ten. Sixteen percent of the communities with gangs believed the gangs consisted of more than fifty people, 12% estimated twenty-six to fifty people, and 32% reported twenty-five or fewer. According to Major et al., about 75% of gang members were juveniles. Females made up 20% of Indian country gang members. A mix of both males and females existed in 82% of the gangs. About 10% of gangs on reservations were thought to be female-dominated. Nearly four out of five gang members on reservations were of Native American, Alaskan Native, or Aleut descent. The other 22% were of other ethnic or racial backgrounds, most notably Hispanics and non-Hispanic whites.

Some researchers classify gangs not according to their racial/ethnic makeup but according to what purposes they serve and their organizational structures. The *National Victim Assistance Academy Textbook* (June 2002, http://www.ojp.usdoj.gov/ovc/assist/nvaa2002/toc .html) by the Department of Justice, Office for Victims of Crime, outlines gang research conducted by the sociologist Carl S. Taylor. Taylor categorized gangs into three types: scavenger gangs, which act spontaneously and lack organization, have frequent changes in leadership, tend to have members who are low achievers, and are regarded unfavorably by other types of gangs; territorial gangs, which are highly organized, prone to fighting to establish turfs, who use formal initiations, and are formed mainly for social reasons; and corporate gangs, which are highly structured, engage in drug trafficking, require members to live by a strict set of rules with harsh punishments for those who break them, and whose members can be considered actual "gangsters." Members of corporate gangs tend to be more intelligent than members of scavenger and territorial gangs, but they may lack formal schooling.

Reasons for Joining a Gang

Why juveniles, youths, and even adults participate in gangs is the subject of much study in the United States. Studies include those by James C. Howell of the NYGC, in *Youth Gangs: An Overview* (August 1998, http://www.ncjrs .gov/pdffiles/167249.pdf) and in *Youth Gang Programs and Strategies* (August 2000, http://www.ncjrs .gov/pdffiles1/ ojjdp/171154.pdf); and Wyrick and Howell (see above). Although the reasons vary greatly among gang members, there are a few basic motives. It is important to note, however, that even though these factors may cause some people to join gangs, they do not prompt most people to do so. Some of the most common reasons to join a gang are:

- Feeling marginalized by society and seeking a commonality with others in similar situations

- Wanting power and respect

- Having friends involved in gangs

- Desiring a sense of belonging when it is not available through a traditional family setting

- Seeking safety and/or protection from bullies, rival gangs, family members, or others

- Having power in numbers

- Ending poverty and joblessness by turning to criminal activities, such as stealing and drug trafficking

- Needing to feel a sense of purpose

- Having trouble or a disinterest in school

- Living in neighborhoods or communities where other troubled youth roam the streets

- Adding organization and structure to one's life

- Having feelings of low self-esteem that are diminished through encouragement from other gang members

Karl G. Hill, Christina Lui, and J. David Hawkins tracked juveniles in Seattle, Washington, over the course of several years to learn more about their involvement in gang-related activities. They reported their findings in "Early Precursors of Gang Membership: A Study of Seattle Youth" (*Juvenile Justice Bulletin*, December 2001). During the multiyear study, Hill, Lui, and Hawkins tracked a group of 808 fifth-graders through age eighteen. They learned that 15.3% (124 students) joined a gang between the ages of thirteen and eighteen. Of those joining gangs, 69% stayed in a gang for less than one year, whereas 0.8% of study participants who joined a gang at age thirteen were still in a gang at age eighteen.

According to Hill, Lui, and Hawkins, those children who stayed in a gang for several years "were the most behaviorally and socially maladjusted," often exhibiting "early signs of violent and externalizing behavior (e.g., aggression, oppositional behavior, and inattentive and hyperactive behaviors)." Children who associated with antisocial peers were more than twice as likely to remain in a gang for more than one year. The *National Victim Assistance Academy Textbook* reports that gangs are starting to recruit younger members, sometimes as young as seven or eight years old.

Hill, Lui, and Hawkins identify various risk factors potentially leading to gang involvement. These include having a learning disability, access to marijuana, low academic achievement, other youth in trouble living in the neighborhood, and a living arrangement that includes one parent along with other unrelated adults.

GANGS IN SCHOOLS

The presence of street gangs is a growing concern in U.S. schools. Various educators and students—urban, suburban, and rural—acknowledge the presence of gangs in their schools. Such gangs are often involved in illegal activities, such as violence, drugs, and weapons trafficking. Gang presence in schools often leads to fear among students who are not affiliated with a gang and may encourage nongang members to join one to gain protection. In schools with significant gang presence, the level of violence is frequently higher than in schools with less gang presence.

Rachel Dinkes et al., in *Indicators of School Crime and Safety: 2006* (December 2006, http://www.ojp.usdoj.gov/bjs/pub/pdf/iscs06.pdf), address the issue of street gangs on school campuses. In 2005, 36% of urban students were most likely to acknowledge the presence of street gangs at school during the previous six months. (See Figure 8.4.) Suburban students (21%) and rural students (16%) followed. Even though law enforcement officials surveyed in the NYGS stated that gang membership held steady in the early 2000s, an increasing number of students reported gang activity at school; in 2001, 20% of students reported gangs at school, whereas in 2005, 24% of students reported gangs at school. This increase was apparent in urban schools (29% in 2001 versus 36% in 2005), suburban schools (18% in 2001 versus 21% in 2005), and in rural schools (13% in 2001 versus 16% in 2005).

According to Dinkes et al., the percentages of students reporting gangs in public schools far eclipsed the number in private schools. In 2005 a quarter (25%) of students in public schools reported gang activities at their schools, whereas only 4% of private school students did. Students at public schools were more likely to report the presence of gangs than were students at private schools, regardless of the school's location.

In terms of race and ethnicity, Hispanics in urban schools (48%) were the most likely group to acknowledge gangs at school, whereas white rural students (14%) were the least likely. (See Figure 8.5.) Hispanic students were the most likely to report the presence of gangs at school and African-American students were the second most likely in urban areas and rural areas, whereas African-American students were the most likely to report the presence of gangs at suburban schools (35%), followed by Hispanic students (32%).

FIGURE 8.4

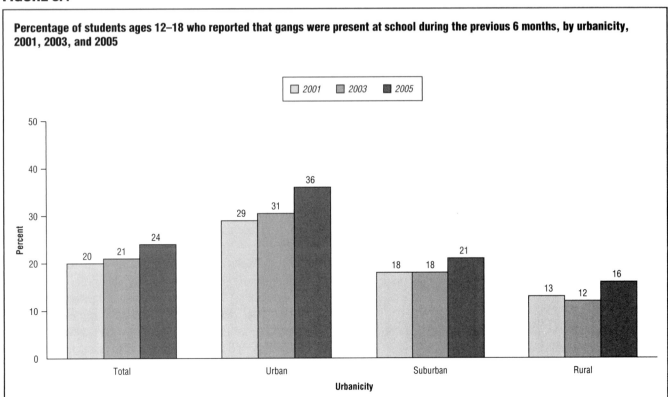

Percentage of students ages 12–18 who reported that gangs were present at school during the previous 6 months, by urbanicity, 2001, 2003, and 2005

Note: All gangs, whether or not they are involved in violent or illegal activity, are included. "At school" includes the school building, on school property, on a school bus, or going to and from school. In 2005, the unit response rate for this survey did not meet National Center for Education Statistics standards; therefore, interpret the data with caution. Population sizes for students ages 12–18 are 24,315,000 in 2001; 25,684,000 in 2003; and 25,811,000 in 2005.

SOURCE: Rachel Dinkes et al., "Figure 8.1. Percentage of Students Ages 12–18 Who Reported That Gangs Were Present at School during the Previous 6 Months, by Urbanicity: Various Years, 2001–2005," in *Indicators of School Crime and Safety: 2006*, U.S. Department of Education, National Center for Education Statistics, and U.S. Department of Justice, Bureau of Justice Statistics, December 2006, http://www.ojp.usdoj.gov/bjs/pub/pdf/iscs06.pdf (accessed March 5, 2007)

FIGURE 8.5

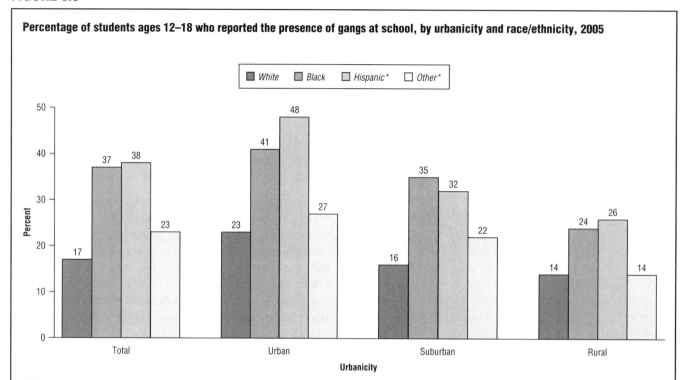

Percentage of students ages 12–18 who reported the presence of gangs at school, by urbanicity and race/ethnicity, 2005

*Other includes American Indian, Alaska Native, Asian or Pacific Islander, and more than one race. For this report, non-Hispanic students who identified themselves as more than one race were included in the other category. Respondents who identified themselves as being of Hispanic origin are classified as Hispanic, regardless of their race.
Note: All gangs, whether or not they are involved in violent or illegal activity, are included. "At school" includes the school building, on school property, on a school bus, or going to and from school. In 2005, the unit response rate for this survey did not meet National Center for Education Statistics standards; therefore, interpret the data with caution. Population size for students ages 12–18 is 25,811,000 in 2005.

SOURCE: Rachel Dinkes et al., "Figure 8.2. Percentage of Students Ages 12–18 Who Reported That Gangs Were Present at School during the Previous 6 Months, by Urbanicity and Race/Ethnicity: 2005," in *Indicators of School Crime and Safety: 2006*, U.S. Department of Education, National Center for Education Statistics, and U.S. Department of Justice, Bureau of Justice Statistics, December 2006, http://www.ojp.usdoj.gov/bjs/pub/pdf/iscs06.pdf (accessed March 5, 2007)

Indicators of Gang Presence at School

In "Youth Gangs in Schools" (*Juvenile Justice Bulletin*, August 2000), James C. Howell and James P. Lynch note that even in elementary and secondary schools, youth gangs can present serious crime problems. They describe various studies that asked surveyed students to explain why they believed gangs were present in their schools. The students' responses included:

- The gang has a recognized name (80%).

- The surveyed student has spent time with gang members (80%).

- The gang members wear clothing or other items identifying their group (71%).

- The gang marks or tags its turf with graffiti (56%).

- The gang committed acts of violence (50%).

- The gang has a recognized territory/turf (47%).

- The gang members have tattoos (37%).

- The gang members have a recognized leader (33%).

Gangs and Drugs at School

Howell and Lynch comment on the connection between drug availability and gang presence at school. They note, "Where none of the drugs was easy to get, only 25 percent of surveyed students said gangs were present. This percentage increased from 42 percent when only one drug was readily available to 69 percent when seven drugs were readily available, and then dropped slightly when eight or nine drugs were readily available." When eight and nine drugs were available at school, the percentage of students reporting gangs increased to 63% and 62%, respectively. It is unclear whether the availability of drugs was because of the gang activity, or if the presence of gangs was part of an underlying problem that contributed to the availability of drugs as well. As Dinkes et al. note, "The availability of drugs on school property has a disruptive and corrupting influence on the school environment." They also report that 25% of high school students reported that drugs were available to them on school property.

Gang Criminality at School

Howell and Lynch report survey respondents' impressions about the presence of gangs in school and its relationship to crime. According to Howell and Lynch, "The students reported that most of the gangs they see at school are actively involved in criminal activities. About two-thirds of the students reported that gangs are involved in none or only one of three types of criminal acts: violence, drug sales, or carrying guns. Nevertheless, students said that a small proportion of gangs in schools (8 percent) are involved in all three types of crimes, and these gangs are probably responsible for the most disruption and violent victimization in and around schools." Howell and Lynch indicate that other studies include a variety of other criminal activities known to be perpetrated by gang members.

Howell and Lynch also stated that gangs contribute substantially to victimizations at school. It is believed that some students join gangs to avoid persecution by gang members. For them, gang membership serves as a form of protection from other students who may have threatened them or wished them harm.

GANG CRIME AND VIOLENCE
Homicides

Egley, Howell, and Major explain that the impact and severity of gang activity in an area is often measured by the numbers of gang-related homicides. The term *gang-motivated homicides* refers to those murders that further the interests of a gang, whereas *gang-related homicides* generally refers to murders where a gang member is either a perpetrator or the victim. Most localities use the broader gang member–based definition, rather than the motive-based definition, when classifying a homicide as gang related.

According to Egley, Howell, and Major, there is a clear relationship between population size and gang-related homicides. More than 90% of law enforcement agencies serving communities of less than twenty-five thousand reported no gang-related homicides between 1999 and 2001, as did 74% of law enforcement agencies serving communities of twenty-five thousand to fifty thousand people. Of law enforcement agencies in these smaller communities that did report gang-related homicides, most had no more than two. Slightly more than half (51%) of law enforcement agencies in communities of fifty thousand to one hundred thousand people reported no gang-related homicides, and another third of agencies in these communities reported no more than two.

Most gang-related homicides are concentrated in large cities. Egley, Howell, and Major note that in cities with a population of one hundred thousand or more, 78% reported gang-related homicides. At the same time, fully a quarter of these cities reported ten or more gang-related homicides between 1999 and 2001.

Some evidence suggests that even though the number of active gangs and gang membership is holding steady or declining, gang violence is getting worse. Egley and Ritz indicate that two cities, Los Angeles and Chicago, reported that more than half of the homicides in those cities were considered gang related, whereas the remaining 171 cities that responded to the survey considered approximately a quarter of all homicides to be gang related. The number of gang homicides in these cities in 2004 was 11% higher than the annual average of gang-related homicides over the past eight years.

In *Homicide Trends in the United States* (June 29, 2006, http://www.ojp.usdoj.gov/bjs/pub/pdf/htius.pdf), James Alan Fox and Marianne W. Zawitz note that between 1976 and 2004 gang-related homicides increased eightfold, from 129 in 1976 to 1,025 in 2004 (down from a high of 1,362, in 1993). Homicides were far more likely to be gang related in large cities (69.5%), followed by suburban areas (16.7%), small cities (13%), and rural areas (0.7%).

The *National Victim Assistance Academy Textbook* notes that "youthful gang members have 'no fear of death' and often *how they die* is what is important in gang dynamics. This factor contributes to retaliatory gang violence and criminal acts that are increasingly violent in nature."

Drug Trafficking and Other Crime

Gangs use drug trafficking as a major source of financial gain. According to the *2005 National Gang Threat Assessment*, 31.6% of all law enforcement respondents to the NYGS reported that gangs in their communities were highly involved in selling drugs in their communities. Law enforcement agencies believed this was especially true in the distribution of marijuana (64.8%), followed by crack cocaine (47.3%), methamphetamine (39.1%), powdered cocaine (38.2%), heroin (27.9%), and MDMA (23.7%). Gangs in the West and the Northeast are believed to be more likely to be involved in selling drugs than are gangs in the South and the Midwest.

Most law enforcement agencies do not keep detailed statistics about gang involvement in other types of crime. As a result, C. Ronald Huff of Ohio State University conducted a study on gang involvement in crime and reported his findings in *Criminal Behavior of Youth Gangs and At-Risk Youths* (March 1998, http://www.ncjrs.gov/pdffiles/fs000190.pdf). Huff interviewed fifty gang members in four communities: Aurora and Denver, Colorado; Broward County, Florida; and Cleveland, Ohio. As a control, Huff also interviewed fifty youths from each area who represented the at-risk population but who were not gang members. The results of the one-time, confidential interviews indicated that gang members were significantly more involved in crime than nonmembers.

Huff notes that 58.3% of Colorado and Florida gang members and 44.7% of Cleveland gang members acknowledged that they had personally stolen cars. The control group youths self-reported a much lower car theft rate. In Colorado and Florida that rate was 12.5%, and in Cleveland it was 4.1%. Huff also asked about drive-by shootings. He reports that 40% of Cleveland gang members claimed to have participated in a drive-by, compared with 2% of those in the control group. Among Colorado and Florida gang members, 64.2% acknowledged that members of their gangs had committed homicide. That number was far less among control-group members, 6.5% of whom reported that their friends had killed someone.

Huff indicates that gang members were much more likely than nonmembers to own guns. In the study communities, more than 90% of gang members stated that their peers had carried concealed weapons, and another 80% admitted that members had taken guns to school. About half of the control-group members had friends who had carried a concealed weapon, whereas one-third acknowledged that friends had taken guns to school.

According to the *National Victim Assistance Academy Textbook*, when it comes to crime and punishment, gang members have learned to "work the system": "Experience shows that incapacitation of individual gang members is not sufficient to control gang crime because removing individuals does not diminish the influence of the gang on the street. In addition, gangs have learned the procedural differences between juvenile and adult court and have used these to their advantage. Since gangs consist of both juvenile and adult members, many gangs have come to use juveniles extensively in the commission of crimes. This ensures lenient penalties for adjudicated juvenile offenders."

CONSEQUENCES OF BEING IN A GANG

Being in a gang can be dangerous. Former members can tell many stories about the difficulties one encounters in gang life. Besides living a life with the potential for more violence and crime than the average youth would experience, many other consequences exist. Although such consequences might vary considerably among individuals, Terence P. Thornberry, David Huizinga, and Rolf Leober, in "The Causes and Correlates Studies: Findings and Policy Implications" (*Juvenile Justice*, September 2004), and Dana Peterson, Terrance J. Taylor, and Finn-Aage Esbensen, in "Gang Membership and Violent Victimization" (*Justice Quarterly*, December 2004), address some of the most commonly encountered consequences:

- Becoming a school dropout
- Having little opportunity to secure a good, legal job
- Being unable to hold a steady job
- Becoming antisocial; having difficulty socializing outside the gang
- Having an increased likelihood of being a victim of violent crime
- Entering motherhood or fatherhood at an early age
- Ending up in prison or jail for gang crimes
- Developing a dependency on drugs and/or alcohol
- Experiencing a higher risk of premature death

CHAPTER 9
CRIME AND VIOLENCE IN THE SCHOOLS

School is supposed to be a safe haven where young people can go to learn the basics of mathematics, literature, science, and other subjects, without fearing for their safety, feeling intimidated, or being harassed. Although school administrators and teachers work toward making the environment safe and secure, crime and violence do find their way into the hallways and classrooms and onto school grounds. Despite media emphasis on topics such as school shootings, fatal violence at schools is relatively low. Nonfatal crime, however, occurs in far greater numbers, sometimes even more frequently at school than away from school.

Safety is and will continue to be a concern at schools. A rash of school shootings and bomb threats that occurred in the 1990s, and that continue to occur in the 2000s, brought increasing attention to school safety issues and what must be done to protect students; two particularly troubling incidences are the shootings at Colorado's Columbine High School in 1999 and the more recent tragedy on the college campus of Virginia Tech in the spring of 2007, in which a student killed thirty-two people and then himself. Various studies on school violence and crime were issued in the late 1990s and early 2000s as researchers examined past trends and tried to predict patterns for the future. Surveys range from how many children bring weapons to school to how many children are injured in fights, are afraid to go to school, or are subjected to disciplinary actions. Educators, school administrators, parents, and students themselves remain vigilant in striving to make schools safe places where youth are able to learn and prepare for the future.

How much crime and violence exist at schools today? Has it increased or decreased in recent years? What effect did the Columbine High School shootings have on students and public opinion in general? Is there a danger that students, educators, and school officials will underreport school crime and violence to police?

VIOLENT DEATHS AT SCHOOL

During the 2004–05 school year there were forty-eight school-associated violent deaths in elementary and secondary schools, including twenty-one homicides and seven suicides. (See Table 9.1.) The most school-associated deaths (including staff, students, and nonstudents) in any year of the study was fifty-seven, which occurred during both the 1992–93 and 1997–98 school years. Still, the 2004–05 number was significantly higher than the thirty-five deaths in each of the previous two school years.

Between July 1, 1992, and June 30, 2005, some 582 school-associated violent deaths occurred across the United States, including 316 homicides of school-age children. Despite the understandable fear generated by the media coverage of events, the possibility of being shot at school is minimal. As Rachel Dinkes et al. note in *Indicators of School Crime and Safety: 2006* (December 2006, http://www.ojp.usdoj.gov/bjs/pub/pdf/iscs06.pdf), "In each school year, youth were over 50 times more likely to be murdered and almost 150 times more likely to commit suicide when they were away from school than at school." However, Americans were shocked by the rash of school shootings in the 1990s and some were afraid to send their children to school. The shootings at Columbine High School, in particular, weighed heavily on many students' and parents' minds.

Columbine High School

The tragedy began around 11:10 a.m. on April 20, 1999, as the senior Eric David Harris arrived at the student parking lot at Columbine High School in Littleton, a suburb of Denver, Colorado. A short time later, Dylan Bennet Klebold, Harris's friend and classmate, arrived. Carrying two large duffel bags, they walked together to the school cafeteria. Each of the bags contained a twenty-pound propane bomb, which was set to detonate at exactly 11:17 a.m. Harris and Klebold looked for an inconspicuous place to

TABLE 9.1

Number of school-associated violent deaths by location, 1992–2005

Year	Total student, staff, and nonstudent school-associated violent deaths[a]	Homicides of youth ages 5–18		Suicides of youth ages 5–18	
		Homicides at school[b]	Total homicides[c]	Suicides at school[b]	Total suicides[d]
1992–93	57	34	2,689	6	1,680
1993–94	48	29	2,879	7	1,723
1994–95	48	28	2,654	7	1,767
1995–96	53	32	2,512	6	1,725
1996–97	48	28	2,189	1	1,633
1997–98	57	34	2,056	6	1,626
1998–99	47	33	1,762	4	1,597
1999–2000[e]	36	13	1,537	8	1,415
2000–01[e]	30	11	1,466	4	1,493
2001–02[e]	40	16	1,468	6	1,400
2002–03[e]	35	18	1,515	9	1,331
2003–04[e]	35	19	1,437	3	1,285
2004–05[e]	48	21	—	7	—

— Not available.

[a]School-associated violent deaths include a homicide, suicide, legal intervention (involving a law enforcement officer), or unintentional firearm-related death in which the fatal injury occurred on the campus of a functioning elementary or secondary school in the United States, while the victim was on the way to or from regular sessions at school or while the victim was attending or traveling to or from an official school-sponsored event. Victims include students, staff members, and others who are not students, from July 1, 1992, through June 30, 2005.

[b]Youth ages 5–18 from July 1, 1992, through June 30, 2005.

[c]Youth ages 5–18 from July 1, 1992, through June 30, 2004.

[d]Youth ages 5–18 in the calendar year from 1992 to 2003.

[e]Data are preliminary and subject to change.

Notes: "At school" includes on school property, on the way to or from regular sessions at school, and while attending or traveling to or from a school-sponsored event.

SOURCE: Rachel Dinkes et al., "Table 1.1. Number of School-Associated Violent Deaths, Homicides, and Suicides of Youth Ages 5–18, by Location: 1992–2005," in *Indicators of School Crime and Safety: 2006*, U.S. Department of Education, National Center for Education Statistics, and U.S. Department of Justice, Bureau of Justice Statistics, December 2006, http://www.ojp.usdoj.gov/bjs/pub/pdf/iscs06.pdf (accessed March 5, 2007)

leave their bomb-concealing bags among the hundreds of other backpacks and bags there. After choosing a spot, Harris and Klebold returned to the parking lot to wait for the bombs to detonate.

Part of their plan was aimed at diverting the Littleton Fire Department, the Jefferson County Sheriff's Office, and other emergency personnel away from the high school as the pair stormed the school. To achieve this, they had planted pipe bombs three miles southwest of the high school set to explode and start grass fires. As the explosions began, Harris and Klebold prepared to reenter the school, this time via the west exterior steps. That location is the highest point on campus and allows a view of the student parking lots and the cafeteria's entrances and exits. Both Harris and Klebold, dressed in black trench coats, concealed 9mm semiautomatic weapons from view. As they approached, the pair pulled out shotguns from a duffel bag and opened fire toward the west doors of the school, killing seventeen-year-old Rachel Scott.

After entering the school, they roamed the halls, library, and cafeteria, among other areas, killing twelve other victims, including a teacher, before finally killing themselves. In the process they also injured twenty-three other students physically and many others emotionally. The details of the event are outlined in *The Columbine High School Shootings: Jefferson County Sheriff Depart-ment's Investigation Report* (May 15, 2000), by the Jefferson County Sheriff's Department. Since that time, more documents and videotapes have been made available to the victims' families, the media, and others as well.

Investigations after the Columbine shootings focused on incidents in the boys' past that might have indicated the potential for such violent behavior. Among the people most surprised by the shootings were Klebold's family. Tom Klebold, Dylan's father, told investigators that his son had never showed any interest in guns. The Klebolds told authorities that Dylan had been accepted at the University of Arizona and had planned to study computer science. Klebold's friends and teachers described him as a nice, normal teenager. However, authorities also learned that Klebold and Harris were often subjected to harassment and bullying from other students. Much discussion of this fact was reported by the media, which prompted various research organizations to look into the effects of bullying on juveniles. Some wondered if the ridicule from other students had prompted Harris and Klebold to seek revenge.

Federal Bureau of Investigation Investigates School Shooters

Previous school shooting incidents had prompted the Federal Bureau of Investigation (FBI) to spend two years researching this phenomenon. In *The School Shooter:*

A Threat Assessment Perspective (1999, http://www.fbi .gov/publications/school/school2.pdf), Mary Ellen O'Toole of the FBI asserts that the profile of a school shooter cannot be determined, nor is it possible to create a checklist of the warning signs indicating the next juvenile who will bring lethal violence to school. O'Toole's intent, however, is to assist school personnel and others in assessing threats and to keep any planned violence from occurring.

O'Toole uses a four-pronged approach in assessing "the totality of the circumstances" known about a student in four major areas: the student's personality, family dynamics, school dynamics, and social dynamics. O'Toole states, "If an act of violence occurs at a school, the school becomes the scene of the crime. As in any violent crime, it is necessary to understand what it is about the school which might have influenced the student's decision to offend there rather than someplace else."

According to O'Toole, the FBI has established the following factors in making this determination:

- The student's attachment to school: The student appears to be "detached" from school, including other students, teachers, and school activities.

- Tolerance for disrespectful behavior: The school does little to prevent or punish disrespectful behavior between individual students or groups of students.

- Inequitable discipline: Discipline is inequitably applied (or has the perception of being inequitably applied) by students and/or staff.

- Inflexible culture: The school's culture is static, unyielding, and insensitive to changes in society and the changing needs of newer students and staff.

- Pecking order among students: Certain groups of students are officially or unofficially given more prestige and respect than others.

- Code of silence: Few students feel they can safely tell teachers or administrators if they are concerned about another student's behavior or attitudes. Little trust exists between students and staff.

- Unsupervised computer access: Access to computers and the Internet is unsupervised and unmonitored. Students are able to use the school's computers to play violent computer games or to explore inappropriate Web sites, such as those that promote violent hate groups or give instructions for bomb-making.

Despite the factors that might indicate a school would be more likely to be the site of a deadly incident, O'Toole emphasizes again in "School Shootings: What You Should Know" (October 2006, http://www.fbi.gov/ page2/oct2006/schoolshootings100606.htm) that there might be nothing that can be done to prevent a violent incident from occurring. However, she states that school personnel should be vigilant, paying attention to students' moods and behaviors and taking all threats seriously.

SECURITY AND DISCIPLINE

After Columbine, as students, teachers, and parents became more worried about school safety, U.S. schools began implementing security measures to try to prevent future violent incidents. According to Dinkes et al., in the 2003–04 school year 83% of public schools locked some doors and monitored unlocked doors during school hours, 98% required visitors to check in, and 1% required students to pass through a metal detector each day. Security cameras were used in monitoring 28% of primary schools, 42% of middle schools, and 60% of secondary schools. More security measures tended to be used in high schools: 13% of all high schools performed random metal detector checks on students, 59% randomly used dogs to detect drugs, and another 28% used other random sweeps to check for drugs. Critics of increased surveillance in schools contend that bullying, stalking, and harassment present the real risk to students and believe that stronger counseling and early intervention programs are urgently needed.

In fact, efforts to decrease violence in schools have had mixed results. Dinkes et al. find that victimizations declined from 73 per 1,000 students in 2003 to 55 per 1,000 students in 2004. However, the number of homicides of youth at school in the 2004–05 school year was actually higher than in 2000–01 (21 and 11, respectively). (See Table 9.1.) In 2004 students were the victims of about 1.4 million nonfatal crimes at school, including 582,800 violent crimes—107,400 of which were serious violent crimes such as rape, sexual assault, and aggravated assault. In addition, 10% of male students and 6% of female students reported being threatened or injured with a weapon on school property. What follows is a closer look at these statistics.

Disciplinary Problems and Actions

Schools contend with a wide range of disciplinary problems that can affect the safety and positive educational experience of students and staff alike. These include bullying, gang activities, verbal abuse of teachers, disrespectful acts against teachers, widespread disorder in the classroom, cult or extremist group activities, and racial tension. The National Center for Education Statistics of the U.S. Department of Education reviews such disciplinary problems in its School Survey on Crime and Safety (SSOCS). Its 2003–04 survey finds that 27% of public schools experienced problems with student bullying. (See Figure 9.1.) Bullying was a particular problem in middle schools; 42% of middle schools reported bullying was a problem. Undesirable gang activities were a problem in 17% of public schools, and student disrespect for teachers was a problem in 19% of public schools. Gang activities

FIGURE 9.1

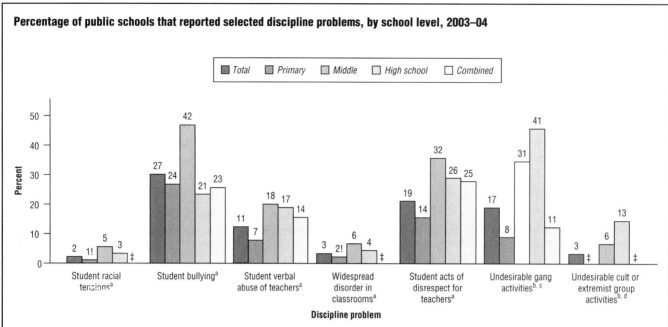

Percentage of public schools that reported selected discipline problems, by school level, 2003–04

!Interpret data with caution.
‡Reporting standards not met.
[a]Includes schools that reported the activity happens either once a week or daily.
[b]Includes schools that reported the activity has happened at all at their school during the school year.
[c]A gang was defined for respondents as "an ongoing loosely organized association of three or more persons, whether formal or informal, that has a common name, signs, symbols or colors, whose members engage, either individually or collectively, in violent or other forms of illegal behavior."
[d]A cult or extremist group was defined for respondents as "a group that espouses radical beliefs and practices, which may include a religious component, that are widely seen as threatening the basic values and cultural norms of society at large."
Notes: Either school principals or the person most knowledgeable about discipline issues at school completed the School Survey on Crime and Safety questionnaire. Primary schools are defined as schools in which the lowest grade is not higher than grade 3 and the highest grade is not higher than grade 8. Middle schools are defined as schools in which the lowest grade is not lower than grade 4 and the highest grade is not higher than grade 9. High schools are defined as schools in which the lowest grade is not lower than grade 9. Combined schools include all other combinations of grades, including K–12 schools. "At school" was defined for respondents to include activities that happen in school buildings, on school grounds, on school buses, and at places that hold school-sponsored events or activities. Respondents were instructed to respond only for those times that were during normal school hours or when school activities or events were in session, unless the survey specified otherwise. Population size is 80,500 public schools.

SOURCE: Rachel Dinkes et al., "Figure 7.1. Percentage of Public Schools Reporting Selected Discipline Problems That Occurred at School, by School Level: 2003–04," in *Indicators of School Crime and Safety: 2006*, U.S. Department of Education, National Center for Education Statistics, and U.S. Department of Justice, Bureau of Justice Statistics, December 2006, http://www.ojp.usdoj.gov/bjs/pub/pdf/iscs06.pdf (accessed March 5, 2007)

were most prevalent at high schools (41%), whereas disrespect for teachers occurred most often in middle schools (32%).

Student verbal abuse of teachers was reported in 11% of public schools, including 18% of middle schools and 17% of high schools. (See Figure 9.1.) Three percent of public schools reported disciplinary problems with undesirable cult or extremist group activities, and another 3% reported widespread disorder in classrooms. Relatively few public schools (2%) reported problems with student racial tensions.

One of the ways that schools attempt to deal with safety issues is to take serious disciplinary action against students committing crimes and violent acts. Dinkes et al. note that almost half (46%) of public schools took at least one serious disciplinary action against a student in the 2003–04 school year. Three quarters (74%) of these actions involved out-of-school suspensions lasting five days or more, 21% involved transfers to specialized

schools, and 5% were removals with no services for the remainder of the school year.

These serious disciplinary actions were taken for a variety of offenses. About a third (32%) of public schools took serious disciplinary actions in response to physical attacks or fights. (See Figure 9.2.) Another 22% took these actions in response to insubordination; 21% were taken in response to the distribution, possession, or use of illegal drugs; and 9% were taken in response to the distribution, possession, or use of alcohol. Another 17% were taken in response to the use or possession of a weapon other than a firearm, and 4% were taken in response to the use or possession of a firearm or explosive device.

NONFATAL CRIMES

Between 1992 and 2004 the rate of nonfatal crimes against students between the ages of twelve and eighteen at school (in the building, on school property, and en route to and from school) has generally declined. (See Figure 9.3.)

FIGURE 9.2

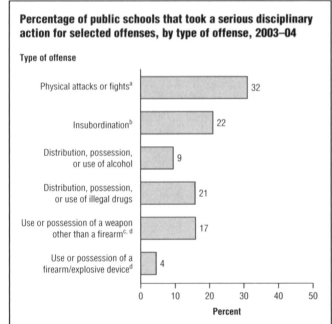

Percentage of public schools that took a serious disciplinary action for selected offenses, by type of offense, 2003–04

Type of offense

Type of offense	Percent
Physical attacks or fights[a]	32
Insubordination[b]	22
Distribution, possession, or use of alcohol	9
Distribution, possession, or use of illegal drugs	21
Use or possession of a weapon other than a firearm[c, d]	17
Use or possession of a firearm/explosive device[d]	4

[a]Physical attacks or fights were defined for respondents as "an actual and intentional touching or striking of another person against his or her will, or the intentional causing of bodily harm to an individual."
[b]Insubordination was defined for respondents as "a deliberate and inexcusable defiance of or refusal to obey a school rule, authority, or a reasonable order. It includes but is not limited to direct defiance of school authority, failure to attend assigned detention or on-campus supervision, failure to respond to a call slip, and physical or verbal intimidation or abuse."
[c]A weapon was defined for respondents as "any instrument or object used with the intent to threaten, injure, or kill. Includes look-alikes if they are used to threaten others."
[d]A firearm or explosive device was defined for respondents as "any weapon that is designed to (or may readily be converted to) expel a projectile by the action of an explosive. This includes guns, bombs, grenades, mines, rockets, missiles, pipe bombs, or similar devices designed to explode and capable of causing bodily harm or property damage."
Notes: Either school principals or the person most knowledgeable about discipline issues at school completed the School Survey on Crime and Safety questionnaire. Serious disciplinary actions include removals with no continuing services for at least the remainder of the school year, transfers to specialized schools for disciplinary reasons, and out-of-school suspensions lasting 5 or more days, but less than the remainder of the school year. Respondents were instructed to respond only for those times that were during normal school hours or when school activities or events were in session, unless the survey specified otherwise. Population size is 80,500 public schools.

SOURCE: Rachel Dinkes et al., "Figure 18.2. Percentage of Public Schools That Took a Serious Disciplinary Action for Specific Offenses, by Type of Offense: 2003–04," in *Indicators of School Crime and Safety: 2006*, U.S. Department of Education, National Center for Education Statistics, and U.S. Department of Justice, Bureau of Justice Statistics, December 2006, http://www.ojp.usdoj.gov/bjs/pub/pdf/iscs06 .pdf (accessed March 5, 2007)

National Crime Victimization Survey (NCVS) data show that although thefts often occur more frequently at school than they do away from school, the reverse is true of violent crimes, including those that are serious violent crimes, such as sexual assault, rape, aggravated assault, and robbery. In 2004 the number of nonfatal crimes against students at school had decreased to 1,445,800, including 107,400 serious violent crimes. (See Table 9.2.)

Some students are more likely to be victimized at school than are others. In 2004 males experienced a higher rate of crime than females did in general (57 and 52 per 1,000 students, respectively), although females experienced a higher rate of theft (35 per 1,000) than did males (31 per 1,000). (See Table 9.2.) In general, younger students had a higher rate of victimization than did older students; in 2004, 64 per 1,000 students aged twelve to fourteen experienced nonfatal crimes at school, compared with 46 per 1,000 students aged fifteen to eighteen. White students (60 per 1,000) and African-American students (60 per 1,000) were more likely to experience nonfatal crimes at school than were Hispanic students (39 per 1,000).

Physical Fights, Injuries, and Forcible Rape

According to the Centers for Disease Control and Prevention (CDC), in "Youth Risk Behavior Surveillance—2005," 35.9% of students nationwide reported being in one or more physical fights anywhere—not necessarily at school—during the last twelve months in 2005. (See Table 9.3.) Male students were more likely to report this behavior (43.4%) than female students (28.1%). A higher proportion of African-American students (43.1%) and Hispanic students (41%) acknowledged fighting than did white students (33.1%). The proportions of students fighting, however, decreased as students got older. Ninth graders (43.5%) fought the most, followed by tenth graders (36.6%), eleventh graders (31.6%), and twelfth graders (29.1%).

Dinkes et al. report that whereas 35.9% of students acknowledged physically fighting, only 13.6% of students fought on school property. More male students (18.2%) than female students (8.8%) engaged in fights on school property, and more Hispanic students (18.3%) and African-American students (16.9%) than white students (11.6%) reported this behavior. The incidence of fighting on school grounds decreased by age in a similar pattern to physical fighting in general.

About 3.6% of students noted that they had been injured in a physical fight in 2005 and required treatment by a doctor or nurse one or more times in the last twelve months, including 4.8% of male students and 2.4% of female students. (See Table 9.3.) African-American students (5.4%) and Hispanic students (5.3%) reported a higher percentage of injuries than did white students (2.4%).

More students reported physical injury at the hands of a date than in physical fights. Overall, in 2005, 9.2% of students said that they had been physically hurt by a boyfriend or girlfriend on purpose (hit, slapped, or otherwise physically hurt) one or more times in the last twelve months, including 9.3% of female students and 9% of male students. (See Table 9.3.) African-American students (11.9%) were most likely to be hurt by a dating partner, followed by Hispanic students (9.9%) and white students (8.2%). In "Youth Risk Behavior Surveillance," the CDC also finds that the higher the grade level, the higher the percentage of students were getting hurt by a

FIGURE 9.3

Rate of nonfatal crimes against students ages 12–18 per 1,000 students, by type of crime and location, 1992–2004

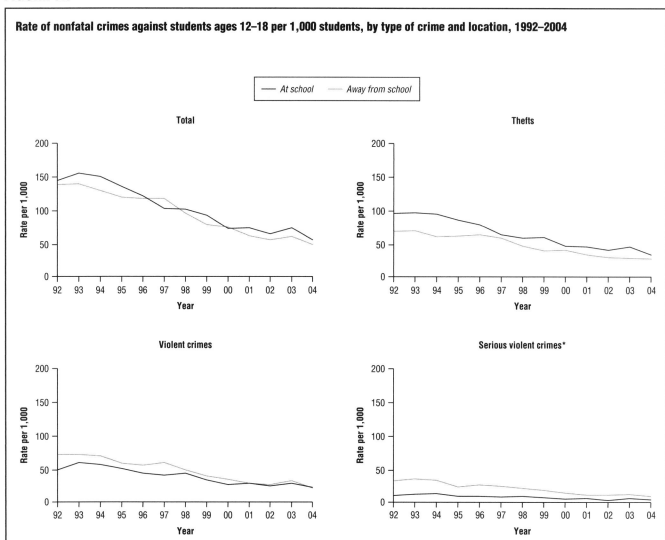

*Serious violent crimes are also included in violent crimes.
Notes: Serious violent crimes include rape, sexual assault, robbery, and aggravated assault. Violent crimes include serious violent crimes and simple assault. Total crimes include violent crimes and theft. "At school" includes inside the school building, on school property, or on the way to or from school. Population sizes for students ages 12–18 are 23,740,000 in 1992; 24,558,000 in 1993; 25,327,000 in 1994; 25,715,000 in 1995; 26,151,000 in 1996; 26,548,000 in 1997; 26,806,000 in 1998; 27,013,000 in 1999; 27,169,000 in 2000; 27,380,000 in 2001; 27,367,000 in 2002; 26,386,000 in 2003; and 26,372,000 in 2004.

SOURCE: Rachel Dinkes et al., "Figure 2.1. Rate of Student-Reported Nonfatal Crimes against Students Ages 12–18 per 1,000 Students, by Type of Crime and Location: 1992–2004," in *Indicators of School Crime and Safety: 2006*, U.S. Department of Education, National Center for Education Statistics, and U.S. Department of Justice, Bureau of Justice Statistics, December 2006, http://www.ojp.usdoj.gov/bjs/pub/pdf/iscs06.pdf (accessed March 5, 2007)

dating partner—7.4% of ninth graders, 8.7% of tenth graders, 9.9% of eleventh graders, and 11.1 % of twelfth graders reported having been intentionally hurt by a dating partner in the past twelve months in 2005.

The CDC asked students if they had ever been forced to have sexual intercourse, or had been forcibly raped. Overall, 7.5% of students acknowledged being forcibly raped—10.8% of female students and 4.2% of male students. (See Table 9.3.) African-American students were the most likely to report being victimized in this way (9.3%), followed by Hispanic students (7.8%) and white students (6.9%). The oldest high schoolers were the most likely to have experienced forced sexual intercourse in

the past twelve months (9%), compared with 6.1% of ninth graders. These results highlight the high level of sexual and dating violence experienced by high school students.

Bullies and Bullying

Most people can recall certain individuals or a group of children at school being identified as bullies. Such behaviors are not new to schools. Bullies harass certain kids they know will not fight back, including pushing students against lockers and taking their lunch money or other personal possessions; pulling gags to humiliate others and cause extreme embarrassment; shoving others

TABLE 9.2

Rate of student-reported nonfatal crimes against students ages 12–18 at school and rate of crimes per 1,000 students, by selected characteristics, 2004

Student characteristic	Number of crimes				Rate of crimes per 1,000 students			
	Total	Theft	Violent	Serious violent[a]	Total	Theft	Violent	Serious violent[a]
At school								
Total	1,445,800	863,000	582,800	107,400	55	33	22	4
Sex								
Male	776,800	416,400	360,400	58,800	57	31	27	4
Female	669,000	446,600	222,400	48,700	52	35	17	4
Age								
12–14	812,200	433,200	379,000	65,000	64	34	30	5
15–18	633,600	429,800	203,800	42,400!	46	31	15	3!
Race/ethnicity[b]								
White	951,700	550,000	401,700	77,800	60	35	25	5
Black	236,600	132,400	104,200	17,300!	60	34	26	4!
Hispanic	194,900	133,700	61,200	*	39	27	12	*
Other	62,600	46,900	15,700!	*	38	29	10!	*
Urbanicity								
Urban	443,600	239,700	203,900	41,400!	62	33	28	6!
Suburban	745,600	488,800	256,800	55,200	51	33	17	4
Rural	256,600	134,500	122,100	*	57	30	27	*
Household income								
Less than $15,000	103,900	37,500	66,400	*	45	16	29	*
$15,000–29,999	154,400	77,400	77,000	*	41	21	21	*
$30,000–49,999	238,100	152,500	85,600	*	50	32	18	*
$50,000–74,999	346,000	178,900	167,000	33,400!	84	44	41	8!
$75,000 or more	397,200	281,700	115,500	26,800!	62	44	18	4!

!Interpret data with caution.
*Reporting standards not met.
[a]Serious violent crimes are also included in violent crimes.
[b]Other includes American Indian, Alaska Native, and Asian or Pacific Islander. Respondents who identified themselves as being of Hispanic origin are classified as Hispanic, regardless of their race.
Notes: Serious violent crimes include rape, sexual assault, robbery, and aggravated assault. Violent crimes include serious violent crimes and simple assault. Total crimes include violent crimes and theft. "At school" includes inside the school building, on school property, or on the way to or from school. Population size for students ages 12–18 is 26,372,000 in 2004. Detail may not sum to totals because of rounding and missing data on student characteristics. Estimates of number of crimes are rounded to the nearest 100.

SOURCE: Rachel Dinkes et al., "Table 2.2. Number of Student-Reported Nonfatal Crimes against Students Ages 12–18 at School and Rate of Crimes per 1,000 Students, by Selected Student Characteristics: 2004," in *Indicators of School Crime and Safety: 2006*, U.S. Department of Education, National Center for Education Statistics, and U.S. Department of Justice, Bureau of Justice Statistics, December 2006, http://www.ojp.usdoj.gov/bjs/pub/pdf/iscs06.pdf (accessed March 5, 2007)

out of their way; threatening violence or setting up derogatory Web sites about other students; sending threatening or insulting text messages; and disrupting class and making threatening gestures, even toward teachers. Jill F. DeVoe and Sarah Kaffenberger of the American Institutes for Research indicate in *Student Reports of Bullying: Results from the 2001 School Crime Supplement to the National Crime Victimization Survey* (July 2005, http://nces.ed.gov/pubs2005/2005310.pdf) that some studies divide these bullying behaviors into two categories: direct and indirect. Direct bullying behaviors include physical and verbal attacks and harassment. Indirect bullying behaviors include subtle actions that might be hard for those not directly involved to recognize. These would include psychological activities, such as those previously mentioned, as well as obscene gestures, hurtful facial expressions, and turning friends against each other.

During the late 1990s bullying at schools became a major issue of concern for parents, educators, police, lawmakers, and students as increasing numbers of people perceived that bullying had become more aggressive and hurtful. In addition, a rash of school shootings shocked the nation in the 1990s. Many of the school shooters, mainly middle school and high school white males, complained of being bullied, victimized, and harassed frequently. They said that they had grown tired of being picked on and struck back. In fact, DeVoe and Kaffenberger find that students who had been bullied were more likely than other students to carry weapons to school (4% and 1%, respectively). However, most of the victims of school shootings are not the bullies who have harassed the shooters, but average students caught in the cross fire of angry classmates.

DEFINITION AND CHARACTERISTICS OF BULLYING. In *Educational Forum on Adolescent Health: Youth Bullying* (May 3, 2002, http://www.ama-assn.org/ama1/pub/upload/mm/39/youthbullying.pdf), Missy Fleming and Kelly J. Towey of the American Medical Association explain that bullies are most often males, although girls do engage in bullying behaviors as well. Boys are most

TABLE 9.3

Percentage of high school students who experienced violence through a physical fight, dating, or forced sexual intercourse, by sex, race/ethnicity, and grade, 2005

Category	In a physical fight[a]			Injured in a physical fight[a, b]			Dating violence[d]			Forced to have sexual intercourse[e]		
	Female	Male	Total	Female	Male	Total	Female	Male	Total	Female	Male	Total
	%	%	%	%	%	%	%	%	%	%	%	%
Race/ethnicity												
White[c]	24.7	41.2	33.1	1.7	3.1	2.4	8.5	8.0	8.2	10.8	3.1	6.9
Black[c]	37.7	48.9	43.1	3.5	7.4	5.4	12.0	11.8	11.9	11.5	7.1	9.3
Hispanic	32.5	49.5	41.0	3.2	7.5	5.3	9.0	10.9	9.9	9.4	6.4	7.8
Grade												
9	37.2	49.6	43.5	3.4	5.8	4.6	7.7	7.0	7.4	8.7	3.5	6.1
10	27.6	45.2	36.6	1.9	4.3	3.1	9.7	7.8	8.7	10.7	3.8	7.2
11	25.0	38.2	31.6	1.9	4.0	3.0	9.4	10.4	9.9	11.6	4.2	7.9
12	20.3	38.0	29.1	2.3	4.2	3.2	10.7	11.4	11.1	12.7	5.3	9.0
Total	**28.1**	**43.4**	**35.9**	**2.4**	**4.8**	**3.6**	**9.3**	**9.0**	**9.2**	**10.8**	**4.2**	**7.5**

[a]One or more times during the 12 months preceding the survey.
[b]Injuries had to be treated by a doctor or nurse.
[c]Non-Hispanic.
[d]Hit, slapped, or physically hurt on purpose by their boyfriend or girlfriend during the 12 months preceding the survey.
[e]When they did not want to.

SOURCE: Adapted from "Table 8. Percentage of High School Students Who Were in a Physical Fight and Who Were Injured in a Physical Fight, by Sex, Race/Ethnicity, and Grade," and "Table 10. Percentage of High School Students Who Experienced Dating Violence and Who Were Ever Physically Forced to Have Sexual Intercourse, by Sex, Race/Ethnicity, and Grade," in "Youth Risk Behavior Surveillance—United States, 2005," *Morbidity and Mortality Weekly Report*, vol. 55, no. SS-5, June 9, 2006, http://www.cdc.gov/mmwr/PDF/SS/SS5505.pdf (accessed February 25, 2007)

likely to use physical and verbal abuse, frequently on a one-on-one basis. Girls typically use verbal and psychological tactics. Female bullies often refrain from one-on-one contact, preferring to work in groups. This might include circulating a "slam book" about another person, which is a notebook containing derogatory remarks about the victim written by the bullying group, or e-mailing embarrassing pictures taken by cell phones in locker rooms to a large group of girls. Male victims of bullying are typically bullied by other males, but female victims may be bullied by either male or female students. In some instances mixed groups will work together to harass other kids.

Fleming and Towey note that bullies look for situations where they can gain power over someone else through intimidation and threats. Sometimes they work alone; other times they work in groups. Some bullies surround themselves with weaker kids who act as henchmen. Bullies seek out situations to harass others in places such as playgrounds and school hallways that are not being supervised by adults. In this way there are no adult witnesses to either stop the act or report it to school authorities.

According to Fleming and Towey, bullies are typically impulsive, have difficulty controlling anger, are easily frustrated, fail to follow rules, and view violence in a positive light. Individual risk factors include a lack of warmth from parents, a lack of parental supervision, and harsh, corporal discipline or child maltreatment. In addition, some schools have higher rates of bullying than do others because there is inadequate adult supervision or because teachers and staff have indifferent or accepting attitudes toward bullying.

In general, Fleming and Towey explain that victims of bullies are passive victims. They are quiet people, cautious, sensitive, and insecure, with few friends to step in and help them out of a bullying situation. They have difficulty standing up to people during confrontations, so bullies perceive them to be safe and easy targets. Male victims tend to be physically smaller and weaker than their peers. Any children who have been victims of child maltreatment are also more likely to be victimized by bullies. However, it is important to note that any student can become a victim of bullying, and the fault lies with the bully, not with the victim.

As the prevalence of bullying increases and more parents and educators grow concerned, various studies are being conducted to learn more about bullies, victims, and the frequency of such occurrences. Dinkes et al. report that in 2005, 28.1% of twelve- to eighteen-year-olds reported being bullied at school during the previous six months—27.1% of males and 29.2% of females. (See Table 9.4.) According to DeVoe and Kaffenberger, bullying appears to be on the rise; four years earlier, in 2001, only 14% of twelve- to eighteen-year-olds reported being bullied at school during the previous six months.

TABLE 9.4

Percentage of students ages 12–18 who reported being bullied at school during the previous 6 months, by location, injury, and selected student and school characteristics, 2005

Student or school characteristic	Total	Location of bullying				Students who were injured[a]
		Inside school	Outside on school grounds	School bus	Somewhere else	
Total	28.1	79.0	27.8	8.1	4.9	24.0
Sex						
Male	27.1	77.6	28.5	8.7	4.4	30.6
Female	29.2	80.4	27.0	7.5	5.3	17.7
Race/ethnicity[b]						
White	30.0	80.6	27.9	7.6	4.7	24.4
Black	28.5	77.3	25.2	10.8	4.3!	25.9
Hispanic	22.3	74.8	28.7	6.2	4.8	21.7
Other	24.6	76.7	31.2	9.4!	7.9!	20.8
Grade						
6th	36.6	68.2	36.9	7.6	4.7!	32.3
7th	35.0	81.0	30.0	14.2	2.9	31.7
8th	30.4	79.4	24.8	10.4	4.0	27.0
9th	28.1	81.7	28.0	5.1	5.0	21.0
10th	24.9	80.1	23.3	5.4	4.4!	21.2
11th	23.0	80.3	26.9	4.5!	7.2	14.5
12th	19.9	80.0	24.9	4.4!	8.5	12.7
Urbanicity						
Urban	26.0	76.9	28.4	6.5	5.4	23.0
Suburban	28.9	78.5	28.2	8.9	5.2	24.6
Rural	29.0	83.6	25.7	7.6	3.0!	23.8
Sector						
Public	28.6	79.4	27.5	8.3	4.9	24.4
Private	22.7	73.9	31.5	‡	4.2!	18.0

!Interpret data with caution.
‡Reporting standards not met.
[a]Injury includes bruises or swelling; cuts, scratches, or scrapes; black eye or bloody nose; teeth chipped or knocked out; broken bones or internal injuries; knocked unconscious; or other injuries. Only students who reported that their bullying incident constituted being pushed, shoved, tripped, or spit on were asked if they suffered injuries as a result of the incident.
[b]Other includes American Indian, Alaska Native, Asian or Pacific Islander, and more than one race. For this report, non-Hispanic students who identified themselves as more than one race were included in the other category. Respondents who identified themselves as being of Hispanic origin are classified as Hispanic, regardless of their race.
Notes: "At school" includes the school building, on school property, on a school bus, or going to and from school. In 2005, the unit response rate for this survey did not meet National Center Education Statistics standards; therefore, interpret the data with caution. Population size for students ages 12–18 is 25,811,000 in 2005. Location totals may sum to more than 100 because students could have been bullied in more than one location.

SOURCE: Rachel Dinkes et al., "Table 11.2. Percentage of Students Ages 12–18 Who Reported Being Bullied at School during the Previous 6 Months, by Location of Bullying, Injury, and Selected Student and School Characteristics: 2005," in *Indicators of School Crime and Safety: 2006*, U.S. Department of Education, National Center for Education Statistics, and U.S. Department of Justice, Bureau of Justice Statistics, December 2006, http://www.ojp.usdoj.gov/bjs/pub/pdf/iscs06.pdf (accessed March 5, 2007)

In 2005 white students reported the most problems with bullies (30%). (See Table 9.4.) Hispanic students (22.3%) and African-American students (28.5%) reported slightly less trouble. Reports of being bullied diminished with age; 36.6% of sixth graders but only 19.9% of twelfth graders reported being victimized by bullies.

DeVoe and Kaffenberger present survey results of students aged twelve to eighteen who reported being bullied at school. They find that factors in the school environment affected the incidence of bullying. Students who said there were gangs at school were more likely than other students to report being bullied (21% and 13%, respectively). Likewise, students who reported security guards or police officers in their schools were less likely than other students to report being bullied (13% and 16%, respectively). Hall monitoring by staff was also associated with fewer students being bullied (14% and 18%, respectively).

EFFECTS OF BULLYING/BEING BULLIED. According to DeVoe and Kaffenberger, bullied students are more likely to engage in a variety of behaviors than students who have not been bullied, including fearing attack, truancy from school or skipping classes, not participating in after school activities, carrying weapons, and engaging in physical fights. Students might be afraid to attend school and practice avoidance behaviors such as finding the shortest routes to school or to different places within the school in an attempt to prevent an attack. Being victimized by a bully may also lead to aggressive and/or antisocial behavior.

In the news release "Bullies, Victims at Risk for Violence and Other Problem Behaviors" (April 14, 2003, http://www.nichd.nih.gov/news/releases/bullies.cfm), the National Institute of Child Health and Human Development (NICHD) notes that "both children who bullied and their victims were more likely than youth who had never been involved in bullying to engage in violent behaviors themselves." The NICHD indicates that boys who acknowledged bullying others at school at least once each week had an increased level of carrying a weapon to school in the last month (43.1%), carrying a weapon in general (52.2%), being involved in frequent physical fighting (38.7%), and being injured in fighting (45.7%). Male bullies who attacked their victims away from school were even more likely to engage in these behaviors. The NICHD concludes, "It appears that bullying is not an isolated behavior, but a sign that children may be involved in more violent behaviors."

CYBERBULLIES. In "Bullies Move beyond the Schoolyard" (*Youth Violence and Juvenile Justice*, 2006), Justin W. Patchin and Sameer Hinduja report that with the advent of the Internet and the increased use of cell phones among students, bullies have found a new way to taunt their victims: cyberbullying, also called digital bullying or Internet bullying. Instead of abusing their victims at school, on the playground, or en route to and from school, bullies are now able to taunt their victims day and night via today's technology. Victims report receiving hateful and hurtful instant messages, e-mails, and text messages on their cell phones. Use of such technologies allows the perpetrators to be anonymous, if they so choose.

Some students have become the victims of hate-filled Web sites that discuss why the bullies and his or her friends do not like that certain individual. Visitors to such sites are allowed to add their insults and gossip as well. In some instances visitors have rallied to the defense of the victim and slammed the bully. Through the use of picture phones, bullies have even taken sensitive photos of students in locker rooms, in rest rooms, or while being intimidated. Then the bullies pass them around, either via e-mail or on Web sites. Researchers point out that electronic bullying can be done anywhere and does not involve the bully having any personal contact, especially eye contact, with the victim.

Parents experience difficulty in getting the Web sites removed by service providers, who suggest that they are not in the business of censorship and that the content is protected under the First Amendment, which guarantees freedom of speech. Some parents file lawsuits to get the content taken down. Because of their age, bullies often do not realize that they are legally responsible for what they put in print.

In "Research Summary: Cyberbullying Victimization" (2005, http://www.cyberbullying.us/cyberbullying_victimization.pdf), Sameer Hinduja and Justin W. Patchin find that 34.4% of adolescent respondents had experienced cyberbullying. More than one out of ten (12.6%) reported they

had been physically threatened, and 5% were frightened for their safety as a result. Hinduja and Patchin report that most cyberbullying occurs in chat rooms (55.6%) or through text messaging (48.9%). Victims of cyberbullying reported feeling frustrated, angry, afraid, and sad; only a third (35%) were not bothered by the experience.

PREVENTION PROGRAMS. Schools throughout the country have implemented antibullying programs aimed at bringing the subject out in the open. Antibullying efforts are not only geared toward bullies but also at the students and teachers who do not do enough to stop such aggression from occurring. Some victims claim that there are teachers who allow bullying to occur, even encourage it. Others say they are afraid to tell teachers because the educators just ignore it and tell the victims to toughen up. Still other victims are ashamed that they cannot stop the bullies and will retreat into themselves and internalize it.

One successful antibullying program, the Olweus Bullying Prevention Program (June 13, 2005, http://www.clemson.edu/olweus/), teaches students, parents, and school staff to work together to address the issue. By discussing bullying and its effects, people learn the consequences of bullying on individuals and on the school environment. Rules and plans are developed and enforced. The Office of Juvenile Justice and Delinquency Prevention (OJJDP) notes that the Olweus program is successful in elementary and junior high schools. According to the article "New Approach to Combating Bullies" (CBS News, December 10, 2003), the European schools that use the program have cut bullying by 30% to 70%.

Crimes against Teachers

Teachers sometimes fall victim to crimes at school. Jill F. DeVoe et al. report in *Indicators of School Crime and Safety, 2005* (November 2005, http://www.ojp.usdoj.gov/bjs/pub/pdf/iscs05.pdf) that on average, between 1999 and 2003, 183,400 crimes were committed against teachers each year, including 118,800 thefts, 64,600 violent crimes, and 7,400 serious violent crimes. The average annual rate of crimes was 39 per 1,000 teachers, including 25 thefts, 14 violent crimes, and 2 serious violent crimes per 1,000 teachers. Male teachers had a higher annual rate of crime (43 per 1,000) than did female teachers (38 per 1,000).

Proportionally, DeVoe et al. note that white teachers (41 per 1,000) experienced the most victimizations annually in the 1999–2003 period, followed by Hispanic teachers (38 per 1,000) and African-American teachers (24 per 1,000). High school teachers were more likely to be victimized (58 per 1,000) than were middle/junior high school teachers (41 per 1,000) or elementary school teachers (29 per 1,000). Proportionally, teachers at urban schools were far more likely to be victimized (46 per 1,000) than teachers in suburban and rural schools (33 and 31 per 1,000, respectively).

FIGURE 9.4

Percentage of public and private school teachers who reported that they were threatened with injury or that they were physically attacked by a student from school during the previous 12 months, by urbanicity and school sector, 2003–04

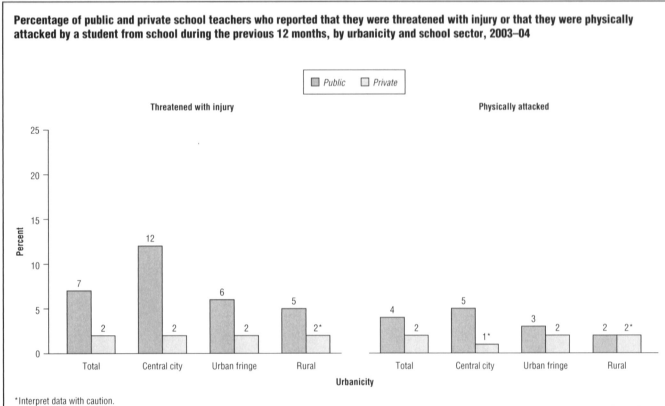

*Interpret data with caution.

Notes: Teachers who taught only prekindergarten students are excluded. The public sector includes public, public charter, and Bureau of Indian Affairs school teachers. Population size for teachers is 3,704,000 in 2003–04.

SOURCE: Rachel Dinkes et al., "Figure 5.2. Percentage of Public and Private School Teachers Who Reported That They Were Threatened with Injury or That They Were Physically Attacked by a Student from School during the Previous 12 Months, by Urbanicity and School Sector: 2003–04," in *Indicators of School Crime and Safety: 2006*, U.S. Department of Education, National Center for Education Statistics, and U.S. Department of Justice, Bureau of Justice Statistics, December 2006, http://www.ojp.usdoj.gov/bjs/pub/pdf/iscs06.pdf (accessed March 5, 2007)

Dinkes et al. report that during the 2003–04 school year, 7% of public school teachers said students from school had threatened them with injury during the last twelve months. However, the rate was far lower at private schools—just 2%. (See Figure 9.4.) Central city public school teachers reported the highest rate of threats (12%), compared with urban fringe (6%) and rural (5%) public school teachers. Dinkes et al. also note that 4% of public school teachers and 2% of private school teachers said they were actually physically attacked by students from school during the twelve months preceding the survey.

Weapons in School

Violence at school makes students feel vulnerable and intimidated. Sometimes it makes them want to carry weapons to school for self-protection. The Gun-Free Schools Act of 1994 required states to pass laws forcing school districts to expel any student who brings a firearm to school. Dinkes et al. report that in 2005, 6.5% of high school students reported they had carried a weapon (a gun, knife, or club) on school property in the last thirty days, down from 11.8% of students in 1993 but higher

than in 2003. (See Table 9.5.) Dinkes et al. also note that the percentage of students who reported carrying a weapon anywhere decreased from 22.1% in 1993 to 17.1% in 2003 before rising again to 18.5% in 2005.

Males were more likely than females to carry weapons on school property in all years reported, moving from a high of 17.9% in 1993 to a low of 8.9% in 2003. They were also most likely to carry weapons anywhere, although this dropped from 34.3% in 1993 to 26.9% in 2003 before rising again to 29.8% in 2005. Females were far less likely than their male peers to carry weapons on school property (5.1% in 1993 and 2.6% in 2005) or anywhere else (9.2% in 1993 and 7.1% in 2005). (See Table 9.5.)

There are various reasons students are carrying fewer weapons to school. Enhanced security measures at school, such as metal detectors and locker searches, added in the wake of the highly publicized school shootings in the 1990s, are partially responsible. Another reason is the stricter punishment given to those found with guns in school. Many schools have adopted zero-tolerance rules, resulting in the immediate expulsion of someone who is found breaking those guidelines.

TABLE 9.5

Percentage of students in grades 9–12 who reported carrying a weapon at least 1 day during the previous 30 days, by selected student characteristics, selected years 1993–2005

Student or school characteristic	Anywhere							On school property						
	1993	1995	1997	1999	2001	2003	2005	1993	1995	1997	1999	2001	2003	2005
Total	22.1	20.0	18.3	17.3	17.4	17.1	18.5	11.8	9.8	8.5	6.9	6.4	6.1	6.5
Sex														
Male	34.3	31.1	27.7	28.6	29.3	26.9	29.8	17.9	14.3	12.5	11.0	10.2	8.9	10.2
Female	9.2	8.3	7.0	6.0	6.2	6.7	7.1	5.1	4.9	3.7	2.8	2.9	3.1	2.6
Race/ethnicity[a]														
White	20.6	18.9	17.0	16.4	17.9	16.7	18.7	10.9	9.0	7.8	6.4	6.1	5.5	6.1
Black	28.5	21.8	21.7	17.2	15.2	17.3	16.4	15.0	10.3	9.2	5.0	6.3	6.9	5.1
Hispanic	24.4	24.7	23.3	18.7	16.5	16.5	19.0	13.3	14.1	10.4	7.9	6.4	6.0	8.2
Asian	b	b	b	13.0	10.6	11.6	7.0	b	b	b	6.5	7.2	6.6!	2.8!
American Indian	34.2	32.0	26.2	21.8	31.2	29.3	25.6	17.6!	13.0!	15.9	11.6!	16.4	12.9	7.2
Pacific Islander	b	b	b	25.3	17.4	16.3!	20.0!	b	b	b	9.3	10.0!	4.9!	15.4!
More than one race	b	b	b	22.2	25.2	29.8	26.7	b	b	b	11.4	13.2	13.3!	11.9
Grade														
9th	25.5	22.6	22.6	17.6	19.8	18.0	19.9	12.6	10.7	10.2	7.2	6.7	5.3	6.4
10th	21.4	21.1	17.4	18.7	16.7	15.9	19.4	11.5	10.4	7.7	6.6	6.7	6.0	6.9
11th	21.5	20.3	18.2	16.1	16.8	18.2	17.1	11.9	10.2	9.4	7.0	6.1	6.6	5.9
12th	19.9	16.1	15.4	15.9	15.1	15.5	16.9	10.8	7.6	7.0	6.2	6.1	6.4	6.7
Urbanicity														
Urban	—	—	18.7	15.8	15.3	17.0	—	—	—	7.0	7.2	6.0	5.6	—
Suburban	—	—	16.8	17.0	17.4	16.5	—	—	—	8.7	6.2	6.3	6.4	—
Rural	—	—	22.3	22.3	23.0	18.9	—	—	—	11.2	9.6	8.3	6.3	—

— Not available.

!Interpret data with caution.

[a]American Indian includes Alaska Native, black includes African American, Pacific Islander includes Native Hawaiian, and Hispanic includes Latino. Respondents who identified themselves as being of Hispanic origin are classified as Hispanic, regardless of their race.

[b]The response categories for race/ethnicity changed in 1999 making comparisons of some categories with earlier years problematic. In 1993, 1995, and 1997, Asian students and Pacific Islander students were not categorized separately and students were not given the option of choosing more than one race.

Notes: "On school property" was not defined for survey respondents. The term "anywhere" is not used in the Youth Risk Behavior Survey questionnaire; students are simply asked how many days they carried a weapon during the past 30 days. Population sizes from the Digest of Education Statistics, 2005 and 2002 for students in grades 9–12 are 13,093,000 students in 1993; 13,697,000 in 1995; 14,272,000 in 1997; 14,623,000 in 1999; 15,061,000 in 2001; 15,723,000 in 2003; and 16,286,000 (projected) in 2005.

SOURCE: Rachel Dinkes et al., "Table 13.1. Percentage of Students in Grades 9–12 Who Reported Carrying a Weapon at Least 1 Day during the Previous 30 Days, by Location and Selected Student and School Characteristics: Various Years, 1993–2005," in *Indicators of School Crime and Safety: 2006*, U.S. Department of Education, National Center for Education Statistics, and U.S. Department of Justice, Bureau of Justice Statistics, December 2006, http://www.ojp.usdoj.gov/bjs/pub/pdf/iscs06.pdf (accessed March 5, 2007)

For some students, obtaining guns is fairly easy. The OJJDP notes that young people attempt various methods to secure guns, including stealing them from cars, houses, apartments, stores and pawnshops, and family members. They also buy guns from family members, drug dealers or addicts, stores, gang members, family friends, and others.

WEAPON USE ON SCHOOL PROPERTY. The percentage of students who report being threatened with or injured by a weapon while at school remained fairly steady between 1993 and 2005. About 7.9% of students in grades nine to twelve reported being threatened or injured with a weapon on school property within the past twelve months in 2005. (See Table 9.6.) This figure was a slight increase from 1993, when 7.3% of students reported being threatened or injured by a weapon. Between 1993 and 2005 the percentage remained in the 7% to 9% range—no clear pattern of improvement or worsening can be seen.

Male students received considerably more weapons threats and injuries in all years surveyed between 1993 and 2005 than did female students. (See Table 9.6.) Among students from different ethnic and racial backgrounds, the victimization rate was highest among Pacific Islanders in 2005, at 14.5%, down from a high of 24.8% in 2001. Native American students (9.8%) and Hispanic students (9.8%) also had fairly high victimization rates. Asian students were the least likely to be threatened by or injured with a weapon in 2005 (4.6%).

The youngest students were the most likely to report being threatened by or injured with a weapon. More than one out of ten (10.5%) ninth graders reported being threatened or injured with a weapon in 2005, compared with 8.8% of tenth graders, 5.5% of eleventh graders, and 5.8% of twelfth graders. (See Table 9.6.) Similar patterns were observed in other years as well. It may be that younger students are viewed as more vulnerable to intimidation and

TABLE 9.6

Percentage of students in grades 9–12 who reported being threatened or injured with a weapon on school property during the previous 12 months, by selected student characteristics, selected years 1993–2005

Student or school characteristic	1993	1995	1997	1999	2001	2003	2005
Total	7.3	8.4	7.4	7.7	8.9	9.2	7.9
Sex							
Male	9.2	10.9	10.2	9.5	11.5	11.6	9.7
Female	5.4	5.8	4.0	5.8	6.5	6.5	6.1
Race/ethnicity[a]							
White	6.3	7.0	6.2	6.6	8.5	7.8	7.2
Black	11.2	11.0	9.9	7.6	9.3	10.9	8.1
Hispanic	8.6	12.4	9.0	9.8	8.9	9.4	9.8
Asian	b	b	b	7.7	11.3	11.5	4.6
American Indian	11.7	11.4!	12.5!	13.2!	15.2!	22.1	9.8
Pacific Islander	b	b	b	15.6	24.8	16.3	14.5!
More than one race	b	b	b	9.3	10.3	18.7	10.7
Grade							
9th	9.4	9.6	10.1	10.5	12.7	12.1	10.5
10th	7.3	9.6	7.9	8.2	9.1	9.2	8.8
11th	7.3	7.7	5.9	6.1	6.9	7.3	5.5
12th	5.5	6.7	5.8	5.1	5.3	6.3	5.8
Urbanicity							
Urban	—	—	8.7	8.0	9.2	10.6	—
Suburban	—	—	7.0	7.4	9.0	8.8	—
Rural	—	—	5.6!	8.3	8.1	8.2	—

— Not available.

!Interpret data with caution.

[a]American Indian includes Alaska Native, black includes African American, Pacific Islander includes Native Hawaiian, and Hispanic includes Latino. Respondents who identified themselves as being of Hispanic origin are classified as Hispanic, regardless of their race.

bThe response categories for race/ethnicity changed in 1999 making comparisons of some categories with earlier years problematic. In 1993, 1995, and 1997, Asian students and Pacific Islander students were not categorized separately and students were not given the option of choosing more than one race.

Notes: "On school property" was not defined for survey respondents. Population sizes from the Digest of Education Statistics, 2005 and 2002 for students in grades 9–12 are 13,093,000 students in 1993; 13,697,000 in 1995; 14,272,000 in 1997; 14,623,000 in 1999; 15,061,000 in 2001; 15,723,000 in 2003; and 16,286,000 (projected) in 2005.

SOURCE: Rachel Dinkes et al., "Table 4.1. Percentage of Students in Grades 9–12 Who Reported Being Threatened or Injured with a Weapon on School Property during the Previous 12 Months, by Selected Student and School Characteristics: Various Years, 1993–2005," in *Indicators of School Crime and Safety: 2006*, U.S. Department of Education, National Center for Education Statistics, and U.S. Department of Justice, Bureau of Justice Statistics, December 2006, http://www.ojp.usdoj.gov/bjs/pub/pdf/iscs06.pdf (accessed March 5, 2007)

are therefore more likely to be targets of students carrying weapons.

HAZING

Like bullying, hazing involves humiliating someone into doing something that he or she would not do normally. In some instances, the hazing act is silly and harmless. However, in the early twenty-first century, parents and educators have become concerned that hazings are getting more and more aggressive and violent. Such hazings, which often occur as initiations to a school or social club, are considered a "rite of passage" to some, just "horseplay" to others, and degrading and devastating to various victims. Some athletic teams claim that hazing is done to toughen up younger players—to help them bond with the team. But unlike bullying, hazing is often done with the consent of its victims. For example, succumbing to peer pressure and wanting to be part of the group or clique, many students will allow themselves to be subjected to humiliating acts that they don't report.

Hazings, however, can go too far and the victims can be seriously harmed. A few victims have even died.

Hazings usually involve older students (veterans) initiating young classmates (newcomers) into the club. The situation can quickly turn violent when the older group gangs up on the younger group, who has no idea what has been planned or what they should expect. Researchers note that students will do things in a mob situation that they would never do on their own.

Several cases of brutal hazings received significant news coverage in 2003, one involving a high school football team and the other concerning senior and junior high school girls. The football incident took place at a training camp over the summer. At camp, several players were allegedly sexually abused with pine cones, golf balls, and broomsticks. Three players were charged in the incident and appeared before a judge, who was to decide if they should stand trial as juveniles or adults. The judge ordered the decision sealed.

The incident involving the teenage school girls occurred in what was supposed to be a "powder puff" football game at a local park. Instead, the younger girls were allegedly beaten, kicked, shoved, and pelted with a variety of objects and liquids, including garbage, mud, paint, animal intestines, feces, and urine. Five girls were taken to the hospital as a result. Fifteen students, who were charged with misdemeanors, were identified through witnesses and a videotape that someone made of the melee. Thirty-two were suspended from school. Although the girls were underage, alcohol was present. Police considered charging some of the girls' parents for providing the alcohol.

More recent incidences of hazing capturing media attention were on college campuses. According to Elaine Corry in "A Fraternity Hazing Gone Wrong" for NPR (November 14, 2005, http://www.npr.org/templates/story/story.php?storyId=5012154), in February 2005 a young man attending Chico State University in California died in a fraternity hazing ritual, where fraternity pledges were forced to do calisthenics in raw sewage while drinking massive quantities of water. The young man died of water intoxication. Felony criminal charges were filed against the fraternity brothers involved in the incident. Other incidences, as reported by StopHazing.org (http://www.stophazing.org/news/index.htm), include a young male student beaten in late 2006 by seven University of South Carolina students who were later arrested, and a 2007 case at Rochester Institute of Technology (RIT) in New York where six students were hospitalized after being forced to drink dangerously high levels of alcohol in order to join the school's rugby team. Eight RIT rugby players faced misdemeanor charges in the latter incident.

Various researchers contend that hazing incidents are underreported. This occurs for several reasons: 1) The victim believes that hazing is an unpleasant, but a necessary part of joining an organization; 2) the victim is threatened into remaining silent; 3) the victim is ashamed and wants to forget the incident occurred; 4) the victim assumes everyone has to endure such acts; or 5) the victim doesn't want to involve parents, school officials, or police because that would bring more trouble from the hazers. Some school administrators, coaches, and parents also play a role in encouraging students to refrain from reporting the incidents saying that they, too, had to endure such rituals. Many schools, however, are developing antihazing programs. In addition to criminal charges being filed in courts, parents of students victimized by hazings have brought lawsuits against schools and the perpetrators of such events.

AVOIDANCE AND FEAR

Edward Gaughan, Jay D. Cerio, and Robert A. Myers of Alfred University, in *Lethal Violence in Schools: A National Study* (August 2001, http://www.alfred.edu/teenviolence/), find that concern about violence is prevalent in school. Some 37% of those surveyed believed that there are "kids at my school who I think might shoot someone." According to Gaughan, Cerio, and Myers, "20 percent of respondents have heard rumors that another student plans to

TABLE 9.7

Percentage of high school students who did not go to school because of safety concerns, by sex, race/ethnicity, and grade, 2005

| Category | Did not go to school because of safety concern[a] | | |
	Female	Male	Total
	%	%	%
Race/ethnicity			
White[b]	4.9	3.9	4.4
Black[b]	9.2	8.2	8.7
Hispanic	9.7	10.7	10.2
Grade			
9	8.1	7.3	7.7
10	7.3	5.3	6.3
11	4.9	4.5	4.7
12	4.5	5.1	4.9
Total	6.3	5.7	6.0

[a]On ≥1 of the 30 days preceding the survey.
[b]Non-Hispanic.

SOURCE: Adapted from "Table 14. Percentage of High School Students Who Were in a Physical Fight on School Property, Who Did Not Go to School Because They Felt Unsafe at School or on Their Way to or from School, and Who Had Their Property Stolen or Deliberately Damaged on School Property, by Sex, Race/Ethnicity, and Grade," in "Youth Risk Behavior Surveillance—United States, 2005," *Morbidity and Mortality Weekly Report*, vol. 55, no. SS-5, June 9, 2006, http://www.cdc.gov/mmwr/PDF/SS/SS5505.pdf (accessed February 25, 2007)

shoot someone, and 20 percent have also overheard another student actually talking about shooting someone at school." Another 8% acknowledged wanting to shoot someone at school themselves. Finally, only about half of the survey participants said they would inform an adult if they overheard someone's plans to shoot another person.

Some students continue to worry about their safety at school. In 2005, 6% of students reported missing one or more days of school in the last thirty days because they believed it was too unsafe at school or going to and from school. (See Table 9.7.) More female students (6.3%) than male students (5.7%) reported this experience. This response to their fear was much higher among Hispanic students (10.2%) and African-American students (8.7%) than it was among white students (4.4%). Younger children reported not going to school because of safety concerns more than did older children; 7.7% of ninth graders, 6.3% of tenth graders, 4.7% of eleventh graders, and 4.9% of twelfth graders reported skipping school because of safety concerns in the previous month.

The NCVS also addresses the issue of fear of attack or harm at school or en route to and from school. Dinkes et al. report that in 2005, 6.2% of students aged twelve to eighteen reported being afraid of attack or harm at school during the previous six months; this was down dramatically from 11.8% of students in 1995. (See Table 9.8.) In 2005 females were slightly more likely to be afraid of harm (6.6%) than were males (5.9%). Hispanic (10.1%) and

TABLE 9.8

Percentage of students ages 12–18 who reported being afraid of attack or harm during the previous 6 months, by location and selected student characteristics, 1995, 1999, 2001, 2003, and 2005

Student or school characteristic	At school					Away from school				
	1995	1999	2001	2003	2005	1995	1999	2001	2003	2005
Total	11.8	7.3	6.4	6.1	6.2	—	5.7	4.6	5.4	5.1
Sex										
Male	10.8	6.5	6.4	5.3	5.9	—	4.1	3.7	4.0	4.5
Female	12.8	8.2	6.4	6.9	6.6	—	7.4	5.6	6.8	5.7
Race/ethnicity*										
White	8.1	5.0	4.9	4.1	4.5	—	4.3	3.7	3.8	4.2
Black	20.3	13.5	8.9	10.7	9.0	—	8.7	6.3	10.0	7.2
Hispanic	20.9	11.7	10.6	9.5	10.1	—	8.9	6.5	7.4	6.1
Other	13.5	6.7	6.4	5.0	6.3	—	5.4	6.6	3.9	5.9 !
Grade										
6th	14.3	10.9	10.6	10.0	9.5	—	7.8	6.3	6.8	5.7
7th	15.3	9.5	9.2	8.2	9.1	—	6.1	5.5	6.7	7.5
8th	13.0	8.1	7.6	6.3	6.9	—	5.5	4.4	5.3	4.9
9th	11.6	7.1	5.5	6.3	5.7	—	4.6	4.5	4.3	3.8
10th	11.0	7.1	5.0	4.4	5.3	—	4.8	4.2	5.3	4.6
11th	8.9	4.8	4.8	4.7	4.5	—	5.9	4.7	4.7	4.1
12th	7.8	4.8	2.9	3.7	3.3	—	6.1	3.3	4.9	5.3
Urbanicity										
Urban	18.4	11.6	9.7	9.5	10.2	—	9.1	7.4	8.1	6.6
Suburban	9.8	6.2	4.8	4.8	4.7	—	5.0	3.8	4.4	4.5
Rural	8.6	4.8	6.0	4.7	5.1	—	3.0	3.0	4.0	4.6
Sector										
Public	12.2	7.7	6.6	6.4	6.5	—	5.8	4.6	5.4	5.1
Private	7.3	3.6	4.6	3.0	3.8	—	5.0	5.1	4.7	4.7

— Not available.

!Interpret data with caution.

*Other includes American Indian, Alaska Native, Asian or Pacific Islander, and, from 2003 onward, more than one race. For this report, non-Hispanic students who identified themselves as more than one race were included in the other category. Respondents who identified themselves as being of Hispanic origin are classified as Hispanic, regardless of their race. Due to changes in racial/ethnic categories, comparisons of race/ethnicity across years should be made with caution.

Notes: "At school" includes the school building, on school property, on a school bus, and, from 2001 onward, going to and from school. For the 2001 survey, the wording was changed from "attack or harm" to "attack or threat of attack." Includes students who reported that they sometimes or most of the time feared being victimized in this way. Fear of attack away from school was not collected in 1995. In 2005, the unit response rate for this survey did not meet National Center of Education Statistics standards; therefore, interpret the data with caution. Population sizes for students ages 12–18 are 23,325,000 in 1995; 24,614,000 in 1999; 24,315,000 in 2001; 25,684,000 in 2003; and 25,811,000 in 2005.

SOURCE: Rachel Dinkes et al., "Table 16.1. Percentage of Students Ages 12–18 Who Reported Being Afraid of Attack or Harm during the Previous 6 Months, by Location and Selected Student and School Characteristics: Various Years, 1995–2005," in *Indicators of School Crime and Safety: 2006*, U.S. Department of Education, National Center for Education Statistics, and U.S. Department of Justice, Bureau of Justice Statistics, December 2006, http://www.ojp.usdoj.gov/bjs/pub/pdf/iscs06.pdf (accessed March 5, 2007)

African-American (9%) students were more likely than white students (4.5%) to feel afraid of attack at school. Younger students were more likely than older students to fear attack or harm at school. Urban students (10.2%) were far more likely than suburban (4.7%) or rural (5.1%) students to report being afraid of attack or harm. Fewer students were afraid of attack or harm away from school than they were at school (5.1% and 6.2%, respectively).

NO CHILD LEFT BEHIND ACT: PERSISTENTLY DANGEROUS SCHOOLS

The No Child Left Behind Act (NCLB) was passed by Congress in 2001 and signed into law by President George W. Bush in January 2002. A reauthorization of the Elementary and Secondary Education Act of 1965, it mandated sweeping changes to the law defining and regulating the federal government's role in kindergarten through twelfth-grade education.

According to the Department of Education (March 6, 2007, http://www.ed.gov/policy/elsec/guid/states/index.html), the law is based on four basic education reform principles:

- Better accountability and assessment
- Flexibility to improve teaching and learning
- More options for parents via choice and charter schools
- Increasing the budget

The NCLB requires that schools demonstrate "adequate yearly progress" toward statewide proficiency goals. The schools that fail to improve will receive corrective action and restructuring measures. Reporting of progress is public, so parents can stay informed about their school and school district. Schools that make or exceed adequate yearly progress are eligible for awards. The ultimate goal is that all children will have a quality education by the 2013–14 school year.

Unsafe School Choice Option

Among the various changes that the NCLB requires is a provision mandating that states work on making schools safer. The Department of Education (November 17, 2004, http://www.ed.gov/nclb/freedom/safety/creating.html) notes:

Under Title IV of ESEA as reauthorized by the No Child Left Behind Act, states are required to establish a uniform management and reporting system to collect information on school safety and drug use among young people. The states must include incident reports by school officials and anonymous student and teacher surveys in the data they collect. This information is to be publicly reported so that parents, school officials and others who are interested have information about any violence and drug use at their schools. They can then assess the problems at their schools and work toward finding solutions. Continual monitoring and reports will track progress over time.

To hold schools accountable for ensuring student safety, the NCLB requires states to create a definition of persistently dangerous schools. States must permit students to have public school choice if their school consistently falls into this category. In addition, student victims of violent crime are also allowed public school choice even if the school is not considered persistently dangerous.

PERSISTENTLY DANGEROUS SCHOOLS: GEORGIA'S EXAMPLE. To illustrate what some states have done to fulfill the NCLB requirements pertaining to persistently dangerous schools, this section focuses on the Georgia Department of Education's (GDOE) efforts. According to the GDOE (2007, http://public.doe.k12.ga.us/aypnclb.aspx?PageReq=About USCO), Georgia defines persistently dangerous schools as:

Any school in which for three consecutive years:

At least 1 student is found by official tribunal action to have violated a school rule related to a violent criminal offense (including aggravated battery, aggravated child molestation, aggravated sexual battery, aggravated sodomy, armed robbery, arson, kidnapping, murder, rape, and voluntary manslaughter) either on campus or at a school-sanctioned event;

At least 2% of the student body or 10 students, whichever is greater, have been found to have violated school rules related to other identified criminal offenses, including non-felony drugs, felony drugs, felony weapons, terroristic threats;

Any combination of [the above]

The GDOE further outlines what happens as a consequence of a school being labeled persistently dangerous:

When a school meets the criteria for three consecutive years, local education agencies (local school districts, herein referred to as LEAs) must within ten school days notify parents of each student attending the school that the state has identified the school as persistently dangerous.

Within 20 school days from the time that the LEA learns that the school has been identified as persistently

dangerous, the LEA must give students the opportunity to transfer to a safe public school, including a safe public charter school, within the LEA.

LEAs must adopt a policy that facilitates the transfer of students who are victims of violent criminal offenses. This policy shall provide that the transfer shall occur within ten school days of the commission of the violent criminal offense, and to the extent possible, shall allow victims to transfer to a school that is making adequate yearly progress and has not been identified as being in school improvement, corrective action, or restructuring.

If deemed persistently dangerous, a school will need to show significant improvements to regain its place on the safe school list. Georgia has specific requirements that such schools must follow, which include taking corrective measures. After a year of showing that it is no longer dangerous, a school can reapply to the GDOE. When it filed its report in 2003, the GDOE indicated that no Georgia schools were deemed persistently dangerous.

Reporting Violence and Crime at School

The National School Safety and Security Services, in "School Crime Reporting and School Crime Underreporting" (2007, http://www.schoolsecurity.org/trends/school_crime_reporting.html), notes that the unsafe school requirement of the NCLB concerns some educators, parents, and police. Some believe that schools will be even more hesitant to report crimes so that they will not be labeled as persistently dangerous. They suggest that by falling into this designation, such schools will undoubtedly lose enrollment and school funds. As such, schools may begin to underreport such crimes so that they maintain a clean rating.

The National Association of School Resource Officers asked its members in 2004 what impact the NCLB would have on school administrators reporting school-based crimes, and Kenneth S. Trump reported the findings in *School Safety Left Behind? School Safety Threats Grow as Preparedness Stalls and Funding Decreases* (February 2005, http://www.schoolsecurity.org/resources/2004%20NASRO%20Survey%20Final%20Report%20NSSSS.pdf). Most of those surveyed (54%) believed it would result in decreased reporting of crimes at schools. The vast majority (86%) said that the number of crimes on school property were underreported to law enforcement.

Dinkes et al. show that many crimes, even violent crimes, committed at school are not reported to the police. During the 2003–04 school year, 81% of public schools experienced one or more violent crimes, but just 44% reported violent crimes to the police. (See Figure 9.5.) Violent incidents included physical attacks, fights with or without weapons, threats of physical violence with or without weapons, rape, sexual battery (other than rape), and robbery with or without weapons. Low-reporting trends also occurred with thefts. Even though 46% of public schools experienced one or more thefts, just 31% reported them to the police.

FIGURE 9.5

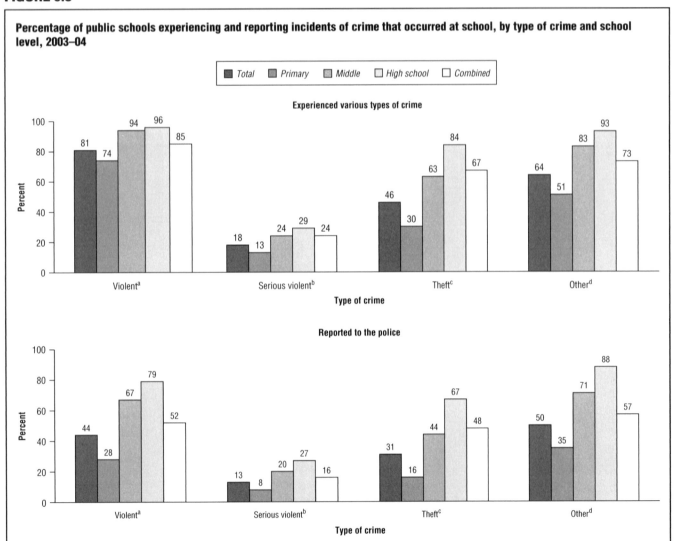

Percentage of public schools experiencing and reporting incidents of crime that occurred at school, by type of crime and school level, 2003–04

[Legend: ■ Total ■ Primary ■ Middle □ High school □ Combined]

Experienced various types of crime

Violentª: 81, 74, 94, 96, 85
Serious violentᵇ: 18, 13, 24, 29, 24
Theftᶜ: 46, 30, 63, 84, 67
Otherᵈ: 64, 51, 83, 93, 73

Type of crime

Reported to the police

Violentª: 44, 28, 67, 79, 52
Serious violentᵇ: 13, 8, 20, 27, 16
Theftᶜ: 31, 16, 44, 67, 48
Otherᵈ: 50, 35, 71, 88, 57

Type of crime

ªViolent incidents include rape, sexual battery other than rape, physical attack or fight with or without a weapon, threat of physical attack with or without a weapon, and robbery with or without a weapon. Serious violent incidents are also included in violent incidents.
ᵇSerious violent incidents include rape, sexual battery other than rape, physical attack or fight with a weapon, threat of physical attack with a weapon, and robbery with or without a weapon.
ᶜTheft/larceny (taking things over $10 without personal confrontation) was defined for respondents as "the unlawful taking of another person's property without personal confrontation, threat, violence, or bodily harm. Included are pocket picking, stealing purse or backpack (if left unattended or no force was used to take it from owner), theft from a building, theft from a motor vehicle or motor vehicle parts or accessories, theft of bicycles, theft from vending machines, and all other types of thefts."
ᵈOther incidents include possession of a firearm or explosive device, possession of a knife or sharp object, distribution of illegal drugs, possession or use of alcohol or illegal drugs, or vandalism.
Notes: Either school principals or the person most knowledgeable about discipline issues at school completed the School Survey on Crime and Safety questionnaire. Primary schools are defined as schools in which the lowest grade is not higher than grade 3 and the highest grade is not higher than grade 8. Middle schools are defined as schools in which the lowest grade is not lower than grade 4 and the highest grade is not higher than grade 9. High schools are defined as schools in which the lowest grade is not lower than grade 9. Combined schools include all other combinations of grades, including K–12 schools. "At school" was defined for respondents to include activities that happen in school buildings, on school grounds, on school buses, and at places that hold school-sponsored events or activities. Respondents were instructed to respond only for those times that were during normal school hours or when school activities or events were in session, unless the survey specified otherwise. Population size is 80,500 public schools.

SOURCE: Rachel Dinkes et al., "Figure 6.2. Percentage of Public Schools Experiencing and Reporting Incidents of Crime That Occurred at School, by Type of Crime and School Level: 2003–04," in *Indicators of School Crime and Safety: 2006*, U.S. Department of Education, National Center for Education Statistics, and U.S. Department of Justice, Bureau of Justice Statistics, December 2006, http://www.ojp.usdoj.gov/bjs/pub/pdf/iscs06.pdf (accessed March 5, 2007)

Proportionally, schools were more likely to report seriously violent incidents to the police, presumably because of the gravity of such offenses. However, even some serious violent crimes were not reported. In the 2003–04 school year, 18% of public schools experienced one or more serious violent crimes, and only 13% reported any serious violent crimes to the police. (See Figure 9.5.)

CHAPTER 10
CRIME PREVENTION AND PUNISHMENT

CRIME PREVENTION

Over the years politicians, law enforcement officials, teachers, parents, and other concerned citizens have examined countless ideas in an effort to decrease youth violence and crime, from holding parents responsible for their children's crimes to having after-school violence prevention programs. The continuing problem of youth crime has many people devoting significant time and resources to end the cycle of violence. A variety of programs have been implemented in the area of prevention, intervention, and suppression. Efforts are ongoing to determine the effectiveness of such programs. The following sections discuss laws that have been enacted as well as a variety of prevention programs, including community prevention programs, law enforcement prevention strategies, and school-based prevention programs, to try to prevent juvenile crime.

Laws Enacted to Prevent Juvenile Crime

HOLDING PARENTS RESPONSIBLE. For many decades civil liability laws have held parents at least partly responsible for damages caused by their children. In addition, child welfare laws included actions against those who contributed to the delinquency of a minor. By the 1990s, in response to rising juvenile crime rates, communities and states passed tougher laws about parental responsibility. In "Parent Liability Child's Act" (2007, http://law.enotes.com/everyday-law-encyclopedia/parent-liability-child-s-act#criminal-responsibility), the *Encyclopedia of Everyday Law* notes that some states now hold parents of delinquent youth criminally liable. However, other, less stringent parental responsibility laws are more common. Alabama, Kansas, Kentucky, and West Virginia require parents to pay court costs for their children adjudicated delinquent. Florida, Idaho, Indiana, North Carolina, and Virginia require parents to pay the costs of caring for, treating, or detaining delinquent children. Idaho, Maryland, Missouri, and Oklahoma require parents to pay restitution to the victims of their children's crimes. Nine states hold parents criminally responsible for storing a loaded firearm in a place that allows minors access to it, and other states hold parents liable if they know their child possesses a firearm and do not confiscate it.

Critics of parental liability explain that victims are just looking for someone to blame. They assert that U.S. law usually holds people responsible for crimes only if they actively participate in the transmission of such acts. They believe that if standard rules of U.S. law are practiced, the prosecutor of a case should have to prove that the parents intended to participate in a crime to be found guilty. Samantha Harvell, Belen Rodas, and Leah Hendey of Georgetown University find in *Parental Involvement in Juvenile Justice: Prospects and Possibilities* (November 8, 2004, http://www.crocus.georgetown.edu/reports/parental.involvement.pdf) that judges and probation officers believe that parents should be more involved in legal proceedings against minors because they feel that the relationship between parent and child often contributes to delinquency. However, judges and probation officers remain somewhat reluctant to use parental sanctions. In fact, the article "UF Study: Americans Give Mixed Reviews to Parental Responsibility Laws" (*University of Florida News*, March 14, 2005) notes that a 2005 survey found that public support for parental responsibility laws was relatively low.

CURFEWS. To break the cycle of youth violence and crime, lawmakers have enacted curfews in various cities, towns, and rural areas across the country. Curfews for young people have existed off and on since the 1890s, when they were enacted to reduce crime among immigrant youth. States and cities often pass curfew ordinances when citizens perceive a need to maintain control over juveniles. Because of the rising rate of juvenile crime in the late 1980s and early 1990s, more than a thousand jurisdictions in the United States imposed youth curfews. Arlen Egley Jr. and Aline K. Major of the National

Youth Gang Survey, in "Highlights of the 2001 National Youth Gang Survey" (April 2003, http://www.ncjrs.gov/pdffiles1/ojjdp/fs200301.pdf), report that 62% of jurisdictions reporting gang problems used curfews or other ordinances aimed at keeping youth from congregating at night. Of those jurisdictions, 86% argued that such laws "demonstrated at least some degree of effectiveness."

Most curfew laws work essentially the same way. They are aimed at restricting juveniles to their homes or property between the hours of 11 p.m. and 6 a.m. weekdays. Such laws usually allow juveniles to stay out a little later on weekends. Exceptions are made for youth who need to travel to and from school, attend church events, or go to work at different times. Other exceptions include family emergencies or situations when juveniles are accompanied by their parents.

Although many people believe that curfews are important in the fight against youth crime, critics of curfew ordinances argue that such laws violate the constitutional rights of children and their parents. They contend that the First, Fourth, Ninth, and Fourteenth Amendment rights of people are endangered by curfew laws, especially the rights of free speech and association, privacy, and equal protection. Opponents also assert that no studies prove curfew laws to be effective. In fact, most studies—such as Patrick Boyle's "Curfews and Crime" (*Youth Today*, November 2006) and Caterina Grovis Roman and Gretchen Moore's "Evaluation of the Youth Curfew in Prince George's County, Maryland" (April 23, 2003, http://www.ncjrs.gov/pdffiles1/nij/grants/200520.pdf)—show that curfews have little effect on youth crime.

Community Prevention and Intervention Programs

Prevention measures are programs aimed at keeping youth, particularly at-risk youth, from beginning a life of crime, joining gangs, and/or otherwise ending up in prison or jail. Intervention programs are designed to remove youth from gangs, criminal activities, and/or patterns of reckless behavior that would ultimately put the youth in prison or jail. Such programs typically include helping the individual build self-esteem, confidence, and socialization skills while offering education, recreation, and job skills assistance.

Although this chapter examines a few of the types of programs available, hundreds of such programs exist throughout the United States, some at the national or state levels, but many at the local/community level. Many involve mentoring—having adults and sometimes other students spend time with at-risk youth to help them explore alternatives to violence and crime. Mentoring programs take on a variety of activities, including sports, recreation, and education. Mentors help their subjects gain self-esteem, conflict resolution abilities, peer pressure resistance skills, and confidence.

Many prevention and intervention programs have seen some success with delinquent and at-risk youth, as noted by individuals who credit such groups with turning their lives around or keeping them from heading into lives of crime and violence. Others have proven to be ineffective. Those that succeed provide alternatives to youth and often a safe place to hang out, make new friends, and learn life skills.

CHICAGO AREA PROJECT. Chicago, like Los Angeles, has been home to many gangs throughout the twentieth century. In an effort to deal with the gang situation on the city's streets, the Chicago Area Project (CAP) was founded in 1934—the nation's first community-based delinquency prevention program. The program, which was designed by the sociologist Clifford R. Shaw (1895–1957), aimed to work with delinquent youth in poverty-stricken areas of Chicago. CAP staff sought to prevent youth from joining gangs and ultimately committing crimes.

To achieve this, CAP advocates believed that improvements needed to be made to neighborhoods and communities. According to CAP (April 9, 2007, http://www.chicagoareaproject.org/aboutus.htm), "The agency believes that residents must be empowered through the development of community organizations so that they can act together to improve neighborhood conditions, hold institutions serving the community accountable, reduce anti-social behavior by young people, protect them from inappropriate institutionalization, and provide them with positive models for personal development." The organization emphasizes that juvenile delinquency in low-income areas is a product of social disadvantages—not a flaw of the individual child or of individuals from certain ethnic or racial backgrounds.

CAP includes more than twenty-nine affiliates and twelve special projects. Continuing to promote self-improvement and self-determination, CAP emphasizes community organizing, advocacy, and direct service. According to CAP, it "has succeeded in arousing in individual citizens a sense of responsibility for the welfare of their children—and a realization that their own united efforts offered the most promising prospect for providing security, protection, and constructive satisfaction of the needs of the children and young people in any community."

BOYS AND GIRLS CLUBS OF AMERICA. Offering a variety of programs to help youth, the Boys and Girls Clubs of America (BGCA; 2007, http://www.bgca.org/) has worked with more than 4.6 million children throughout the United States, Puerto Rico, the Virgin Islands, and U.S. military bases in the United States and abroad. In about four thousand club locations, the group uses forty-seven thousand trained, full-time staff "to enable all young people, especially those who need us most, to reach their full potential as productive, caring, responsible citizens."

The BGCA offers a specialized program called Gang Prevention/Intervention through Targeted Outreach for those aged six to eighteen. Sponsored by the Office of Juvenile Justice and Delinquency Prevention (OJJDP), the outreach program works with delinquent youth and those at risk of becoming delinquent. The goal of the program is to provide educational and fun activities for youth in a safe environment to steer them away from becoming involved in gangs.

VIOLENCE-FREE ZONES. Coordinated by the National Center for Neighborhood Enterprise, violence-free zones help gang members and other violent youths turn their lives around through the adoption of a productive and peaceful lifestyle. A community-based program, the project provides various types of assistance, including life-skills training, mentoring, job assistance, substance abuse help, character development, and family services. To establish a violence-free zone, the National Center for Neighborhood Enterprise and community leaders seek to end youth violence by working with warring gang factions to call a truce.

The first violence-free zone was created in 1997 in the Benning Terrace public housing complex in Washington, D.C. At that time the area was so crime-ridden that people were afraid to leave their homes. The situation became even more desperate after the twelve-year-old Daryl Hall was beaten, kidnapped, and later murdered by warring gang members. Gangs had become so bold they attacked Hall in broad daylight. The National Center for Neighborhood Enterprise, in conjunction with the Alliance of Concerned Men, stepped in and was able to set up meetings between the leaders of the rival gangs. The groups managed to work out a truce.

Aimee Howd reports in "How to Stop Kids from Killing Kids" (*Insight on the News*, April 24, 2000) that when David Gilmore of the D.C. Housing Authority heard about the cease-fire, he joined the cause and offered jobs to some of the youths. Meaningful, legitimate employment proved to be an important asset to the program. Among the jobs available were landscaping, building maintenance, and removing graffiti. Jobs not only provided youth with an income but also with a sense of purpose and belonging. Gilmore estimates that the program saved the city $13 million and that fifteen or more deaths were prevented in the three years following the truce.

Programs have since been launched in Atlanta, Georgia; Prince George's County and Baltimore, Maryland; Dallas, Texas; and Milwaukee, Wisconsin.

Law Enforcement Strategies

OJJDP COMPREHENSIVE GANG MODEL. The OJJDP advocates the use of a comprehensive gang model developed by Irving A. Spergel to combat gangs. Jim Burch and Candice Kane, in the fact sheet "Implementing the OJJDP Comprehensive Gang Model" (July 1999, http://www .ncjrs.gov/pdffiles1/fs99112.pdf), note that the model includes five steps to help gang members and their communities. Steps include mobilizing the larger community to create opportunities or service organizations for gang-involved and at-risk youth; mobilizing outreach workers to connect with youth involved in gangs; creating academic, economic, and social opportunities for at-risk and gang-involved youth; using gang suppression activities and holding youth involved in gangs accountable for their actions; and helping community agencies problem solve at a grassroots level to address gang problems. The model assumes that gang violence is a byproduct of a breakdown in the larger community. According to the OJJDP, in "OJJDP Model Programs Guide" (October 11, 2005, http://www.dsgonline.com/mpg2.5/mpg_index.htm), evaluations of programs based on the OJJDP model show mixed results, although negative results generally result from poor program implementation.

GANG RESISTANCE EDUCATION AND TRAINING. Hoping to reach students before they become involved in gangs and crime, uniformed police officers throughout the country visit middle schools to discuss the life consequences associated with such activities. The thirteen-part curriculum, offered through the Gang Resistance Education and Training (G.R.E.A.T.) program, was initially created by the Phoenix (Arizona) Police Department and the Bureau of Alcohol, Tobacco, and Firearms in 1991. Because that pilot program met with success, G.R.E.A.T. has expanded to all fifty states and the District of Columbia. Among the topics presented are personal, resiliency, resistance, and social skills. The stated goals of the program are to help youth resist peer pressure, have positive attitudes toward law enforcement, learn ways to avoid violence, develop basic life skills, and set positive goals for the future. According to the article "G.R.E.A.T. Middle School Component" (April 27, 2007, http://www.great-online.org/corecurriculum.htm), the G.R.E.A.T. curriculum for seventh graders educates students about gangs, violence, drug abuse, and crime; helps students recognize their responsibilities and learn how to make good decisions; fosters communication skills; and teaches anger management skills.

The effectiveness of G.R.E.A.T. training became the basis for a study conducted by Finn-Aage Esbensen and D. Wayne Osgood, who published their findings in "Gang Resistance Education and Training (GREAT): Results from the National Evaluation" (*Journal of Research in Crime and Delinquency*, 1999). Program participants were said to have developed more negative opinions about gangs and more positive attitudes about police. They also reported experiencing lower rates of victimizations, among other things.

SUPPRESSION PROGRAMS. Another method intended to reduce youth crime and violence is called suppression. This tactic is used by law enforcement agencies throughout the country. Suppression usually involves a show of force, such as saturating an area with many uniformed police officers. The idea is meant to demonstrate to criminals that they are being watched and that criminal activities will not be tolerated. Suppression techniques also include sweeps, where officers sweep through an area rounding up youth and adult offenders. Some suppression programs have proven to be somewhat effective, whereas others have not.

In some areas with high gang activity and violent youth crime, law enforcement personnel have tried suppression techniques. Suppression programs have been tested out in various cities, including Los Angeles, Chicago, and Houston, among others.

The Houston Police Department Gang Task Force is just one example of the many units of this type operating throughout the United States. Working in conjunction with the Mayor's Anti-Gang Office (2007, http://www.houstontx .gov/publicsafety/antigang/index.html), the task force focuses on areas with high gang activity by providing a highly visible presence in an effort to lessen gang violence and crime. Initiatives aim to target, arrest, and incarcerate gang members involved in criminal activities. At the same time, the Anti-Gang Office works with communities, neighborhoods, service organizations, and schools to provide supportive services to at-risk youth, including counseling, job leads, conflict resolution, and recreation programs. The Mayor's Anti-Gang Office has also provided gang awareness training to individuals, including educators, law enforcement personnel, probation officers, and members of the public since 1994. The group makes use of high-tech devices, such as geomapping and tracking systems. These programs help staff keep track of gang locations as well as youth program assistance sites.

Bill White, the mayor of Houston, reports in "Houston Mayor White Oversees Gang Free Schools and Communities Project" (April 10, 2006, http://www.usmayors.org/uscm/ best_practices/usmayor06/HoustonBP.asp) that suppression is generally not successful alone. Houston provides an example of how suppression can be combined with other program elements, in that the Mayor's Anti-Gang Office uses suppression techniques as one element of the OJJDP's comprehensive gang model, "a paradigm that utilizes five core strategies (community mobilization, provision of opportunities, social intervention, suppression, organizational change and development) to address gang issues within a targeted community."

SCHOOL RESOURCE OFFICERS. The School Resource Officers (SROs) program is intended to improve relations between youth and police. The project, designed to prevent and intercept the commission of youth crime and violence, also gives students and police officers the chance to get to know one another. In some areas, children grow up with contempt for or fear of police. The SRO program

works to eliminate these concerns as well as to educate students about the law and provide one-on-one mentoring.

Under the program, a police officer is dispatched to a school as an SRO. The officer works to prevent crime, violence, and substance abuse; makes arrests if necessary during the commission of crimes; counsels students; and conducts classes about law enforcement and school safety. The program calls this the TRIAD concept (police officer, educator, and counselor). To participate as an SRO, candidates must complete a specialized training program. The SRO program is credited with helping reduce youth crime in schools and in the community.

Founded in 1990, the National Association of School Resource Officers (NASRO) has a national membership of nine thousand officers. NASRO holds annual conferences and provides workshops for the SROs about various procedures, techniques, and prevention measures. The group also conducts surveys of its members to learn more about current issues affecting the SROs and schools. For example, Kenneth S. Trump of the National School Safety and Security Services, in *School Safety Left Behind? School Safety Threats Grow as Preparedness Stalls and Funding Decreases: NASRO 2004 National School-Based Law Enforcement Survey* (February 2005, http://www.schoolsecurity.org/resources/ 2004 %20NASRO%20Survey%20Final%20Report%20 NSSSS.pdf), notes that over a third of the SROs (37.4%) believed that gang activity in their schools had increased, another third (38%) believed gang activity had remained the same, and only 8.4% believed gang activity had decreased.

School-Based Prevention Programs

STUDENTS AGAINST VIOLENCE EVERYWHERE. After Alex Orange was shot and killed in Charlotte, North Carolina, while trying to stop a fight in 1989, his classmates at West Charlotte High School decided to organize the group Students against Violence Everywhere (SAVE). SAVE (2006, http://www.nationalsave.org/main/statistics. php) has grown far beyond Orange's high school; in 2006 it had more than 1,650 chapters with 189,000 student members. The organization is active in elementary, middle, and high schools across the United States. Members have their own "colors": orange for Alex Orange and purple for peace and nonviolence.

The group focuses on violence prevention and on helping kids gain life skills, knowledge, and an understanding of the consequences of violence and crime. SAVE helps members overcome negative peer pressure situations through the development of positive peer interactions. It also plans safe activities, including cosponsorship of the National Youth Violence Prevention Campaign (2007, http://www.violencepreventionweek.org/). During the weeklong campaign participants spend each day focused on one aspect of violence prevention. For example, the first day seeks to "promote respect and tolerance," and other days focus on anger management, conflict resolution, school and community safety, and unity.

BIG BROTHERS BIG SISTERS IN SCHOOL. The Big Brothers Big Sisters program has been serving children for over one hundred years. The organization provides one-on-one mentoring services to young people (aged five to eighteen) throughout the United States. Big Brothers Big Sisters seeks to help youth perform better at school, stay clear of drugs and alcohol, improve their relationships with others, and avoid lives of crime and violence. Under the main program, a child is paired with an adult who spends time with him or her several times each month on outings, which can include sports, recreation, visits to museums or parks, and so on. Through the experience, the "Bigs" help the "Littles" develop life skills, confidence, and self-esteem.

Big Brothers Big Sisters has also developed programs for school children. Through the group's outreach program, volunteers visit schools weekly to provide one-on-one mentoring to students needing help. In addition, high school students also gain experience mentoring elementary school children through the High School Bigs program. While helping older students develop skills working with children, the project helps younger children bond with teens closer to their own age and see that they, too, can grow up to lead productive lives. According to the *Big Brothers Big Sisters Report to the Community, 2005* (2006, http://www.bbbs.org/), the organization provided assistance to 234,000 children in 2005, a 5% increase over the year before, through 440 local Big Brothers Big Sisters agencies.

PUNISHMENT

Juvenile Justice

In *Juvenile Offenders and Victims: 2006 National Report* (March 2006, http://www.ojjdp.ncjrs.gov/ojstatbb/nr2006/downloads/NR2006.pdf), Howard N. Snyder and Melissa Sickmund of the National Center for Juvenile Justice (NCJJ) indicate that juvenile court generally has original jurisdiction in cases involving youth who are under age eighteen when the crime was committed, when the youth is arrested, or when the offender is referred to the court. In 2004 thirty-seven states and the District of Columbia considered the oldest age for juveniles to be seventeen. Ten states—Georgia, Illinois, Louisiana, Massachusetts, Michigan, Missouri, New Hampshire, South Carolina, Texas, and Wisconsin—used sixteen—meaning that youth aged seventeen are under the jurisdiction of criminal courts. In Connecticut, New York, and North Carolina the age was set at fifteen—in other words, sixteen- and seventeen-year-olds are tried in criminal court.

When youth crime surged in the 1980s, many citizens called for changes in the juvenile justice system. According to Snyder and Sickmund, forty-five states made it easier to transfer juveniles from the juvenile justice system to the criminal justice system, thirty-one states made a wider variety of sentencing options for juveniles available, forty-seven states either changed or removed confidentiality provisions of the juvenile justice system, twenty-two states passed laws that enhanced the rights of victims of juvenile crime, and new programs for juveniles were developed in most states. As a result of these changes, more juveniles were tried as adults in the criminal justice system. Codes regulating state juvenile justice systems now tend to strike a balance between prevention/treatment goals and punishment rather than focusing mainly on rehabilitation.

If the court deems that it is in the interests of the juvenile and the public, juvenile courts in some states may retain jurisdiction over juvenile offenders past the ages discussed earlier. Thus, such courts can handle juvenile offenders until they turn twenty in thirty-three states and the District of Columbia. Snyder and Sickmund note that Florida uses age twenty-one, Kansas uses age twenty-two, and California, Montana, Oregon, and Wisconsin use age twenty-four as the cutoff. Extended jurisdiction, however, may be limited by legislation to specific crimes or certain juveniles. Hence, the question of "who is considered a juvenile" does not have one consistent, standard answer. In various states exceptions can be made to the age criteria. This is done so that juveniles can be tried as adults or to provide for procedures under which a prosecutor can decide to handle an offender as a juvenile or an adult.

DOES IT WORK? From 1996 to 2005 the murder rate for juvenile offenders consistently declined, dropping 46.8% in that period, and juvenile arrests for violent crimes—murder, forcible rape, robbery, and aggravated assault—were at their lowest rate since 1980. (See Table 10.1.) In 2005 only 739 juveniles were arrested for murder and nonnegligent manslaughter, compared with 1,388 in 1996. As such, some public officials believe that efforts to reduce crime through adult sentencing were working. However, many experts attribute the murder rate decline to expanded after-school crime prevention programs, the decline of crack cocaine and violent gangs, and big-city police efforts to crack down on illegal guns.

A 1987 Florida study discussed by Donna M. Bishop et al., in "The Transfer of Juveniles to Criminal Court: Does It Make a Difference?" (*Crime and Delinquency*, April 1996), suggests that juveniles tried in adult courts were likely to be rearrested more quickly and more often than juveniles who went to juvenile court. The study compared the rearrest rates of juveniles transferred to criminal court with a matched sample (similar crimes, past court experience, age, gender, and race) of those

TABLE 10.1

Ten-year arrest trends by age and offense, 1996–2005

[8,009 agencies; 2005 estimated population 178,017,991; 1996 estimated population 159,290,470]

| | Number of persons arrested | | | | | | | | |
| | Total all ages | | | Under 18 years of age | | | 18 years of age and over | | |
Offense charged	1996	2005	Percent change	1996	2005	Percent change	1996	2005	Percent change
Total[a]	8,619,699	8,244,321	−4.4	1,703,500	1,278,948	−24.9	6,916,199	6,965,373	+0.7
Murder and nonnegligent manslaughter	9,564	7,989	−16.5	1,388	739	−46.8	8,176	7,250	−11.3
Forcible rape	18,745	15,129	−19.3	3,202	2,392	−25.3	15,543	12,737	−18.1
Robbery	80,980	67,841	−16.2	25,318	16,791	−33.7	55,662	51,050	−8.3
Aggravated assault	315,405	282,003	−10.6	46,124	36,967	−19.9	269,281	245,036	−9.0
Burglary	220,798	180,973	−18.0	85,248	47,416	−44.4	135,550	133,557	−1.5
Larceny-theft	905,963	692,593	−23.6	319,161	182,813	−42.7	586,802	509,780	−13.1
Motor vehicle theft	100,318	82,160	−18.1	42,957	19,755	−54.0	57,361	62,405	+8.8
Arson	11,598	9,716	−16.2	6,506	4,915	−24.5	5,092	4,801	−5.7
Violent crime[b]	424,694	372,962	−12.2	76,032	56,889	−25.2	348,662	316,073	−9.3
Property crime[b]	1,238,677	965,442	−22.1	453,872	254,899	−43.8	784,805	710,543	−9.5
Other assaults	756,129	737,475	−2.5	137,850	142,957	+3.7	618,279	594,518	−3.8
Forgery and counterfeiting	72,103	70,738	−1.9	5,433	2,600	−52.1	66,670	68,138	+2.2
Fraud	255,162	193,539	−24.2	6,947	4,779	−31.2	248,215	188,760	−24.0
Embezzlement	10,152	12,087	+19.1	880	751	−14.7	9,272	11,336	+22.3
Stolen property; buying, receiving, possessing	91,832	82,771	−9.9	26,647	13,902	−47.8	65,185	68,869	+5.7
Vandalism	190,069	168,366	−11.4	87,907	63,697	−27.5	102,162	104,669	+2.5
Weapons; carrying, possessing, etc.	123,016	112,054	−8.9	31,067	26,834	−13.6	91,949	85,220	−7.3
Prostitution and commercialized vice	48,936	41,641	−14.9	723	870	+20.3	48,213	40,771	−15.4
Sex offenses (except forcible rape and prostitution)	56,484	52,410	−7.2	10,620	10,437	−1.7	45,864	41,973	−8.5
Drug abuse violations	830,684	1,034,844	+24.6	117,400	106,150	−9.6	713,284	928,694	+30.2
Gambling	6,352	3,446	−45.7	563	395	−29.8	5,789	3,051	−47.3
Offenses against the family and children	84,459	72,623	−14.0	4,839	3,067	−36.6	79,620	69,556	−12.6
Driving under the influence	877,727	816,243	−7.0	11,000	10,550	−4.1	866,727	805,693	−7.0
Liquor laws	364,792	348,974	−4.3	95,686	76,756	−19.8	269,106	272,218	+1.2
Drunkenness	446,767	335,730	−24.9	14,821	9,094	−38.6	431,946	326,636	−24.4
Disorderly conduct	420,232	379,439	−9.7	112,697	116,422	+3.3	307,535	263,017	−14.5
Vagrancy	16,424	17,376	+5.8	1,998	1,395	−30.2	14,426	15,981	+10.8
All other offenses (except traffic)	2,062,908	2,269,707	+10.0	264,418	220,050	−16.8	1,798,490	2,049,657	+14.0
Suspicion	4,025	2,569	−36.2	1,453	360	−75.2	2,572	2,209	−14.1
Curfew and loitering law violations	119,407	87,658	−26.6	119,407	87,658	−26.6	—	—	—
Runaways	122,693	68,796	−43.9	122,693	68,796	−43.9	—	—	—

[a]Does not include suspicion.
[b]Violent crimes are offenses of murder, forcible rape, robbery, and aggravated assault. Property crimes are offenses of burglary, larceny-theft, motor vehicle theft, and arson.

SOURCE: "Table 32. Ten-Year Arrest Trends: Totals, 1996–2005," in *Crime in the United States 2005*, U.S. Department of Justice, Federal Bureau of Investigation, September 2006, http://www.fbi.gov/ucr/05cius/data/table_32.html (accessed March 5, 2007)

retained in the juvenile system. Of the transferred youth, 30% were rearrested, compared with 19% of the non-transferred ones. Transferred youth who were rearrested had committed a new offense within an average of 135 days of release, compared with an average of 227 days for youth processed in juvenile courts.

Youth on Trial: A Developmental Perspective on Juvenile Justice (Thomas Grisso and Robert G. Schwartz, eds., 2000) discusses some of the problems in transferring juveniles to adult court. The authors note that juveniles have a harder time than adults when making "knowing and intelligent" decisions at many junctures in the criminal justice process. In particular, problems occur when waiving Miranda rights, which allow the juvenile to remain silent and talk to a lawyer before responding to questions posed by police. When a juvenile waives such rights, this can lead to much more serious consequences in adult court than in juvenile proceedings. The authors assert that "questions must be raised regarding the juvenile's judgment, decision-making capacity, and impulse control as they relate to criminal culpability" in adult proceedings. Before deciding if a youth can be held accountable as an adult for a particular offense, according to researchers and experts in child development, it is important to understand an adolescent's intellectual, social, and emotional development.

Juvenile Arrests

According to statistics maintained by the Federal Bureau of Investigation (FBI), the property and violent crime arrest rate for juveniles aged ten to seventeen began to rise during the 1980s. As recorded in the FBI's Property Crime Index and Violent Crime Index, arrests per one hundred thousand juveniles in that age bracket decreased for both property and violent crime from around 1980 to 1983. At that point, property crime arrests began a gradual increase and violent crime started to surge in the late 1980s. Around 1995 arrest rates for both property crime and violent acts began to decrease, with violent crimes seeing the greatest reductions.

Between 1996 and 2005 the number of juveniles arrested for all crimes dropped 24.9%; during this same period arrests of adults increased by 0.7%. (See Table 10.1.) Arrests of juveniles for some offenses declined even more drastically. For example, arrests of juveniles for murder and nonnegligent manslaughter dropped 46.8%, for burglary, 44.4%, for motor vehicle theft, 54%, and for drunkenness, 38.6%. Other offenses dropped much less. For example, arrests for driving while under the influence of alcohol dropped by only 4.1%, for drug abuse violations, by 9.6%, for carrying or possessing weapons, by 13.6%, and for sex offenses other than rape and prostitution, by only 1.7%. Arrests of juveniles for prostitution actually increased by 20.3% during this period.

Crime in the United States 2005 (September 2006, http://www.fbi.gov/ucr/05cius/index.html) reports that 14.1 million arrests were made nationwide in 2005, an increase of 0.2% from 2004. Overall, in 2005, 15.5% of all people arrested were juveniles and 84.5% were adults. Adults were most often arrested for drug abuse violations (928,000 arrests), whereas juveniles were most often arrested for larceny-theft (183,000 arrests). (See Table 10.1.) Adults were proportionally more likely to be arrested for violent crime than were juveniles, whereas juveniles were more likely to be arrested for property crime. In 2005, 84.7% of arrests for violent crime were arrests of adults; however, only 73.6% of arrests for property crime were of adults.

ARRESTS AMONG SPECIFIC AGE GROUPS. *Crime in the United States 2005* also records arrest rate statistics for specific age groups—under fifteen, under eighteen, under twenty-one, and under twenty-five—as shown in Table 10.2. Whereas 15.3% of all people arrested were juveniles in that year, almost half (44.3%) of all people arrested were under age twenty-five, highlighting that crime is often perpetrated by young adults, rather than juveniles. These statistics also show what crimes are more likely to be committed by juveniles rather than by young adults. Table 10.2 compares the number of arrests for these four age groups against the total number of arrests for all ages in 2005. For each offense, it presents the number of actual arrests for each age group as well as what percentage of total arrests falls within each age group.

A high percentage does not necessarily indicate a high number of arrests in a category. Instead, it means that age group was responsible for a high percentage of arrests within that category. For example, 141,035 individuals under eighteen were arrested on drug abuse violations, which was 10.4% of the total arrests in that category. (See Table 10.2.) Compare that to the 16,501 people under the age of eighteen arrested for buying,

receiving, and possessing stolen property. Although the number of stolen property offenses is far less than that of drug abuse violations for those under age eighteen, it represented 16.6% of the total arrests for stolen property. Such percentages help law enforcement personnel identify trends and patterns in juvenile crime.

Two categories that consistently had high arrest percentages among each of the four age groups presented in Table 10.2 were arson and vandalism. Two-thirds of arrests for each of these crimes (66.3%) were of young adults under age twenty-five. Of the 12,012 arrests for arson in 2005, more than a quarter (28.8%) were of youth under age fifteen, almost half (48.6%) were of juveniles under age eighteen, and 58.1% were of people under age twenty-one. Vandalism was less associated with the youngest juveniles. Of the 206,351 people arrested for vandalism in 2005, 15.5% were under age fifteen, 37.2% were under age eighteen, and more than half (52.8%) were under age twenty-one.

Other categories with the highest arrest percentages for those under age fifteen include disorderly conduct (11.9%), larceny-theft (9%), sex offenses, except forcible rape and prostitution (9%), and burglary (8.7%). (See Table 10.2.) The under-age-fifteen group also scored high in two other categories that are not applicable to those over age eighteen: curfew and loitering law violations and runaway arrests. A little more than a quarter of all arrests for curfew violations (28.2%) were of people under age fifteen, and 34.6% of arrests of runaways were of people under age fifteen. Children under age fifteen were the least likely to be arrested for murder (0.9%), forgery and counterfeiting (0.4%), fraud (0.4%), embezzlement (0.3%), prostitution (0.3%), and drunkenness (0.3%).

All arrests for curfew violations and of runaways were of youth under the age of eighteen. Besides arson and vandalism, arrests for disorderly conduct (29.7%), burglary (26.1%), larceny-theft (25.7%), motor vehicle theft (25.5%), and carrying and possessing weapons (23.1%) were particularly likely to be of youth under age eighteen. (See Table 10.2.) Arrests for offenses against the family and children (4.2%), forgery and counterfeiting (3.5%), drunkenness (2.9%), fraud (2.5%), prostitution (1.9%), and driving under the influence of alcohol (1.3%) were the least likely to be of youth under age eighteen.

Despite the overall decrease in arrests of juveniles, Snyder and Sickmund report that delinquency cases handled by juvenile courts nationwide increased to over 1.6 million between 1985 and 2002. Cases involving offenses against people rose to 387,500. (See Figure 10.1.) Cases involving public order offenses increased to 409,800. Cases involving drugs rose to 193,200. In contrast, juvenile court cases involving property offenses decreased to 624,900 during this period.

ARRESTS BY GENDER. In *Juvenile Arrests 2004* (December 2006, http://www.ncjrs.gov/pdffiles1/ojjdp/214563.pdf),

TABLE 10.2

Arrests of persons under 15, 18, 21, and 25 years of age, 2005

[10,974 agencies; 2005 estimated population 217,722,329]

Offense charged	Total all ages	Number of persons arrested				Percent of total all ages			
		Under 15	Under 18	Under 21	Under 25	Under 15	Under 18	Under 21	Under 25
Total	10,369,819	479,926	1,582,068	3,020,386	4,588,884	4.6	15.3	29.1	44.3
Murder and nonnegligent manslaughter	10,335	97	929	2,864	5,129	0.9	9.0	27.7	49.6
Forcible rape	18,733	1,055	2,888	5,585	8,334	5.6	15.4	29.8	44.5
Robbery	85,309	4,986	21,515	39,470	52,915	5.8	25.2	46.3	62.0
Aggravated assault	331,469	15,468	45,150	82,245	132,179	4.7	13.6	24.8	39.9
Burglary	220,391	19,135	57,506	96,832	127,740	8.7	26.1	43.9	58.0
Larceny-theft	854,856	77,340	219,881	343,938	446,320	9.0	25.7	40.2	52.2
Motor vehicle theft	108,301	6,443	27,666	46,376	62,980	5.9	25.5	42.8	58.2
Arson	12,012	3,463	5,834	6,982	7,958	28.8	48.6	58.1	66.3
Violent crime[a]	445,846	21,606	70,482	130,164	198,557	4.8	15.8	29.2	44.5
Property crime[a]	1,195,560	106,381	310,887	494,128	644,998	8.9	26.0	41.3	53.9
Other assaults	958,477	74,377	182,578	275,372	405,867	7.8	19.0	28.7	42.3
Forgery and counterfeiting	87,346	370	3,096	14,245	29,171	0.4	3.5	16.3	33.4
Fraud	231,721	1,033	5,882	27,053	61,432	0.4	2.5	11.7	26.5
Embezzlement	14,097	49	856	3,681	6,220	0.3	6.1	26.1	44.1
Stolen property; buying, receiving, possessing	99,173	4,202	16,501	33,163	49,321	4.2	16.6	33.4	49.7
Vandalism	206,351	31,925	76,817	109,002	136,750	15.5	37.2	52.8	66.3
Weapons; carrying, possessing, etc.	142,878	11,246	33,069	58,278	83,649	7.9	23.1	40.8	58.5
Prostitution and commercialized vice	62,663	163	1,204	7,857	16,524	0.3	1.9	12.5	26.4
Sex offenses (except forcible rape and prostitution)	67,072	6,052	12,196	19,523	26,816	9.0	18.2	29.1	40.0
Drug abuse violations	1,357,841	22,596	141,035	376,106	621,104	1.7	10.4	27.7	45.7
Gambling	8,101	199	1,464	3,085	4,411	2.5	18.1	38.1	54.5
Offenses against the family and children	93,172	1,230	3,901	9,873	21,212	1.3	4.2	10.6	22.8
Driving under the influence	997,338	236	12,956	103,277	296,129	*	1.3	10.4	29.7
Liquor laws	437,923	8,706	92,556	302,455	334,862	2.0	21.1	69.1	76.5
Drunkenness	412,930	1,393	11,816	50,135	116,978	0.3	2.9	12.1	28.3
Disorderly conduct	501,129	59,395	148,795	210,857	284,993	11.9	29.7	42.1	56.9
Vagrancy	24,372	1,082	3,416	5,450	7,558	4.4	14.0	22.4	31.0
All other offenses (except traffic)	2,837,806	70,131	266,885	600,528	1,055,767	2.5	9.4	21.2	37.2
Suspicion	2,747	97	400	878	1,289	3.5	14.6	32.0	46.9
Curfew and loitering law violations	104,054	29,382	104,054	104,054	104,054	28.2	100.0	100.0	100.0
Runaways	81,222	28,075	81,222	81,222	81,222	34.6	100.0	100.0	100.0

[a]Violent crimes are offenses of murder, forcible rape, robbery, and aggravated assault. Property crimes are offenses of burglary, larceny-theft, motor vehicle theft, and arson.
*Less than one-tenth of 1 percent.

SOURCE: "Table 41. Arrests of Persons Under 15, 18, 21, and 25 Years of Age, 2005," in *Crime in the United States 2005*, U.S. Department of Justice, Federal Bureau of Investigation, September 2006, http://www.fbi.gov/ucr/05cius/data/table_41.html (accessed March 5, 2007)

Howard N. Snyder of the NCJJ reports that young males were arrested in far greater numbers than young females between 1980 to 2004 in general. However, juvenile female arrest rates grew proportionately more than did arrests among young males, particularly in violent crime. In 2000 females represented 28% of the juveniles arrested. By 2004 the percentage of juvenile arrests who were female had reached 30%. Even though arrests of both males and females decreased between 1995 and 2004, arrests of females decreased less in most offense categories—and in some categories female arrests increased, whereas male arrests decreased.

For example, between 1996 and 2005 juvenile male arrests for aggravated assault dropped by 23.4%, whereas juvenile female arrests dropped by only 5.4%. (See Table 10.3.) Juvenile male arrests for simple assault dropped by 4.1%, whereas juvenile female arrests increased by 24%. Arrests of juvenile males for drug abuse violations

dropped by 13.6%, whereas arrests of juvenile females for the same offense increased by 14.4%. *Crime in the United States 2005* notes that females accounted for 50% of all arrests for embezzlement and 66.4% of arrests for prostitution, more than any other type of crime.

Crime in the United States 2005 reports that 76.2% of all arrests in the United States were of males (all ages) in 2005. In that year, more than four out of five (82.1%) people arrested for violent crime were male, whereas 68% of those arrested for property crime were male. Between 1996 and 2005 the number of arrests of males dropped 7.6%, whereas the number of arrests of females increased 7.4%. The rate for juvenile males dropped 28.7% during this period, whereas the rate for juvenile females dropped only 14.3%.

According to the FBI's ten-year arrest trends, juvenile males and females engage in many of the same types of

FIGURE 10.1

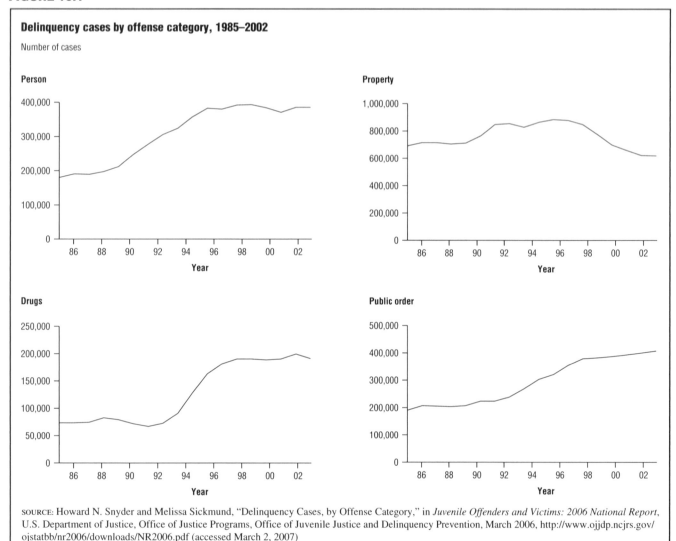

Delinquency cases by offense category, 1985–2002

Number of cases

SOURCE: Howard N. Snyder and Melissa Sickmund, "Delinquency Cases, by Offense Category," in *Juvenile Offenders and Victims: 2006 National Report*, U.S. Department of Justice, Office of Justice Programs, Office of Juvenile Justice and Delinquency Prevention, March 2006, http://www.ojjdp.ncjrs.gov/ojstatbb/nr2006/downloads/NR2006.pdf (accessed March 2, 2007)

crimes. For example, the crime most frequently committed by both males and females was larceny-theft. Although numbers of arrests were down for both males and females in this category in 2005, 105,513 males were arrested, whereas 77,300 females were arrested. As such, juvenile males were responsible for 18% of arrests for larceny-theft, and juvenile females for 11%. Together, juvenile offenders represented 29% of all larceny-theft arrests.

Other areas with high arrest rates of both juvenile males and females include other assault, disorderly conduct, and drug abuse violations. Young males were arrested 95,555 times for other assault charges, whereas young females were arrested 47,402 times for this offense in 2005. (See Table 10.3.) Disorderly conduct resulted in 78,552 young males and 37,870 young females under age eighteen being arrested, and drug abuse violations accounted for the arrests of 86,895 young males and 19,255 young females.

Other crimes most frequently committed by young males and females include liquor law violations (49,116 arrests for

males, 27,640 arrests for females) and curfew and loitering law violations (61,069 arrests for males, 26,589 arrests for females). (See Table 10.3.) Males also saw high numbers of arrests for vandalism (54,939 arrests), whereas young females were arrested 39,809 times as runaways.

Despite the high number of juvenile crimes, arrest rates for youth under age eighteen were down in many categories between 1996 and 2005. Young males experienced the greatest decline in the number of arrests for motor vehicle theft (down 55.3%); buying, receiving, and possessing stolen property (down 50.1%); murder and nonnegligent manslaughter (down 48.5%); and forgery and counterfeiting (down 47.8%). (See Table 10.3.) During this same period young female arrest rates dropped most for forgery and counterfeiting (down 59.3%), gambling (down 51.4%), motor vehicle theft (down 47.1%), and running away (down 43.4%).

Whereas juvenile males experienced decreases in arrests for all crime categories, female juveniles witnessed increases for certain crimes between 1996 and 2005. Arrests

TABLE 10.3

Ten-year arrest trends by sex, 1996–2005

[8,009 agencies; 2005 estimated population 178,017,991; 1996 estimated population 159,290,470]

Offense charged	Male						Female					
	Total			Under 18			Total			Under 18		
	1996	2005	Percent change	1996	2005	Percent change	1996	2005	Percent change	1996	2005	Percent change
Total[a]	6,773,900	6,261,672	−7.6	1,258,168	897,305	−28.7	1,845,799	1,982,649	+7.4	445,332	381,643	−14.3
Murder and nonnegligent manslaughter	8,572	7,114	−17.0	1,290	664	−48.5	992	875	−11.8	98	75	−23.5
Forcible rape	18,512	14,924	−19.4	3,153	2,332	−26.0	233	205	−12.0	49	60	+22.4
Robbery	73,192	60,096	−17.9	22,962	15,118	−34.2	7,788	7,745	−0.6	2,356	1,673	−29.0
Aggravated assault	260,469	224,080	−14.0	36,972	28,312	−23.4	54,936	57,923	+5.4	9,152	8,655	−5.4
Burglary	195,124	153,888	−21.1	76,490	41,672	−45.5	25,674	27,085	+5.5	8,758	5,744	−34.4
Larceny-theft	595,297	421,828	−29.1	212,281	105,513	−50.3	310,666	270,765	−12.8	106,880	77,300	−27.7
Motor vehicle theft	86,405	67,522	−21.9	36,188	16,172	−55.3	13,913	14,638	+5.2	6,769	3,583	−47.1
Arson	9,972	8,114	−18.6	5,794	4,230	−27.0	1,626	1,602	−1.5	712	685	−3.8
Violent crime[b]	360,745	306,214	−15.1	64,377	46,426	−27.9	63,949	66,748	+4.4	11,655	10,463	−10.2
Property crime[b]	886,798	651,352	−26.6	330,753	167,587	−49.3	351,879	314,090	−10.7	123,119	87,312	−29.1
Other assaults	597,763	554,044	−7.3	99,610	95,555	−4.1	158,366	183,431	+15.8	38,240	47,402	+24.0
Forgery and counterfeiting	45,250	43,068	−4.8	3,388	1,768	−47.8	26,853	27,670	+3.0	2,045	832	−59.3
Fraud	137,874	104,201	−24.4	4,536	3,065	−32.4	117,288	89,338	−23.8	2,411	1,714	−28.9
Embezzlement	5,545	5,979	+7.8	486	419	−13.8	4,607	6,108	+32.6	394	332	−15.7
Stolen property; buying, receiving, possessing	78,156	66,459	−15.0	23,140	11,540	−50.1	13,676	16,312	+19.3	3,507	2,362	−32.6
Vandalism	163,890	139,529	−14.9	78,226	54,939	−29.8	26,179	28,837	+10.2	9,681	8,758	−9.5
Weapons; carrying, possessing, etc.	113,685	103,184	−9.2	28,657	24,052	−16.1	9,331	8,870	−4.9	2,410	2,782	+15.4
Prostitution and commercialized vice	20,524	14,615	−28.8	303	202	−33.3	28,412	27,026	−4.9	420	668	+59.0
Sex offenses (except forcible rape and prostitution)	52,296	48,112	−8.0	9,829	9,437	−4.0	4,188	4,298	+2.6	791	1,000	+26.4
Drug abuse violations	688,006	832,707	+21.0	100,568	86,895	−13.6	142,678	202,137	+41.7	16,832	19,255	+14.4
Gambling	5,541	2,942	−46.9	528	378	−28.4	811	504	−37.9	35	17	−51.4
Offenses against the family and children	68,211	55,393	−18.8	3,089	1,894	−38.7	16,248	17,230	+6.0	1,750	1,173	−33.0
Driving under the influence	745,658	658,705	−11.7	9,191	8,187	−10.9	132,069	157,538	+19.3	1,809	2,363	+30.6
Liquor laws	286,425	255,746	−10.7	66,537	49,116	−26.2	78,367	93,228	+19.0	29,149	27,640	−5.2
Drunkenness	391,721	284,892	−27.3	12,156	6,999	−42.4	55,046	50,838	−7.6	2,665	2,095	−21.4
Disorderly conduct	324,503	279,714	−13.8	83,418	78,552	−5.8	95,729	99,725	+4.2	29,279	37,870	+29.3
Vagrancy	12,893	13,752	+6.7	1,654	1,082	−34.6	3,531	3,624	+2.6	344	313	−9.0
All other offenses (except traffic)	1,651,922	1,751,008	+6.0	201,228	159,156	−20.9	410,986	518,699	+26.2	63,190	60,894	−3.6
Suspicion	3,209	2,211	−31.1	1,118	254	−77.3	816	358	−56.1	335	106	−68.4
Curfew and loitering law violations	84,194	61,069	−27.5	84,194	61,069	−27.5	35,213	26,589	−24.5	35,213	26,589	−24.5
Runaways	52,300	28,987	−44.6	52,300	28,987	−44.6	70,393	39,809	−43.4	70,393	39,809	−43.4

[a]Does not include suspicion.

[b]Violent crimes are offenses of murder, forcible rape, robbery, and aggravated assault. Property crimes are offenses of burglary, larceny-theft, motor vehicle theft, and arson.

SOURCE: "Table 33. Ten-Year Arrest Trends by Sex, 1996–2005," in *Crime in the United States 2005*, U.S. Department of Justice, Federal Bureau of Investigation, September 2006, http://www.fbi.gov/ucr/05cius/data/table_33.html (accessed March 5, 2007).

of young females were up for prostitution and commercialized vice (up 59%) and other sex offenses (up 26.4%), driving under the influence (up 30.6%), disorderly conduct (up 29.3%), and for other assaults (up 24%). (See Table 10.3.)

ARRESTS BY RACE. African-Americans are disproportionately arrested in the United States. The U.S. Census Bureau reports in *Race and Hispanic Origin in 2005* (2005, http://www.census.gov/population/pop-profile/dynamic/RACEHO.pdf) that in 2005 the U.S. population was 80.4% white, 12.8% African-American, 4.2% Asian, and 1% Native American or Alaskan Native. Hispanics, who can be of any race, represented 14.1% of the total. *Crime in the United States 2005* notes that 69.8% of all arrested individuals in 2005 were white, 27.8% were African-American, 1.3% were Native American or Alaskan Native, and 1% were Asian or Pacific Islander.

Arrested juveniles exhibited a similar racial distribution; 67.5% of arrested juveniles were white, 29.9% were African-American, 1.3% were Native American or Alaskan Native, and 1.3% were Asian or Pacific Islander in 2005. (See Table 10.4.) Among juveniles, a particularly high proportion of those arrested for driving under the influence (93.3%), violation of liquor laws (91.6%), drunkenness (88.8%), arson (79.1%), vagrancy (79.1%), offenses against the family and children (79%), and vandalism (78%) was white. A particularly high proportion of those arrested for gambling (92.2%), robbery (67.5%), prostitution and commercialized vice (55.8%), and murder and nonnegligent manslaughter (54%) was African-American.

In 2005 juveniles were arrested more for larceny-theft than for any other crime (218,383 arrests). They were also arrested more often for simple assaults (181,114 arrests),

TABLE 10.4

Arrests of juveniles by race, 2005

[10,971 agencies; 2005 estimated population 217,692,433]

Offense charged	Arrests under 18					Percent distribution[a]				
	Total	White	Black	American Indian or Alaskan Native	Asian or Pacific Islander	Total	White	Black	American Indian or Alaskan Native	Alaskan Pacific Islander
Total	1,570,282	1,059,742	469,382	20,490	20,668	100.0	67.5	29.9	1.3	1.3
Murder and nonnegligent manslaughter	924	397	499	18	10	100.0	43.0	54.0	1.9	1.1
Forcible rape	2,851	1,834	969	31	17	100.0	64.3	34.0	1.1	0.6
Robbery	21,460	6,598	14,487	96	279	100.0	30.7	67.5	0.4	1.3
Aggravated assault	44,845	24,951	18,942	487	465	100.0	55.6	42.2	1.1	1.0
Burglary	57,054	38,287	17,663	565	539	100.0	67.1	31.0	1.0	0.9
Larceny-theft	218,383	149,754	61,407	3,176	4,046	100.0	68.6	28.1	1.5	1.9
Motor vehicle theft	27,499	14,798	11,943	349	409	100.0	53.8	43.4	1.3	1.5
Arson	5,787	4,575	1,076	63	73	100.0	79.1	18.6	1.1	1.3
Violent crime[b]	70,080	33,780	34,897	632	771	100.0	48.2	49.8	0.9	1.1
Property crime[b]	308,723	207,414	92,089	4,153	5,067	100.0	67.2	29.8	1.3	1.6
Other assaults	181,114	105,684	71,486	2,063	1,881	100.0	58.4	39.5	1.1	1.0
Forgery and counterfeiting	3,051	2,259	725	18	49	100.0	74.0	23.8	0.6	1.6
Fraud	5,796	3,723	1,981	32	60	100.0	64.2	34.2	0.6	1.0
Embezzlement	849	532	293	8	16	100.0	62.7	34.5	0.9	1.9
Stolen property; buying, receiving, possessing	16,305	8,941	7,019	146	199	100.0	54.8	43.0	0.9	1.2
Vandalism	76,096	59,349	14,961	955	831	100.0	78.0	19.7	1.3	1.1
Weapons; carrying, possessing, etc.	32,949	20,154	12,161	253	381	100.0	61.2	36.9	0.8	1.2
Prostitution and commercialized vice	1,200	501	670	9	20	100.0	41.8	55.8	0.8	1.7
Sex offenses (except forcible rape and prostitution)	11,979	8,534	3,226	110	109	100.0	71.2	26.9	0.9	0.9
Drug abuse violations	139,776	96,207	41,076	1,301	1,192	100.0	68.8	29.4	0.9	0.9
Gambling	1,463	106	1,349	0	8	100.0	7.2	92.2	0.0	0.5
Offenses against the family and children	3,850	3,042	714	80	14	100.0	79.0	18.5	2.1	0.4
Driving under the influence	12,584	11,744	502	223	115	100.0	93.3	4.0	1.8	0.9
Liquor laws	91,800	84,107	4,322	2,535	836	100.0	91.6	4.7	2.8	0.9
Drunkenness	11,401	10,122	951	230	98	100.0	88.8	8.3	2.0	0.9
Disorderly conduct	147,976	87,640	57,331	1,889	1,116	100.0	59.2	38.7	1.3	0.8
Vagrancy	3,416	2,702	676	12	26	100.0	79.1	19.8	0.4	0.8
All other offenses (except traffic)	264,643	190,241	67,221	3,429	3,752	100.0	71.9	25.4	1.3	1.4
Suspicion	400	253	144	2	1	100.0	63.3	36.0	0.5	0.3
Curfew and loitering law violations	103,886	64,881	36,928	876	1,201	100.0	62.5	35.5	0.8	1.2
Runaways	80,945	57,826	18,660	1,534	2,925	100.0	71.4	23.1	1.9	3.6

[a]Because of rounding, the percentages may not add to 100.0.
[b]Violent crimes are offenses of murder, forcible rape, robbery, and aggravated assault. Property crimes are offenses of burglary, larceny-theft, motor vehicle theft, and arson.

SOURCE: Adapted from "Table 43. Arrests by Race, 2005," in *Crime in the United States 2005*, U.S. Department of Justice, Federal Bureau of Investigation, September 2006, http://www.fbi.gov/ucr/05cius/data/table_43.html (accessed March 5, 2007)

disorderly conduct (147,976 arrests), and drug abuse violations (139,776 arrests). The FBI data on arrests by race did not identify arrest rates by Hispanic origin.

DISPOSITION OF JUVENILES ARRESTED. Ann L. Pastore and Kathleen Maguire report in *Sourcebook of Criminal Justice Statistics* (2003, http://www.albany.edu/sourcebook/pdf/t4262004.pdf) that in the 1970s a change occurred in the disposition of arrested juveniles. Statistics for 1972 show that 50.8% of arrested minors were referred to juvenile court, 45% were handled within the police department and then released, and 1.3% were referred to criminal or adult court. In other words, almost half of all arrested juveniles were not formally charged with offenses in either juvenile or criminal court. From 1972 to 2000, however, those referred to juvenile court increased 20%, whereas those handled internally and then released dropped nearly 25%. The percentage of juvenile cases referred to criminal or adult court rose to 7%.

By 2005, 20.2% of arrested juveniles were released after being handled internally within the department, 70.7% were referred to juvenile court jurisdiction, and 7.4% were referred to criminal or adult court. (See Table 10.5.) Also included in Table 10.5 are statistics for the percentage of juveniles referred to a welfare agency (0.4%) and those referred to another police agency (1.3%). Statistics for city-residing juveniles are consistent with the overall totals. In urban areas more juveniles were handled within the department and released than overall (21.1% versus 20.2%), and fewer were referred to criminal or adult court (7% versus 7.4%).

TABLE 10.5

Police disposition of juvenile offenders taken into custody, 2005

[2005 estimated population]

Population group		Totalª	Handled within department and released	Referred to juvenile court jurisdiction	Referred to welfare agency	Referred to other police agency	Referred to criminal or adult court	Number of agencies	2005 estimated population
Total agencies:	Number	660,974	133,664	467,288	2,461	8,808	48,753	5,138	120,999,116
	Percentᵇ	100.0	20.2	70.7	0.4	1.3	7.4		
Total cities:	Number	553,741	116,983	389,513	1,903	6,330	39,012	3,926	85,869,567
	Percentᵇ	100.0	21.1	70.3	0.3	1.1	7.0		

ªIncludes all offenses except traffic and neglect cases.
ᵇBecause of rounding, the percentages may not add to 100.0.

SOURCE: Adapted from "Table 68. Police Disposition of Juvenile Offenders Taken into Custody, 2005," in *Crime in the United States 2005*, U.S. Department of Justice, Federal Bureau of Investigation, September 2006, http://www.fbi.gov/ucr/05cius/data/table_68.html (accessed March 5, 2007)

Juveniles in Custody

The OJJDP classifies juveniles in residential placement into three categories: committed, detained, and under a diversion agreement. According to the OJJDP (2007, http://ojjdp.ncjrs.org/ojstatbb/glossary.html), "Committed . . . includes juveniles in placement in the facility as part of a court-ordered disposition [and] those whose cases have been adjudicated and disposed in juvenile court and those who have been convicted and sentenced in criminal court. Detained . . . includes juveniles held prior to adjudication while awaiting an adjudication hearing in juvenile court, as well as juveniles held after adjudication while awaiting disposition or awaiting placement elsewhere. . . . Diversion . . . includes juveniles sent to the facility in lieu of adjudication as part of a diversion agreement."

Snyder and Sickmund note that of the 109,225 juvenile offenders in residential placement overall in 2003, 74% were committed, 25% were detained, and less than 1% were under diversion agreements. The largest group, committed, was sent to residential placement by juvenile courts. Those being detained were part of a transitory population— those awaiting hearings, awaiting the disposition of their cases, or awaiting transfer to a different type of facility. It is likely that some of the detained individuals were later sent to prison or jail. People in confinement under diversion agreements have entered detention voluntarily. In other words, the juvenile may have volunteered to go to a detention center to avoid going to juvenile court.

DETENTION. About one out of five juveniles are put in detention as their cases are processed in juvenile court. Detention may be used if the youth is judged to be a threat to the community, will be at risk if returned to the community, or may not appear at an upcoming hearing if released. Snyder and Sickmund report that the number of delinquency cases involving detention increased 42% between 1985 and 2002, from 234,600 to 329,800. The largest increase was for drug cases (140%), followed by crimes against people (122%), and public order cases

(72%). The number of juveniles detained in property cases declined by 12% during this period. Figure 10.2 shows that the percent of juveniles who were detained for these cases fluctuated between 1985 and 2002 but did not experience much change overall.

Snyder and Sickmund find that the use of detention increased more for females than for males between 1985 and 2002 (87% and 34%, respectively). However, males continued to be more likely than females to be detained, despite the increase in the use of detention for female juvenile offenders. Likewise, the use of detention increased more for African-American youth between 1985 and 2002 (64%) than it did for white youth (32%). Although a larger number of white youth than African-American youth were detained, African-American youth were proportionately more likely than white youth to be detained. This disparity was greatest in drug cases—African-American youth were more than two times more likely than white youth to be detained for these offenses.

RESIDENTIAL PLACEMENT. Youths sentenced under the jurisdiction of juvenile courts could be generally confined in residential placement facilities. According to Snyder and Sickmund, 96,655 juvenile offenders were confined in public and private juvenile correctional, detention, and shelter facilities. (See Table 10.6.) Excluded from this category are juveniles in prisons and jails. Melissa Sickmund of the NCJJ finds in *Juvenile Residential Facility Census, 2002: Selected Findings* (June 2006, http://www.ncjrs .gov/pdffiles1/ojjdp/211080.pdf) that the number of juvenile offenders in custody decreased 7% between 2000 and 2002, probably because of the substantial decline in the number of juvenile arrests since the mid-1990s.

Sickmund reports that in 2002 group homes made up 38% of all facilities and held 12% of all juveniles in residential placement, reflecting their relatively small size; detention centers made up 26% of all facilities and held 40% of all juveniles in residential placement, reflecting these centers' relatively large size. Other types

FIGURE 10.2

Number and percent of juvenile delinquency cases involving detention, 1985–2002

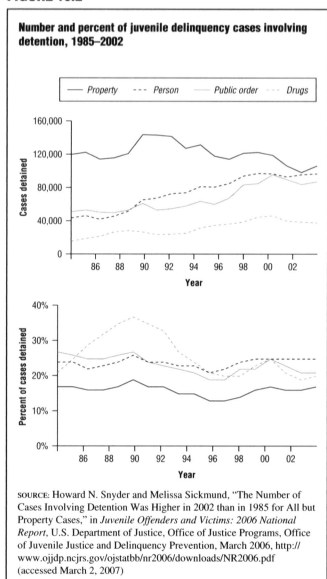

SOURCE: Howard N. Snyder and Melissa Sickmund, "The Number of Cases Involving Detention Was Higher in 2002 than in 1985 for All but Property Cases," in *Juvenile Offenders and Victims: 2006 National Report*, U.S. Department of Justice, Office of Justice Programs, Office of Juvenile Justice and Delinquency Prevention, March 2006, http://www.ojjdp.ncjrs.gov/ojstatbb/nr2006/downloads/NR2006.pdf (accessed March 2, 2007)

erty (burglary, theft, auto theft, arson, or other property offenses), 8% were held for drug offenses, 10% were held for public order offenses, and 15% were held for technical violations.

The number of juveniles held in residential placement declined by 8% between 1997 and 2003. (See Table 10.6.) In a few cases, however, the number of juveniles held in residential placement increased. The number of juveniles held for sexual assault increased by 34%, the number held for simple assault increased by 22%, and the number held for underage drinking increased by 27%. The greatest decline (54%) was in the number of juveniles held for criminal homicide.

Sickmund notes that in 2002 states with the largest number of youth under twenty-one in residential facilities included California (17,294), Florida (8,508), Texas (8,371), Pennsylvania (5,080), Ohio (4,480), and New York (4,455). These five states housed 47% of all juveniles in residential detention. States with the smallest number included Vermont (61), Hawaii (112), and New Hampshire (234). However, such data need to be considered in relation to the size of the population of these states; the rate of juvenile offenders in custody per 100,000 youth measures the likelihood of juvenile incarceration by state. In 2002 the states with the highest juvenile custody rates included Wyoming (688 per 100,000 youth), South Dakota (640 per 100,000 youth), the District of Columbia (599 per 100,000 youth), Louisiana (496 per 100,000 youth), and Florida (473 per 100,000 youth).

DEMOGRAPHICS OF THOSE IN RESIDENTIAL PLACEMENT. According to Snyder and Sickmund, in 2003 juvenile detention facilities were home to a disproportionately larger number of males (85%) than females (15%), although the proportion of females had increased slightly from 13% in 1991. Of the males in confinement, more than one-third (35%) had committed offenses against people and 29% had committed property offenses. Females were less likely to commit person offenses (30%) and property offenses (21%) than males were. Proportionally, among person offenses, females were more likely to commit simple assault than males (14% and 7%, respectively), but far less likely to commit sexual assault (1% and 9%, respectively). Among property offenses, a larger proportion of males were being held for burglary (12%) than were females (5%). Females were substantially more likely to be held for status offenses (13%) than were males (4%), including ungovernability (5% of females and 1% of males), running away (5% of females and 0% of males), and truancy (2% of females and 1% of males). However, the proportion of female status offenders dropped from 33% in 1991 to 13% in 2003.

Snyder and Sickmund also report that in 2003, 61% of juveniles in custody nationwide were members of minority groups. More than a third of offenders in custody were African-American (38%), 19% were Hispanic, 2% were

of residential facilities included shelters, diagnostic centers, boot camps, wilderness camps, and training schools. Six out of ten (60%) facilities were privately run; the rest were run by state or local government.

The OJJDP divides juvenile crimes into delinquency offenses and status offenses. Delinquency offenses are acts that are illegal regardless of the age of the perpetrator. Status offenses are acts that are illegal only for minors, such as truancy and running away. About 95% of juveniles in residential placement in 2003—91,831 out of a total of 96,655—were delinquents. (See Table 10.6.) The other 5% were status offenders (truants from school, noncriminal ordinances and rules violators, out-of-control youths, curfew violators, and runaways). According to Snyder and Sickmund, a third (34%) of juveniles in residential placement were held for offenses against people (homicide, sexual assault, robbery, and aggravated or simple assault), 28% were held for offenses against prop-

TABLE 10.6

Juvenile offenders in residential placements by offense, 2003

Most serious offense	Juvenile offenders in residential placement, 2003			Percent change 1997–2003		
	Type of facility			Type of facility		
	All	Public	Private	All	Public	Private
Total offenders	96,655	66,210	30,321	28%	212%	3%
Delinquency	91,831	64,662	27,059	−7	−12	11
Person	33,197	23,499	9,671	−6	−13	21
Criminal homicide	878	803	73	−54	−56	−28
Sexual assault	7,452	4,749	2,698	34	20	68
Robbery	6,230	5,157	1,073	−33	−35	−22
Aggravated assault	7,495	5,745	1,741	−21	−24	−7
Simple assault	8,106	4,984	3,113	22	21	25
Other person	3,036	2,061	973	38	22	87
Property	26,843	18,740	8,073	−16	−18	−10
Burglary	10,399	7,481	2,904	−17	−21	−7
Theft	5,650	3,793	1,848	−22	−26	−12
Auto theft	5,572	3,756	1,812	−15	−14	−16
Arson	735	514	220	−19	−25	0
Other property	4,487	3,196	1,289	−4	−4	−6
Drug	8,002	4,851	3,137	−12	−23	15
Drug trafficking	1,810	1,284	522	−37	−41	−24
Other drug	6,192	3,567	2,615	0	−14	28
Public order	9,654	6,782	2,866	0	−5	11
Weapons	3,013	2,346	665	−28	−29	−24
Other public order	6,641	4,436	2,201	20	16	29
Technical violation	14,135	10,790	3,312	14	5	56
Status offense	4,824	1,548	3,262	−29	−11	−36
Ungovernability	1,825	253	1,570	−36	−45	−34
Running a way	997	417	577	−33	−14	−43
Truancy	841	207	634	−37	−49	−32
Curfew violation	203	65	138	5	−18*	21
Under age drinking	405	210	186	27	86	−10
Other status offense	553	396	157	−14	98	−64

*Percent change is based on a denominator less than 100.
Note: Total includes juvenile offenders held in tribal facilities.

SOURCE: Howard N. Snyder and Melissa Sickmund, "In 2003, Public Facilities Held 64,662 Delinquents and Private Facilities Held 27,059 Delinquents on the 2003 Census Date," in *Juvenile Offenders and Victims: 2006 National Report*, U.S. Department of Justice, Office of Justice Programs, Office of Juvenile Justice and Delinquency Prevention, 2006, http://www.ojjdp.ncjrs.gov/ojstatbb/nr2006/downloads/NR2006.pdf (accessed March 2, 2006)

Native American, and 2% were Asian. About four out of ten (39%) juveniles in custody were non-Hispanic white. Another 1% fell into the other category, which includes those of multiple races. Snyder and Sickmund also provide data on the number of detained juveniles per 100,000 juveniles in the general population for each of the racial/ethnic categories, except the other category. The custody rate for African-American juveniles was highest (754 per 100,000 youth), followed by Native American juveniles (496 per 100,000 youth) and Hispanic juveniles (348 per 100,000 youth). The rate was relatively low for white juveniles (190 per 100,000 youth) and Asian juveniles (113 per 100,000 youth).

Incarcerated Juveniles

In *Prison and Jail Inmates at Midyear, 2005* (May 2005, http://www.ojp.usdoj.gov/bjs/pub/pdf/pjim05.pdf), Paige M. Harrison and Allen J. Beck of the U.S. Bureau of Justice Statistics indicate that 6,759 juveniles were in prison or jail in 2005. According to Snyder and Sickmund, in 2004 youth aged seventeen and younger accounted for about 1% of all jail inmates; an estimated 7,083 youth were held in adult jails on June 30, 2004. The number of juveniles being held in state prisons had declined from 5,309 in 1995 to a low of 2,266 in 2005. (See Table 10.7.)

Of the 2,266 juveniles in state prisons as of mid-2005, 2,175 (or 96%) were male. (See Table 10.7.) This figure represents a drop of 1,546 male juveniles since 2000. Although females were a small percentage of the juveniles incarcerated in state prison each year during this period, their numbers decreased as well, from 175 in 2000 to 91 in 2005. Overall, the number of juveniles in state prison dropped by 3,043 from 2000 to 2005.

Six states claimed more than 100 juvenile inmates in mid-2005—Connecticut (383), New York (223), Florida (185), North Carolina (169), Texas (167), and South Carolina (120). (See Table 10.8.) Between 2004 and 2005 Connecticut saw a 19.3% increase in juveniles in state prison, and South Carolina saw a 5.3% increase. The other states saw a decrease, with the largest decrease (20.5%) being in

TABLE 10.7

Number of inmates under age 18 held in state prisons, by gender, 1995, and 2000–05

	Inmates under age 18		
Year	Total	Male	Female
2005	2,266	2,175	91
2004	2,485	2,375	110
2003	2,741	2,627	114
2002	3,038	2,927	111
2001	3,147	3,010	137
2000	3,896	3,721	175
1995	5,309	—	—

— Not available.

SOURCE: Paige M. Harrison and Allen J. Beck, "Table 5. Number of Inmates under Age 18 Held in State Prisons, by Gender, June 30, 1995, and 2000–05," in *Prison and Jail Inmates at Midyear 2005*, U.S. Department of Justice, Bureau of Justice Statistics, May 2006, http://www.ojp.usdoj.gov/bjs/pub/pdf/pjim05.pdf (accessed March 5, 2006)

TABLE 10.8

States with the highest number of prisoners under age 18, midyear 2004–05

	Number of prisoners under age 18		Percent
	6/30/05	6/30/04	change
Connecticut*	383	321	19.3%
New York	223	225	−0.9
Florida	185	214	−13.6
North Carolina	169	192	−12.0
Texas	167	210	−20.5
South Carolina	120	114	5.3

*Includes local jail inmates under age 18.

SOURCE: Paige M. Harrison and Allen J. Beck, "Number of State Inmates under Age 18 Continues to Decline," in *Prison and Jail Inmates at Midyear 2005*, U.S. Department of Justice, Bureau of Justice Statistics, May 2006, http://www.ojp.usdoj.gov/bjs/pub/pdf/pjim05.pdf (accessed March 5, 2006)

Texas. Three states reported no juvenile inmates in state prisons and another nineteen states reported having ten or fewer juvenile inmates in state prison in 2005.

In the fact sheet "Youth under Age 18 in the Adult Criminal Justice System" (June 2006, http://www.nccd-crc.org/nccd/pubs/2006may_factsheet_youthadult.pdf), Christopher Harney of the National Council on Crime and Delinquency reports that both the number of juveniles being admitted to state prisons and the proportion of people under age eighteen in prisons have been dropping since the mid-1990s. Nearly two-thirds (62%) of these youth have been convicted of a violent offense. However, Harney points out that "the practice of sentencing youth as adults most seriously impacts African American, Latino, and Native American youth" and that juveniles convicted in the adult system receive little or no rehabilitative programming and are more likely to recidivate (go back to criminal behavior) than youth convicted of similar offenses in the juvenile system.

Recent breakdowns of juveniles in state and federal prisons by race are not available. However, among the 27,500 (26,300 male and 1,200 female) imprisoned young adults aged eighteen to nineteen in 2005, 12,200 (11,800 male and 400 female) were African-American (44%), 7,700 (7,200 male and 500 female) were white (28%), and 5,800 (5,600 males and 200 females) were Hispanic (21%). (See Table 10.9.) Of those who were eighteen to nineteen years old in 2005, the rate of incarceration for African-Americans was 1,920 per 100,000 males and 61 per 100,000 females; for Hispanics the rate was 791 per 100,000 males and 38 per 100,000 females; and for whites the rate was 274 per 100,000 males and 20 per 100,000 females. (See Table 10.10.)African-American juveniles have a much higher rate of incarceration than do white juveniles.

TABLE 10.9

Number of sentenced prisoners under state or federal jurisdiction, by gender, race, Hispanic origin, and age, 2005

	Number of sentenced prisoners							
	Males				Females			
Age	Total[a]	White[b]	Black[b]	Hispanic	Total[a]	White[b]	Black[b]	Hispanic
Total	**1,362,500**	**459,700**	**547,200**	**279,000**	**98,600**	**45,800**	**29,900**	**15,900**
18–19	26,300	7,200	11,800	5,600	1,200	500	400	200
20–24	218,700	62,700	94,200	50,400	11,900	5,300	3,600	2,300
25–29	244,800	67,000	106,600	59,600	15,300	6,700	4,700	2,900
30–34	224,200	69,800	92,000	51,100	17,400	8,100	5,100	2,900
35–39	207,200	72,300	81,600	41,600	19,400	9,000	6,000	3,000
40–44	185,200	70,900	71,000	31,600	16,500	7,800	5,100	2,400
45–54	189,800	76,300	71,100	29,500	13,800	6,500	4,300	1,800
55 or older	63,500	32,900	17,600	9,000	3,000	1,800	700	300

Note: Based on estimates by gender, race, Hispanic origin, and age from the 2004 Survey of Inmates in State Correctional Facilities and updated from jurisdiction counts by gender at yearend 2005. Estimates were rounded to the nearest 100.
[a]Includes American Indians, Alaska Natives, Asians, Native Hawaiians, other Pacific Islanders, and persons identifying two or more races.
[b]Excludes Hispanics and persons identifying two or more races.

SOURCE: Paige M. Harrison and Allen J. Beck, "Table 10. Number of Sentenced Prisoners under State or Federal Jurisdiction, by Gender, Race, Hispanic Origin, and Age, Yearend 2005," in *Prisoners in 2005*, U.S. Department of Justice, Bureau of Justice Statistics, November 2006, http://www.ojp.usdoj.gov/bjs/pub/pdf/p05.pdf (accessed March 5, 2007)

TABLE 10.10

Number of sentenced prisoners under state or federal jurisdiction per 100,000 residents, by gender, race, Hispanic origin, and age, 2005

	Number of sentenced prisoners per 100,000 residents							
	Males				Females			
Age	Total[a]	White[b]	Black[b]	Hispanic	Total[a]	White[b]	Black[b]	Hispanic
Total	**929**	**471**	**3,145**	**1,244**	**65**	**45**	**156**	**76**
18–19	619	274	1,920	791	29	20	61	38
20–24	2,016	948	6,345	2,493	118	85	248	137
25–29	2,342	1,098	8,082	2,618	153	113	339	158
30–34	2,234	1,172	7,726	2,450	177	138	391	165
35–39	1,953	1,067	6,630	2,255	185	134	435	184
40–44	1,641	923	5,472	1,975	145	102	345	164
45–54	899	493	3,136	1,327	63	41	163	85
55 or older	208	135	697	416	8	6	19	13

Note: Based on estimates of the U.S resident population on January 1, 2006, by gender, race, Hispanic origin, and age. Detailed categories exclude persons identifying with two or more races.
[a]Includes American Indians, Alaska Natives, Asians, Native Hawaiians, other Pacific Islanders, and persons identifying two or more races.
[b]Excludes Hispanics and persons identifying two or more races.

SOURCE: Paige M. Harrison and Allen J. Beck, "Table 11. Number of Sentenced Prisoners under State or Federal Jurisdiction per 100,000 Residents, by Gender, Race, Hispanic Origin, and Age, Yearend 2005," in *Prisoners in 2005*, U.S. Department of Justice, Bureau of Justice Statistics, November 2006, http://www.ojp.usdoj.gov/bjs/pub/pdf/p05.pdf (accessed March 5, 2007)

JUVENILES IN JAIL. Between 1995 and 2005 the number of juveniles in local jails fell from 7,800 to 6,759, for a decrease of 13%. (See Table 10.11.) In 2005, 5,750 of 6,759 juveniles held in local jails were being held as adults (85%), whereas 1,009 were being held as juveniles (15%). In 1995 a smaller proportion of juveniles in local jails were being held as adults (76%, or 5,900)—meaning they were either being held for trial in adult criminal court or they had been convicted as adults. Even though the number of juveniles being held in local jails had declined between 1995 and 2005, the overall number of inmates had actually risen from 507,044 in 1995 to 747,529 in 2005, for an increase of 47%.

IMPRISONING ADULTS AND JUVENILES TOGETHER. A number of human rights organizations and juvenile justice groups point out the risks associated with incarcerating juveniles with adults. Among the chief concerns is that being held with hardened adult prisoners will likely cause youth offenders to become more violent, more tough, and repeat offenders. Instead of rehabilitation and education, such juveniles will be subjected to more physical and sexual abuse and violence, increasing their likelihood of showing violent tendencies when they eventually return to society.

In addition, youth in adult prisons and jails are vulnerable to violence. Amnesty International notes in *Betraying the Young: Human Rights Violations against Children in the U.S. Justice System* (November 20, 1998, http://web.amnesty.org/library/index/ENGAMR510571998) that "youth in prison are notoriously a common target of sexual and physical assault by adult inmates." Vincent Schiraldi and Jason Zeidenberg of the Center on Juvenile and Criminal Justice, in *The Risks Juveniles Face When They Are Incarcerated with Adults* (1997, http://www.cjcj.org/pubs/risks/risks.html), echo this sentiment: "Young people slated to be placed in adult prisons and jails are more likely to be raped, assaulted, and commit suicide."

Organizations also point out that juveniles are exposed to attack not only by adult inmates but also by prison guards. Reasons for this can include the juveniles' small stature, lack of confidence, and inexperience at living confined with hardened criminals. Juveniles sometimes resort to suicide because they may give in to despair more quickly.

ADULT TIME FOR ADULT CRIME? Although the public favored tougher penalties for juveniles in the 1990s, as juvenile crime decreases, these attitudes appear to be changing. The survey "New NCCD Poll Shows Public Strongly Favors Youth Rehabilitation and Treatment" (February 2007, http://www.nccd-crc.org/nccd/pubs/zogby PR0207.pdf), which was conducted by Zogby International for the National Council on Crime and Delinquency, finds that the American public supports rehabilitation and treatment for young people, not prosecution in adult criminal courts or incarceration in adult jails or prisons. Nine out of ten people surveyed believed this approach might help prevent crime in the future, and seven out of ten believed imprisoning juveniles in adult facilities would increase the likelihood that they would commit future crimes. Most people believed that youth should not be automatically transferred to adult court, but that such transfers should be handled on an individual basis.

Children and the Death Penalty

Until 2005 convicted criminals could be executed for crimes they committed as juveniles. Victor L. Streib of Ohio Northern University reports in *The Juvenile Death Penalty Today: Death Sentences and Executions for*

TABLE 10.11

Average daily population and the number of men, women, and juveniles in local jails, midyear 1995, 2000, and 2004–05

	1995	2000	2004	2005
Average daily population[a]	509,828	618,319	706,242	733,442
Number of inmates, June 30	507,044	621,149	713,990	747,529
Adults	499,300	613,534	706,907	740,770
Male	448,000	543,120	619,908	646,807
Female	51,300	70,414	86,999	93,963
Juveniles[b]	7,800	7,615	7,083	6,759
Held as adults[c]	5,900	6,126	6,159	5,750
Held as juveniles	1,800	1,489	924	1,009

Note: Data are for June 30. Detailed data for 1995 were estimated and rounded to the nearest 100.
[a]The average daily population is the sum of the number of inmates in a jail each day for a year, divided by the total number of days in the year.
[b]Juveniles are persons held under the age of 18.
[c]Includes juveniles who were tried or awaiting trial as adults.

SOURCE: Paige M. Harrison and Allen J. Beck, "Table 9. Average Daily Population and the Number of Men, Women, and Juveniles in Local Jails, Midyear 1995, 2000, and 2004–05," in *Prison and Jail Inmates at Midyear 2005*, U.S. Department of Justice, Bureau of Justice Statistics, May 2006, http://www.ojp.usdoj.gov/bjs/pub/pdf/pjim05.pdf (accessed March 5, 2007)

Juvenile Crimes, January 1, 1973–February 28, 2005 (October 7, 2005, http://www.law.onu.edu/) that between 1973 and 2005 twenty-two offenders were executed for crimes they committed when they were younger than eighteen. The U.S. Supreme Court has considered many cases concerning the practice of executing offenders for crimes they committed as children. In *Eddings v. Oklahoma* (455 U.S. 104 [1982]) the Court found that a juvenile's mental and emotional development should be considered as a mitigating factor when deciding whether to apply the death penalty, noting that adolescents are less mature and responsible than adults and not as able to consider long-range consequences of their actions. In this case, the Court reversed the death sentence of a sixteen-year-old who had been tried as an adult.

Subsequent Supreme Court rulings have further limited the application of the death penalty in cases involving juveniles. In *Thompson v. Oklahoma* (487 U.S. 815 [1988]), the Court found that applying the death sentence to an offender who had been fifteen years old at the time of the murder was cruel and unusual punishment, concluding that the death penalty could not be applied to offenders who were younger than sixteen. However, the following year the Court found in *Stanford v. Kentucky* (492 U.S. 361) that applying the death penalty to offenders who were age sixteen or seventeen at the time of the crime was not cruel and unusual punishment.

The Court was asked to reconsider this decision in 2005. In *Roper v. Simmons* (543 U.S. 551), the Court set aside the death sentence of Christopher Simmons by a vote of five to four, concluding that the "Eighth and Fourteenth Amendments forbid imposition of the death penalty on offenders who were under the age of 18 when their crimes were committed." Snyder and Sickmund note that few states applied death penalty provisions to juveniles at the time of the *Roper* decision, even though twenty states allowed juveniles to be sentenced to death under the law.

IMPORTANT NAMES
AND ADDRESSES

Alan Guttmacher Institute
1301 Connecticut Ave. NW, Ste. 700
Washington, NY 20036
(202) 296-4012
1-877-823-0262
FAX: (202) 223-5756
E-mail: info@guttmacher.org
URL: http://www.guttmacher.org/

America's Second Harvest
35 East Wacker Dr., #2000
Chicago, IL 60601
(312) 263-2303
1-800-771-2303
URL: http://www.secondharvest.org/

Child Trends
4301 Connecticut Ave. NW, Ste. 350
Washington, DC 20008
(202) 572-6000
FAX: (202) 362-8420
URL: http://www.childtrends.org/

Children's Defense Fund
25 E St. NW
Washington, DC 20001
(202) 628-8787
1-800-233-1200
E-mail: cdfinfo@childrensdefense.org
URL: http://www.childrensdefense.org/

**Federal Interagency Forum on Child
and Family Statistics**
URL: http://www.childstats.gov/

**National Center for Children in Poverty
Columbia University, Mailman School of
Public Health**
215 W. 125th St., Third Fl.
New York, NY 10027
(646) 284-9600
FAX: (646) 284-9623
E-mail: info@nccp.org
URL: http://www.nccp.org/

**National Center for Education Statistics
U.S. Department of Education
Institute of Education Sciences**
1990 K St. NW
Washington, DC 20006
(202) 502-7300
URL: http://www.nces.ed.gov/

**National Center for Missing and
Exploited Children**
Charles B. Wang International Children's
Building
699 Prince St.
Alexandria, VA 22314-3175
(703) 274-3900
FAX: (703) 274-2200
URL: http://www.missingkids.com

National Center for Victims of Crime
2000 M St. NW, Ste. 480
Washington, DC 20036
(202) 467-8700
FAX: (202) 467-8701
URL: http://www.ncvc.org/

National Crime Prevention Council
1000 Connecticut Ave. NW, Thirteenth Fl.
Washington, DC 20036
(202) 466-6272
FAX: (202) 296-1356
URL: http://www.ncpc.org/

**National Institute on Drug Abuse
National Institutes of Health**
6001 Executive Blvd., Rm. 5213
Bethesda, MD 20892-9561
(301) 443-1124
E-mail: Information@nida.nih.gov
URL: http://www.nida.nih.gov/

**National Youth Gang Center
Institute for Intergovernmental Research**
PO Box 12729
Tallahassee, FL 32317-2729

(850) 385-0600
FAX: (850) 386-5356
E-mail: nygc@iir.com
URL: http://www.iir.com/nygc/

**National Youth Violence Prevention
Resource Center**
PO Box 10809
Rockville, MD 20849-0809
1-866-723-3968
FAX: (301) 562-1001
E-mail: NYVPRC@safeyouth.org
URL: http://www.safeyouth.org/

**Office of Juvenile Justice and
Delinquency Prevention**
810 Seventh St. NW
Washington, DC 20531
(202) 307-5911
URL: http://www.ojjdp.ncjrs.org/

**Office of National Drug Control Policy
Drug Policy Information Clearinghouse**
PO Box 6000
Rockville, MD 20849-6000
1-800-666-3332
FAX: (301) 519-5212
URL: http://www.whitehousedrugpolicy.gov/

Office of the U.S. Surgeon General
5600 Fishers Lane, Rm. 18-66
Rockville, MD 20857
(301) 443-4000
FAX: (301) 443-3574
URL: http://www.surgeongeneral.gov/

Urban Institute
2100 M St. NW
Washington, DC 20037
(202) 833-7200
URL: http://www.urban.org/

RESOURCES

Many government agencies in Washington, D.C., publish timely information on their programs and the American population. The U.S. Census Bureau publishes statistics on American life in its *Current Population Reports*, including *Grandparents Living with Grandchildren: 2000* (Tavia Simmons and Jane Lawler Dye, October 2003), *Children's Living Arrangements and Characteristics: March 2002* (Jason Fields, June 2003), *Income, Poverty, and Health Insurance Coverage in the United States: 2005* (Carmen DeNavas-Walt, Bernadette D. Proctor, and Cheryl Hill Lee, August 2005), *Fertility of American Women: June 2004* (Jane Lawler Dye, December 2005), *America's Families and Living Arrangements: 2003* (Jason Fields, November 2004), *Who's Minding the Kids? Child Care Arrangements: Winter 2002* (Julia Overturf Johnson, October 2005), *Custodial Mothers and Fathers and Their Child Support: 2003* (Timothy S. Grall, July 2006), and *Educational Attainment in the United States: 2003* (Nicole Stoops, June 2004).

The Federal Interagency Forum on Child and Family Statistics, in *America's Children in Brief: Key National Indicators of Well-Being, 2006* (2006), provided invaluable data on many aspects of children's health and well-being. The U.S. Department of Health and Human Services provided a wide assortment of statistical data concerning health issues. Its Centers for Disease Control and Prevention (CDC) issues the *Morbidity and Mortality Weekly Report*, which focuses on various aspects of death and disease. The CDC's "Youth Risk Behavior Surveillance—United States, 2005" (June 2006) was the source of survey information on risk behaviors among American high school students. The CDC is also a leading source of AIDS statistics with its quarterly *HIV/AIDS Surveillance*.

Child Health USA 2005 (2005), published by the Maternal and Child Health Bureau, reports the health status and needs of American children. *Child Maltreatment 2004* (2006) counts cases of child abuse reported to state child protective agencies. The Administration for Children and Families provided data on child support collections as well as reports from the *Adoption and Foster Care Analysis and Reporting System (AFCARS) Report* (September 2006).

The Social Security Administration, Office of Policy, offered helpful statistics on children receiving Supplemental Security Income in 2002. The Bureau of Labor Statistics, which is part of the U.S. Department of Labor, provided data on employment and unemployment.

The *National Vital Statistics Reports*, published by the National Center for Health Statistics (NCHS), provided statistics on births and infant mortality. The NCHS also published *Health, United States, 2006* (2006), which gives invaluable data on many health conditions, birthrates, fertility rates, and life expectancy.

The U.S. Department of Agriculture provided estimates of expenditures on children from birth through age seventeen. Its Center for Nutrition Policy and Promotion calculates how much it costs to raise a child in *Expenditures on Children by Families, 2005* (Mark Lino, 2006).

The National Center for Education Statistics, which is part of the U.S. Department of Education, published the *Digest of Education Statistics, 2005* (June 2006) and the *Condition of Education, 2006* (June 2006), which provide important statistics on education in the United States.

The Bureau of Justice Statistics provided important information on juvenile crime and victimization in *Key Crime and Justice Facts at a Glance* (January 2007), *Homicide Trends in the United States* (James Alan Fox and Marianne W. Zawitz, June 2006), and *Criminal Victimization, 2005* (Shannan M. Catalano, September 2006), as did the Office of Juvenile Justice and Delinquency Prevention in *Juvenile Offenders and Victims: 2006 National Report* (Howard N. Snyder and Melissa Sickmund, March 2006). The Federal Bureau of Investigation's *Crime in the*

United States 2005 (September 2006) covers crime and victimization.

The Office of Juvenile Justice and Delinquency Prevention (OJJDP) of the U.S. Department of Justice was a valuable resource of information about youth violence, crime, and gangs in the United States. Various sources of the OJJDP provided important data that helped in the compilation of this book. These included *National Youth Gang Survey Analysis* (2006), *The Growth of Youth Gang Problems in the United States: 1970–1998* (Walter B. Miller, April 2001), *2005 National Gang Threat Assessment* (2005), *National Youth Gang Survey, 1999–2001*

Summary (Arlen Egley Jr., James C. Howell, and Aline K. Major, July 2006), "Youth Gangs in Indian Country" (Aline K. Major et al., March 2004), and many articles in the *Juvenile Justice Bulletin*. The annual reports of the National Youth Gang Survey, which is prepared by the OJJDP, were also helpful.

The National Center for Children in Poverty provided information on children in low-income households. Child Trends provided research on adolescent sexual activity. The Alan Guttmacher Institute provided information on abortion rates among teenagers in the journal *Perspectives on Sexual and Reproductive Health*.

INDEX